Laughter's
Gentle
Soul

Laughter's Gentle Soul

THE LIFE OF ROBERT BENCHLEY

Billy Altman

W · W · NORTON & COMPANY

NEW YORK

LONDON

Permission was granted by the Estate of Robert Benchley to quote accurately from
unpublished and published works under the Estate's domain.

For information about permission to reproduce selections from this book, write to
Permissions, W. W. Norton & Company, Inc., 500 Fifth Avenue, New York, NY 10110.

The text of this book is composed in 11.5/14 Berthold Bodoni Light
with the display set in Cheltenham Book and Cheltenham Bold
Composition manufacturing by the Haddon Craftsmen, Inc.
Book design by Margaret M. Wagner

Since this page cannot legibly accommodate all the copyright notices,
pages 371–72 constitute an extension of the copyright page.

Library of Congress Cataloging-in-Publication Data
Altman, Billy.
Laughter's gentle soul : the life of Robert Benchley /
Billy Altman.
p. cm.
Includes bibliographical references (p.) and index.
ISBN 0-393-03833-5
1. Benchley, Robert, 1889–1945. 2. Humorists, American—20th
century—Biography. I. Title.
PS3503.E49Z54 1997
814′.52—dc20
[B] 95-37604
CIP

W. W. Norton & Company, Inc., 500 Fifth Avenue, New York, N.Y. 10110
http://www.wwnorton.com

W. W. Norton & Company Ltd., 10 Coptic Street, London WC1A 1PU

1 2 3 4 5 6 7 8 9 0

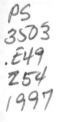

To Israel and Erna Altman
for their love, their humor—and their faith

Contents

Contents

Foreword

"*I am not* a writer and not an actor," Robert Benchley once complained to his friend Harold Ross, editor of *The New Yorker*. "I don't know what I am." The evidence, of course, weighed heavily against him, and on both counts. By the time of his death in 1945 at age fifty-six, Benchley had written enough humorous essays to fill twelve books—that in addition to his twenty years' worth of weekly theater criticism for the original *Life* and Ross's *New Yorker*, as well as countless articles that enhanced the content of virtually every notable periodical to be found on a magazine stand during the first half of the twentieth century. As an actor, Benchley was a featured player in nearly forty motion pictures during the 1930s and '40s, and, more important, the star of nearly fifty of his own short subjects, one of which—*How to Sleep*—won an Academy Award in 1935. Additionally, he was a much-sought-after radio performer who, besides appearing frequently on the top comedy and variety shows of the day, starred for several seasons in his own network program. For a man who considered himself neither a writer nor an actor, he did an awfully good—and frightfully industrious—impersonation of both.

While much evidence suggests that Benchley believed his work on all these various fronts to be ultimately trifling and disposable—one of the running jokes of his life was an unfulfilled desire to write a serious dissertation on England's Queen Anne period—history, which ultimately takes the long view (and has the last laugh), would beg to differ with that assessment. While Benchley, especially after his unintentionally begun career in film and radio made him a highly recognized face in the crowd, dreaded the notion of being thought of as a "funnyman," such has not been the case. History accurately portrays him as "an American humorist," pure and simple, and does so without a trace of the intellectual condescension that Benchley (like so many talented and successful humorists both before and after him) always felt he lived in the shadow of.

That's because his contributions to the world of humor, both on the printed page and on the silver screen, have proved to be unique, significant, and influential—during his lifetime, and far beyond it as well. It would be difficult, if not impossible, to find a writer of humor of the last seven decades who would not confess to having at some point (in the block- and hurdle-filled life that is a writer's lot) gone to Benchley's deep artistic well for inspiration. And his influence as a film actor has been surprisingly resonant—his 1928 film debut, *The Treasurer's Report*, is often cited by scholars as one of the breakthrough events in the advancement of sound pictures, and much of what's come to be known as "situation comedy" can be linked in many ways to the trials and tribulations of his bumbling short-subject persona, Joe Doakes.

Perhaps it's not so remarkable then that, some fifty years after his passing, we remain aware of his presence, whether we're rereading an anthologized essay on the relative merits of, say, "Coffee vs. Gin," watching him on cable television in one of his movie shorts as he exasperatedly grapples with some innocent-looking inanimate object that has suddenly turned against him, seeing some mention of the famous Algonquin Round Table of which he was a charter member in New York during the Roaring Twenties, or hearing some newly unearthed anecdote about his days at the notorious Garden of Allah apartments in Hollywood in the decadent thirties. Benchley and his gentle humor are still with us—and as riotous as ever.

Outside the public eye, his life was riotous too. What started out as an orderly, straitlaced existence neatly in accord with the late-nineteenth-century New England from which he sprang eventually became an increasingly tumultuous and unpredictable juggling act in which he desperately tried, on both coasts, to keep in the air all the myriad people, places, and things he often far too nonchalantly tossed into simultaneous and separate orbits. As another friend, the playwright Robert Sherwood noted, "His life represented some of the strangest reversals of moods and habits I have ever observed in one human being. Together with many others, I saw him in various contrasting characters: as a methodical, teetotaling, nonsmoking, galosh-wearing, penurious, homebound commuter . . . as a violent crusader for civil rights . . . a passionate pacifist, and (so help me!) an ardent prohibitionist; and, finally, as a laboriously irresponsible flaneur or court jester of the Café Society belt, of Hollywood or Antibes. He could wear the motley, all right, but he always remained indelibly the same person: Benchley."

It was in an attempt to uncover, as well as to understand, as many of these contrasting characters as possible that the challenge of writing this biography of Robert Benchley was undertaken. Whatever the extent to which that effort has been successful, of one thing I am certain: If you derive even half as much pleasure from reading about Robert Benchley as I know you could get from reading or watching him without any interference from me, I'll be more than satisfied.

Billy Altman

Acknowledgments

My heartfelt thanks to the following people who helped me, in some capacity, to navigate my journey through the maze of Robert Benchley's life:

Maragalo Gillmore and Albert Hackett, for sharing recollections and insights about the New York theater and the Algonquin Round Table of the 1920s.

Eve Arden, John Carradine, Natalie Schafer, Gloria Sheekman, and especially Sheilah Graham, for their reminiscences about Hollywood in general and the Garden of Allah in particular during the 1930s and '40s.

Brendan Gill, William Maxwell, and William Shawn for their thoughts on Robert Benchley's *New Yorker* career, and to Mr. Shawn, Henry F. S. Cooper, and librarian Helen Stark for their aid in my research at the *New Yorker* offices.

Herbert Nusbaum and the business affairs office at then MGM-UA Pictures, for allowing me to look through production and legal files pertaining to Benchley's film work for the Metro-Goldwyn-Mayer studios, and for quietly bending the rules so that I was able to have screened for me all of Benchley's MGM shorts.

Raymond Rohauer, for showing me, at his own home, his private collection of some of Benchley's Fox and Paramount shorts, including *The Treasurer's Report* and *The Sex Life of the Polyp*.

Dorothy Parker's biographer, Marion Meade, whose kindred-soul encouragement and endless contacts proved indispensable, and James

Gaines, author of the Round Table overview *Wit's End*, for his many helpful leads.

The New York Public Library and the New York Public Library Newspaper Annex for assistance in researching Benchley's work as a journalist and columnist for the *New York Tribune* and the *World*, as well as his work for *Vanity Fair;* the Billy Rose Theater Collection at the Lincoln Center Library for the Performing Arts for making available its Gertrude Benchley collection, which includes personal scrapbooks of her husband's professional career as well as items relating to Benchley's theatrical activities while attending Harvard University; the Library of the Academy of Motion Picture Arts and Sciences and the Margaret Herrick Library for credits and other production-related information regarding Benchley's film career; the Museum of Broadcasting (now the Museum of Television and Radio) for assistance in researching Benchley's radio career; the Columbia University Library for help in researching Benchley's work for *Life* magazine; and Columbia's Oral History Research Office for assistance in researching taped interviews with Marc Connelly, Dorothy Parker, Donald Odgen Stewart, and Frank Sullivan.

The Office of the Mayor of Worcester, Massachusetts, for help in researching matters pertaining to the career of Charles Benchley.

The Estate of Robert Benchley, which kindly gave me access to Benchley's papers in the archive at Boston University's Mugar Memorial Library. However, they have not authorized this biography, nor have they endorsed my interpretations of Benchley's life or work.

Dr. Howard A. Gotlieb and his staff at the Mugar Memorial Library department of Special Collections, and in particular, researcher Charlie Niles.

Special thanks to Henry Edwards for putting me in touch with my first agent, Ron Bernstein, and to Ron for his diligence in helping to get this book off the ground. To Tom Wallace, Mary Cunnane, and Amy Cherry, my three editors on this at times seemingly endless labor of love, I am inordinately indebted, not only for their individual editing skills and helpful comments, but for the truly saintly extent of their collective patience. As the final editor on the project, Amy deserves special credit for taking a manuscript that was turned in over so long a period, and gently but firmly helping to shape it into one (I hope) cohesive entity.

Acknowledgments

I cannot adequately express in words my gratitude to Tom Wallace. Not only did he show enormous confidence in me by taking the original plunge on this book, but he has continued to demonstrate that confidence by wanting me for a client after making the transition from editor to agent. Given how long it's taken me to finish this work, I am genuinely humbled by his ongoing trust in my abilities—and hope in the future to prove myself more worthy of that trust.

For inspiration, guidance, advice, and, above all, friendship, during the many years that this project has taken to complete, my continued thanks to Barbara and Emily Bader, Mitchell Cohen, Joe Fernbacher, Woody and Lori Graber, my sister Eileen and my brother-in-law Michael Hecht, Joe Kane and Nancy Naglin, Richard Lally, Lee Lowenfish, Andy and Ria McKaie, Richard Meltzer and Irene Forrest, John Milward, Jeff and Diane Nesin, Hal and Marion Persons, Terry and Diane Rafferty, and Nick Tosches.

And, finally, to my extraordinary wife and best friend, Joyce, to whom I said sometime in the latter part of the 1980s that I did not want to begin a family until I'd finished this book—thank you, and our now six-year-old daughter, Emma, for not listening to me.

Laughter's
Gentle
Soul

1
Lemon Drops Around Us Are Falling

THEY SAY JENNIE BENCHLEY DENTED A FENDER

BORN Isle of Wight, September 15, 1807. Shipped as cabin boy on the *Florence J. Marble*, 1815. Arrested for bigamy and murder in Port Said, 1817. Released, 1820. Wrote *A Tale of Two Cities*. Married Princess Anastasia of Portugal, 1831. Children: Prince Rupprecht and several little girls. Wrote *Uncle Tom's Cabin*, 1850. Editor of *Godey's Lady's Book*, 1851–56. Began *Les Misérables*, 1870, finished by Victor Hugo. Died 1871. Buried in Westminster Abbey.

—*Autobiography* by Robert Benchley, c. 1930

In fact, his origins were exactly the kind that one would expect of a son of late-1880s New England—Worcester, Massachusetts, to be precise, where, on September 15, 1889, Robert Charles Benchley was born. The first Benchley to arrive in America—one William Benchley of Merthyr Tydfil, Glamorgan, Wales—did so several years before the colonies rose up in revolt against the king of England, and by the 1840s William's descendants had moved the family from Smithfield, Rhode Island, to industrial Worcester, the "Heart of the Commonwealth," as the town's motto proclaimed. Henry Weatherly Benchley, William's great-grandson and Robert's grandfather, was a fairly well known local politician who, after helping to found the Republican Party in the eastern portion of the United States, served first as a representative to the state senate and later, in the mid-1850s, as Massachusetts's lieutenant governor.

It's entirely possible that Henry Benchley could have gone even further in politics, but his sense of outrage at the way the South was conducting its social business led the widowed politician (his wife, Julia, had died in 1854) to leave his two sons, Charles and Julian, in the care of relatives and head off for Texas, where he eventually was arrested, tried, and jailed for operating a station on the underground railroad that was helping escaped slaves flee to the North. He died in Houston shortly after the end of the Civil War, but left enough of a mark on the area that, years later, a small community near Houston rose up bearing the name of Benchley, Texas.

Perhaps the fact that his father had been imprisoned by Confederates stimulated fourteen-year-old Charles Henry Benchley to lie about his age and in 1863 gain a place in the Massachusetts Voluntary Militia's 1st Battalion of Heavy Artillery in the War Between the States. Charlie distinguished himself enough to be promoted to corporal before the conclusion of the war, and he apparently enjoyed military service enough that, when he turned eighteen, he enlisted for a four-year tour of duty in the U.S. Navy. After he completed his Navy hitch, Charlie Benchley settled down to civilian life in Worcester in the early 1870s with his new bride, the former Maria Jane (Jennie) Moran, whose lineage on her mother's side, like Benchley's, dated back to Revolutionary stock, and whose father had come to America from Northern Ireland. In March 1876, the couple's first son, Edmund Nathaniel, was born, and the family remained a threesome for some thirteen years, until Jennie's unexpected second pregnancy resulted in the birth of baby Robert, a brown-haired, blue-eyed boy who was welcomed into the Benchley household with both surprise and delight—especially by Edmund, who gleefully carried his little brother all around the house and often rocked him to sleep in his arms before handing him over to Charlie, who, in turn, gave the child to Jennie for final inspection before bedtime (a practice which came to be known around the Benchley premises as "first, second, and third relief").

By all indications, it was Jennie, not Charlie, who was the dominant force in the family. Charlie Benchley was familiar to many residents of Worcester as the quiet and kindly mayor's clerk, and it was a sign of his efficient and accommodating nature that, although he was, like his father, a Republican, he stayed at his post in City Hall regardless of which party was in power, and was still on the job after thirty years and twelve different mayors at the time of his death in 1923. A short, stocky man with a bald head, thick mustache, and pince-nez glasses, Charlie also was the city's soldier's relief agent, which meant that his office was often filled with needy or down-on-their-luck ex-servicemen looking for assistance of some form or other, for it was common knowledge that Charlie Benchley would reach into his own pocket before allowing a fellow veteran to leave his office empty-handed.

Common knowledge, that is, until Jennie found out about her husband's philanthropy and started picking up Charlie's weekly paycheck herself. "His friends don't like me, but his creditors love me," she was known to say, and proudly, too. That she sometimes laughed as she said it sheds at least some light on the complex personality of Mrs. Charles H. Benchley. Strong-minded to the point of intolerance and indefatigably strong-willed as well, Jennie Benchley kept Charlie on a weekly allowance that barely covered his carfare, thus enabling her not only to keep a good limit on his charitable donations, but also to discourage him from lingering downtown for post-workday rounds of drinks with friends at Worcester taverns. Charlie had begun to drink during his soldier days, but Jennie flatly refused even to acknowledge his predilection—in fact, the one time she discovered a pint of whiskey that Charlie had hidden in the house, the staunchly anti-alcohol Jennie ceremoniously poured it down the drain and later boasted to friends that "he didn't say a word about it." She was, however, a woman who often found it hard not to be rather amused by her own harsh manner and stern demeanor. After being run down by an ice truck once, she greeted well-wishers at the hospital she was taken to after the accident with a matter-of-fact "They *say* I dented a fender." And while the Benchley home was literally dry, it did often sparkle with the wry, clipped humor that Charlie and Jennie Benchley and their two boys shared.

Edmund, in fact, was a bit of a prankster, as demonstrated by the time when little Robert, needing to learn a poem to recite in kindergarten, came to his older brother for guidance. The next day, when Robert returned home, he had clutched in his hand a terse note from his teacher to his parents concerning proper classroom behavior. The letter confused Charlie and Jennie—what on earth could the boy have done?—and they asked Robert if he could explain what had prompted it. The youngest Benchley confessed that the verse Edmund had taught him didn't seem to have pleased the teacher at all—a verse which, it turned out, went: "My mother-in-law hath lately died / For her my heart doth yearn / I know she's with the angels now / 'Cause she's too tough to burn." And before long, Robert was finding that he didn't have to rely on Edmund to let the family wit get him into trouble, as when he led a Sunday school hymn reading and substituted the word "lemon" for "mercy" in the phrase "mercy drops around us are falling." In both instances, neither Benchley boy was reprimanded by his parents; indeed, the lemon-drop incident was noteworthy more for Jennie's reaction to the reprimand received by Robert than for the actual "sacrilegious" jest, as Mrs. Benchley, displaying her customary protectiveness of her children, marched straight over to the teacher's house and berated the woman for not appropriately appreciating her son's attempt to "make the hymn a bit more cheerful."

Like most young boys, Robert eagerly counted the weekdays until the arrival of Friday, when, as he noted in a reminiscence many years later, the Benchley house filled with the comforting smells of a New England weekend.

> We began getting whiffs as early as Friday evening, when the bread was "set" on the kitchen table and the beans "put to soak" nearby. The smell of the cold bread-dough when the napkins were lifted from the pans always meant "no school tomorrow," and was a preliminary to the "no school today" smells of Saturday. . . .
>
> On Saturday morning early these "no school today" smells began to permeate the kitchen, and, as the kitchen was the sole port of entry and exit during the morning's play outside, they became inextricably mixed up with not only cooking, but "duck on the rock," "Indian guide," and that informal scrimmaging which boys indulge in back yards, which goes by the name of either baseball or football according to the season of the year. . . .
>
> In New England, of course, the leit motif among the Saturday smells was the one of beans baking, but the bread and pies ran a close second. . . . Then, along about eleven-thirty, the noon dinner began to heat up. . . . it usually took the combined form of cabbage, turnips, beets and corned beef, all working together in one pot, with the potatoes, to make the "New England boiled dinner." That put a stop to any other smells that thought they were something earlier in the morning.

In 1894, the tall, good-looking Edmund graduated from high school, and through the influential help of Massachusetts Senator George Frisbie Hoar, he received an appointment to the West Point

Military Academy. During the next few years, the family often took the long trip from Worcester across to New York State and over the Hudson River to visit Edmund, who, like most cadets at the time, rarely was granted leaves or furloughs. There they would stand and watch the afternoon marching drills, an event which the prideful Benchleys enjoyed even more after Edmund joined the color guard. Once Edmund's regiment, marching into the camp chapel, found itself distorting its neat files so as avoid trampling a little sailor-suited boy standing right in their path and waving to his embarrassed older brother. About the only negative aspect of the visits was that Robert, who was always fearful of loud noises, became terribly frightened by the sound of the sunset gun, and would usually run away and hide from everyone around the time of its firing.

In the spring of 1898, the Spanish-American War broke out, and Edmund Benchley's class was graduated ahead of schedule so that they could be sent into action in Cuba. After returning to Worcester for a few days in late April so he could properly say goodbye to his family and friends, the newly commissioned lieutenant went off to join the U.S. infantry stationed in Tampa, Florida. For a time, it appeared that Edmund's battalion would never have to take part in the actual fighting. "There is a feeling here that if we don't go before next week we won't go until fall, by which time it may well be over," he wrote to his parents in late May. "The officers here say it's the rashest foolishness sending us over there now and nobody would do it who knew anything about the matter. It doesn't seem to trouble anybody down here whether they go or not. . . . I never saw such a happy-go-lucky crowd."

The next week, however, the orders to sail did come, and before long Edmund was on a boat headed to Santiago, Cuba. "There was great disappointment on board when it was learned what our destination was," he wrote while still at sea near the end of June, "because everybody realizes the strategic value of Porto Rico and in case of the very probable termination of the war we would have something to show for our troubles and expense. One thing is certain—our stay in Santiago will be comparatively short. . . . We are to land at a place about thirty miles this side of Havana at Guantanamo; it is already in our possession and we will probably go into camp and sit there and wait for the enemy to surrender. I don't think it is the policy of our commanding officer to be very aggressive. . . .

"Please don't worry if you don't hear from me once a week for awhile," he concluded. "Until we get definitely located, mail communication is likely to be rather irregular."

At the same time that Edmund was writing that letter, Jennie and Charlie were each sending off their own notes of parental concern and support. "I have come to the conclusion that it is not best to take too much stock in the papers," wrote Charlie on June 25. "They all, without any exception, exaggerate and magnify reports when the simple truth without any coloring is bad enough. Your mother nearly goes wild when she reads some of the reports. She is bound to pick out and brood over the discouraging ones and not consider the favorable ones in the least. . . . I saw by this morning's paper that the advance of Shafter's army had had a brush with the dagoes, and that ten were killed and fifty wounded, among them several officers. . . . God grant that the fighting will not be severe by the time you are at the front." On June 28, Jennie wrote: "Sometimes I feel as if I couldn't breathe when I think of where you are. If only I could help you in some way. . . ." Included with her letter were three pencil drawings by eight-year-old Robert, depicting a U.S. ship with a "Don't tread on me" flag flying from its mast, a politician making a speech while a cloud marked "peace" approached from above, and Uncle Sam rolling up his sleeve and making a fist, warning Spain to leave Cuba alone.

As it turned out, Edmund's letter from aboard ship was never mailed, and the young officer never received the last two letters his parents wrote him. On the Fourth of July, while the distinctive aroma of firecrackers filled the Benchleys' Worcester neighborhood, a newspaper reporter knocked at the door of Jennie and Charlie's home and delivered the grim news that their twenty-two-year-old son had been killed defending his country.

After landing in Cuba and setting up camp near Santiago, Edmund's company had marched into the battle of Fort San Juan at dawn on July 1, and the front line which he was a part of crossed the San Juan River under heavy fire from Spanish magazine guns, resulting in many casualties. At that point, according to the report filed by company commander Captain L. W. Kennon, "the brush was so thick that the other companies could not be seen, and the Colonel directed them to be brought up at once so that a full line of attack could be formed. He called Lieut. Benchley and directed him to re-cross the river—it had to be waded, being about waist deep—and carry orders to the battalion and company commanders to bring their troops forward at once. He started immediately on this important and dangerous duty and had succeeded in giving the orders to several of the commanders when he received a bullet through the heart, killing him instantly."

The terrible news of Edmund's death, coming as it did amid the ceaseless battlelike sounds and smells of Independence Day cele-brations, was just too much for Jennie to bear. She began screaming uncontrollably, and it was several hours before her sister Lizzie, sum-moned from her nearby home by a distraught Charlie, was able to get her even slightly calmed down. When she finally appeared to have regained her senses, the first clear words she spoke were frighteningly blunt. *"Why couldn't it have been Robert?"* she cried—an outburst that so troubled those friends and relatives at her side that it was decided it would probably be best if Lizzie took Robert over to her house until his mother was back in her right mind again. (For the rest of his life, Robert would hate the sound of firecrackers—a grim reminder of the day he found out his brother was dead.)

It was a few days before Robert was able to return home. Some-how during that time, news of what Jennie Benchley had said got out among her neighbors, and it was quite a while before the gossip and behind-the-back chatter finally subsided. But whether it was pri-marily out of remorse over what she'd said, a need to repair the hurt she'd caused, or the instinctive protectiveness of a mother who'd al-ready lost one child, Jennie Benchley soon was devoting much of her considerable energies to pampering Robert. She would allow no one to say a bad word about him or to him, encouraged his interest in drawing and music (he had his own mandolin and banjo by the time he was fourteen), and waited on him hand and, literally, foot; it wasn't until he was in high school that Jennie stopped tying his shoes for him. And while Jennie obsessively showered him with attention, Robert dealt with Edmund's death by trying to follow in his brother's footsteps, developing intensified interest in reading, drawing, dramatics, and charity work—hoping to be, for his mother's sake, as much like Edmund as possible.

Besides his mother, there was another woman whose relationship with Robert was significantly altered by Edmund's death. Lillian Duryea, who came from a wealthy starch-manufacturing family in Nyack, New York, frequently accompanied her two sisters on trips to West Point, where they provided company for young and eligible cadets at social affairs. It was there that she had met Edmund, and the two saw a great deal of each other throughout his stay at the academy. After Edmund was killed, Lillian announced to a somewhat stunned Jennie and Charlie Benchley that she and Edmund had been secretly engaged; moreover, she said, the two had planned to do a great many things for young Robert after they were married, and now that Edmund was gone, she felt it was up to her to keep her dead fiancé's dreams alive by serving as Robert's friend and benefactress.

Although Jennie was a mother not especially tolerant of outside interference in the raising of a child, Lillian's connection to Edmund—as well as the fact that Lillian's headstrong personality was strikingly similar to her own—led Jennie to accept her. (In later years, each of the two women would confide to outside parties that the other was certifiably insane.) Soon Robert was being treated as something of a ward by the prosperous Duryeas. Every week he would dutifully sit down and write his mandatory letter to Lillian, detailing his progress at school and reporting on family news and items of local interest; and every year at the beginning of July, Robert would take the train to Nyack to satisfy Lillian's desire to have him at her side on the anniversary of Edmund's death—a date she observed by drawing all the curtains in the house and spending the entire twenty-four hours mourning in the dark. As Robert grew older, his visits to Nyack became more frequent, and the depression of the July commemoratives was counterbalanced by the gaiety of the Thanksgivings and Christmases he often spent as a guest of the Duryea family, as well as several New York vacations that Lillian took him on in which Robert got his first taste of the Broadway theater and his first glimpse of the hustle and bustle of New York City life.

Although Robert always noted in the diaries he began keeping during his adolescent years how much gratitude he felt toward Lillian and her family for the continued kindness they showed him, he seems to have regarded his part-time membership in high-society circles as simply an exciting extra, but separate, part of what was to him a most happy and contented life as a middle-class Worcester teenager. That he felt this way was most likely a result of his mother's influence, since, from his very early years, the devoutly religious Jennie usually made a point not only of taking Robert to church with her but also of getting him to take part in the various Protestant charity activities that she was often engaged in. These regular reminders of the existence, and needs, of the poor helped instill in him both a sense of responsibility toward others and what his mother felt was a proper perspective on his own role in the world.

The neighborhood church played an important role in turn-of-the-century life in small-town American life, and it isn't surprising that Robert's diaries reveal a special regard for Sundays and their many church-related activities. A typical Sunday would begin with his taking part in morning services from his usual seat in the last row. From there it was on to his Sunday-school classes, the end of which would signal lunchtime, to be enjoyed either back at home or at his Aunt Lizzie's house, where he'd visit with his cousin Dot and sample the latest batch of wondrous cookies baked by Lizzie's Swedish cook. In late afternoon, he would return to church for the meeting of the Christian Endeavor group. With the other members of the religious youth organization he would sing hymns, recite short prayers, and then listen to the morally uplifting messages of visiting lecturers such as the crusading prohibitionist Carrie Nation, whose (as his diary described it) "red hot talk" Robert enthusiastically absorbed.

Sundays also were deemed the time for proper social interactions between the teenage boys and girls of Worcester, and the conclusion of Christian Endeavor gatherings was always marked by a town ritual in which the young men would ceremoniously request the honor of seeing that their favorite girl made it safely home. And for Robert Benchley that meant a leisurely walk through Worcester's friendly streets with one Gertrude Darling, whose family owned several wool-manufacturing mills and who had been Robert's classmate since third grade and his special friend almost as long as they'd known each other. As Gertrude later recalled to their son Nathaniel, her interest in Robert first came about for a variety of reasons, not the least of which was his virtually unsurpassed skill at making all the other kids laugh, either as the owner/operator of a neighborhood Punch and Judy puppet theater (the puppets had been given to Robert by Lillian Duryea shortly after Edmund's death) or through the amusing drawings that adorned all of his notebooks and school papers (and that he sometimes shyly left on Gertrude's desk as a present). Then there was the sympathy one always felt while watching him try to deal with even the simplest mechanical chore—for Robert, even something as seemingly uncomplicated as the sharpening of a pencil could turn into an arduous and exhausting battle from which he'd emerge only with point blunt and pride bruised.

At Worcester's South High, where he was president of both his freshman and junior class (Gertrude was his v.p. in those years), Robert distinguished himself in numerous areas—among other things, he managed the track team, served as treasurer for the school's dramatic club, and provided mandolin and banjo accompaniment for student minstrel shows and dances. Perhaps his most noteworthy achievement came the night during his sophomore year when, while acting as an extra for a traveling repertory company, he single-handedly stopped the show without uttering a single line of dialogue. The production was a medieval costume drama, and Robert's small role as a guard required that he wear a brass collar with long spikes sticking out. Halfway through the final act, while the action heated up onstage, he accidentally leaned against the backstage switch panel and blew out every fuse in the theater. That he wasn't electrocuted was to his friends and family a good reason to count their blessings; that the next day he announced his temporary retirement from professional theatrical work was for the show's producers a good reason to count theirs.

In early June 1907, while Robert was finishing his junior year, Lillian came to town to discuss Robert's future with Jennie and Charlie. Earlier that spring, in a letter to Robert, she had suggested that he allow her to lend him the money to go away to a prep school for his senior year, the idea being that he would then stand a better chance at gaining admission to one of New England's finer colleges. Robert, however, had dismissed the idea. "No doubt the living with a crowd of fellows would be a good thing," he wrote back to her, "but it is the preparation for the book side of college and not the social side that I ought to prepare for first, and there are few better places than Worcester for that. Our high schools stand as high as any preparatory schools in the region."

Within a few days after receiving his response, however, the determined Miss Duryea was sitting in the Benchleys' family room in Worcester pleading her case before a higher authority. While Robert sat by the door inside his bedroom upstairs straining to hear, Jennie and Lillian argued for better than an hour—Lillian extending her loan offer to include the cost of any four-year university Robert desired to attend, and the prideful Jennie insisting that, if it came to it, Robert would work his way through college. Eventually, the two women reached a compromise: Jennie would allow Lillian to be the one to determine the course of Robert's educational future, but whatever money she wound up spending would have to be considered an outright gift, and not a loan.

The prep school Lillian decided on for Robert was the Phillips Exeter Academy in Exeter, New Hampshire, and she took him there in mid-June to arrange for his taking the entrance examinations and to help him select a prospective room at one of the academy's residence halls. Although Robert had been having a great deal of difficulty with Latin in high school, he managed to pass Exeter's Latin exam after a few days of concentrated studying. This would have been the cause of great joy were it not for the fact that because of his turning all of his attention to that language, he failed the French test rather badly. Fortunately, though, Robert's principal at South High had sent in such a glowing reference ("I don't think we have ever received a recommendation which spoke so enthusiastically of a boy's character and ability," Exeter's assistant principal remarked in a letter to Lillian) that he was accepted anyway, and assigned a room in the Gilman House dormitory.

The summer of 1907 was a hectic one for Robert. At home in Worcester during the last two weeks of June, he saw a great deal of Gertrude, as the knowledge that he'd be going off to boarding school in the fall intensified what had blossomed from a childhood friendship into a serious relationship. It was a relationship that, during July in Nyack, Lillian apparently did her best to undermine by trying to kindle an affair between Robert and a friend of hers from Georgia named Lucy Hilton, whose family owned a summer home not far from the Duryeas. (Apparently, Lillian was holding on to the hope that Robert, though much younger than she, would somehow grow up to take Edmund's place by her side, and that a brief romance with some other girl would provide grounds for a breakup with Gertrude.) At the beginning of August, Robert returned home to spend several weeks playing his mandolin and reading at his usual voracious pace while Gertrude and her father (her mother had died when she was twelve) vacationed in Massachusetts. In mid-August, it was Jennie's turn to get some time alone with her son, as she took him for a week away to the seaside at Falmouth Heights; the very next week, Lillian again took over, treating Robert to a boat trip to Nova Scotia aboard the S.S. *Rosalind*. He got back to Worcester on September 8, leaving just enough time to pack his trunks and say goodbye to his family, and Gertrude, before heading off for Exeter.

If Lillian thought that attending a prestigious boarding school would cause Robert to aspire toward a more upscale lifestyle, she was mistaken. And, by the same token, if Jennie thought that being sent away to school would make Robert appreciatively homesick, she was also mistaken. Simply put, Robert thought boarding school was a pip. For the first time in his life, he was out from under the overly watchful eye of all female figures, and he found the rough-housing camaraderie of an all-boys school a new and enjoyable experience. His marks reflected this new touch of wildness. During his year at Exeter, Robert's grades were, at best, undistinguished (his highest average during the three semesters was a B-, and in his final term he received D's in three of his seven subjects). But he took part in a great variety of extracurricular activities, including the Mandolin Club, the Dramatic Club, the school yearbook, and the literary magazine, for which he drew comic illustrations. He demonstrated his independence when his English teacher told the class that for their senior paper they could tackle any topic that struck their fancy. While his fellow students went off to the library to delve into Swift, Milton, or Shakespeare, Robert took advantage of this opportunity for self-expression by paying several visits to the local undertaker. The result was a painstakingly researched, thoroughly detailed essay entitled "How to Embalm a Corpse," for which his instructor gave him an A— possibly for "astonished."

Robert's year at Exeter went swiftly, and as it did, the question of which college he should apply to loomed ever larger. For a brief time, he thought about seeking admission to Yale, but after several visits to the Harvard campus with Lillian, who would often arrange to meet Robert in Boston on Saturdays and spend the day with him, he set his sights there. In early May, Robert went over to Cambridge with Roger Hoar (son of the senator who had helped Edmund get his West Point appointment) and selected a room in a dormitory at Mount Auburn and Plympton streets that would be his if he passed Harvard's entrance tests. On June 15, a gangly Robert—standing just under six feet tall and weighing but 135 pounds—graduated from Exeter, with his parents and Lillian in attendance; one week later, after a cram-ming session to erase a year's worth of bad study habits, Robert went to Harvard to take the three-day battery of tests that composed the school's admissions exam. At the end of the month, he found out that he'd been accepted. Robert Benchley was going to be a Harvard man.

As had happened the previous summer, Lillian Duryea whisked Robert away for much of July and August. After the obligatory July 1 observances were completed, Lillian and Robert left Nyack and trav-eled by boat to Nantucket Island, where they spent a week at a sea-side inn in Siasconset celebrating Robert's acceptance to Harvard. In early August, Jennie again took him for a short stay at Falmouth, and then it was Lillian's turn once more, as she and Robert set off for a sightseeing trip through the Great Lakes and Canada's Thousand Is-lands region. Robert finally returned home to Worcester in early Sep-tember, and he spent virtually all of the next few weeks by the side of a very subdued Gertrude Darling.

Tragedy had struck the Darling family back in June; the day be-fore her graduation from South High, her father had suddenly died, and it turned out that he had been greatly in debt, resulting in the loss not only of the family's manufacturing mills but also of their house on May Street. In the spring, Gertrude had been admitted to Smith College. For a while she wasn't sure she would be able to go, but her older brother Albert offered to help her with money for her education, and her married sister Florence Reed offered her a room in her home to stay in when back from school. And when Robert reaffirmed his affection and love for her the day before she headed off to college, she was further reassured.

In a summer filled with great excitement and anticipation over his future, the only truly discordant note came in the form of an IOU that Lillian asked him to sign the last time he saw her in Nyack prior to leaving for Cambridge and collegiate life. The document, dated September 10, 1908, consisted of one lone sentence: "I hereby promise to pay to Lillian C. Duryea such amounts as I shall receive from her for the payment of college expenses." Besides making him affix his signature to the promissory note, Lillian made Robert agree verbally to two other conditions for the loan: first, that the terms of the repayment would be at the sole discretion of the lender; and second, that Robert promise that he would never tell his mother about the transaction.

Exactly what Lillian Duryea's motives were is unclear. Perhaps she had always intended that the money be a loan, and had only told Jennie that it would be a gift in order to end an argument she feared she'd otherwise lose. Or perhaps she felt that by solidifying his dependence on her, she could be assured that he would remain close to her, and could hope that as he matured into manhood, he might begin to see her in a romantic light. In any event, five days short of his nineteenth birthday, a confused but resigned Robert signed the IOU and vowed to keep the deal a secret. And whether the financing of it was ultimately going to be determined a gift or a loan, Robert Charles Benchley was going to be the first in his family's lineage to get an Ivy League education.

2
For the Love of Ivy

"I'D HATE TO HAVE TO BE HUMOROUS EVERY DAY"

The story goes that one afternoon during his college career, Robert Benchley, Harvard Class of 1912, and a fellow Delta Upsilon fraternity brother were walking along Beacon Street in Boston when Benchley suddenly turned to his companion and said, "Let's go get the davenport."

Ringing the doorbell of the most expensive-looking brownstone on the block, the two young men soon found themselves face to face with the butler. "Is the master at home?" Benchley asked.

"Not at the moment, I'm afraid," answered the man. "What did you wish to see him about?"

"Actually, we don't have to see him," replied Benchley. "We've just come for the davenport."

"The davenport, sir?" responded the butler.

"Yes," said Benchley, peering past the man and into the house. His eyes fell on a large old sofa sitting in the middle of the drawing room. *"That* one."

Soon the two were back on Beacon Street, with the davenport. After half a block of strenuous hauling, Benchley called out to his friend at the other end to stop. "I think," said Benchley, "that we should now deliver the davenport."

The maid answering the bell at the second house opened the door. "We're here with the davenport," said Benchley. "Where do you want it?"

"Why—there, I guess," replied the puzzled maid, pointing to an open area in the hallway.

Fifteen minutes later, two Harvard boys were aboard a trolley car headed back to Cambridge, laughing themselves silly.

As it would turn out, Robert Benchley was in some pretty fair company as a member of the Harvard 1912 chapter of the D.U. fraternity. Among his brothers were Joseph P. Kennedy, later to become chairman of the U.S. Maritime Commission, first chairman of the Securities and Exchange Commission, U.S. ambassador to England, and father of a President and three senators; James Buell Munn, future dean of the Washington Square College of New York University; and Clarence Randall, an eventual steel magnate and foreign trade policy adviser to Dwight Eisenhower. And among his classmates and Harvard friends were Frederick Lewis Allen, who went on to become *Harper's* editor in chief; Gluyas Williams, the *Harvard Lampoon* illustrator whose drawings graced practically every Benchley book collection ever published; and John Reed, later to achieve more than his share of fame as author of the chronicle of the Russian revolution *Ten Days That Shook the World* and notoriety as the only American to be buried in Moscow's Red Square.

Benchley was taken into D.U. in the spring of his freshman year, a year which set the tone for his entire career at Harvard in that he spent so much of his time on extracurricular activities and outside interests that his schoolwork was often frantically completed at the very last possible moment. It wasn't that he didn't enjoy his classes, because he did; it was just that he had a hard time fitting them into his overcrowded calendar. Before his first university term was over, Benchley already had joined the Mandolin Club and had been taken aboard by the *Lampoon* staff as a cartoonist. (His first published drawing featured two elderly women holding their noses while staring into an open garbage can, with the caption "Ain't it offal, Mabel?") His appetite for the theater was growing insatiable; besides auditioning for several dramatic clubs, he periodically ventured into Boston on weekday evenings to sit in the inexpensive balcony seats ("the gods," as they were called) at local playhouses and watch such stars as Charlotte Walker and Lew Fields touring with their latest shows. As for the weekends, they offered a myriad of choices: Benchley could go home to Worcester by trolley, a two-hour ride, and visit his parents and, perhaps, see Gertrude if she too was home for the weekend; he could take advantage of Lillian's usual standing offer to spend Saturdays together in Boston; or else he could just stick close to campus and try to get some studying done.

Luckily for Benchley, although he rarely sat around his room on the first floor of 52 Plympton Street for very long without being distracted by someone or something, he always did manage to get enough work done to satisfy even the most demanding of his instructors. In his freshman year—and, for that matter, throughout his entire four years at Harvard—it helped that, unlike a good many of his fellow undergraduates, the strictly raised Benchley abstained from such standard collegiate pastimes as drinking, smoking, and cardplaying. His

ability to tune out the often considerable noise around him and concentrate on work he needed to get done enabled him to do fairly well
in his classes even though he never seemed to be devoting all that
much study time to them. (Dormitory mate H. Towner Deane recalled
that once, during his junior year, Benchley was some twelve books
behind in the assigned reading for an English class, and caught up
in one all-night session in which he memorized chapter summaries
of every single book. "It was quite a joke to him that he stood rather
well in the final exam," wrote Deane.

Early on at Harvard, Benchley established a pattern of drawing on
personal experiences and his own background as the basis for many
of his assigned essays. In a freshman philosophy class, for example,
he most often wrote about religious issues and questions of faith. In
one paper, called "On Belief in God," he described what he termed
"my theory of heaven and hell":

"A man whose advantages have placed in his grasp a finer perception of right and wrong must follow a much higher course of action than the man whose better self has never had a chance to grow,
stunted by poverty, ignorance or misfortune, but an erring from these
higher paths of duty will cause an inner sense of shame and remorse
that will suffice for a hell for the man. According as a man lives up
to his light he has a sense, a subtle higher sense of spiritual satisfaction, and according to his [sins] and the dictates of his conscience he
has a torturing sense of self-degradation. So some slight violation of
the spiritual law by a man who has been brought by a higher perception of self will cause as much mental suffering for himself as a
far more devious erring on the part of a man whose spiritual growth
has been stunted through circumstances and misfortune."

Similarly, for an assignment in a government class, Benchley examined his hometown's powerful temperance movement (Worcester
was one of the first major U.S. cities to elect to go dry) and analyzed
its effectiveness in a paper entitled "Is No-License Advisable in
Worcester?" "Does no-license succeed in elevating the moral and
physical condition of the community?" he wrote. "Does it improve
the financial condition of the city and individual? Can it be successfully enforced? I believe the affirmative of all these questions to be
true. . . . In Worcester is a police squad of one lieutenant and eight

patrolmen; since May 1 there have been 150 arrests for violation of the local prohibition law. Of these, 125 have been convicted. The chief of police states that 94% of the number of drunks on Worcester streets are arrested, and the city hospital notes that the number of commitments to the alcoholic ward has been reduced from 169 to 68. Additionally, the number of deaths from delerium tremors and acute alcoholism has decreased from 14 to 3. . . . Liquor in Worcester may be obtained only through a process of registration, the records of which are not only under the town's supervision but are also open to the public for inspection. . . ."

While these papers reflect the high moral tone that Benchley's up-bringing had developed in him, it is significant that while he could have been regarded by his peers as something of a prude, he wasn't. "Bob's chuckling friendliness, his catholic tolerance, and his fun-loving nature made it impossible for any of the fast set to regard him as a prig," classmate Oscar Hausserman reflected in a 1955 letter to Robert's son Nathaniel. Furthermore, he noted, Benchley had an un-usually well-rounded relationship with all the differing segments of the Harvard student body. "His intelligence and his understanding and his gift for articulating his humorous observations of the passing show precluded the great middle class of dull, good boys from claiming him as one of their own, notwithstanding the fact that he didn't drink or smoke or play around with luscious ladies. And his quality of mind and his gift of expression were recognized by his scholarly classmates and precluded them from regarding him as a low-brow."

That "gift for articulating his humorous observations" began to manifest itself publicly not long after Benchley was taken in by D.U. At fraternity meetings, he increasingly found himself being called upon to entertain house members and visitors with one of his mock travelogues or satirical political "orations." Ever since boyhood, Benchley had loved to make faces in the mirror, and his talent at pick-ing up the mannerisms and speech patterns of adults was the source of much hilarity among his schoolmates, who often would be in stitches over his good-natured imitations of teachers, parents, and clergy. By the time he'd reached Harvard, Benchley had several "rou-tines" worked up, and his performances of them at the Delta Upsilon house left lasting impressions on the fraternity audience, as evidenced by Hausserman's vivid recollections:

> Bob's travel talks required as props nothing but an ordinary sized plain white handkerchief tacked high upon the wall, and a long pointer. The handkerchief served as the map of the region explored by Benchley, the head of an adventurous expedition which presumably had, before his lecture at the D.U. Club, already received world-wide acclaim. Benchley's manner was that of a gentle but quietly pleased with himself expert explorer not unwilling to talk about himself and his achievements and assuming as a matter of course that his prosaic stay-at-home listeners were interested in every detail of planning and of actual operation that led to the ultimate and exciting success of the dangerous and intricate expedition. So, using the long pointer, he would spot on the blank white surface of the tacked up handkerchief the starting point of the trip; and then, with slow, painstaking care trace the exact route followed by the party, interrupting himself frequently with rather confusing asides describing in pseudo-scientific jargon the nature and amount of his curious equipment, or repeating some quaint or amusing remark of a native or of a member of his group. . . .
>
> As for Bob's "political" speeches about "what we are doing down there in Washington," they parodied the type of pompous government official engaged in some movement or work which was in the public eye. At the request of his club-mates to tell them about his work in the nation's capital, he would take a stand in front of the group, pull out his watch and, holding the time-piece in his hand so that he wouldn't be late in catching his train back to Washington, he would then launch forth on what "we" were trying do "down there" and the progress "we" had made to date. He was always unctuous, kindly, jovially condescending and ready to chuckle with a falsely deprecating or modestly boastful smirk over the little human touches that sometimes cropped up in the great enterprise. We never knew exactly what the enterprise was, and we felt in our "little man" way that the great man was a bit muddled and obscure, but we were inclined to attribute all this to the protesting warning of the watch in his hand which was telling him that he ought not to be wasting his valuable time on us yokels but ought to be getting back to Washington in a hurry to resume the great work which he was so now lithesomely and modestly outlining. Sometimes the overall aim of this profound work was to

"make men out of boys—or girls (chuckling correction). I mean, of course, vice versa as the case may be." Sometimes the ultimate aim was to "build strong bodies" or to "make for a better understanding of things" or for "a better appreciation of the great outdoors" or to "enable our boys and girls to see things as they should be seen."

As it turned out, the Delta Upsilon fraternity house was just one of many places where Benchley began to make a name for himself as both a performer and a campus wit. His "talks" grew so popular that, in time, most student organizations viewed it as something of a necessity to include a Benchley appearance in their entertainment programs, and, soft touch that he was, Benchley almost always accepted the invitations. ("He never played hard to get when his talents were requested," noted H. Towner Deane, "and the demand for his presence increased as time went on.") By his junior year, the "act" was even playing off-campus; a 1910 Harvard Club meeting in Boston featured, among its after-dinner speakers, one R. C. Benchley, giving a travel lecture entitled "Through the Alimentary Canal with Gun and Camera."

Besides his solo performances as a speaker, Benchley also took part in numerous theatrical ventures of a more traditional nature, as barely a term went by that he wasn't in the midst of rehearsals or performances of some play or other. As a member of D.U., he participated in the fraternity's theater club's annual Elizabethan Revivals, in which he was always given a comic role. Part of the fun of appearing in the D.U. theatricals was that performances of each year's production weren't limited to the Cambridge campus; there was always one performance at a theater in Boston, and then the company would "take to the road" for one or two nights at other colleges in the region. Thus, Smith freshman Gertrude Darling was able to see a bewigged Robert on stage in April 1909 when D.U.'s presentation of George Chapman's *Al Fooles* came to Northampton. (This, by the way, was one of two free trips to Smith that Benchley was able to make that year; the other was when Harvard's Mandolin Club came to town the previous month for a concert with the Smith College Glee Club, which Gertrude was a member of.) And Benchley received quite a thrill in his senior year when the fraternity's production of Nicholas

Udall's *Ralph Roister Doister*, in which he played the lead role, was presented at the Opera House theater in his old stamping grounds, Exeter, to commemorate the three hundredth anniversary of its very first performance in Exeter, England. Virtually the entire Philips Exeter Academy, students and faculty, packed the hall, and when it was over, alumnus Benchley experienced for the first time the exhilaration of a standing ovation.

Besides the fraternity plays, Benchley was featured in several Harvard Dramatic Club presentations—including *The Horse Thieves, The Heart of the Irishman,* and *The Scarecrow*—as well as numerous Hasty Pudding shows and Stylus Club play parodies. Typical of these was an April 1910 production of *Rumeo and Julep,* a play described in its program notes as "a lamentable and lugubrious tragedy in four heartrending, tearcompelling and sobextracting accidents, by the late Mr. Francis Acrostic Bacon of Stratford-un-even, carefully abridged, curtailed, condensed and expurgated by Mr. Anthony (99 44/100% Pure) Constalk under the benign and maternal auspices of the Blotch and Awed Sorority, Lmtd. of Paris, Boston and Back Bay," in which Benchley starred as Rumeo W. Waverly-Waverly "of the House of Montaubun, captivated in the snarls of Julep's coiffure."

Still, Benchley did not really earn his reputation at Harvard as an actor or a writer. He was known mainly as a funny public speaker, and quite the practical joker—besides the davenport affair, classmate Laurence McKinney recalled that Benchley once boarded a Harvard-bound trolley out of Boston, stuck his leg stiffly into the aisle, and began wincing if anyone touched it; when the trolley reached Harvard Square, several people helped him off and accompanied him back to his dorm room—and, while he was recognized around Cambridge as one of the guiding forces behind the *Lampoon,* his work there consisted almost exclusively of drawing cartoons and providing comic illustrations for other people's copy, not his own.

Ironically, it was the very fact that he was looked upon as an illustrator and not a writer that made Benchley's election to the presidency of the *Lampoon* in January 1911 something of a shock. Traditionally, the post went to the foremost writer on the staff, and Benchley, who'd been appointed art editor back in the fall, was both surprised and humbled when the election results came in and showed him to be the overwhelming choice. Just how much this meant to him was reflected by the thoughts he put down that night in his diary: "It will mean a lot of work and a lot of worry and responsibility for it is a responsible position, yet I am very happy to be given it—not least of all because Mother will be so proud—and Gertrude too—and maybe my course will seem a little more worth while to Lillian. I never dreamed when I was a struggling freshman toiling over bum jokes that I would someday be the dreaded censor of others—I trust I remember enough of how I felt, to be as nice as Hallowell [Bob Hallowell, Benchley's first editor at the *Lampoon*] was to me then. It is the biggest thing so far in my college course, but it doesn't seem so big now that I've got it—I can see lots bigger things that I ought to do, a 'cum laude' for instance."

Being voted president of the Lampoon was but the first of many unexpected honors bestowed on Benchley during his junior year. Although he didn't know it at the time of the election, the *Lampoon* presidency automatically made him a member of Harvard's student council, and though he certainly would have been happy with just those two positions, the next two months saw him elected president of the Signet Society literary club, vice president of both the Dramatic Club and the D.U. fraternity, and a member of Hasty Pudding. In March, he was invited to a Papyrus Club dinner at a hotel in Boston, and, as he disclosed in his diary, "when I got there I found out that I had been elected a member. I didn't know what the club was beforehand, but during the dinner I gleaned that it is quite a body of literary men in Boston; I appear to be the only undergraduate in it. I think," he concluded, "that I'm getting over being surprised at the impossible things that are happening."

As Benchley had recorded in his diary, most of his noteworthy achievements at Harvard were not specifically related to academic endeavors. He knew that, in general, Lillian Duryea was not pleased with the path that his college career was taking. Indeed, at the beginning of the 1910 school year she had tried—unsuccessfully—to persuade Benchley to transfer to a more prestigious residence hall, in the apparent belief that he was being held back by his circle of friends at Holworthy Hall. "She did try to bring pressure as to his habits and associates," H. Towner Deane wrote many years later in a reminiscence to Nathaniel Benchley, "and junior year she very much wanted him to live in Beck Hall, then the habitation of the wealthy whom we thought a little stuffy. Bob managed to resist in a way that did not interrupt the flow of funds, as he seemed perfectly satisfied with his roommates and his conditions of living." The matter seems to have caused considerable tension between the two, a tension that remained until the spring, when Lillian, seeking to patch things up, invited Benchley to join her, along with two of her friends (one male, one female) and a local minister, for a summer-long sightseeing excursion to Europe.

Benchley found Lillian's offer characteristically double-edged. He'd barely been able to see Gertrude or his family during the course of the entire winter and spring, and now he was being enticed to leave the country for two months—two months in which he'd be dependent on Lillian for virtually everything. Still, he'd never traveled outside North America before, and since it was entirely likely that he'd never again be afforded such an opportunity, he knew he'd be foolish to turn it down. So, putting a good face on it, he accepted. And once he'd been able to see with his own eyes all the natural and man-made splendors of England, Holland, Germany, Austria, Italy, Switzerland, France, Spain, and Portugal—places he'd been reading and dreaming about his entire life—he was glad he had. Everywhere he found something to enjoy, from the Cheshire Cheese in London ("the old inn on Fleet Street where Dr. Johnson and his club used to hang out") to the White Cliffs of Dover ("In the moonlight they made another picture that more than lived up to expectations"), and from a resort beach in Amsterdam ("the surf was great—just like Maine, only warmer—and if I hadn't been watched by two life guards who blew a horn at me every time I got out of bounds I would have had the time of my life") to Montreux's Castle of Chillon ("The lace that Byron didn't have in mind when he wrote his 'Prisoner' "), Benchley found himself enveloped in history, culture, and beauty.

Only once during the sixty-four-day excursion was Benchley uncomfortable, and that was when, after leaving Paris, Lillian decided to split from the group for a few days and take Robert to Spain. For one thing, he had no desire to be in the country that was responsible for his brother's death. After witnessing a bullfight in Madrid, he wrote, "I left wishing I could touch a button that would topple the whole place over on top of the crowd and bury them all. . . . A nation that tolerates that is a degenerate nation and deserves to sink into the oblivion that it is in." Three days later, though, he confessed to his diary, "Since Madrid, I have seen so many sad, intelligent and attractive faces and had evidence of such innate courtesy and pride that my feeling toward the Spanish people has entirely changed to an attitude of great respect (when I can forget the bullfight)."

Moreover, there was the fact that before they left Paris, Lillian had arranged for a woman to accompany her and Robert to Spain as a chaperon. Since Benchley was at this point nearly twenty-two years old, he accepted the woman's presence as far as outward appearances were concerned, but it still bothered him a bit when, every now and then, Lillian would chide him for being "heartless and cold" to her. In his own mind, Benchley felt that being with Lillian helped maintain a connection between himself and Edmund, and he usually was able to convince himself that all of her attention to him was motivated by her feelings toward Edmund, and that she cared for him as the substitute older sibling he'd been robbed of by Edmund's death. Every once in a while, though, as on this side trip to Spain, he had to confront the fact that his and Lillian's relationship was more complex than he really wished it to be—and it was at those times that he found his only recourse was to indeed appear "heartless and cold," though he didn't find that characterization either appropriate or accurate. He simply didn't know what else to do. Gertrude was the only girl he'd ever cared about "that way," and he didn't see that changing, then or ever. Sometime soon, they would marry, just as everyone in Worcester expected them to—and Lillian would have to accept that if she wanted to remain his friend.

There was another issue that made him uncomfortable at several points during the trip, and that was when Lillian attempted to bring up the subject of Benchley's plans for employment after graduation— a subject he diverted the conversation from as best he could each time it was brought up. With talents lying in several different directions, Benchley knew that he could probably make a go of it at *something*— but exactly what? Illustrating? Perhaps writing, as some had suggested? Or maybe some form of civil service? He simply couldn't decide one way or another, and, between his full complement of classes and assorted extracurricular activities, he managed to avoid making many inquiries about possible job opportunities during the fall term. But as the months slipped away and the calendar turned to January 1912, he realized that the inevitable couldn't be postponed any longer. He simply had to try to secure a job, and soon.

Throughout the first three months of the new year, Benchley was in a total quandary as he sought to determine a proper course for himself. "Today, for the first time, I seriously considered teaching English as a possible step," he wrote in his diary on January 15. "In it I see my ideal life more than in any other line I have considered." To that end, he sought advice from Harvard's dean of the Faculty of Arts and Sciences, LeBaron Russell Briggs. "He said he thought I'd do better at a boy's school," noted Benchley, "but that, wherever I went, I'd have to spell better." Armed with this provisional endorsement, Benchley used the new typewriter he'd just purchased to fill out "what seemed like thousands of blanks" for teaching positions in the region.

Satisfied that that particular avenue was being adequately pursued, Benchley next went to see "Copey"—Harvard's legendary and beloved English professor Charles Townsend Copeland—who "urged me to go to New York and see the real American life." Copeland, and several others, had suggested writing as a possible vocation; it was a suggestion that Benchley found both intriguing and intimidating. In mid-January he received a letter of inquiry from an editor at the *Boston Journal*, "asking me to try writing humorous comments or articles on current topics for a special column," but Benchley politely declined, commenting—rather ironically—that he'd "hate to have to be humorous every day." The offer did, however, encourage him enough to mail a story he'd written, "The Doodlebugs Who Eat Grapes," along with some accompanying drawings, off to *St. Nicholas Magazine*, a move he described as "my first missile hurled at the wall of the world's literature." And for a brief period of time, he and fellow Lampooner Gluyas Williams entertained the idea of channeling their love of the theater into the formation of a freelance dramatic reviewing team, in which Benchley would provide the criticisms and Williams the illustrative caricatures, but they soon agreed that such aspirations were totally unrealistic. (As it turned out, less than ten years later, both of them would be firmly established in exactly this kind of work.)

Another person who recommended writing as a good choice for a career was his former classmate John Reed, who was in New York working as a newspaper reporter. Benchley, at Copey's behest, wrote to him for possible leads on vacancies at any of the numerous dailies published there. "Better a whiff of Gotham than a cycle of Back Bay!" the always exuberant Reed responded in a letter dated February 19.

I should say, to most people, and to you above all, "N'Yawk's the place." I think, without doubt, that you are destined to shine some day on the staff of Life. [This was an allusion to an enormously successful parody of the weekly humor magazine that had been published by the *Lampoon* under Benchley's editorship the previous year.] But of course one does not attain that in twenty minutes. If Copey can give you letters, try to get connected with an evening paper like the Sun or the World. The pay is not so high as with a morning paper, but you'll have your evenings free to write or go to the theatre. Besides having all sorts of channels to perhaps get into a humorous "column"—there is an excellent market for the kind of thing you do so well on Lampy. . . . I really think your bent is satire, and we have no satirists. . . . If you could get on a magazine, that would be fine for one who found newspaper life too strenuous, as I do; but chances are rare in that line.

In short, Old Lady Opportunity is permanently domiciled hereabouts. She only *visits* in other cities. . . . Here and now I extend you an invitation, also on behalf of my colleagues, Messrs. Rogers (Class Poet '09), who is a contributing reporter on the Brooklyn Eagle, Andrews '10, now advertising O'Sullivan's Rubber Heels, Osgood '11, now foreclosing widows and orphans on the Lawyers Mortgage Company—I repeat I invite you to live in our house, 42 Wash Squ Sou', room costing $3.50 per week—with use of our sun-parlor—meals at Childs and Ferrari's. I will guarantee that you get a good room and fair treatment; the water pipes burst about once a month, and the gas-light is not what it should be, but who cares? BOHEMIA! O BOHEMIA!

While Benchley mulled over the notion of an exciting, but expensive, life in New York City, he continued to explore opportunities closer to home. He went out to the Groton School in late February at the invitation of the school's director, the Rev. Dr. Endicott Peabody, but as the two discussed the possibility of Benchley's joining the faculty, he realized that Peabody was looking for someone who could give Groton a long-term commitment and that, deep down, he saw teaching only as a temporary means of supporting himself. "I am afraid," he confessed privately after the meeting, "that I enjoyed my talk with Mr. P more than the prospects for my teaching."

March provided something of a respite from the pressures of job-hunting, primarily because Benchley was completely absorbed in work on the final two amateur productions of his college career—the aforementioned *Ralph Roister Doister*, in which he starred, and a Hasty Pudding show called *Below Zero*, written by one of his best friends, Laurence McKinney. ("My last appearances in college theatricals—a total of nine shows," Benchley noted in his diary. "It has been enjoyable, but it has also wasted much good time.") In fact, Benchley was so busy with his shows and the *Lampoon* that it wasn't until the very end of the month, when Reed came to Cambridge for a visit and once again tried to persuade him to move down to New York, that a guilt-ridden Benchley once again started focusing his energies on the task of finding a job.

Unfortunately, things only became more confused in April. Bliss Perry, Benchley's Comparative Literature teacher, had recommended that he think about the publishing field, and to that end, Benchley went to see a man at the Curtis Publishing Company's advertising department in Boston, where there was supposedly a vacancy. "It took him an hour and a half to tell me that the job in question—the editorship of an advertising magazine—was already filled," wrote Benchley, "and to dilate upon the general history and prospects of advertising as such. He advised me not to teach, but to try and get into some agency to write copy." The ad man recommended that Benchley return with a portfolio of his work for the "higher-ups" to look at, since one never knew when something might open up.

A few days later, while Benchley was still thinking about whether it was worth the trouble of putting together a scrapbook for what seemed to be a rather unlikely possibility, he heard about, and quickly received an interview for, a staff writer's position on a business trade publication, but when he found out that taking the position meant relocating to Chicago, he withdrew his application. ("Truthfully," he confided in his diary afterward, "I doubt that I could write persuasive business articles anyway.")

The very next day, on April 10, Benchley met Dr. Peabody at the Union Club in Boston, and as the two walked around Boston Common and Commonwealth Avenue, Peabody offered him the only position available at Groton—that of French instructor. Knowing that he was utterly unqualified to teach the subject, Benchley declined as respectfully as possible, telling Peabody that his "zeal for teaching had weakened considerably of late," but he sensed that Peabody wasn't pleased about what had ended up being a considerable waste of time and effort on his part. "We parted with only one thing definite," he wrote of the meeting, "and that is that I do not teach at Groton."

The experience did prove to be helpful, however, in that it made Benchley realize that he really *didn't* have any particular "zeal" for teaching, and that he was just going through the motions for outward appearances. He sent off letters to the headmasters of Andover and his alma mater, Exeter, informing the only two other schools that had expressed any interest in him that he'd decided not to become a teacher. With at least one less thing to worry about, he put together the requested scrapbook of clippings, dropped them off at the Curtis offices, and started gathering letters of reference and introduction from several of his professors. He was going to follow John Reed's advice and use some of his final spring break vacation time to investigate employment prospects in New York.

Benchley spent three long days in New York City absorbing both disappointments and pain. The disappointments stemmed from the fact that virtually all the people he'd hoped to see were not around when he showed up at their offices. On four different occasions, he went downtown to try to gain an audience with the editor of the *World*, Ralph Pulitzer, but was rebuffed each time, and his trip to the *Collier's* office proved equally fruitless; the editor, he was told, was off traveling in Europe. Even Reed was out when he went to see him at his desk at the *American Magazine*. As for the pain, that was the result of his encounters with Dr. Converse, a dentist whom Lillian

Duryea arranged for him to visit for a checkup. Converse found so much inside his mouth that required attention that Benchley spent several hours of each of his three days in town sitting open-jawed and white-knuckled in the dentist's chair. His one "triumph" was a five-minute chat with Mr. Dodd of the Dodd, Mead & Co. publishing firm, who politely told him that there was absolutely nothing available, but that he'd be happy to let him know if anything came up, although that was highly unlikely. With battered molars and a bruised ego, Benchley left New York for a weekend at Northampton, where an understanding Gertrude helped to console him.

Returning to Cambridge with what he hoped was a better sense of direction now that New York seemed to have eliminated itself as a place to begin a professional career, Benchley received some encouraging news when he went back to the Curtis offices in late April to pick up his scrapbook. He was brought in to meet Richard Walsh—an old Lampooner who, it turned out, had the job that Benchley had originally applied for. Walsh told him that there was a good possibility that the company might need someone in about six months. Not long after that, Benchley heard a rousing speech on the subject of careers in social work delivered by Oliver Cutts, one of the directors of the Civic Service League, and learned that there were immediate openings in Philadelphia, where the organization was based. Benchley found the idea of social work very appealing, and decided to apply for admission to the league's one-year apprentice program. Even if he eventually chose to do something else, he figured, he'd at least be spending the time in a worthwhile activity. "With a social service job," he wrote, "I could look any man in the eye and say that my job was just as good."

Buoyed by a more promising outlook on the employment front, Benchley felt confident enough to proceed with some more personal matters. To no one's surprise, and everyone's delight, Benchley and Gertrude Darling announced their engagement on May 10 in Northampton. (Actually, not quite *everyone* was completely pleased by the news. As it happened, one of Lillian Duryea's sisters was married to the head of Smith's history department, and after news of the engagement spread all the way to Nyack, the woman came to offer congratulations. "You must understand if Lillian isn't too enthusiastic about this," she told Gertrude. "Robert is her one ewe lamb, you know.") The only immediate change in their courtship was that, as an engaged student, Gertrude was now allowed to visit with Benchley in a private sitting room at her dormitory residence, rather than only in the more public Haven House parlor. But any official marriage plans were, at this point, out of the question: first Benchley would have to find not only a bona fide job, but one sufficient to support at least two people.

On May 21, Benchley received a letter from Oliver Cutts offering him the civic service job in Philadelphia. He went to seek Bliss Perry's advice, and the professor strongly suggested that he take it, pointing out that since the Curtis Publishing Company had a branch office in Philadelphia, Benchley could stay in touch with the firm and perhaps do some work for it on the side if he so desired. "Of course, he strongly advised me *not* to go into publishing," Benchley noted, "as it was too commercialized to suit a man who liked books for themselves." Over the course of the next two weeks, Benchley slowly concluded that the apprentice program was probably his best bet, especially since the only other offer he'd received during this time was for a secretarial job at the Boston Museum of Fine Arts, which had sounded potentially interesting but was paying a disappointingly low starting salary of $800 a year. So, on June 7, during the period between the official end of classes and the beginning of finals week, he went to Philadelphia, where he was to be treated to lunch at the St. James Hotel by several of the Civic Service League's bigwigs. The food was marvelous, and the directors all seemed like nice men, but by the time coffee and dessert were being served, Benchley was inwardly wishing he'd never made the trip; all the talk at the table was about the nobility of young men like Benchley who were willing to make civic service their life's work. On the train ride back from Pennsylvania, he realized that once again he was fooling himself as well as others. Loftier goals were fine, but he simply wasn't sure enough about what he wanted to do with his future to make any long-term commitments one way or other. All he could be absolutely certain of was that he needed a job that would provide a decent day's wage for a decent day's work. Nothing more and nothing less—at least for now.

With that in mind, Benchley began to reconsider the Boston Museum of Fine Arts. The director, Arthur Fairbanks, had offered Benchley the job on the spot when he'd interviewed for it, but with the pay so low, Benchley had flatly refused. When he got back to Massachusetts from Philadelphia, however, Fairbanks notified him that he'd been able to get the board of trustees to approve a substantially higher salary for Benchley—$1,200 a year. Fairbanks, it seems, had been able to argue successfully that in addition to performing his secretarial duties, Benchley could help the museum raise funds and promote itself through what he termed "social service educational assignments"—i.e., making speaking appearances on behalf of the museum, acting as a tour guide for visiting dignitaries, and being of service to the various museum executives and patrons. Benchley was impressed by Fairbanks's industriousness, and by the fact that he was at last being pursued for a job with no long-term strings attached. He told Fairbanks he'd let him know one way or the other as soon as his finals were over.

As might have been expected, Benchley hadn't done much preparation for his exams, and what little spare time he did manage to find during the last few hectic weeks of the school term was mainly occupied by preparations for the Ivy Oration speech, which, as *Lampoon* president, he was required to make at the close of commencement exercises. Compounding all of this was a very bad cold that he had caught during the trip to Philadelphia, which knocked him so out of commission that he wound up taking several of his exams in his dormitory room with a proctor at his bedside. Benchley's weakened condition was, no doubt, at least partially responsible for his failure in the Government 4 (International Law) final exam—a failure which, technically, prevented him from being included in Harvard's 1912 graduating class. Then again, Benchley had been doing so miserably in the course all semester that perhaps *no* answer might have been preferable to the one he did provide for the exam's last essay question. Thoroughly at a loss as to how to tackle the topic of the legal dispute between the United States and Great Britain over the rights to the waters off the Newfoundland coast, Benchley decided to argue the matter from the perspective of a concerned third party—the fish. Nascent environmentalist that he might have been, the government department was not sufficiently amused to pass him, and it wasn't until the following spring, when his F was erased from the record by way of two substituted extra English classes, that Benchley officially received his bachelor's degree.

Nonetheless, he did manage to shed his cold, as well as his worries, in time for his Ivy Oration speech on June 20 at Soldiers' Field. Traditionally, this humorous talk was the final speech of Graduation Day, and its contents were printed in the year's final edition of the *Harvard Lampoon*. Benchley had faithfully auditioned it under the sanctioned tutelage of one of the speech department's professors, but the opportunity to skewer the whole process of speechmaking on both the written and oral fronts was just too tempting. As published, his speech ("divided," he noted, "into three quarters, or halves") featured an introduction that ended with these words:

"Here it was Class Day, and there I was, in my room playing the organ. Quickly I drew on a pair of shoes and my cap and gown, and breaking into a run—and a perspiration—soon found myself, unless I am mistaken, here."

When he actually delivered it, though, it came out sounding more like this:

"Here it was Class Day, and there I was, in my room playing with my—I mean, playing with *an* organ. Quickly I drew on a pair of shoes— that is, I didn't really *draw* them, you see, even though I can draw a fair pair of shoes when I have a good mind to, or even when I have a bad mind to—and threw up, rather threw *on* my cap and gown, and breaking into a nun, er, a *run*, and a perspiration, soon found myself, unless I am mistaken, [looks down] here. [Moves several inches to the left.] Or, perhaps, *here*."

Having been preceded by the usual tedium of Graduation Day pomp and circumstance, this genial, irreverent address ("You men have gone through much," he noted, "besides your allowances") was a refreshing tonic to the audience, which laughed continuously throughout the speech and applauded loudly at its conclusion.

For Benchley, the Ivy Oration was a fitting climax to a college career spent primarily in the pursuit of good times. Now, however, it was time to set foot in the real world. Gertrude, herself now a college graduate, was heading for Lewiston, Pennsylvania, to spend the summer as a private tutor, and, he, too, had to begin making his own living. On June 29 he notified Dr. Fairbanks of his decision, and the Boston Museum of Fine Arts had a new secretary.

3
Heaven Won't Protect the Working Man

"A SERIOUS DISTASTE FOR MERCHANDISING PROBLEMS"

On a weekday afternoon in early September 1912, Robert Benchley sat nervously in a box seat at Fenway Park watching a baseball game between the Boston Red Sox and the Washington Senators. Although the tense action on the field could have been responsible for his condition—the Red Sox were, after all, fighting for the American League pennant—it wasn't. In fact, Benchley was hardly paying attention to the game at all. What he was paying attention to, and what was causing him no small amount of anxiety, was the elderly woman in the seat next to him, who was cheering on pitcher Rube Marquard and the rest of the hometown heroes with such exuberance and abandon that nearly everyone in the surrounding section of stands was staring their way.

Just a few hours before, Benchley had been quietly going about his business on his second official day at a desk in the Museum of Fine Arts when he was told that one of the institution's most important patrons, a Mrs. Gardner, was coming for a visit. No other museum administrator was at the office when she arrived, and the only instructions he'd received were to see to it that whatever the visiting dignitaries wanted, they get. And what this woman wanted, evidently, was someone to accompany her to a baseball game. So this was what the board of trustees had meant by "social service educational assignments"!

Benchley had spent most of the summer at home in Worcester, fighting sweltering heat, his annual hay fever attacks, and the tedious translating of a French catalog of paintings that the museum had acquired for exhibition in the fall. Right after hiring him, Dr. Fairbanks had left town on business. In a letter detailing Benchley's responsibilities until his return, he'd placed Benchley in the hands of one of the museum's other administrators, a Mr. Carter. "If he needs your help in any matters, he may ask you for it," Fairbanks had written. "I expect to be back on October 1, and the normal work may begin at that time." As Benchley quickly discovered, though, there seemed to be precious little about working at Boston's Museum of Fine Arts that could be described as normal.

In mid-August, as he neared completion of the translation, Benchley came into town to ask Carter some technical questions concerning the preparation of the catalog and to discuss what would be his regular office hours, which were scheduled to begin the first week of September. Carter suggested that the two of them, along with two other museum officials, go to lunch. Benchley sat quietly listening to three disgruntled men whine over what they felt was the terrible state of affairs at the museum. The only time they acknowledged his presence was when one or another of them would turn his way and inquire if he had any idea what he was getting himself into coming to such a badly run organization. "Why on earth are you coming to work here, anyway?" asked one of them. "The museum certainly is no place for someone like you." Benchley looked to Carter for some sign of reassurance, but none was forthcoming; all the administrator would say was that if Dr. Fairbanks wanted him to begin office hours in September, then a work space would be provided for him. But no mention of specific duties came up, and Benchley returned to his parents' home in Worcester befuddled. He hadn't been particularly impressed with any of the people he'd met; they didn't seem like the sort one would expect to find at a cultural institution. "Art for art's sake does not seem indigenous to an art museum evidently," he commented in his diary. "I shall wait results with interest."

The translating of the catalog, though drudgery, had at least been something concrete for Benchley to work on. But Fairbanks's vague orders—"You will report to the museum and spend your time in study of objects, records, and whatever else you will, and I hope that you will be able to gain some familiarity with those objects kept on exhibition," the director had written him—and the cool reception given him by the rest of the museum staff left Benchley feeling very lonely and misplaced. His days were a strange combination of the boring and the unpredictable. He'd spend hours trying to keep himself awake leafing through old museum records or wandering through the halls examining various objects, and then quite suddenly he'd be conscripted to conduct a group of visiting schoolchildren on a tour of the Egyptian wing or to cater to the whims of special patrons like Mrs. Gardner. As for his nights, they consisted mainly of attending shows by himself at Boston theaters or reading the classics and writing letters to Gertrude from the study room at the D.U. fraternity house, where he was temporarily staying until he could save up enough money to rent a furnished room. For one of the first times in his life, he experienced a true sense of loneliness. "It's no fun hanging college pictures alone when you're out of college," he wrote. "It kind of made me sick to my stomach."

As it turned out, though, this situation was not to last very long. Before the first week of September ended, Benchley received a glimmer of hope in the form of a meeting with the Curtis Publishing Company's Richard Walsh. The two had kept in touch over the summer—at Walsh's request, Benchley had done some freelance copywriting for the company's newspaper ads—and it seemed that Walsh's statement to him several months previous about a possible job opening in the advertising department had indeed been true. The company was considering starting up a house organ for its advertising department out of its New York offices, and Benchley's name had come up as a possible editor. Was he interested?

With both the *Ladies' Home Journal* and the *Saturday Evening Post* under its aegis, the Curtis Publishing Company was one of the nation's most successful magazine publishing houses. Founded by Cyrus H. K. Curtis in the late 1800s, the company was headquartered in an imposing block-long building overlooking Philadelphia's Independence Square and had various branch offices, including one in New York's Metropolitan Building near Madison Square. Benchley knew that living in New York would be expensive, but he also knew that he was suffocating at the museum. And the job would get him into the publishing world—even if it was through the not especially literary side door of the advertising wing.

Benchley told Walsh that he certainly *was* interested, and a week later he traveled to New York to be interviewed by one of Curtis's advertising directors, Stanley Latshaw. Latshaw liked him so much that before the day was over, Benchley wound up taking a train to Philadelphia for a tour of the Curtis plant, where the new publication, *Obiter Dicta*, was to be printed. Upon his return to Boston, Walsh informed him that the job was all but his, and that as soon as the paperwork was finished, it would be official. On October 2, he received a note from Walsh confirming that he was being hired as editor of the Curtis house organ: Come October 17, he was expected to be at the Curtis office in New York, ready to work.

Arthur Fairbanks had just the previous day returned to Boston, and Benchley felt guilty about giving immediate notice, but the director was understanding and wished him luck. There was a scheduled meeting of the museum committee that afternoon, and Fairbanks asked Benchley to record the minutes, which he dutifully did, noting in his diary later that evening how ironic it was that his first official act as Fairbanks's secretary was also his last. The "normal" work had finally come, but much too late for him to want to stay.

During the next two weeks, Benchley made preparations for the move to New York. He had no place to live, but again the Duryea family lent a hand. Although Benchley had seen little of Lillian since she'd come to Cambridge for the graduation ceremonies the previous June, they had continued corresponding regularly, and when it happened that Lillian was sailing to Europe the same morning that Benchley had his New York interview with the Curtis people, Benchley had risen early and taken a ferry to Hoboken to see her off. When Lillian found out about the job possibility, she told Benchley that she'd ask her mother if, should Benchley get the job, the family might be able to put him up until he could get himself proper accommodations in the city. When the job offer was firm, Benchley wrote Mrs. Duryea, who sent back word that she'd be delighted to have the company. Benchley arrived in Nyack on the evening of the 16th, dined with Mrs. Duryea, checked the train schedule for the next morning's trains into the city, and made ready for his new life in New York. His diary entry for the day was predictably reflective. "Here we are," he wrote, "taking a second start in the Big Game. I don't know whether I'll like the new work or whether I can do it, but some how I'm not much worried. . . . When I read this in twenty-five years let me bear in mind that right now I have every helpful influence behind me and every advantage before me and if I don't make good it will be through my own fault, for I've got as good a chance as a man ever had."

As his diary entry for October 17 details, Benchley spent most of his first day as a workingman in New York City scurrying around town in a frenzy of activity:

Went down to the city on the 8:13, which landed me at the Metropolitan Building a trifle late, but very vigorous. I spent the morning with

Mr. Walsh. . . . He got me out some of the material at hand for "Obiter Dicta" and left me alone in luxury, with the wind howling around the 18th story of the Tower. At 12 went across the street to a cafe-lunch and had a teutonic dish of pigs knuckles and sauerkraut. Then went down to the 23rd St. Y.M.C.A. and got some membership blanks and asked about rooms. Went up to the Harvard Club and wrote a couple of notes and saw Bob Hallowell. Took the bus down to Washington Square where I investigated #42 South where Jack Reed lives and wants me to come. I wasn't much impressed with anything but the gloominess of it and the dirtiness of the Park opposite. It may be bohemian but I'll bet it's unsanitary. Came back to the office and spent the rest of the p.m. sorting over the "Obiter Dicta" material and listening to Mr. Latshaw's ideas on the textile advertisers. . . . Caught the 5:34 up to Nyack, and spent the evening till nine pumping the pianola. Retired then and meditated on my lodging prospect. At night the Y.M. certainly has a big lead over Bohemia.

By the end of the week, Benchley had made his choice, and on the 21st he took a $5-a-week room at the Y.

Since the Curtis advertising division had never tried to publish a house organ before, definitive decisions from the department heads were hard to come by, resulting in Benchley's having to sit on his hands quite a bit during his first few months on the job. So as not to make it appear that he wasn't doing the requisite amount of work, Benchley's superiors started using him as an ad copywriter, even though the inexperienced Benchley showed little flair or instinct for this type of writing. He was put onto various textile accounts, but with little success; he thought he'd come up with a suitably snappy campaign slogan for the Columbia Cufturn Shirt Company—"A shirt is no cleaner than its spotted cuff"—but the idea was summarily dismissed. Eventually, he found the closest thing to a niche in the department composing letters designed to persuade manufacturers to buy advertising space in Curtis publications.

Life at the Y was fairly uneventful, so Benchley soon began spending most of his free time at the Harvard Club, where he could count on animated conversations with fellow alumni, enjoy a decent meal (so long as his credit held out, that is; he often had to have other members cover for him when he was unable to settle the previous week's accounts), and while away the hours reading books from the club's well-stocked library of classics. Gertrude was still in Lewiston working as a tutor for the Woods family.

Benchley surveyed several of his coworkers and friends on the question of how much it would take to start housekeeping in New York. Most everyone he talked to gave him the same figure of $2,000, which was a seemingly unattainable $500 more than his yearly salary. Clearly, he needed either to get a raise or to start saving, but as he'd just started at his job, a raise was out of the question. His accumulated wealth after he bought his Christmas presents in December amounted to a grand total of twenty cents, so it was clear that as long as he was living in New York, marriage to Gertrude would have to be postponed.

Benchley began 1913 by taking care of some unfinished business—his college makeup exams—and trying to start a new one—that of a spare-time freelance writer. In late January, he took several days' vacation from work and returned to the Harvard campus for his curriculum-completing tests in English and Comparative Literature. Benchley knew he'd passed a certain critical juncture in his life when the news that he'd finally graduated (he officially received his degree on March 8) excited him far less than the letter that came for him at the D.U. fraternity house notifying him that his unattended bank account in Cambridge still had a balance of $14.05 left in it. Several weeks later, he decided to proceed with an idea he'd had for a story—a serious story—that he hoped to sell to a magazine. "I made beginnings tonight on what I hope will be my first great literary success," he wrote in his diary on February 15, "a powerful, yet cynical, and very evenly written sketch which I think I shall call 'The Socialist.' Just why I chose to write about that I can't say, except that ever since fall I've wanted to write about the men that wrap themselves up in newspapers to sleep in the park."

While Benchley did succeed in completing "The Socialist," the piece proved unsalable; there was, understandably, little interest in an unrelievedly depressing story of a bum who rants and raves about the need for man to share his wealth with those less fortunate—in this case, the bum on the adjoining bench won't donate any spare insulatory sheets of old newspaper to his needy neighbors—until he himself stumbles upon a pile that some other wretched soul has hidden away. It turns out that there's more than enough in the pile for one person, but as soon as the man's hands fall upon the booty, he becomes exactly like the selfish bum he was berating moments before; the story ends with him cheerfully stuffing his pockets with his newfound riches and turning a deaf ear on the whimpering cries and coughs of another freezing man nearby. While "The Socialist" failed to crack the literary marketplace for him, Benchley nonetheless felt good about the experience, and his spirits were considerably lifted when, at the end of March, he made his very first freelance sale ever: *St. Nicholas* magazine sent him a check for $10 for two drawings that his friend Laurence McKinney had wheedled out of him to illustrate McKinney's poem "The Orc and His Globular Isle."

As spring approached, work on *Obiter Dicta* finally began to heat up. The New York office's advertising manager, Edward Hazen, had been designated to serve as "supervisor" for the first issue, but having been given no specific instructions other than to produce "a house organ with punch," Benchley found himself working in the dark. He spent considerable time poring over other companies' internal publications and began piecing together articles about various aspects of the technical and business aspects of publishing, from the latest advances in typography to ways of cultivating better relationships with advertisers to the importance of product placement at magazine stands. After Benchley finished getting a dummy issue prepared and handed it over to Hazen, better than a week went by without any response from the executive. After a bit of investigating, Benchley learned that the dummy was still sitting on Hazen's desk, buried under a pile of other papers. Since he'd already gathered enough material for the second issue, Benchley decided that the best way to proceed would probably be simply to go ahead and get the thing printed, so that some semblance of a production schedule could be followed. Putting a dummy for issue two in Hazen's in-basket, Benchley reclaimed the first-issue dummy and passed it along to the company printer. The premiere edition of *Obiter Dicta* arrived at the advertising department offices in late April. No sooner was it in circulation than the company executives in Philadelphia gave Benchley a detailed criticism in which they described the finished product as "too technical, too scattering, and wholly lacking in punch."

Whether Hazen had looked over the dummy or not Benchley never found out, for Hazen hadn't made one single comment to him during the entire time.

Had Benchley not been introduced to the world of executive responsibility avoidance at the Museum of Fine Arts, perhaps he would have been unnerved by the company's reaction to the first issue of *Obiter Dicta*. But he knew that he was the new kid on the block and, as such, likely to attract precious little support from anyone—the only sympathy shown to him at all came from Walsh, who promised to aid in the selection of articles for the next few issues. He managed to weather the storm, promising his superiors that future editions would meet with their approval now that he better understood what was expected of the publication.

After the initial humiliating reception of the first issue of *Obiter Dicta*, things settled down considerably at Curtis. Benchley's letter-writing skills resulted in his being assigned to head up an in-house information bureau responsible for sending out weekly letters and monthly notebook leaves, and while he continued to struggle editorially with the contents of the magazine (*Obiter Dicta* features included "Selling Through Boys," "Cultivating the Jobber," and "From Cider Press to Rotary"), he slowly became part of the company team. Even a few of his textile ads were accepted, and by icy Hazen no less.

With his career appearing to be on the upswing, Benchley turned to more personal matters. To satisfy his desire for some kind of civic work, he became involved with the Intercollegiate Social Service Committee, an organization that helped run numerous boys' clubs around town. Benchley was assigned to the East Side House on 16th Street near the East River, and every Wednesday night he supervised an evening of games and activities for a group of underprivileged teenage boys. The Sea Gull Athletic Club, as the group came to call itself, proved to be an extremely rewarding experience for Benchley, who was so well liked by the kids (especially after he spent one entire meeting drawing caricatures of historical figures) that they surprised him one night with a "banquet" of sandwiches and ice cream, courtesy of the drugstore run by the brother of one of the club members.

It was also at this time that Benchley finally got Gertrude to let him buy her a proper engagement ring. She knew that he couldn't afford one, and that marriage was still way off in the future, but it had been a year since they'd officially announced their engagement, and he felt that her patience had to be rewarded with something. So one afternoon when he had to go down to Philadelphia on business, Gertrude came by train from Lewiston and met him there, and the two went shopping. They found a ring they both liked in the window of a downtown jewelry store, but when they went inside to price it, they found they'd been admiring a diamond solitaire ring costing $150 more than the $60 Benchley had scrimped together. When the jeweller balked at extending credit, the determined Benchley went over to the Curtis offices and borrowed the money against his salary. It meant that he wasn't going to see another paycheck for the next seven weeks—it would take the generosity of friends like Walsh and Freddy Allen to help him pay for his room and meals—but once he'd placed the ring on Gertrude's finger, all thoughts of practical considerations simply melted away.

At the start of the summer of 1913, Benchley was given new responsibilities by the Curtis Publishing Company. The gingham business was noticeably livelier in Ohio and Pennsylvania than it was in New England, and Benchley was dispatched on a three-week, thirty-two-city fact-finding mission to discover why that was. At each stop, Benchley interviewed manufacturers, merchants, and buyers, and though he came back from the trip with no real conclusions, his employers found the multitude of data he submitted in his report impressive, and he soon found himself traveling extensively, investigating such things as heightened pianola sales in the mid-Atlantic states and magazine subscription scams at state fairs. Generally, he was able to plot his own itinerary, and so he made regular sweeps through the Worcester area, where he could not only stay with his parents and save a few days' expense money, but also see Gertrude. Her tutorial job in Lewiston had ended, and she was now living at the nearby Millbury, Massachusetts, farm of her friend Katharine Colton's parents.

Had Benchley been able to continue working in this sort of troubleshooting capacity, things might have stayed manageable for him at Curtis. But with fall came the seasonal increase in the copywriting load, and once again Benchley was spending days contemplating the philosophical dilemmas of "Advertising Anatomy," "Advertising and Luxuries," and "Advertising and the High Cost of Living," as well as trying to think up original ways to promote printer's ink producers and carpeting manufacturers. Once again his ideas and articles were being met with the familiar uncommitted responses. In late September, Dick Walsh took Benchley out to lunch and told him that changes were in the air, and that there were doubts that Benchley was sufficiently interested in the job to be the right man for it. Walsh told him that the company bigwigs were unconvinced that he was capable of the kind of "serious writing" that the firm expected from its copywriters.

Over the next few weeks, Benchley tried to concentrate on his work, but his mind kept wandering. He thought of many things: of several very "serious" articles that he was trying to complete in his limited spare time—one an antiwar treatise, the other a fictional account of a day in the life of a subway motorman; of why, although he tried, he seemed unable to overcome "my serious distaste for these merchandizing problems and agency situations"; of how much he missed the city of Boston, and Gertrude; and of what he wished he was doing for a living. "Had a long dream, as I sat at my desk," he noted in his diary on October 6. "I thought how much I'd like to be dramatic critic for 'Life.' If I am to change my work, I need to do it soon, before I have my family."

In mid-October, as Benchley came to the end of his first year at Curtis—he asked for a small raise, but was told that none would be forthcoming—he reflected in his diary on the general conditions of his life. Financially, he was a bit in the red, as the small fortune he'd spent on Gertrude's ring still had him owing about $80 to friends, but he wasn't overly concerned, and he felt fine both physically and mentally ("I think I have improved through business experience and fairly wide reading," he noted). In several other areas, however, he was dissatisfied. "I must face the fact that I haven't lived up to expectations in my work," he confessed. "I haven't put enough into it, and while it has been interesting, it hasn't been absorbing. I have been lazy at it, as I have at all other things. Morally, I have lost rather than gained—both in will power and perception—due, I think, to a loosening grip on spiritual introspection. I find myself reverting only occasionally to inspirations that I used to frequently fall upon. The work in the settlement house is the only thing of which I am proud."

The Curtis Publishing Company traditionally held its annual convention in Philadelphia at the end of October, and Benchley's Harvard reputation as an after-dinner speaker led to Latshaw's asking him to help organize and oversee the program for the convention's main dinner on the 29th. Hoping that the sense of humor that the firm generally frowned upon in his writing would serve him better in the context of a friendly banquet, Benchley decided to play what he was sure would be recognized as a great practical joke. Several weeks before the dinner, Benchley went out for lunch one day and returned wearing a fake beard, a wig, and a pair of eyeglasses. After walking through the Curtis corridors and past everyone from Walsh to Latshaw without being recognized, he decided that the trick could indeed by carried off.

On the night of the company banquet, Cyrus Curtis, president of the Curtis Publishing Company, found himself seated on the dais next to an odd-looking gent going by the name of John J. Constantine, head of an advertising concern based in Seattle, Washington. Although Curtis had met Benchley a few times, the pleasantries he exchanged with Mr. Constantine assured Benchley that the disguise was indeed working. Only Walsh and the toastmaster knew what Benchley was up to when, having been introduced to the audience, he proceeded to make a vigorous speech denouncing most of Curtis's advertising practices. In the middle of the speech, which was being met with dead silence, Benchley started to criticize the company's censorship policy, and a flushed Cyrus Curtis began to rise to his feet and had to be physically restrained by several people. After a few more agonizing minutes, Benchley finally flung off his disguise, launched into several rousing choruses of "Heaven Will Protect the Working Girl," and heard a very slight smattering of sparse, nervous laughter. It wasn't until later in the evening, when Benchley returned to the podium and performed one of his old travelogue routines, that he managed to slip out of the noose he'd placed his neck into.

The year 1913 ended with Benchley still looking for a raise and, because of the banquet fiasco, feeling even less secure about his position at Curtis and disturbed because the work gave him so little satisfaction. He began to do volunteer work for the Urban League investigating living conditions at uptown tenements, and also decided to take the little money he'd saved for Christmas presents for his family and donate it to the East Side House's Holiday Fund, which was buying gifts for needy neighborhood children. He wrote the Harvard Alumni Appointments Office to request that he be notified of any possible social-service-related job openings in the Boston area. Feeling that at least he was trying to better his life, Benchley returned to Worcester for the holidays. As was a custom of the time, on New Year's Eve he and Gertrude leaped into the air just before the stroke of midnight. When they landed, it was 1914.

Benchley started the new year with one firm resolution—to marry Gertrude Darling by June. They'd been engaged for over a year and a half, and even though he had not yet succeeded in finding a job he wanted to keep or keeping a job he didn't want long enough so that he could comfortably find another one he did want, he knew he couldn't make her wait much longer. Their time together had grown scarce since their respective graduations from college, and while it did add a romantic flavor whenever she'd arrange for a day off from tutoring and meet him at the train station in either Philadelphia (if he needed to go there for meetings) or New York, there was always a certain frenzied, hurried air as well. Eventually, there'd be a train for one of them to catch, and then they'd be planning the next rendezvous. Marriage, Gertrude hoped and Benchley agreed, would change all that—forever.

At work, where things appeared to be calming down once again, he instructed the payroll department to withhold $10 of his weekly salary, so that he could accumulate some sort of savings with which to begin married life. Dick Walsh spoke on Benchley's behalf to Latshaw to see if he might finally get a raise, and it was primarily because of Walsh's assurances that the board of directors was certain to approve one that Benchley turned down an offer to serve as business manager of the *American Journal of Public Health* back in Boston for the same salary he was already making—$1,500 a year. But at the end of February, an embarrassed and apologetic Walsh told him not only that a raise was out of a question, but that the company had decided to reorganize the department and that several positions—including Benchley's—were likely to be eliminated. "Dick assured me that there was nothing to hurry about," he noted on February 27, "but to wait until I find just what I want. . . . It really comes as a relief, for I have felt all along that I was stalling, and I have ached to get into something where I could write what I wanted, and not boost advertising in which I had but faint faith myself. I feel ten pounds lighter—but worried about that wedding in June."

On March 7, Benchley lunched with another coworker, Earl Derr Biggers, who suggested that he try out for one of the New York newspapers. Biggers was friends with the *Tribune*'s popular columnist Franklin P. Adams, known far and wide as the redoubtable F.P.A., creator of "The Conning Tower"—a daily potpourri of theatrical gossip, outrageous punnery, and literary bon mots drawn mainly from the contributions of a dedicated flock of aspiring young writing hopefuls whom Adams never paid but whose careers invariably profited from the prestigious exposure. Biggers volunteered to check with Adams to see if the *Tribune* might need anyone, and Benchley told him to go ahead, even though he felt he wasn't really cut out to be a newspaperman. If he had his choice of publishing jobs, he told Biggers, he'd much prefer working at a magazine—some place like the *Century*, whose editor, Frank Crowninshield, Benchley had met the previous summer. Crowninshield was one of the few editors he'd talked with who actually encouraged him to keep trying his hand at writing. But he knew there were no openings there—or anywhere else, for that matter. Nonetheless, Biggers did manage to get Benchley an audience with Adams, and the dour-looking but courteous columnist introduced him to the managing editor, Mr. Gilbert, who was, Benchley noted, "indefinite but smiling." In the meantime, Benchley prayed that some miracle might get him back to Boston.

On March 11, Benchley received a letter from the secretary of the Harvard Alumni Association Appointment Office—a letter that seemed to have dropped from the heavens. "My Dear Mr. Benchley," it began.

Mr. Richard Russell (Harvard '01) of Wm. A. Russell & Brother, 50 State Street, Boston, general managers for a number of well-known paper, pulp and cotton manufacturing concerns, has an interesting position for which you have been suggested. . . . Roughly the position is along welfare lines; that is, Mr. Russell wishes a man to act as secretary for an association, or club, composed of the various heads of departments. This secretary must be interested in the workmen and can help them to improve themselves, and is both social and educational. The position requires a man with a good deal of initiative, for he must really create the position.

Mr. Russell expects to be in New York in about two weeks and can arrange to see you at that time. If, however, you would like to go over the situation with him before then and can come to Boston, Mr. Russell will pay your expense. . . .

Within three days, Benchley was in Boston to meet with Richard Russell. As had been outlined in the letter, the company was looking for an educated, socially responsible man to oversee company civic activities, organize social events, and help the mills' employees with family problems. The salary was $1,800 a year. Benchley could hardly believe his good fortune. "I'm going to have to wait until after I've had my cold bath in the morning," he joked in his diary. "It looks like a chance to do some real good—and also will give me time to write some things on the side." He took his bath the next morning, still had the offer in front of him, and so went back to Russell and accepted the job. He was going home to take a job he could be proud of—and he could go ahead with his wedding plans.

Benchley returned to New York on the 16th and gave Latshaw his notice of resignation. Ironically, Biggers came into his office that very day to tell him that Adams had been in touch, and that it looked as if there was indeed going to be a reporter's job opening up at the *Tribune*. Benchley thanked him for his efforts, but told him that he'd made up his mind about returning to Massachusetts. On April 3, his last day at the Curtis offices in the Metropolitan Tower building, the payroll department gave him a check for his final week's work, as well as an extra one for $140, the result of his self-imposed $10-a-week savings program. At six o'clock, he was taken to a nearby restaurant, where Latshaw, Walsh, and the rest of his office mates treated him to a surprise farewell dinner. They presented a deeply touched Benchley with copies of two new H. G. Wells books, *The World Set Free* and

Social Forces in England and America. After stopping off at the Harvard Club for goodbyes, Benchley caught the 11:15 for Worcester.

Benchley began working for the Russell Company in early April and found a room to share with Harvard classmate George Gray at 88 Charles Street in Boston. Richard Russell had been correct when he'd told Benchley that the job would entail all kinds of skills. The new welfare secretary found himself trying to put together a company information booklet one week, investigating supposed improprieties by local Catholic charities the next, and interviewing Lithuanian undertakers about their thoughts on education the week after that. His assignments were scattered, and he often went days without being given specific things to do, but all in all Benchley was content. As promised, he had plenty of free time to work on original stories; he submitted manuscripts to *Harper's Weekly*, the *Atlantic*, *Life*, and other magazines. And he was able to start making preparations for the wedding, which was to be on the first Saturday in June.

Over the course of the next month, Benchley and Gertrude prepared for the beginning of their life together. They worked out a family budget based on Benchley's salary, and after determining that $32 a month was what they could afford to spend on housing, they set out to look for an apartment. They saw one in Belmont for $28 that they liked, and were set to take it when Benchley bumped into Arthur Beane, secretary of Phillips Brooks House, a Harvard-affiliated settlement house where Benchley had done volunteer work during college. Beane and his family were going away for the summer, and he generously offered Benchley free use of his Cambridge apartment on Brattle Street until the fall. On June 1, Benchley cleared out his few belongings from the Charles Street rooming house and deposited them at 51 Brattle Street.

Robert Benchley and Gertrude Darling were married on Saturday, June 6, 1914, at Piedmont Church just outside Worcester, with the Rev. Dr. Henry Stiles Bradley officiating. Gertrude was given away by her brother, Albert Willis Darling, and attended by both a maid—Catherine Faulker—and a matron—Katharine Colton Coes—of honor. Laurence McKinney was the best man, and Frederick Allen, Huntington Faxon, George Gray, and Arthur Stone served as ushers. Just a few minutes after seven o'clock, a somewhat jittery Benchley took the wedding ring from his even more jittery best man—McKinney was positioned directly over a hot-air vent, and was positive that the gold band was going to fall down the shaft—and placed it on Gertrude's finger. After better than a two-year engagement, they were finally husband and wife.

4
A Brief History of Chinese Football

"ARE YOU NUTTY ABOUT BOSTON . . . ?"

O_n the Saturday before the 1914 Thanksgiving holiday, Robert and Gertrude Benchley spent several hours standing on a street corner in front of the *Boston Transcript* building, braving the late-fall chill to watch a huge animated scoreboard re-create the play-by-play account of the annual Harvard-Yale football game. The Benchleys hadn't missed a single Harvard game all season, but with their bank account reading a lowly $1.40, a trip to New Haven to witness the official opening of the Yale Bowl was out of the question. Being part of the crowd across from the *Transcript* offices, they decided, would be the next-best thing.

The news from the scoreboard was good. In fact, it was stupendous. It seemed that Yale's football coach, Frank Hinkey, had tried to combat the superiority of that year's Harvard squad by introducing a new offensive wrinkle, the lateral pass—but the play kept backfiring on the home team as the boys from Eli kept fumbling the ball away and into the hands of their rivals from Cambridge. When the final gun was mercifully fired, an embarrassed Hinkey hurried his players off the field while Harvard and the thousands of its fans who'd come to Connecticut to cheer the team on wildly celebrated the Crimson's 36–0 win.

The shutout against Yale put the finishing touches on one of the finest gridiron campaigns in Harvard history, and a few days later, the organizers of the university's annual football dinner approached Benchley about making an after-dinner speech at the affair. He merrily accepted the invitation. Benchley spent about a week weighing various possible subjects and approaches for his talk, trying to come up with something novel for the occasion—after all, a season as special as the one the Harvard football team had just completed merited a special kind of commemoration. And then he had an idea.

With the aid of Dean Briggs and several fellow alumni, Benchley devised an elaborate hoax. A local storekeeper named Chin Willy, outfitted in an expensive tailored suit and a pair of gold-rimmed spectacles, was presented to the football players, students, assorted alumni, and faculty on hand at the Copley Plaza Hotel on the night of December 11, 1914, as "Professor Soong, of the Imperial University of China." Somberly, Briggs explained that since the erudite professor spoke almost no English, his speech would be translated by alumnus Benchley, who just happened to be fluent in Chinese. With that, the dean turned to the "professor" and, after an exchange of courteous bows, escorted the guest speaker to the podium.

Mr. Chin—a native of Canton who'd been in America for at least thirty years, and who spoke English as fluently as anyone in the room—had been instructed by Benchley to simply say anything at all that came into his mind, as long as it was in Chinese, and to keep talking until he felt a slight tug at his trouser leg, the signal for him to stop. Chin spoke for a while, and stopped when he received the signal, and then Benchley rose to "interpret." Up until that moment, only a few people had any idea that something was amiss. But then Benchley began his "translation."

"The professor has honored us by giving a brief history of Chinese football," he said, "with special emphasis on the development of the lateral pass. This play was known to the Chinese as the kaew chung, but as in no instance was it ever known to gain over three yards—and that in the wrong direction—it was abandoned in the year 720. Its last use was in the game between the University of Canton and University of Tong, in which game the latter university had the unique distinction of scoring forty-four points on itself entirely through safeties resulting from the use of the lateral pass."

With the sound of laughter beginning to be heard, Benchley signaled Chin to continue. After several moments, the tug came, and Benchley stood up and again spoke. "One thing that was not quite clear to Professor Soong in watching the Harvard-Yale contest was the remarkable restraint displayed by the Yale men in their tackling of the Harvard runners. In the game as he knew it, the idea was to tackle a runner and get him down that way as quickly as possible, but Yale coach Hinkey seemed to pursue the moderate policy of letting a Harvard man run until he tripped himself up or fell from utter exhaustion and *then* to have his men tackle him, en masse. He thinks that this good feeling shows how much farther the sport is advanced in this country."

At that point, Benchley announced that the professor would be happy to entertain questions from the audience. One by one, Benchley's "plants" rose from their seats and asked the questions he'd supplied for them, the volume of laughter increasing with each successive answer. "We have time for just one final question," said Benchley after a while, "as Professor Soong has to catch the midnight train for New York. If you please, sir."

"Professor," a young man called out, "what, in your opinion, is the main reason that Harvard was able to beat Yale so handily this year, and what do you think is the essential factor that can enable Harvard to maintain its superiority over Yale in the years to come?"

After Benchley "repeated" the question, Chin began his reply. He talked for about a minute. Receiving no signal from Benchley, he kept talking. And talking. And talking. He talked about his family. He discussed the importing trade. He even told a few off-color Chinese jokes. Finally, after more than five minutes, he felt the tug, and stopped.

Benchley stood up, looked around the room, smoothed his jacket, straightened his tie, and cleared his throat. "He says, 'Hinkey,' " he said, and sat back down.

The Chinese professor caper, as it came to be known, caused quite a stir. Several local newspapers wrote up the incident (the *Boston Post* went so far as to hail Benchley as "one of the greatest humorists of all time at Harvard"), and as the story spread, Benchley found himself in demand on the banquet circuit again, just as he'd been during college.

Of the various speaking engagements he made over the course of that winter and spring, one in particular stood out. It occurred at a gathering of Navy officers at Boston's Wardroom Club in January. Posing as an assistant to Secretary of the Navy Josephus Daniels, Benchley didn't think it would take long for the officers to get the joke and realize that his "unofficial unveiling" of the Secretary's new plan to "broaden and democratize" the Navy by doing away with virtually all of the privileges of commissioned personnel was a complete farce. He was wrong, though; his officious look and serious manner had the officers thoroughly convinced that the Navy was actually going to make them join the enlisted men for communal messes and post-shore-leave physical examinations for signs of social diseases—and they were rather angry about it. By the time he got around to the proposed changes in the Naval Academy curriculum (the new Navy, he promised, would stop presenting trophies for gunnery marksmanship and instead encourage competition in such areas as Aesthetics, Philosophy, and Harmony and Counterpoint), many of the officers were openly booing him. With memories of the Curtis convention fiasco flashing through his mind—and a dinner roll or two breezing past his ear—Benchley nervously pressed on. Eventually, when he beat a fist on the table to emphasize the seriousness with which the new Navy was going to view the offense of "splitting infinitives without written permission from Washington," several of the men laughed loudly, and he let go a smile. *Finally*, they'd caught on. By the end of the speech, the officers were on their feet applauding. But it had been a close call.

While Benchley certainly enjoyed his popularity as an after-dinner speaker (he got so good at it that at a Harvard Club banquet in Chicago that winter, Harvard's President Lowell insisted he appear *before* Benchley, not after him), there was another area in which, during this period, he received even greater personal satisfaction. The October 1914 issue of *Vanity Fair* included his first-published professional magazine piece, an article that Benchley had originally titled "No Matter from What Angle You Look at It, Alice Brookhausen Was a Girl Whom You Would Hesitate to Invite into Your Own Home," and that editor Frank Crowninshield had run under the more manageable heading "Hints on Writing a Book." The piece was a parody of the then-current "real life" tales written by nonwriters. Benchley's protagonist relates his struggles in attempting to overcome the obstacles that stand between him and a surefire best-selling book. Obstacles like a typewriter:

"Even now that I can express, with only a few misplaced dollar signs, that stirring exhortation for all good men to rally round the party standard," confesses the novice author, "I don't think that the letters on the average key-board are arranged with anything more definite in mind than a general scheme of getting them all on. The man who placed the letter 'C' within such easy striking distance of the letter 'V' certainly could have no sense of proportion or he would have realized what ungainly looking words 'suvvumb' or 'vough' would be. And as for 'K' and the question mark, 'wor?ing' is one of my favorite descriptive words. It has that elusive quality which, to me, is a mark of good writing. . . ."

After finally accepting that he has to use the typewriter, the narrator moves on to his next hurdle—a subject. After deciding that "the presence of immorality on the stage seems a good field to stir things up," he goes to the theater at which "the most 'frank' of the 'present-day problem' plays was running—entirely in the interest of my story, of course." Unfortunately, when he gets to the box office, the bored ticket seller tells him that the show is sold out for that night and the only seat he can get is behind a chandelier and for a performance five weeks ahead. He promptly purchases that seat even though he doesn't really want to, because "like the weak-kneed craven that I am I was seized with a panicky fear of appearing impecunious before this man who was apparently so much in touch with the theatrical world."

On the way home, though, he begins to berate himself for buying the ticket. "I ran over in my mind all the clever retorts I might have handed him instead of my two dollars. There were so many that I couldn't possibly have used all of them on this one occasion; it would have necessitated going back again and again, each time asking ingenuously for seats and each time coming back at him with an acrid taunt more clever than the one before, until he should break down and beg me to let myself be placed on the regular free list. And how the people who would be waiting in line back of me would enjoy my sallies! How they would hail me as a champion of the long-suffering public with my keen wit! There might be some editor in the line who, hearing my ringing echoes of Voltaire at his best, would take me aside and say, 'A man who has such a facile power to lampoon sham and fraud should do some work for me. I have a series of articles in mind—.'

"At this point I walked into a hydrant, and on replacing my hat I realized that whatever the possibilities for my poignant sarcasm might have been, the fact still remained that I was in possession of one ticket behind a chandelier for five weeks from Tuesday which I did not want and which I had accepted without a murmur. . . . By the time I reached home I was so disgruntled at the whole affair that I had resolved not to attend the performance at all—in fact to throw the whole thing over and let the stage and its immorality and the public all go hang."

"Hints on Writing a Book," for which Benchley received $40, displayed a number of qualities that would eventually be recognized as characteristic of his brand of humor. Benchley's narrator regularly drifts off onto irrelevant tangents, and is more confused than angered by the way life deals him its seemingly indiscriminate blows. In several ways, the piece was also rather prophetic. That fall, the Benchleys moved into a building at 117 Church Street in Watertown. They had a ground-floor apartment, which meant that they had to tend to their own heating needs. As the temperature outside decreased, hostilities between Benchley and the basement furnace increased; by December, the relationship was classifiable as major warfare. Unschooled in the proper way to start fires and keep them going, Benchley stubbornly refused to seek advice (he didn't want to appear not to know what he was doing), and the result was that he and Gertrude regularly woke up shivering in the early morning, the fire having gone out in the middle of the night. Benchley had problems loading the coal into the furnace. He had problems removing the dead ashes. When he needed a blazing fire, few of the pieces of coal would stay lit. And when all he wanted was a bit of heat, an immense fire would rage, untended. One morning he became so frustrated that he gathered all the kindling he could find and methodically lit every individual piece of coal and his adamance about completing the mission was such that he totally lost track of time and wound up an hour late for work.

Another part of "Hints on Writing a Book" that turned out to be prophetic was Benchley's fantasy of being asked by an editor to write about the theater. Late in December, old Curtis colleague Dick Walsh came to town and suggested to Benchley that he see an acquaintance of his named Ernest Greuning, managing editor of the *Boston Traveler*, in regard to some possible theater reviewing work. That he did, and while it turned out that there wasn't any pay involved for the position of fill-in reviewer (free tickets were all he would receive for his efforts), Benchley reasoned that the exposure in a real newspaper would make it worthwhile. Besides, he loved the theater so much that he'd probably be buying tickets to many of the shows anyway; if nothing else, he'd save some money. Several days later, a favorable review of the play *Seven Keys to Baldpate* appeared on the drama page of the *Traveler*. Robert Benchley was now a published, if uncompensated, theater critic.

Meanwhile, Benchley's work at the Russell Company continued to proceed along the same amorphous lines as when he'd first joined the company the previous spring. For months Richard Russell had been assuring him that there would eventually be a great deal of important work to be done for the Russell Club, the organization of department heads from the five company mills that Benchley was to help oversee and guide. But the only club activity that took place during Benchley's first year with the firm was an October picnic held at Mr. Russell's farm in North Andover, at which, during a break from the clams, lobsters, corn, and sweet potatoes, the sixty-five members unanimously elected him secretary and treasurer. As most of the Russell Club's agenda kept getting delayed or postponed, Benchley busied himself with all manner of odds and ends: writing up accident reports and surveys of the pulp industry and composing the company bulletin; making up "safety first" signs in different languages for those mills with non-English-speaking employees ("The printers had quite a time with all the Polish 'Z' 's," he noted); taking responsibility for the formation of an inter-mill baseball league, finding available fields, and serving as the league's official scorer; and delivering—without any disguises or masquerades—the company's annual report at the yearly business conference.

It was while preparing the company's annual report in the spring that Benchley began to understand why Mr. Russell had been continually shelving the Russell Club projects. Business at the mills was down, and projections for the upcoming fiscal year indicated that things were almost certain to get worse before they got better. The Russell Club, and, indeed, his own position of welfare secretary had been created during a time of expected expansion; without that expansion, the future of both looked bleak.

In August, he and Gertrude went off to Scarboro Beach, Maine, for a two-week vacation not far from where they'd honeymooned the previous year, and Benchley did his best to keep up a cheerful front. Gertrude had become pregnant during the latter part of the winter, and the two spent their time much as they had always spent it—going for long walks, reading aloud to each other from the classics, and discussing their aspirations for the future. His position at Wm. A. Russell had grown less secure with each passing month, but Gertrude continued to express her faith in him regardless of what happened with this particular job, and he continued to be buoyed by her quiet resolve and strength of character. In his heart, he was always afraid that everything could unravel at the drop of a hat, but Gertrude continually worked to push those fears aside. In many ways, he admired her as much as he loved her—perhaps even more than he loved her.

It wasn't long after they'd returned from their holiday that Mr. Russell finally ended the uncomfortable speculation and formally informed Benchley that if business didn't pick up considerably, he was going to have to terminate Benchley's job as of the end of November. It was several days before Benchley was able to summon up the strength to tell Gertrude. Each night he'd return home from work to find her calmly knitting baby clothes for the child that was due to be born right around the time he was going to be losing his job, and his heart would nearly break.

Gertrude took the news as he knew she would—she tried to reassure him that he shouldn't worry about her, and expressed her complete confidence in his ability to find another, and better, job. But Benchley wasn't sure about his ability to do *anything* correctly in the world of work. He knew that the jobs he'd had since graduating from college hadn't led him down any paths he was particularly satisfied with, and he certainly couldn't support a family as a practical-joking after-dinner speechmaker. Writing was still the career he dreamed of, but he was not confident about his chances of making it in the field. He loved reviewing plays for the *Traveler*, but that didn't pay, and his many attempts at writing serious articles ("real" stories, as he referred to them in his diary) had all resulted in nothing—judging from the ever-growing pile of rejection slips—but failures. *Vanity Fair* was the only publication buying articles from him, and he certainly couldn't make a living selling pieces sporadically to just one magazine.

In September, a visit from Dick Walsh brightened Benchley's spirits. Shuttling between the Curtis offices in Boston, New York, and Philadelphia, Walsh knew people at newspapers in all three cities, and he offered to ask around on Benchley's behalf—that is, if Benchley would be willing to take a reporter's job if that was all that was available. Eighteen months previous, feeling that he possessed neither the instincts nor the temperament to be a decent reporter, Benchley had balked at the chance to work for the *New York Tribune*. His feelings hadn't really changed since then, but in his present financial situation, he knew he couldn't afford to say no if such an opportunity arose again. "I'm game for anything at this point," Benchley told his friend, "provided it carries a living wage for three." If some paper would give him a chance, he'd try to make a go of it. In early October, Walsh wrote with news that he'd spoken to Frank Adams, and that the columnist, remembering Earl Derr Biggers's glowing recommendation back when Benchley was at the Curtis Company, had promised to see what he could come up with. A few days later, on October 6, Benchley received a brisk and encouraging note from Adams. "Are you nutty about Boston . . . ?" he asked. "I don't know what there is here, definitely, but I think I can land you if you want to come. They're tight about money for starters, but liberal enough after worth is proven. Which is to say that any man who is worth $150 a week to them can grab off $60 like finding it. On other papers, it would be $45. They'd probably offer you $35 to start."

Benchley received Adams's letter at work, and he spent most of the day mulling over its contents and staring at the wall in his office. The *Tribune* was a morning paper, and the likely opening, a reporter's job, would almost certainly mean a workday that began in the early afternoon and ended late at night—hardly a comfortable schedule for a man with a new family. Wherever they lived (and a small apartment would be the best they could hope for in an expensive, crowded city like New York), Gertrude and the baby would be by themselves most nights, and he knew that would be hard on them. Benchley returned home and showed Gertrude the letter, and the two talked things over. "She took it like the good sport she is," Benchley noted in his diary, "but even with her willing, I don't think I want to do this. The job is simply not compatible with a young family, and I'd rather have the young family." He scolded himself for the turn of events at Wm. A. Russell. "I do not feel that it is so much my fault as that of conditions and the fact that Mr. Russell had no regular job for me," he wrote, "but I might have, through forcing, made myself valuable along other lines. . . . Spiritually, I am atrophied through disuse. . . . I still have to find myself."

The next morning, Benchley dashed off a note to Adams, telling him that he certainly was interested, but asking if he could wait until mid-November—after the baby was born—to make a final decision. Adams agreed, and during the next four weeks Benchley sought advice from most of his friends about the *Tribune*'s offer. Walsh told him that if the paper really wanted him, he could probably get a little more money or, at least, better hours. The *Traveler*'s Ernest Greuning, after trying to get his paper to make Benchley an offer ($15 a week was the best it would do), told him that a stint as a reporter—even if it was only for a few months—was an absolute necessity if he wanted a future in newspaper work, and if that was the case he shouldn't think twice. He even talked to Mr. Russell, who told him that he could stay with the company until January if that would help any.

While Benchley still hadn't completely made up his mind about his immediate future by November 13, another member of the household had. At a little after noon that day in 1915, six-pound-one ounce Nathaniel Goddard (named after Benchley's great-grandfather, a Millbury, Massachusetts, deacon) was born.

Gertrude was still at Newton Hospital when, several days later, a telegram arrived from Adams. He was coming to Boston for the weekend and wanted to meet Benchley on Saturday at the Copley-Plaza. "Your future hangs on the result," Adams wrote, and over breakfast that Saturday (they would have had lunch were it not that neither wanted to miss the Harvard-Yale game that afternoon), he outlined the details of that possible future. Although the only position open at the newspaper was technically that of a city reporter, there was soon going to be a new Sunday supplement called the *Tribune Magazine* that he, Adams, was going to be overseeing, and he wanted Benchley, who'd been highly touted by everyone he'd talked to, to be part of the small staff working on it. He knew Benchley was reluctant to start out as a reporter, but he promised him it would only be a matter of months before the change would come, and that he could get him a starting salary of $40 a week—$5 better than the usual rate.

Cheering on the inside, Benchley told Adams that he had to talk it over with Gertrude, but that he was fairly certain he wanted the job. And later that day, cheering on the outside, he and Adams watched Harvard crush Yale again, 41–0. With his wife and newborn baby still in the hospital, Benchley invited Adams back to the empty apartment, and his guest ended up spending the weekend, thus leading to the first of what would ultimately be scores of Benchley appearances in Adams's running *Tribune* series, the celebrity-studded "Diary of Our Own Samuel Pepys." "Unpacking my portmanteau," Adams wrote on Monday, November 22, "I found I had forgot only my hair-brush and my shaving-brush, which I did leave at Mr. R. Benchley's, and I hope he will not try to convince me I did naught of the sort." A few days later, Adams received the brushes in the mail—along with Benchley's acceptance of the *Tribune* offer.

While the holiday season that year proved to be a humble one for the Benchleys (the family Christmas dinner, shared by visiting grandparents Jennie and Charlie, was conspicuously devoid of roast turkey, and the few presents Benchley and Gertrude scraped together money to buy were the ones for little Nathaniel), their spirits remained high as they prepared for the new year. "Read the morning-after scene in the *Christmas Carol* and, as usual, cried," Benchley wrote in his diary on December 25, 1915. "Not at the sad parts, but at the parts that are so glad that they shut off your wind." On the 30th, the apartment at 177 Church Street was cleared out, and the threesome headed off to Cambridge, where friends had invited Gertrude and the baby to stay until Benchley was settled in New York. At the stroke of midnight on the 31st in the Cambridge home of Marian and Hans Miller, Gertrude Benchley gently picked up sleeping Nathaniel and jumped into the air. Her husband couldn't. He was in an upper berth aboard the midnight express somewhere along the rail route between Boston and New York, and would have hit his head.

5
Ecstasy of Conceit

"YOU LIVE IN MANHATTAN;
THE CHANCES ARE YOU'RE A MOLE"

Shortly before Robert Benchley left Massachusetts to go to work for the *New York Tribune*, he received a note from Franklin P. Adams that included some advice about how he should conduct himself around the newspaper's Nassau Street offices in downtown Manhattan. "Don't forget to tell folks that you're a reporter with nothing else in prospect," wrote Adams. Plans for the special Sunday section still hadn't officially been approved, he explained, and with office politics and hiring practices being what they were, "rumors of the Sunday thing [will] only make it harder to move over when the time comes." Since Benchley followed Adams's advice, it's not known how much of a surprise it was to city editor Robert MacAlarney when, in the middle of March, Benchley was transferred over to the staff of the fledgling *Tribune Magazine*. One thing is fairly certain, though. Whether it was a surprise or not, it certainly was a relief—to Benchley and perhaps even more to the city desk.

"The worst reporter, even for my age, in all of New York City" was how Benchley, in later years, characterized his brief turn as a general assignment reporter for the *Tribune*. The assessment was a bit severe; given his complete lack of experience going in, he really didn't do that bad a job. It was just that there were certain kinds of stories, and certain kinds of news-gathering assignments, that he wasn't very good at. When it came to interviewing a New Jersey woman who, after being blind for many years, had mysteriously recovered her eyesight on her eightieth birthday, or a bus conductor who greeted his daily passengers with poetry recitations, Benchley had no difficulties whatsoever. But when he was told to find out about some sticky domestic situation on Long Island, or to investigate the report of a white girl being physically attacked by a black youth near Morningside Park, he'd travel to the site of the stories in dread of having to do what every good reporter must do—namely, pry. More often than not in such situations, he'd purposely arrive late at his destination, in the hope that the people he was supposed to see would already have departed. If he was unfortunate enough to locate them, he'd introduce himself by saying, "I'm from the *Tribune*—you don't really want to talk to a reporter, do you?" and pray that they wouldn't. If all went well—i.e., no interview—he'd call the office to say there was no story and get reassigned to the steamship-arrival or lost-dog detail, relieved that he didn't have to invade anyone's privacy just to fill a few inches' worth of type in the back pages of the paper.

Sometimes, the plan worked, as was the case with the uptown racial incident: The girl refused to talk to *any* reporters, so he was off the hook. Other times it didn't. His Long Island misadventure came about when he was dispatched to Freeport to check on a divorced couple, the hook of the story being that the two were living next door to each other. Benchley was hoping that neither the husband nor the wife would grant him an interview, but both parties did. First he went to see the husband, who cheerfully led him into a noisy living room filled with guests, talked his ear off for better than an hour, and insisted on showing him some magic tricks he'd learned since the split. Benchley finally escaped and went to see the wife, who was quiet and sad and just wanted to be left alone. She was living a scant fifteen feet from her ex-husband, she explained, because that was the only available place she'd known about at the time of the breakup. "The most unpleasant assignment I have had," an annoyed Benchley wrote in his diary after several wrenching hours of drafts and rewrites back at the office. "I felt that it was none of my, or the paper's, business."

It didn't take long for the city editors to realize that Benchley wasn't doing very well on the domestic-squabble beat—people he said were never home when he called were being quoted in every paper *but* the *Tribune*, it seemed—and by February he was switched over to the lecture circuit, where he fared much better. Naturally curious, and with varied interests, Benchley didn't at all mind having to cover lectures by inventor Guglielmo Marconi, luncheons honoring opera singer Enrico Caruso, and dinners given by the Society of Illuminating Engineers for electronics wizard Thomas Edison. In mid-February, however, he was stuck with an ongoing feature story involving a little girl, the United States Navy, and the war that had been raging in Europe for the past two years, and working on it gnawed at his conscience so much that he gave serious consideration to quitting the newspaper business altogether.

Marjorie Starret was a local schoolgirl who somehow got the idea that maybe, if she saved up all her pennies, she could buy a battleship for her country to use just in case America had to enter the war.

In no time, the girl and her piggy bank were being publicized and promoted all over town, and the *Tribune*—a paper whose pro-intervention editorials had bothered Benchley even before he'd begun working there—rallied to young Marjorie's cause. The *Tribune* decided to help in the formation of a "Battleship Fund," and space was reserved daily for news of Marjorie and her fund—space that had to be filled by the designated Battleship Fund reporter, Benchley. Every day for more than a month, Benchley had to follow the trail of the little girl and her battleship. When a minister in Brooklyn mentioned Marjorie in a Sunday sermon, Benchley had to write it up; when a "Battleship Benefit" was held on Wall Street, Benchley had to write it up; and when new contributors sent in pledges and letters of support, Benchley had to write it up. And as he wrote the stories up, he seethed inside.

Benchley had been a patriotic youngster himself when his brother, Edmund, marched off to war in 1898 and never returned. But as he got older, and learned for himself that the Spanish-American War had been fought for little reason other than to show off the United States' military might, Benchley became a determined, passionate pacifist. During the summer of 1914, when Austria first declared war on Serbia and Germany invaded Belgium, he'd written in his diary that war between countries couldn't be seen as anything but a horrible step backward for civilization. "I can't really believe it possible that they really will fall back so far into the Middle Ages after having come so far," he'd lamented. Even after the British ship *Lusitania* was sunk off the Irish coast by a German submarine in May 1915, with 124 Americans among the almost 1,200 dead, Benchley had continued to defend President Wilson's policy of diplomacy and nonintervention. He was distressed by all the war-mongering and flag-waving going on around him ("How could I have ever been thrilled by brass buttons?" he asked himself after having to cover a 7th Regiment review at a downtown armory), and yet how could he say anything publicly at this point? He was helping stir the fires with his articles!

On March 20, just as he was about to explode (some Wall Streeters had donated a bull to the Battleship Fund, and Benchley had been instructed to research its pedigree), Adams broke the news that the *Tribune Magazine* was finally getting off the ground. As of the fol-

lowing Monday, Benchley would be working on the Sunday section—
and only the Sunday section. Feeling as if a great burden had been
lifted off his back, Benchley glided though his last week's assignments,
Battleship Fund and all, and on his last day in the newsroom he gave
city editor MacAlarney a note thanking him for his patience in putting
up with him.

During his first two months back in New York, Benchley lived in
a furnished room at 154 East 37th Street, and while he only got to
see Gertrude and the baby on his days off at the Miller home in Cambridge, where they were still staying, he had little time to be lonely.
When he wasn't working he could usually be found in the company
of Adams or several other *Tribune* employees—most notably sports editor (and fellow Harvard alumnus) Heywood Broun, and drama editor (and fellow Adams protégé) George S. Kaufman. Adams and his
wife, Minna, took Benchley under their wing virtually from the moment he came to town, treating him to meals at the fancier restaurants in Manhattan and getting him free tickets to the many shows
he was dying to see. At the Hippodrome, he listened to John Philip
Sousa's band and saw the great Pavlova dance, and at the Astor he
enjoyed his first George M. Cohan revue.

Adams also ingeniously managed to introduce Benchley to a whole
slew of local intelligentsia within a week of his arrival in New York.
Every year the Contribunion, a club composed of contributors to
F.P.A.'s "Conning Tower" column in the *Tribune*, held a dinner for all
those whose work had appeared during the previous twelve months.
Although Adams never paid any of the writers who supplied the
puns, jokes, and verses that helped fill his column, it was his custom
to single out one favorite contribution every year and reward its author with a gold watch, traditionally bestowed at the annual dinner,
which took place at a saloon over Scheffel's Hall at Third Avenue and
17th Street. Adams himself never attended, choosing instead to send
emissaries in his place, and on January 6, 1916, he deputized Benchley to serve as presenter.

Music composer and critic Deems Taylor (who wrote for Adams
under the pseudonym "Smeed") happened to be that year's recipi-
ent, and he was probably as puzzled as anyone else in the room when
an unknown young man introduced by poet Clarence Wood as "the

Bringer of the Watch" stood up and informed the audience that, as one of the leading authorities in his field, it was a great honor to be able to speak on this particular evening on the history and development of the timepiece. This group was nothing like the Navy crowd back in Boston; Benchley had scarcely begun to describe the invention of the vest-pocket sundial ("delayed for several days by heavy rains") before the collection of literati were laughing heartily.

By evening's end, Benchley had met many of New York's best-known newspaper and magazine writers and editors, and he returned to his room that night with his feet barely touching the ground. Over the course of the next few months, many of these acquaintances grew into friendships, and once work on the *Tribune Magazine* began in late March, Benchley began to feel, for the first time in his adult life, as if he really belonged somewhere. He managed to find a reasonably priced three-room sublet at 152 East 22nd Street, near Gramercy Park, and Gertrude and Nathaniel at last were able to move to the city and join him. His home life and career were, he hoped, finally on track together.

The eight-page *Tribune Magazine* debuted on April 9, under a parenting nucleus consisting of Adams (supervisory editor), former *Puck* editor Arthur Folwell (editor), Benchley (chief writer), and artist William Hill, and the staff was rounded out over the next few months with the addition of writer Deems Taylor and artist Rea Irvin. Although not technically a humor magazine—topical issues like prison reform, immigration, and the socialist movement were regularly addressed, and Alice Duer Miller's "Are Women People?" column railed noisily at the inequality between the sexes—the *Tribune Magazine* leaned heavily on satires, parodies, and humor pieces for the bulk of its contents. Regular features included Montague Glass's ethnic dialect stories, Folwell's parodies of famous poems, Hill's editorial-like full-page drawings commenting on urban matters, and Irvin's "This Day in History" cartoon series depicting such momentous events as "The day the cocktail was perfected."

At first, Benchley was responsible for writing two articles a week for the magazine—a book review and a feature story. For the reviews, Adams instructed Benchley to seek out (in Adams's words) "the phoniest books" he could find, and then critique them as one would a major literary work. It probably came as quite a shock to the authors of *Courtship Made Easy* and *Spalding's Official Baseball Record* to see their work receiving coverage in a major newspaper. Of course, reading the reviews gave them an even bigger shock. "There runs through it a note that is reminiscent of Freud in its insistence on the significance of dream stimuli," Benchley wrote of *Pettengill's Perfect Fortune-Teller and Dream Book*. "In fact, in its first editions, Professor Pettengill's work antedates that of Freud although the latter had never made any public acknowledgment of his indebtedness."

When it came to the features, Adams gave Benchley carte blanche: As long as the piece dealt with some interesting aspect of metropolitan life, he could write about anything he felt like. For years, Benchley had racked his brains trying, with precious little success, to come up with marketable story ideas. But now he was among people whose sensibilities were very similar to his—he, Adams, and Folwell could spend hours sharing their admiration of writers like George Ade, Stephen Leacock, and P. G. Wodehouse—and almost all of his suggestions were met with encouragement and support. Adams's confidence in him, as well as the highly fertile atmosphere at the *Tribune Magazine*, inspired Benchley tremendously, and his work quickly reflected it. On May 16, just five weeks after the magazine's premiere issue, Benchley was awarded a byline—usually reserved for columnists and celebrity writers—for a story called "A Piece of Roast Beef," and soon most of his Sunday features were, in the vernacular of the newspaper business, "signed." He might have had few instincts as a straight reporter, but given the opportunity to approach subjects subjectively, he was soon tackling matters as diverse as the fiftieth anniversary of chewing gum, the history of fire escapes, the art of toasting, and the ins and outs of professional panhandling, and doing so with an ease and a verve that delighted both his peers at the magazine and the *Tribune* readership.

His flair for the absurd emerged in such pieces as "Our Own Science Page"—an investigation which addressed such burning questions as "Did Prehistoric Man Walk on His Head?" and "Do Jellyfish Suffer Embarrassment?"—and "Shakespeare Explained," wherein one nondescript line from *Pericles* ("What ho! Where is the music?") is besieged by hordes of "illuminating" footnotes such as the following:

" '*Ho!*' In conjunction with the preceding word doubtless means 'What ho!' changed by Clarke to 'What hoo!' In the original MS. it reads 'What hi!' but this has been accredited to the tendency of the time to write 'What hi!' when 'What ho!' was meant. Techner also maintains that it should read 'What humpf!' Cf. Ham. 5:0. 'High-ho!' ")

There were several themes that Benchley returned to again and again in his Sunday stories, themes that struck responsive chords in anyone having to live and work in a big city, such as public transportation and eating establishments. In "All Hoops Abandon, Ye Who Enter Here," Benchley took the fashion angle in examining the possible consequences of the transportation department's decision to build new city buses under a formula that allowed for only two square feet of room per passenger ("What if these should come back in fashion?" read the caption to a picture Benchley had dug up at an old print shop showing a group of women all wearing hoop skirts). He wondered about the long-term effects of subterranean travel on humans in "You Live in Manhattan; the Chances Are You're a Mole." Lunch counters—the bane of many an office worker's existence—came in for special attention with articles like "How Many Miles Do You Walk at Lunch?" (complete with map) and "Coffee, Megg and Ilk, Please" in which Benchley's protagonist tries unsuccessfully to overcome his meekness and place his desired order at a boisterous luncheonette:

> I have any number of witnesses who will sign statements to the effect that my voice changed about twelve years ago, and that in ordinary conversation my tone, if not especially virile, is at least consistent and even. But when I give an order at a soda fountain, if the clerk over-awes me at all, my voice breaks into a yodel that makes the phrase "Coffee, egg and milk" a pretty snatch of a song, but practically worthless as an order. If the counter is lined with customers, I might just as well save time and go home and shake up an egg and milk for myself, for I shall not be waited on until every one else has left the counter and they are putting the nets over the caramels for the night. . . .
>
> I [finally] decide that the thing for me to do is to speak up loud and act brazenly. So I clear my throat, and, placing both hands on the counter, emit what promises to be a perfect bellow: "COFFEE, MEGG and

ILK." This makes just about the impression you'd think it would, both on my neighbors and the clerk. . . . At this I withdraw to the other end of the counter, where I can begin life over again with a clean slate, [but] I am suddenly confronted by an impatient clerk. . . . "What's yours?" he flings at me. I immediately lose my memory and forget what it was that I wanted. . . . There is a big man edging his way beside me who is undoubtedly going to shout "Coca-Cola" in half a second. So I beat him to it and shout "Coca-Cola," which is probably the last drink in the store I want to buy. But it is the only thing I can remember at the moment, is spite of the fact that I have been thinking all morning how good a coffee, egg and milk would taste.

"Coffee, Megg and Ilk, Please" ("my timid man story" was how Benchley described it in his diary) was published in early September, by which time the Benchley family had moved from the apartment in Manhattan to a house in suburban Crestwood, just north of New York City. The sublet on East 22nd Street had been a nightmare for Gertrude: Not only were the three rooms (kitchen, dining room, and bedroom) oppressively small, but all the windows faced either fire escapes or brick walls. The first month, especially, while Benchley was still working on the reporters' evening shift, had been devastating; it was too cold for her to go out with the baby for very long during the day, and sitting around the apartment at night after Nathaniel fell asleep, she would worry about Benchley's safety on the dark city streets. Benchley told her she should try to get out by herself, but the few times she'd allowed herself to leave the baby with the janitor's daughter, she'd worried the whole time about something horrible happening while she was gone.

It was true what they always said about New York—visiting was fine, but she couldn't imagine ever feeling comfortable living there. The pace, the noise, the congestion, the sheer numbers of people—it was simply too much for her. She hardly knew anyone in New York to begin with, and while her husband made friends easily, she did not, and she was soon feeling both isolated and alienated. She never complained openly—she saw how hard Benchley was working, and how much he seemed to be invigorated by precisely the bustling atmosphere that she found so suffocating. Moreover, having seen Benchley spend his childhood and adolescence under two domineering women, Jennie and Lillian, she was determined not to be like them; as both his wife and his friend, she wanted him to feel that he could make his own decisions and live his life the way he wanted. Still, she couldn't keep everything bottled up inside without something giving way, and when Benchley arrived home from work late one night and found her wrapped in blankets suffering from chills that turned out to be the result of sheer nervousness, he realized he'd better find his family a decent place to live, and fast.

As it turned out, another of Benchley's Harvard friends, Russell Stiles, was working in New York and also looking for a home outside town for him and his fiancée, Viola Sullivan. After scouting around Rye, Mamaroneck, New Rochelle, and White Plains, Miss Sullivan discovered two two-story brown stucco houses side by side that were renting for $45 a month in Crestwood. As usual, the family bank account was barely in two figures, so Benchley borrowed $100 each from Adams and Dick Walsh to cover moving expenses and various deposits. Their furniture was shipped down from Boston, and after sending Gertrude and Nathaniel back to Worcester one last time, Benchley spent the first two weeks of May taking the train to Westchester every few evenings to unpack their crates and fix the place up.

On May 15, Benchley spent his last night at the 22nd Street apartment. He had been planning to go up to Crestwood after work to drop off Nathaniel's baby bathtub and do a final cleanup, but over dinner at Grand Central Station, Deems Taylor talked him into checking the bathtub in a locker and going to a burlesque show at the Rialto. The next morning, he threw whatever was left in the apartment into a duffel bag, taxied up to Grand Central, retrieved the bathtub, and caught the 8:25 up to Crestwood. As recorded in his diary, the day went thusly: "Spent the morning cleaning up the top floor, making the bed and the last few sweeping touches. Ordered groceries, too. In on the 12:12 and ate lunch. . . . Worked (in the office) on various things only to leave again at three to meet Gertrude and the son on the train from Worcester. As it was pouring and gave no indication of letting up, I decided to lodge the family at the Algonquin Hotel. Left them there and went back to the paper for awhile. Ate dinner with Gertrude in the hotel with inter-course dashes upstairs to listen at Nathaniel's door. Spent the early part of the evening in the bath-room so as not to disturb him and turned in about nine." The next day they moved into the Crestwood house: Nathaniel finally had his own room, Gertrude had trees and a garden to look out on instead of brick walls and fire escapes, and Benchley had train schedules to memorize.

While riding in on the 9:34 from Crestwood one morning, Benchley spotted a familiar figure waiting on the platform at the Bronxville station. It was Lillian Duryea, whom Benchley hadn't seen or heard from in quite some time. Their relationship had been drastically different ever since Benchley announced his engagement to Gertrude. At first she would simply stop him whenever he started to discuss his marriage plans, acting as if Gertrude barely existed. But then Benchley brought his fiancée to Nyack to meet Lillian's mother while she was out of town, and that, he learned later, infuriated her. Since Benchley looked upon Mrs. Duryea as something of a surrogate grandmother, he saw nothing at all wrong with what he'd done. If Lillian was troubled, he reasoned, then it was up to her to say something about it. She didn't, however, and as correspondence and visits between the two dwindled and began to show signs of strained formality, he realized that whatever warmth there'd been between them was now cooling rapidly.

In early 1914, after he hadn't heard from her for more than six months, Mrs. Duryea told him that Lillian was going to marry a man named Wilbur Baldwin, an old suitor of hers who was in the process of getting a divorce from his first wife. The Baldwins had been living with Wilbur's aged father near the Duryea home, and according to Gertrude, "all Nyack's sympathy was with the first Mrs. Baldwin," who continued to live with and care for her father-in-law after Wilbur took off for Reno. Benchley had sent Lillian an invitation to his wedding, but she had written back telling him that her own wedding—a private ceremony, with no guests—was scheduled just a week before his, and so she wouldn't be able to attend. Along with the note came a silver tray as a wedding present.

By June 1916, contact between the two had grown so minimal that it was only through Lillian's mother that they were finding out anything of each other's activities. But Benchley did know that Lillian and Wilbur Baldwin had settled in Bronxville, not too far from Crestwood, and that there was a chance he might run into her. On the morning that he saw Lillian come aboard the train headed to New York, Benchley motioned to her, but she pretended not to notice him. "She sat down in the seat directly in front of me," Benchley recorded in his diary, "but as she has no desire for diplomatic relations, I didn't force myself over the back of the seat." They rode the rest of the trip without saying a word to each other, and when they reached Grand Central Station, Benchley waited until she was well on her way before getting up to leave the train.

A month later, Benchley again spotted Lillian on his morning train, but this time she was accompanied by Wilbur Baldwin and she did come over, initiating what Benchley noted in his diary as "our first conversation in two years." Lillian wasn't looking to rekindle the friendship, however. She merely wanted to let him know that her mother had suddenly grown quite ill and wasn't expected to live much longer. Benchley went to visit Mrs. Duryea shortly thereafter and saw that Lillian wasn't exaggerating; his old friend was near death. In late September, the Duryea family matriarch passed away, and Benchley's sense of loss was deep. "If I could feel that some of Mrs. Duryea would live in me," he wrote in his diary after the funeral in Nyack, "it would be enough to assure my soul of immortality." The family home, he learned, was going to be sold, and after the funeral Benchley took a melancholy final walk around the grounds where he'd felt welcome since he was a little boy.

To counteract his sadness, Benchley threw himself into his next *Tribune* article, which sought to determine if hotel bellboys ever found the people they were paging. The story, researched at the Biltmore and written on the train going to and from the memorial services in Nyack, was published in October under the title "Call for Mr. Kenworthy" and drew praise from Benchley's colleagues at the *Tribune*—especially Adams, who suggested that he do *all* his writing on the way to funerals.

"Call for Mr. Kenworthy" represented something of a breakthrough for Benchley in that he was able to get in some satirically stinging blows against the phonies and snobs he saw on both sides of the front desk at many of the city's "better" hotels:

In order that no expense should be spared, I picked out a hotel with poor service, which means that it was an expensive hotel. . . . I picked out a boy with a discouraged voice, who seemed to be saying, "I'm calling these names—because this is my job—if I wasn't calling these—I'd be calling out cash totals in an honor system lunchery—but if anyone should ever answer to one of these names—I'd have a poor spell."

Allowing about fifteen feet between us for appearance's sake, I followed him through the lobby. He had a bunch of slips in his hand and from these he read the names on the pages.

"Call for Mr. Kenworthy—Mr. Shriner—Mr. Bodkin—Mr. Blevitch—Mr. Kenworthy—Mr. Bodkin—Mr. Kenworthy—Mr. Shriner—Mr. Kenworthy—Mr. Blevitch—Mr. Kenworthy."

Mr. Kenworthy seemed to be standing about a 20 per cent better chance of being located than any of the other contestants. Sometimes that was the only name he would call for mile upon mile. It occurred to me that perhaps Mr. Kenworthy was the only one wanted, and that the other names were just put in to make it harder, or to give body to the thing.

But when we entered the bar the youth shifted his attack. The name of Kenworthy evidently had begun to cloy . . . he dropped Kenworthy and called: "Mr. Blevitch. Call for Mr. Blevitch—Mr. Shriner—Mr. Bodkin—Mr. Blevitch—"

But even this subtle change of tactic failed to net him a customer. We had gone through the main lobby, along the narrow passage lined with young men waiting on sofas for women who would be forty minutes late, through the grill, and now had crossed the bar, and no one had even raised an eyebrow. . . .

As we went through one of the lesser dining-rooms, the dining-room that seats a lot of heavy men in business suits holding cigarettes, who lean over their plates the more confidentially to converse with their blond partners, in this dining-room the plaintiff drew fire. One of the men in business suits, who was at a table with another man and two women, lifted his head when he heard the sound of names being called.

"Boy!" he said, and waved like a traffic officer signaling, "Come!"

Eagerly the page darted forward. Perhaps this was Mr. Kenworthy! Or better yet, Mr. Blevitch.

"Anything here for Studz?" asked the man in the business suit, when he was sure that enough people were listening.

"No, sir," sighed the boy. "Mr. Blevitch, Mr. Kenworthy, Mr. Shriner, Mr. Bodkin?" he suggested, hopefully.

"Naw," replied the man, and turned to his associates with an air of saying, "Rotten service here—just think of it, no call for me!"

On we went again . . . the boy slid past the coat-room girl at the exit (no small accomplishment that) and down a corridor, disappearing through a swinging door at the end. . . . I dashed after him.

At first, like the poor olive merchant in the *Arabian Nights* I was blinded by the glare of lights and the glitter of glass and silver. . . . I had entered by a service entrance into the grand dining-room of the establishment, where, if you are not in evening dress, you are left to munch bread and butter until you starve to death and are carried out with your heels dragging, like the uncouth lout you are. . . .

Now, mind you, I am not ashamed of my gray suit. I like it, and my wife says that I haven't had anything so becoming for a long time. . . . As a gray suit it is above reproach. As a garment in which to appear single-handed through a trapdoor before a dining-room of well dressed Middle Westerners it was a fizzle from start to finish. Add to this the fact that I had to snatch a brown soft hat from my head when I found out where I was, which caused me to drop the three evening papers I had tucked under my arm, and you will see why my up-stage entrance was the signal for the impressive raising of several dozen eyebrows, and why the captain approached me just exactly as one approaches another when he is going to throw him out. . . .

I saw that anything that I might say would be used against me, and left him to read the papers I had dropped. One only lowers one's self by having words with a servitor.

Gradually I worked my way back through the swinging doors to the main corridor and rushed down to the regular entrance to wait there until my quarry should emerge. Suppose he should find all his consignees in the dining-room! I could not be in at the death then, and would have to falsify my story to make any kind of ending at all. And that would never do.

Once in a while I would catch the scent, when, from the humming depths of the dining-room, I could hear a faint "Call for Mr. Kenworthy" rising above the click of the oyster shells and the soft crackling of the "potatoes Julienne" one against another. So I knew that he had not failed me, and that if I had faith and waited long enough he would come back.

And, sure enough, come back he did, and without a name lost from his list. I felt like cheering when I saw his head bobbing through the melee of waiters and bus-boys who were busy putting clean plates on the tables and then taking them off again in eight seconds to make room for more clean plates. Of all discouraging existences I can imagine none worse than that of an eternally clean plate. There can be no sense of accomplishment, no glow of duty done, in simply being placed before a man and then taken away again. It must be almost as bad as paging a man who you are sure is not in the hotel. . . .

It was in the grill that the happy event took place. Mr. Shriner, the one of whom we expected least, suddenly turned up at a table alone. He was a quiet man and not at all worked up over his unexpected honor. He signaled the boy with one hand and went on taking soup with the other, and learned, without emotion, that he was wanted on the telephone. He even made no move to leave his meal to answer the call, and when last seen was adding pepper with one hand and taking soup with the other. I suspect that he was a "plant," or a plain-clothes house detective, placed there to deceive me.

We had been to every nook of the hotel by this time, except the writing-room, and, of course, no one would ever look there for patrons of the hotel. Seeing that the boy was about to totter, I went up and spoke to him. He continued to totter, thinking, perhaps, that I was Mr. Kenworthy, his long-lost beau-ideal. But I spoke kindly to him, and offered him a piece of chocolate-almond bar, and soon, in true reporter fashion, had wormed his secret from him before he knew what I was really after.

The thing I wanted to find out was, of course, just what the average is of replies to one paging trip. So I got around to it in this manner: Offering him another piece of chocolate-almond bar, I said, slyly: "Just what is the average number of replies to one paging trip?"

I think that he had suspected something at first, but this question completely disarmed him, and, leaning against an elderly lady patron, he told me . . . perhaps one in six. . . . And I found that he had not painted the lily in too glowing terms. I followed other pages that night—some calling for "Mr. Strudel," some for a "Mr. Carmickle," and one was broad-minded enough to page a "Mrs. Bemis." But they all came back with that wan look in their eyes and a break in their voices.

And each one of them was stopped by the man in the business suit in the downstairs dining-room and each time he considered it a personal affront that there wasn't a call for "Studz."

Some time I'm going to have him paged, and when he comes out I shall untie his necktie for him.

"We are happier and better off this Christmas Eve than I ever dared hope last Christmas Eve when we were breaking up housekeeping without knowing where we would set up again," Benchley wrote in his diary near the end of 1916. Gertrude was the happiest she'd been since they'd married. She showed little interest in going into the city, but seemed pleased that he was doing well now in a job that enabled him to go to work and come home at reasonable hours. Though the family was still in debt, those debts had at least been consolidated, thanks to a generous $300 loan from Gertrude's friend Mrs. Colton which was used to repay Walsh and Adams and settle a much-in-arrears Harvard Club bill. Benchley's good work at the *Tribune* was rewarded in mid-December with a $5 raise, and *Vanity Fair*'s Frank Crowninshield was giving him regular assignments that were good for another $55 a month. His pride received a boost when Adams came back one day from a lunch with Stephen Leacock and told him that the popular British humorist had mentioned how much he enjoyed Benchley's writing ("Ecstasy of conceit!" he noted in his diary), and his sense of civic duty was fulfilled when *Collier's* editor Mark Sullivan accepted an editorial he'd written supporting the Prohibition movement—a piece, he told Sullivan in an accompanying note, he hoped would help "in the fight to smash the rummies."

Benchley's attitude toward drinking had, to a great extent, been shaped by what he saw in his own home growing up. He knew that his father drank, and that his mother detested it. It was a weakness of character, to be sure, but it was a weakness for which he could forgive his father; after all, he rationalized, were it not for the Civil War, his father would never have been around so many people who drank, and surely would never have started were it not for the awful things he experienced as a soldier. But he saw how men acted when they were drunk, how they became crude and disrespectful, how their sense of decorum and propriety diminished. Once he had been in a restaurant in Boston and watched as a group of eight men were toasting each other. In front of each of them was a whiskey and a glass of water, and Benchley commented to his friends at the table, "Look! They have to wash away the taste of it with water!" The five-course lunch he was eating cost fifty cents; the whiskey was fifteen cents a shot. "Remarkable, isn't it?" he asked. "Those men are paying a dollar twenty for eight glasses of water!" And Gertrude had seen him react angrily during their college years when, after the two had come back from a walk along the Charles River on a cold, damp day, someone at the D.U. house offered Gertrude a hot toddy. In fact, so strong were his views on drinking that he'd loudly supported a Prohibition Party candidate in the Massachusetts gubernatorial election in 1915. (He'd also voted in favor of another controversial movement—woman suffrage.)

As the new year began, Benchley's career continued on a high note. In January, when *Vanity Fair*'s regular theater critic, P. G. Wodehouse, went off to the West Coast on leave, Crowninshield asked Benchley to pinch-hit, and he responded with a column in which he referred to Russian actress Alla Nazimova, the star of a somewhat lewd disaster called '*Ception Shoals*, as the play's "leading spermatozoa." In February, Benchley again substituted for Wodehouse, but his most memorable theater experience that month had nothing to do with reviewing. There happened to be at the time a hit show called *The Thirteenth Chair* in which, during the course of a lights-out séance, a dead body mysteriously appeared onstage. After seeing the show, *Tribune Magazine* editor Folwell got an idea for a report on the life of a Broadway corpse. The result was that on February 13, 1917, twenty-seven-year-old R. C. Benchley made a one-night-only appearance in the role of the dead body. The part, Benchley found out, had its own peculiar demands: He had to crawl from the back of a fake fireplace out to his mark in almost total darkness without bumping into anything or anyone, and once he was lying in place, he had to resist the gnawing temptation to open an eye.

Benchley's piece on the experience turned out well enough that shortly thereafter, when the circus came to town, Folwell again decided that Benchley was just the man to give *Tribune* readers an insider's view of things. Soon Benchley found himself on the floor of Madison Square Garden, riding around the ring on the back end of a fire engine wearing a wig, a fake nose, a painted-on frown, a broadly striped suit, and a pair of big floppy shoes. Everything went along smoothly until Benchley was asked to hop aboard the trick exploding bus. At that point he decided that self-preservation was the better part of professional duty, and he quickly repaired to the safety of the dressing rooms. He didn't shrink from his fears when it came time to write the story, however: Its guilty title was "Uneasy Lies the Head That Plays the Clown."

While the *Tribune* continued to treat him well—an offer from a Harvard Club friend to become publicity director for the Red Cross in Washington for nearly $4,000 a year, relayed to Adams, resulted in another raise, upping his pay to $60 a week—Benchley continued to be bothered by the paper's coverage of the war in Europe. In early February, the United States broke off diplomatic relations with Germany, which had just announced its intention to ignore any attempts to restrict submarine warfare, and Benchley was so horrified by the giddy excitement with which the *Tribune*'s editorials demanded that Wilson immediately declare war that he again contemplated handing in his resignation. "I can't help feeling that Germany will not give us cause [to enter the war]," he wrote in his diary at this time, "although that's the way I felt in August, 1914. I am hovering between a desire to see German Prussianism buried for the good of the future world's peace, and the feeling that if war is wrong, it is wrong, and no pratings of honor can justify it. The second is my real belief . . . if we can find justification for this war, justification can always be found for future wars." He made up his mind that if he got drafted, he would only serve in defense of home soil: "I will never carry war into another country," he vowed, "not even if I were to be shot for refusing." He'd already seen enough of war's horrible legacy in his own life; one war had driven his father to drink, and another had robbed him of his brother. (As it turned out, he didn't have to test the measure of his convictions. In June, after war had been declared, he went to register for the draft but was deferred immediately because of his wife and child.)

Although a great many Americans were, in some part, of German extraction, anti-German sentiment began to run quite high in the winter and spring of 1917, and, predictably, most German-Americans grew distraught and distrustful of their neighbors in return. One day, amid some distressing news from across the Atlantic, Benchley went for a haircut downstairs from the *Tribune* office and was shaved by a "grouchy German barber," who scared him so much, he wrote in his diary, that "I feared that I might be the unlucky American to precipitate an international crisis." He later felt better when, after signing up with the local Big Brother office, he helped provide some companionship for several months for a young German boy whose father had recently died, leaving him the only male in an eight-child household. It was only coincidence that the child was German, but it made Benchley feel that he was doing a doubly good deed.

On Monday, May 28, after spending the early morning putting the finishing touches on a *Vanity Fair* piece, Benchley took a late-morning train into New York and arrived at the *Tribune* building a little before noon. Walking into the *Tribune Magazine* offices, Benchley felt something in the air. Young Irwin Edman, a writer who'd been working as Deems Taylor's substitute while Taylor was away on sabbatical, was sitting quietly at his desk, staring at the closed door to Frank Adams's office, where, he told Benchley, Arthur Folwell had been summoned some twenty minutes previously. Some more time passed, and then Adams opened his door and asked Benchley and Edman to come in. The ever cheerful Folwell had a look on his face that Benchley knew meant only one thing—somebody was getting fired. Then Adams spoke, and Benchley wished he'd never gotten out of bed that morning.

Benchley knew that there had been rumblings over the previous few months that *Tribune* publisher Ogden Reid was growing increasingly unhappy with the magazine's content and generally irreverent tone. At times, Reid had told associates, it seemed as though the magazine was making fun of the rest of the paper. Even Adams, however, seemed a bit shocked by the news he had to break to them— that the *Tribune Magazine* with its entire staff was being terminated in two weeks. The official line was that the magazine was going under because of economic contraints—at least that's what vice president and general manager George Rogers said to Adams when he lowered the boom. Whether they believed that or not, Adams told his three colleagues, was up to them. He certainly didn't.

News of the impending demise of the *Tribune Magazine* brought many writers and editors down to the office for sympathy calls during its final two weeks of existence. Everyone Benchley ran into assured him that he'd have no trouble whatsoever finding work, but the reality was that after sending out a multitude of inquiries to other papers and magazines, Benchley found himself without a single offer for a salaried position. For some time Crowninshield had hinted that the managing editor's post at *Vanity Fair* would be opening up soon, and that he thought Benchley would be the perfect candidate for the post. But when Benchley went to see him and told him he would actually be free very shortly, Crowninshield, embarrassed, confessed that publisher Condé Nast had another man in line for the position, and that he couldn't overrule his boss. Perhaps down the line, he said. In the meantime, he'd try to give Benchley as much freelance work as possible.

In desperation, Benchley allowed a friend to get him an appointment with a man from the Metro Film Corporation in regard to possible caption writing, but it turned out that there was nothing immediate for him, and he only halfheartedly asked the movie executive to keep him in mind if anything turned up. From everything he'd heard about the picture business, it didn't seem like a career he'd be interested in pursuing. "I am not too keen for the prospects to come through," he wrote in his diary, "not quite being reconciled to mixing up in circles which must consist of the country's most frothy and inconsequential citizens."

On Sunday, June 3, Benchley sat at home working on his final article for the *Tribune Magazine*—fittingly, it was about looking for a job—and late in the afternoon he went for a walk down near the Bronx River. "Every once in a while I would have to stop and think of where next month's food is coming from," he wrote in his diary, "and wonder if, by next Sunday, I will have anything more definite to build on. I hope so, for Sunday is a bad day to be out of a job." The ensuing week, however, brought no miracle job offers, and Benchley awoke on the morning of the 10th with a blank future staring him in the face. Every editor he'd spoken to had told him that although he had no jobs to offer, he'd love to see possible freelance contributions from Benchley. Well then, Benchley decided, a freelance writer he would be.

6

Rough Sledding on the
Field of Honor

AND OTHER STEPS TOWARD UTOPIA

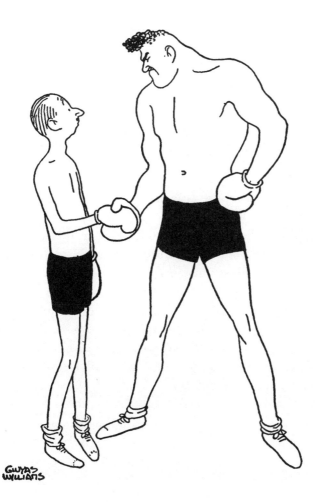

Had Robert Benchley the freelancer simply continued writing the kinds of stories that Robert Benchley the *Tribune Magazine* staffer churned out each and every week for more than a year, it's altogether possible that he could have begun building a successful career as a self-employed writer in the summer of 1917. But, just as in 1914, when he'd made his first tentative stabs at cracking the publishing field, Benchley believed that he needed to produce "serious" stories in order to be considered a "real" writer. When he started working from home in mid-June, his only committed assignments were from *Vanity Fair*, as Frank Crowninshield, keeping his word about providing him with work, had commissioned him to do two stories per month. (Since the magazine's standard policy was not to use more than one article per issue by any outside contributor, his extra pieces were published under the pseudonym Brighton Perry.) These articles, which Benchley considered "fluffs," rarely required more than one draft and were done quickly and efficiently. When he turned to the "important" stories, though, the ones he hoped to sell to prestigious publications like *Harper's* or the *Atlantic*, his pace turned slow and deliberate. While *Vanity Fair* and *Collier's* were both successful magazines, their breezy style and modernist outlook kept them, Benchley thought, from being taken seriously as important journals. *Harper's*, the *Atlantic*, the *Saturday Evening Post*—that was where articles of substance and import invariably appeared. Humor was fine, in its place; the dearth of it in these magazines proved that. And, he assumed, serious writing mandated a serious approach to the craft of writing. Feeling that he was working for a different and much more demanding reading market, he slaved over sentences for hours at a time, and sometimes came away from a full day's writing with only a lone page satisfactorily completed. And yet, despite his best efforts, these articles failed to attract much interest.

By the middle of August, all Benchley had to show for two months of hard work was $60 from *Vanity Fair* and a disappointing collection of rejection slips. He'd managed to finish only two uncommissioned articles, and neither proved marketable. One was a story that, according to his diary, was about "home-made scenes in reading literature," and though Benchley had painstakingly tried to tailor it especially for the *Atlantic*, it was returned with shocking alacrity. *Harper's* got to see it next, and it met the same fate there. The other story was an art museum piece that Benchley had wanted to do ever since his strange experience at the Boston Museum of Fine Arts, but by the time he sent it off to New York agent Paul Reynolds, the article had swelled to an unwieldy twelve thousand words. After Reynolds and then the *Saturday Evening Post* passed on the piece, Benchley retired it—and his career as a freelancer. The hunger that a few months earlier he'd said would be the only thing to drive him back to salaried employment finally manifested itself. Throughout most of June and July, the family had been staying at Red Farm, the Millbury, Massachusetts, home of Katharine Coes's mother, Mrs. Samuel Colton, and though he greatly appreciated Mother Colton's ongoing kindness, Benchley knew that they couldn't stay there indefinitely. He *had* to find a regular job.

Benchley went down to New York to talk to Frank Adams. If anyone knew of any jobs in newspapers, magazines, or the theater, it would be him. Adams told him he'd try to find out if anything was out there, and a few days later he wrote to announce that Dave Wallace, press agent for Broadway producer William A. Brady, was about to resign his position and was looking for a replacement to recommend to Brady. Adams was sure that Benchley could get the job if he wanted it, but he cautioned him to think it over carefully before applying. Brady did pay fairly well, Adams conceded—Benchley could probably get a starting salary of $75 a week—but he wasn't sure the money would be worth the aggravation. "Even if you get it," he wrote, "you won't like it. He [Brady] is a bad boy—crooked, I imagine, and a souse, I know."

On August 21, Benchley came down to New York, and after getting some last-minute advice from both Adams and Crowninshield, he was taken by Wallace to see William Brady. The interview lasted all of five minutes. The producer bluntly stated that he knew little of Benchley and that he was uncertain he could do the job as expected. If he wanted to try it, Brady told him, he'd better know right at the outset that there were "no clocks on this job"; he'd be on call virtually all day and night. Benchley told him he understood, and it was agreed that Brady would "try him out" for a while at the $75 he was asking for. "Come back here a week from today," the producer said as he abruptly rose from his desk to show Benchley to the door. "You start then."

As it turned out, Frank Adams was all too accurate in his prediction that Benchley wouldn't like working for William Brady. Benchley found virtually everything about the man distasteful—not the least of which was (as Adams had warned) his propensity for being drunk a good deal of the time. How much of Brady's coarse and rude behavior was attributable to his drinking and how much was just part of his basic nature, Benchley really couldn't figure out. All he knew was that the job was a source of constant aggravation and tension. The producer kept him on the run at all hours.

Brady had three shows in production—one running in New York, one on the road, and one in rehearsal—and it fell to Benchley to take care of all the publicity for each of them. He was expected to supply press releases, news, and feature material to the drama editors of each of the eighteen New York dailies for the shows in town, as well as arranging for coverage in other cities for the road show. And since the fickle producer was constantly changing dates for openings and deciding to pull or alter ads at the last minute, Benchley often found himself on a frantic merry-go-round, running from one newspaper office to another trying to change information he'd delivered only hours before. Brady's warning that his press agent would have to be available day and night was no joke, either. During one stretch, Benchley went two weeks without being able to go home for dinner, and several times Gertrude had to travel in from Crestwood to bring him a set of evening clothes to change into in his small office at Brady's theater, the Playhouse.

At various points that fall, Benchley had major run-ins with Brady. The first occurred when Benchley left for home immediately after the opening of *The Land of the Free* without checking in with Brady—who seemed to be much too tight to discuss anything. The transgression resulted in a sound verbal thrashing the next morning. A week later, when the Sunday newspapers devoted what Brady felt was grossly insufficient space to news of the upcoming opening of *Eve's Daughter* (which just happened to star his wife, actress Gladys George), he called Benchley at home and berated him at such length that Benchley decided that he'd quit the very next day. And he would have, except that when he showed up at the theater the next afternoon, Brady acted as if the phone conversation had never taken place. Benchley realized Brady had been intoxicated when he'd called, and his anger passed over to pity when Brady, forgetting that Benchley was a teetotaler, asked him to go have a drink with him. Benchley declined, and when Brady left to go to a local bar, he sat alone in his office and thought seriously about what he should do. As it stood, the job simply wasn't worth what he was having to endure for his $75 a week. It was mid-October, and he'd been with Brady all of seven weeks. It felt like an eternity.

Intent on getting out, Benchley sent out letters to friends and colleagues to see if they knew of any job openings. On November 1, Frederick Allen wrote him from Washington, D.C., that there seemed to be a number of vacancies in the U.S. government's Council of National Defense, where he was working, and that Benchley should come down to apply for a position. When Benchley phoned Brady to ask for two days off, the producer demanded to know why, and Benchley told him the truth. Brady angrily barked words to the effect that Benchley couldn't work for him and the government at the same time, and promptly hung up. When Benchley called back, Brady was gone, so he gave the assistant a message to pass on: As soon as someone could be found to take his place, he'd be quitting.

The next day, Benchley took the train down to Washington. As Allen had indicated, there were several jobs available within the department, all involving press relations and publicity. He saw one official at the council's main division about a public relations post, and then another at the Hoover Food Administration, where a similar spot was open, but sensing that he wasn't likely to be offered either job, he returned to New York disappointed. Although he and Brady were barely speaking, it didn't look as if Brady was hurrying to find anyone to take his place, so he continued his work while Allen kept an eye out for news of any openings. Brady was having his troubles. *Eve's Daughter* had been an instant failure, and he tried to rebound by thrusting Gladys George into a new play called *L'Elévation*. The show opened on November 14 to generally good notices, but it didn't attract much business. And on the 24th, during a sparsely attended performance, Brady's assistant came into Benchley's office to notify him that Brady was going to close *L'Elévation* the following week, that Miss George would take the rest of the season off, and that Brady had decided to do without the services of a press agent for the time being. In other words, Brady was accepting Benchley's resignation—effective immediately.

Fortunately for Benchley, it wasn't more than a week later that Freddy Allen got him an interview with the Aircraft Board's chairman, Howard Coffin, who was looking for a publicity director. The meeting went well, and Benchley was put up in a hotel for several days so that he could be interviewed by other senior officials. The board members explained to him that much of his "publicity" work would involve trying to keep military secrets *out* of the newspapers, and that there would be a lot of rumor-squelching as well. It all sounded a bit mysterious to Benchley, but with the United States now formally at war, he understood that some secrecy was necessary, and he agreed that he would do the best he could. He knew that taking the job meant compromising some of his principles, but he also knew he had to provide for his family, and he rationalized that in working for the government he would be doing his patriotic duty while still remaining a pacifist. And if his work in any small way helped the war end sooner, it would be worth it.

Right after New Year's Day, 1918, a telegram arrived at Crestwood telling Benchley that he was officially hired and that he was expected in Washington to begin work as soon as possible. Since Benchley hadn't been completely certain that he was getting the job, he hadn't looked for a place for the family to live, and so it was decided that Gertrude and Nathaniel would move in with Katharine Coes at her Worcester home until Benchley found something. And, because of his track record over the previous five and a half years, it was agreed that the wisest thing to do would be to sublet the Crestwood house.

Benchley arrived in Washington on January 9, one day after President Wilson outlined his Fourteen Points peace program to Congress. "As a general summary of what's wrong with the world they are admirable," he wrote in his diary, "but if we are going to wait on their complete fulfillment the war will be a long time going." On the morning of the 10th, he reported to the Aircraft Board office. One of the

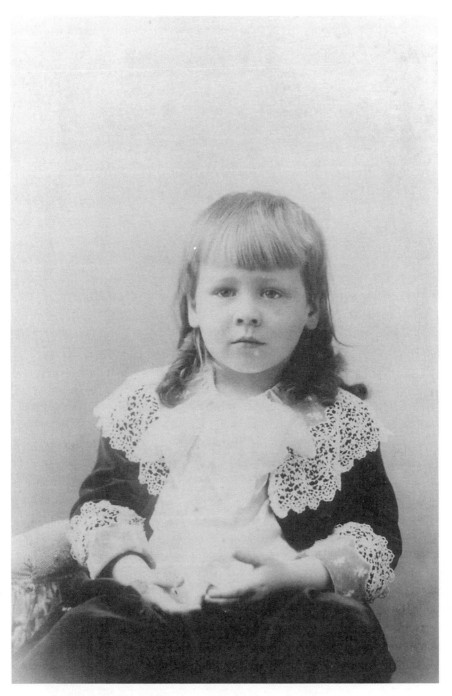

Robert Charles Benchley, age two, 1891.

Jennie Moran Benchley.

Charles Henry Benchley.

With his brother, West Point cadet
Edmund Benchley, c. 1897.

With Lillian Duryea,
c. 1900.

Enjoying himself along
the Hudson River near
Nyack, 1901.

At South High School, Worcester, 1904. Benchley is at left in the next to the last row; Gertrude Darling is at bottom right.

Midway through his college career at Harvard, 1910.

Appearing (at left)
in the title role of
the Delta Upsilon
fraternity production
of *Ralph Roister
Doister*, 1911.

Honeymooning with
Gertrude near Scarboro
Beach, Maine, 1914.

Perusing the latest issue of the undertaker's trade paper, *The Casket*, with Dorothy Parker, 1919.

Benchley (with duster) and Parker (with broom), giving a mock military salute to *Vanity Fair* editor Frank Crowninshield, 1919.

OPPOSITE.
At the *Life*
offices, early
1920s.

The suburban homeowner:
in Scarsdale with sons
Bobby (left) and Nathaniel,
snow shovel and pipe,
1925.

Trying to escape
from driving teacher
Edward Brady in
Lesson No. One,
1929.

On the way to Europe with Gertrude
aboard the S.S. *Bremin*, 1929.

With Charles McArthur, Beatrice Ames Stewart, and Stewart's husband, Donald Ogden Stewart (face not visible in picture), apparently discussing something of almost serious import, mid-1930s.

Laughing—as usual—in the presence of Marc Connelly, mid-1930s.

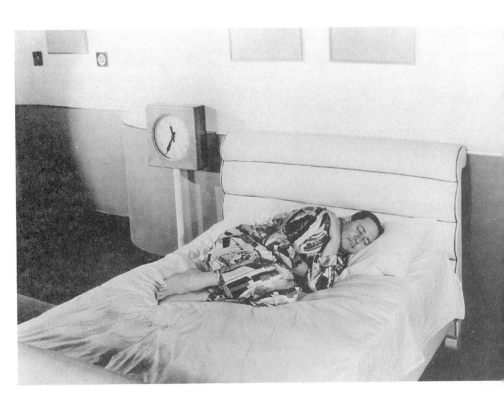

Demonstrating the "Supine Curl" in *How to Sleep*, 1935.

"This position is a favorite with drunks . . . . "

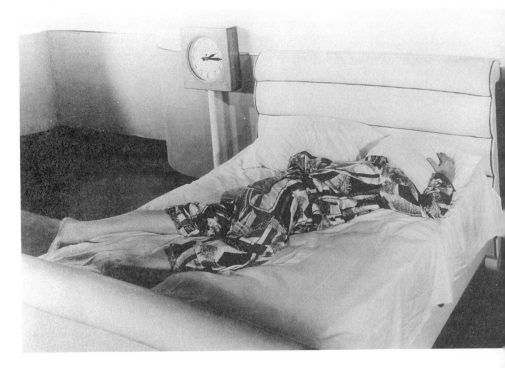

Explaning where all the money goes in *How to Vote*, 1936.

Eyeball to eyeball with three-year-old Ricardo Cezon in *A Night at the Movies*, 1937.

"Dr." Benchley (left), encountering a suspiciously familiar looking patient in *Mental Poise*, 1938.

Wincing at a bad pun while producer Martin Gosch looks on during a rehearsal for the *Melody and Madness* radio show, 1939.

OPPOSITE. Outside his apartment at the Garden of Allah, late 1930s.

With Joel McCrea, and a reluctantly ordered
glass of milk, in Alfred Hitchcock's *Foreign
Correspondent*, 1940.

As Deanna
Durbin's
father in
Nice Girl?,
1941.

Touring the Walt Disney studios in
The Reluctant Dragon, 1941.

Playing ring toss with Rosalind Russell
in *Take a Letter, Darling*, 1942.

As Joe Doakes, about to get it from
Ruth Lee in *My Tomato*, 1943.

With Shirley
Temple in *Kiss
and Tell*, 1945.

OPPOSITE.
Relaxing at
the Garden in
the late
1940s.

directors, Jack Paine, showed him around and generally outlined his duties. Then he was taken to the office of a man named Steel, who told him that there seemed to be a lot of whispering going on about airplane production being far behind schedule, and that a much-vaunted aircraft engineering project, the Liberty Motor, was rumored to be a major failure. Benchley gathered that he was to try to counteract this gossip—although Steel had given no indication whatsoever that the rumors weren't true.

A few days later, however, he met Coffin at the director's house and was assured that the Liberty Motor was not a bust but a great—and so far secret—success, and that although plane production was nowhere near the 100,000 that had been predicted, those planes already in service were more than sufficient for the level of fighting being done at the front in Europe. Benchley asked Coffin if he knew just how many planes actually *had* been produced, and Coffin said several thousand—although none of them were part of the 100,000 everyone was talking about. Those were fighter planes; the ones that had been built were training planes. And as soon as the pilots were schooled in flying them, the actual fighter craft would be manufactured. So if anyone asked, Coffin told him, he should stress that training-plane production was proceeding just fine, and be careful not to discuss the fighters. In the meantime, he wanted Benchley to begin getting the good word out about the Liberty Motor.

The Aircraft Board operated under the aegis of the Signal Corps, and Benchley quickly began to comprehend the true meaning of red tape when he innocently tried to order a few things for his office. In order to keep track of coverage of the Aircraft Board's activities, he'd need a scrapbook to keep clippings in, but when he tried to buy one he was told that he had to buy six of them, and could only get them from a government-contracted firm in New York. When he attempted to purchase a national newspaper directory, he was informed that the transaction required the solicitation of bids from a minimum of three suppliers. And although Coffin had hoped it wouldn't happen, Benchley was ordered by the chief of the Signal Corps to clear all news stories with corps officials—regardless of subject matter—before releasing them to the press. After the officials axed a report on the training of homing pigeons, Benchley realized he'd have to overstep authority every now and then or else *nothing* would come out of his office. Which seemed to be the way the Signal Corps wanted it.

Toward the end of March, Benchley began to understand why the military people were so nervous about publicity. By accident one day, a young pilot training in Texas who was in Washington on leave happened to overhear Benchley telling some newspapermen about the wonderful training planes, and the young man confided in one of the secretaries at the office that such was not the case at all, at least not at the training field where he was stationed. Down in Texas, there weren't enough planes for the cadets to fly, and those that were used were shoddily built, resulting in numerous crashes and many injuries. Several pilots, he confessed, had been killed.

In a confidential note a few days later, the secretary relayed to Benchley the story the pilot had told her, and Benchley, aghast, tried to take action. "If the information I get from headquarters is not true," he noted, "I had better get out of here and not continue to relay lies to the press." Feeling uncomfortable, he wrote up a report of what he'd heard and sent it off to the Signal Corps liaison officer, Major Stedman Hanks, along with a plea for a more frank relation between the Signal Corps and the Aircraft Board. "If I can get something started there, it will be the only worthwhile thing I have done on the job," he wrote in his diary, "but I am afraid that no one in the Signal Corps will take it seriously." He was right; the major never even acknowledged receiving the report, and although Benchley had asked him to forward it to more senior officials, he was positive that Hanks had simply let it die on his desk.

In early April, after news of the nonexistent 100,000 fighter planes finally emerged—General Pershing, seeing all the new German planes flying unchallenged in the European skies, had angrily wired Washington that unless the planes were really on the way, they'd better knock off all the talk about them—a hastily organized Senate investigating committee officially condemned the aircraft program as a failure, and steps were undertaken to relieve the Signal Corps of responsibility for airplane production and maintenance. On the 24th, Benchley learned that Howard Coffin's departure from the board was imminent; a copper manufacturer named Ryan was being brought in to replace him, and it looked as though they were going to clamp down even more severely on press relations. Coffin said he was sure that Benchley could stay on, but he wasn't certain exactly what he'd be doing. Benchley had heard that one before.

While all of this was going on, Benchley received a prefectly timed offer. Ernest Greuning, the managing editor of the *Boston Traveler* who had used Benchley as a theater reviewer a few years before, was working for the War Trade Board when Benchley arrived in Washington, and he'd helped the Benchleys find a house near his family's in Chevy Chase, Maryland. The two households had grown quite close over the course of February and March—Greuning's two children and Nat Benchley were constant playmates—and Greuning often came to Benchley's assistance when the latter had his inevitable troubles with the coal-eating heat monster in the basement. Then Greuning accepted an invitation in April to return to newspaper work in New York as managing editor of Benchley's former paper, the *Tribune*. When he left, he told Benchley that he had the authority to hire anyone he pleased, and that if Benchley wanted to work there again, he'd be only too happy to bring him back. Hearing of the Aircraft Board troubles, Greuning wrote Benchley to tell him that the paper was contemplating a Sunday pictorial supplement and that he could be the editor if he wanted the job.

On May 1, Benchley took the train to New York to talk to Greuning about the new Sunday section. Greuning told him he could start him at $75 a week (the government had been paying him $60), with a guarantee of a raise to $100 after three months if all went well. Benchley accepted on the spot, and returned to Washington to hand in his resignation from the Aircraft Board. "In view of the fact that my government work now consists chiefly of drawing pay," he wrote in his diary, "I have no compunction against withdrawing, and since I am going to be working with Ernest, there are no compunctions about going back on the *Trib*." Having gone through a myriad of jobs in such a short time, he also had no illusions about what the future might bring. "After many buffetings," he mused, "[I have] reached a calloused state where I don't look ahead to a permanent holding of any one job for more than six months. And, from what I know of the *Trib*, I am not in for long. Hi-ho!" Greuning wanted him to start as soon as possible, and after the Aircraft Board agreed to let him leave on short notice, he said goodbye to Gertrude and Nat (the Crestwood house was sublet until September, so they were to stay in Washington until he found an interim place for all of them) and took the May 4 midnight train to New York.

The *Tribune Graphic*, a predecessor of the rotogravure sections that would soon be part of most newspapers' Sunday editions, was a twelve-page pictorial supplement that Benchley, under Greuning's supervision, was solely responsible for creating and editing. He had a $200-a-week budget for purchasing photos, and after selecting those pictures he wished to use, he personally arranged the layouts, wrote all the captions, and oversaw the production process.

During the first few weeks, all went well. Greuning, who was living in Bay Shore, Long Island, once again found Benchley a house to rent near his own, and soon Gertrude and Nat were able to leave Washington. The train ride into the city took almost two hours, and Benchley and Greuning often spent the time talking over their ambitious plans for the *Graphic*. The *Tribune*'s hierarchy—publisher/editor Ogden Reid, general manager Rogers, and assistant editor Garet Garrett—seemed satisfied with the contents. Even Rogers, who'd never once spoken to Benchley during his first go-round at the paper, not even when he fired him, came downstairs one afternoon and complimented him on one of his captions.

Feeling that their work was being approved, Greuning and Benchley soon began to discuss ways of expanding the section's horizons. They were always encouraged to give ample space to coverage of the war—a weekly full-page feature called "The Field of Honor" carried pictures of American soldiers killed in action—and when Benchley received in the mail a picture showing a regiment of Negro infantrymen who were being decorated for bravery in France, he showed it to Greuning and they decided to run it. Not by itself, however. They'd recently received another, altogether different photograph with a Negro in it, and they thought that juxtaposing the two photos might make for a provocative page. They were correct. The page, as planned, was provocative enough that it literally stopped the presses. As soon as Ogden Reid saw it being printed, he hit the ceiling and ordered it destroyed.

As laid out by Benchley, the top half of page two of the *Tribune*

Graphic's June 9 issue showed the regiment of black American soldiers fighting in France, and the caption beneath the picture noted that two of the troops, Henry Johnson and Needham Roberts, had recently been decorated with the French War Cross for bravery in the field, and that the entire organization had distinguished itself in recent battles. The bottom half of the page showed a black man in Georgia being murdered by a very large crowd of whites. The caption read: "At the left, a mob of representative citizens of the South are engaged in the manly sport of burning a Negro. The old-fashioned Southern gentleman nearest the pyre is taking advantage of the emboldening presence of a thousand other gentlemen of the old school to apply a red hot iron to the victim. Since the United States entered the war, the South has indulged its passion for chivalry to the extent of 219 lynchings and burnings of Negro men and women, many of them accused of no particular crime except that of color. Governor Dorsey of Georgia recently gave it as his opinion that the only way to stop this lynching will be to appeal to the Negro element of the South to be more decent! A bill has, nevertheless, been introduced into Congress making lynching a Federal crime, a move which will win the support of all Americans who value the splendid loyalty of our colored citizenry throughout the nation's history."

The lynching picture never saw the light of day. On Friday, the day the pictorial section was to go to press, Benchley was called in for a meeting with Reid, Rogers, and Garrett. The picture, he was angrily informed, would not be running in that Sunday's—or any Sunday's—*Graphic*. A picture such as this one would serve no purpose other than to stir dissent among Americans, and that, Benchley was told, was unacceptable during a time of war. Running a picture of a lynching was, well, it was *pro-German*, Reid told him. While a new press cylinder was being fitted, Benchley was ordered to find something to substitute for the offending photo. He grabbed the first thing he found on his desk—a picture of some racehorses—wrote up a small blurb, and handed it in to Garrett and Rogers, who stared at him with such contempt that he told Greuning later in the day he was sure they had it in for him.

As it turned out, it was Garrett who was out to get him. The assistant editor started loudly criticizing the *Graphic*, questioning Benchley's choice of pictures as well as the captions. Most of his comments dealt with war-related items, as he consistently sought to prove that the "pro-German" slant Reid hinted at was indeed manifesting itself in the pictorial section. A simple shot of the Kaiser was assailed as showing him to be "normal," thus, Garrett contended, "weakening the public's hate for him, which must be fanned high." A street-scene picture from Berlin was attacked as being a fraud—"too many young men not in uniform," Garrett sneered. It had to be an old picture, taken before the war, and not, as Benchley claimed, a recent photo. So it went. In early July, Benchley was going to run a picture of a German U-boat picking up survivors of a ship it had just sunk, and Garrett not only had it blocked from publication, but launched an investigation to find out if the Dutch picture agent Benchley was using for many of his war photos might be a spy. When Benchley found out about it, he called up some of his former colleagues in Washington and had an Army intelligence officer call Garrett to set him straight.

Ernest Greuning continued to defend Benchley, and that led Garrett to believe that the managing editor himself should be investigated. A reporter named Lynch was asked to see what he could come up with on Greuning, and although he produced only a few rumors about possible German ancestry and the fact that a man in a Manhattan building where Greuning had been renting an apartment had been arrested for running a German-owned paper, Garrett was able to convince Rogers that Greuning's presence on the paper was "an embarrassment" to such a patriotic newspaper as the *Tribune*. On the evening of July 12, without being given any chance to repudiate the rumors, Greuning was told he was being dismissed. Benchley found out the next morning, and before lunch he'd typed up three copies of the following letter:

Mr. Ogden Reid
Mr. Rogers
Mr. Garrett

Gentlemen:
    Without any rational proof that Dr. Greuning was guilty of the burlesque charges made against him (except the heinous one of living at 324 West 103d St.), you took steps, which on the slightest examina-

tion could have been proven unwarranted, to smirch the character and newspaper career of the first man in three years who has been able to make the *Tribune* look like a newspaper.

I haven't the slightest idea who is boss of this sheet, so I am sending this resignation to three whom I suspect.

Robert C. Benchley

As soon as he'd delivered the letters to the offices of the addressees, Benchley walked out of the *Tribune* building, never to return. As for Greuning, Garrett had apparently never bothered to check with the War Trade Board, where his managing editor had worked before coming to the *Tribune*, and after Greuning saw to it that his name was officially cleared by the Department of Justice, he started a slander suit against the newspaper, enlisted in the Army, and went off to Europe to fight for the United States. After the war, he entered politics, and he eventually became quite well known—as governor of Alaska.

The day after he resigned from the *Tribune*, Benchley went to see Bug Farwell, an executive of the Liberty Loan organization. Like the U.S. Savings Bond programs they foreshadowed, Liberty Loans were started to help fill America's war chest, and their various drives raised billions of dollars. Benchley had met Farwell not long after he'd first gone to Washington to work for the Aircraft Board, and Farwell had told him that since the loan program was always in need of press liaisons, he should get in touch if he was ever back in New York and wanted to work for the organization. Benchley had filed the offer away in the back of his mind, and when the reality of his quitting the *Tribune* sank in, he decided on a hunch to see if Farwell was still interested. Farwell was delighted to hear from him. The fourth Liberty Loan drive had a target goal of almost $6 billion, and the organization needed all the help it could get. Benchley knew that he would have to keep his pacifist beliefs under wraps yet again were he to get the job, and he briefly grappled with himself over whether to apply. But he knew that his choice of fields was limited by both experience and opportunity, and that his loud exit from the *Tribune* virtually ensured that he wasn't going to be snatched up by any newspaper in the near future. So, within three days, Benchley was interviewed, hired, and at work at the Liberty Loan offices in Manhattan at a salary of $65 a week. His primary job was to help generate publicity for the loan drive through the solicitation and placement of newspaper and magazine articles about the organization, and occasionally he helped compose copy for posters and ads.

Benchley had been with the Liberty Loan program less than four months when Armistice was declared on November 11, 1918. The news broke in the middle of the night, and like many Americans all across the country, the Benchleys were awakened by the sounds of gongs and bells signaling the end of the war. Throwing coats over their bed-clothes, Benchley and Gertrude roused Nathaniel, called on their neighbors the Stiles, and raced over to where the townspeople were lining up to ring the Crestwood fire bell. Benchley did little sleeping the rest of the night. He was naturally overjoyed that the fighting was over. But he couldn't help wondering if the end of the war meant the end of the Liberty Loan program as well. As it turned out, it didn't. A fifth drive had begun in October, and after a reorganization of the press department, Benchley was not only asked to stay, but was pro-moted to assistant publicity director. As the year came to an end, Benchley calculated the family finances and discovered, much to his surprise, that he'd finally gotten out of debt. He'd earned over $5,000 in 1918—enough to owe $160 of income tax!

The first few months of the new year were among the most per-sonally and professionally peaceful that Benchley had known in quite some time. Work at the Liberty Loan program, while not particularly stimulating—without any pressing emergencies, the entire fund-raising process was proceeding at a snail's pace—was at least pleasant. His freelance writing began to pick up a bit when Deems Taylor joined the editorial staff of *Collier's* and contracted him to start getting into print all of his uproarious stories about man-eating furnaces, weed-filled gardens, off-key community sings, bridge disasters (four-handed, that is), and other peculiar aspects of suburban life. There was no doubt the extra money was going to come in handy, for Gertrude learned in January that she was going to have another baby.

It was also in January that the proposed Eighteenth Amendment to the U.S. Constitution—the prohibition of the manufacture, sale, or transportation of intoxicating liquors—was ratified by enough states to assure its passage into law. The effective date was to be January of the following year, and nondrinker Benchley expressed in his diary the hope that in the interim "the millions which the liquor interests are preparing to spend in contesting the constitutionality of it will not avail to change it." As far as Benchley was concerned, the outlawing of alcohol was a blessing from heaven, "a step toward Utopia." Just a few months before, when he'd been ill with a touch of influenza, he'd been shocked when his doctor prescribed a tablespoon of whiskey every few hours. He went along with the doctor's orders for two days, until he looked in the mirror and saw that the end of his nose had turned red—like those of the rummies he saw in saloons!

In late March, when Deems Taylor left *Collier's*, the magazine's managing editor, William LeBaron, approached Benchley about taking over the vacant associate editor post. Armed with the offer, Benchley went to see Frank Crowninshield on April 4. For almost two years, Crowninshield had been "promising" him that one day he'd be the managing editor of *Vanity Fair*—which Benchley considered a classier magazine than *Collier's*—and Benchley decided to give him a final chance to make good before agreeing to take the *Collier's* job. Crowninshield seemed genuinely perturbed about the possibility of Benchley's joining the staff of a competing magazine, and he told Benchley he'd talk to publisher Condé Nast right away about hiring him. He asked Benchley to return to his office later that day, and in the afternoon, after some coaching by Crowninshield, Benchley went to see Nast. Nast had told Crowninshield on numerous occasions that he thought *Vanity Fair* needed to take itself a little more seriously, and when Benchley replied to a Nast inquiry about the future of the magazine by discussing the need for a somewhat less frivolous outlook, he knew by the expression on Nast's face that the job was his. They agreed on a salary of $100 a week, with the stipulation that Benchley would write no more than two freelance articles a month for any other periodical.

After a starting date of May 19 was set, Benchley informed the Liberty Loan people of his plans, and though they were sorry to see him go they wished him well. Actually, the loan program had been doing a lot of work recently in settlement houses, and Benchley felt a twinge of guilt about leaving the organization just as it was beginning to get into the kind of social work that he found fulfilling. Then again, working as the managing editor at a magazine where he truly believed he'd be blissfully happy was something he'd often dreamed of. And now he was ready to try to live that dream.

7
Contributions for
Miss Billie Burke

INSIDE THE *VANITY FAIR* LION'S DEN WITH GUN AND TARDY SLIP

Their editor in chief, Frank Crowninshield, would somewhat bemusedly refer to the three of them in later times as "those amazing whelps." Observers of the literary hierarchy of the twenties were about to recognize them as founding members of the famous Algonquin Round Table. Yet to their boss, publisher Condé Nast, they all too quickly became more trouble than he thought they were worth. Suffice it to say that when the eight-month experiment in heightened irreverence was abruptly concluded by a firing and two resultant resignations, about all one could say with absolute certainty was that from the last ten days of May 1919 until the end of January 1920, Robert Benchley had indeed served as managing editor of the highly respected monthly *Vanity Fair,* and that the remainder of the editorial staff during that time consisted of one Dorothy Parker and one-and-then-some Robert Sherwood.

If Benchley had harbored any gnawing doubts about his qualifications for the job of managing editor of *Vanity Fair,* they were rapidly erased by Crowninshield's great show of confidence as he was led through his interview with publisher Nast. It was, after all, Crowninshield who had purchased the first freelance article Benchley had ever sold back in 1914, and Crowninshield's unfailing belief in him was certainly one of the primary reasons that Benchley, amid an avalanche of rejection slips, had continued to pursue writing as a profession.

Frank Crowninshield—"Crownie," as he was known by Benchley, Parker, Sherwood, and a host of other "young whelps" whose careers he helped along—was a suave, Paris-born, European-educated, white-haired man whom Nast had entrusted with the supervision of both the highly successful fashion-oriented *Vogue* and the less successful but prestigious *Vanity Fair.* Crowninshield prided himself on being a keen purveyor and benefactor of young talent, and as proof of that, one had to look no further than the desk next to Benchley's—a desk occupied by the magazine's new drama critic, Dorothy Parker.

She'd been born Dorothy Rothschild in West End, New Jersey, on August 22, 1893, the fourth and youngest child of J. Henry Rothschild, a Jewish clothier, and his Christian wife, the former Eliza Marston, a public school teacher. She arrived in the world some two months prematurely; it was, she would eventually contend, "the last time I was early for anything." Educated first at Manhattan's Blessed Sacrament Academy—which she later claimed she was "expelled from for a lot of reasons, among them my insistence that the Immaculate Conception was spontaneous combustion"—and then at a girls-only finishing school in Morristown, New Jersey, the bright, shy Miss Rothschild found herself orphaned when her father passed away shortly after her graduation from the Jersey school in 1911; her mother had died during Dorothy's infancy. Bereft of both family (she detested her stepmother, refering to her always as "the housekeeper") and home (her father had left her virtually penniless), she took up residence in an Upper West Side boardinghouse, where she supported herself by playing piano at night for a dancing school and spent her days writing light verse which she hoped someday to sell to magazines.

In 1916, one of her works found its way to Crowninshield, who not only purchased it for the pages of *Vogue* but went so far as to offer her steady employment there as well, for a salary of $10 a week. Dorothy quickly accepted, and was soon diligently devoting her skills as a compact, precise wordsmith to the task of writing captions for the magazine, providing *Vogue*'s pictures with such lyrical accompaniment as "Brevity is the soul of lingerie—as the petticoat said to the chemise."

By the next year, however, her life had begun to change drastically, both professionally and personally. Early in 1917 she'd married tall, handsome Eddie Parker, a Wall Street stockbroker born and bred in the upper crust of Hartford, Connecticut, society, but no sooner had they begun to enjoy life as a couple when the United States entered World War I and Eddie enlisted. It was that all-too-briefly-known Eddie Parker to whom Dorothy would write almost every day of the fifteen months that he was to spend abroad in service with the 33rd Ambulance Division; it was quite another Eddie Parker, psychologically torn apart by the war and now burdened with a severe drinking and drug problem, who would return home from France in late 1919, and from whom Dorothy would soon thereafter become forever estranged.

It was also during 1917 that Crowninshield, sensing Dorothy's ennui and lack of challenge at *Vogue*, shifted her over to the *Vanity Fair* staff. Here she began to flourish, contributing verse, commentary, humor, almost anything she pleased, to the magazine's pages. By the time Benchley arrived, she had taken over the theater critic's post from regular reviewer P. G. Wodehouse, who was overseas on an extended leave of absence.

Mrs. Parker was not yet the famous, feared, and fawned-over high priestess of the Algonquin Vicious Circle, effortlessly chopping down overgrown egos with a single well-turned, well-placed phrase. She was not yet—in that patented "girl's best friend is her mutter" notch-above-a-whisper manner—letting loose on unsuspecting lessers such devastating put-downs as "If all those girls were laid end to end, I wouldn't be at all surprised" and "That woman speaks eighteen languages, and can't say 'no' in any of them." She was, rather, at the time Benchley met her, a generally quiet, solitary figure whose amusements were mostly conducted for no one else's benefit but her own, as evidenced by the practical joke she played on one of *Vanity Fair's* staffers in 1918.

"One of the editors had a map over his desk with little flags on it to show where our troops were fighting," she recalled many years later to the *Paris Review*. "Every day he would get the news and move the flags around. I was married, my husband was overseas, and since I didn't have anything better to do, I'd get up half an hour early and go down and change his flags. Later on, he'd come in, look at his map, and get very serious about spies being everywhere, shout a lot, and spend his morning moving his little pins back in position."

Completing the troika at *Vanity Fair* was a young man who'd shown up looking for work just two days after Benchley himself had begun, a young man impossible to ignore—unless you could ignore someone who stood six feet, six and a half inches tall, weighed about 170 pounds when thoroughly soaked, sported size seventeen shoes, and paraded around the streets of New York wrapped in a kilt. Benchley wrote in his diary on May 21: "Just met Bob Sherwood, who presented his six feet five or ten in candidacy for a job."

It hadn't taken long for Robert Emmet Sherwood to make an impression on the world. He checked in at birth in New Rochelle, New York, on April 4, 1896, at fifteen pounds. And it wasn't simply size that set him apart. By age five, the imaginative young Sherwood was solemnly explaining to peers that his great height was attributable to the fact that he'd been born one year old already, and the future Pulitzer-winning playwright was already directing and starring in his own self-penned dramas (much to the inconvenience of his family, whom he usually recruited as cast members).

School had posed no particular problem for Sherwood; at Harvard, his father had been one of the founders and the first president of the *Lampoon* and an active member of Hasty Pudding, and the family name enabled Sherwood to squeeze his elongated frame through Cambridge's hallowed halls even though he rarely studied and had the poor grades to prove it. Coming to Harvard did little to change his work habits; he was soon excelling only in extracurricular activities and all but ignoring his textbooks and classes. Sherwood remained at Harvard only through his junior year—a campaign distinguished academically only by his continuous journey into, out of, and back into the ranks of probation. When he ran off to Montreal to enlist in the Canadian army in the middle of 1917, it was just in time; he was about to be removed from the rolls of the university anyway, war or no war.

Sherwood would no doubt have preferred to join the American armed forces, but both the Army and Navy had rejected him as "too tall and too thin" ("The military authorities seemed to think it would be too much trouble to dig trenches deep enough for me," he later complained), so he hopped a train to Canada and joined the 42nd Battalion of the Royal Highlanders, the famed Canadian Black Watch. Sherwood spent half of 1918 fighting in France before being gassed and wounded in the legs by German artillery fire; the Armistice found him in a hospital bed back in Canada. (He would wind up having to deny, for the rest of his life, Benchley's claim that he'd deliberately lain down on his back and been shot while dangling his legs up in a taunting gesture at the enemy.)

It was not out of the blue that Sherwood, dressed in his regimental uniform complete with kilts, had come inquiring about a position at *Vanity Fair*. Crowninshield knew Sherwood's family, and he was also familiar with Robert's activities as *Lampoon* president, especially in regard to a highly successful parody issue of *Vanity Fair* published under his editorship in the spring of 1917—a parody, Sherwood readily admitted, that had been inspired by a burlesque of *Life* engineered and brilliantly executed by 1912 *Lampoon* president Robert C. Benchley.

Actually, the two Roberts had crossed paths once before, when alumnus Benchley had addressed an assemblage of freshmen, including Sherwood, back in 1914. It was a night that Sherwood hadn't forgotten. "Even before he'd said a word," he later noted, "his reputation was so great that everyone was laughing at the very mention of his name." For this lanky young man drawn to humor and writing, "Benchley became a shining objective towards which to strive." And now here they were, about to work side by side, Benchley as managing editor, and Sherwood as editorial assistant (his official title was "drama editor"), with Parker between them. "No young writer," Sherwood wrote years later, "ever had such luck in starting his professional career in such fast company."

Vanity Fair had commenced publication in 1914. Its inaugural issue included an editorial by Crowninshield which pledged that the magazine would be "a month by month record of current achievements in all the arts and a mirror of the progress and promise of American life. . . . *Vanity Fair* means to be as cheerful as anybody. It will look at the electric and diversified life of our day from the frankly cheerful angle of the optimist or, which is much the same, the mock-cheerful angle of the satirist." The *Vanity Fair* that Benchley was hired to help edit in 1919 had strayed very little from Crowninshield's original vision of a responsible arts monthly. Its regular departments fell under the headings "In and About the Theatre," "In the World of Art," "Modern Thoughts on Timely Topics," and "The World Outdoors," and humorous articles were designated "All Seriousness Aside." In addition, a "Miscellaneous" section served as an effective catch-all for everything from pictorial layouts of performing arts celebrities and a "We Nominate for the Hall of Fame" page saluting leaders in "all forms of human endeavor" to a suitably stuffy men's fashion column and cartoon essays casually knocking various social mores.

Benchley quickly learned to handle, adapt, and, if necessary, violate *Vanity Fair*'s format. If Crowninshield really wanted the world covered from the viewpoint of the "cheerful" optimist and the "mock-cheerful" satirist, he'd certainly found the right man for the job in Robert Benchley. "Crowninshield would allow any entertaining writer to say practically anything in *Vanity Fair*, as long as he said it in evening clothes," Benchley realized before very long. Actually, by the time the first issue Benchley worked on (August 1919) was back from the printers, it was apparent that he'd already discerned what kinds of maneuvers he could get away with safely.

The "In *Vanity Fair*" frontpiece that month was entitled "Our Own Contributors' Column" and purported to be "Notes, likely to be of interest, in regard to a few of *Vanity Fair*'s writers and artists." After casually dismissing rival magazines like the *Atlantic* and the *Century* for running "certain pertinent facts about their celebrated contributors such as 'Henry Cabot Lodge is the senior Senator from Massachusetts,'" Benchley proceeded to "detail" some of *Vanity Fair*'s August contributors:

P. G. Wodehouse ("Prohibition and the Drama") only a few months ago reflected—in the buoyancy of his demeanor—the light, whimsical and somewhat fantastic quality discernable in all of his published writings. Then golf, the Great Reaper, came upon him in the night and withered his *bonhomie*, blanched his spirit, blasted his soul. From a literary point of view, the interesting thing now to be said about Mr. Wodehouse is that he uses the overlocking grip, the thumb of the right hand slightly down the shaft, the feet well apart, the belt straining, the head ready to be tossed in the air—like a Nubian lion—at the first impact with the ball.

Dorothy Parker ("The First Shows of Summer") writes from her delightful summer home on West End Ave. "I just know that all your readers will want to hear how we are spending the hot weather. We are roughing it up here, far away from everybody, living the real primitive life. It is so cool and invigorating—we sleep, under blankets, almost every other night, and whenever there is a breeze we practically always get it. The days are spent in pleasant health-giving hours at the office, while the fragrant evenings are passed away close to the great, throbbing heart of Nature, in the open-air movies under the glowing stars. I sincerely wish all your readers could have such a wild, free life as ours."

Robert C. Benchley ("One Hundred Years from Now") is entirely dependent on his hands for his conversational prowess. In telling a funny story, Mr. Benchley introduces a distinctly original line of illustrative gestures, as follows: "It seems there was an Irishman walking down the street (left hand describes an arc) when he met an Englishman (right hand swings high over head). 'Hello,' says Pat (gesture as in treading water). 'Hello,' says the Englishman (shifts into a breaststroke)." By this time—what with considerable footwork incidental to the hand gestures—the raconteur is physically exhausted and has to be carried out before the real point of the story has been reached.

And this was only the beginning. The Benchley piece referred to, "One Hundred Years from Now," was a righteously worded call for proper and fitting recognition of the upcoming hundredth anniversary of "literary giant" John Bartlett ("It is not an exaggeration to say that his words are in everyone's mouth wherever there is any pretense to culture in the English language. . . . The hold which his works have taken on the minds of men cannot be over-estimated"), while another Benchley article, under the pseudonym Brighton Perry, examined the way in which various magazines of opinion would tackle the same intensely controversial topic—the weather. (" 'To call this heat wave a betrayal of all liberal weather principles is simply not enough.'—*The Nation.*")

The spirit apparently was contagious, too. Parker's theater column that month found her describing Ziegfeld Follies star Eddie Cantor as having "a way, peculiarly his, and Al Jolson's own, of putting over a song," and she dealt with yet another of that year's overabundance of "naughty" revues by writing that "its name alone will keep 'Scandals of 1919' with us. It has enormous appeal to the transients. You know yourself that if you came in from Detroit to see a little of the night life of the city, anything called 'Scandals of 1919' would be the first show you'd want to see."

While the editorial tone of the magazine was taking a sharp turn toward the giddy and carefree, camaraderie between the three young editors grew at a swift pace. Underwhelmed by the ostentatious, highly formal fashion in which the Nast organization ran its office and its business, Dorothy and the two Roberts began addressing themselves as "Mr. Benchley," "Mrs. Parker," and "Mr. Sherwood," a practice which would continue for the remainder of their lives whenever one talked about the others—although it should be pointed out that Benchley and Sherwood often called each other "Rob," even though no one else ever did, that Benchley sometimes referred to Sherwood as Sherry, and that Mrs. Parker many times was overheard addressing Benchley as "Fred."

The trio were quick to grasp the value of strength through unity outside the workplace as well as in when the proximity of the *Vanity Fair* offices on 44th Street to the circus-styled Hippodrome began to cause daily nightmares for Sherwood. A visiting troupe of especially ill-tempered midgets were performing at the showplace, and once they discovered Sherwood's presence along 44th Street, they kept a keen eye on the Nast offices around lunchtime, ready to attack the defenseless Sherwood. As soon as they caught sight of him, they would swarm at his knees, pecking at his ankles and humiliating him with crass tall jokes. One day, able to suffer in silence no more, Sherwood begged his colleagues for help. "The midgets were always sneaking up behind him," Parker later reminisced, "and asking him how the weather was up there. 'Walk down the street with me,' he'd asked, and so Mr. Benchley and I would leave our jobs and guide him down the street." And so it was that soon the three of them could be seen traversing the avenue at high noon as one strange unit—the four-foot-eleven Parker, the six-foot Benchley, and their friend the skyscraper—combining for a sight best described by Nathaniel Benchley as "a walking pipe organ."

As the frequency of shared lunch hours increased, so did the reputation of the spot the three frequented the most. The dining room at the Algonquin Hotel had just begun to draw a daily clientele of both established and up-and-coming literati, and Benchley, Parker, and Sherwood started to fall in regularly with a group that included former *Stars and Stripes* editor Harold Ross, *Tribune* columnist Franklin P. Adams, and *New York Times* drama critic Alexander Woollcott.

Benchley and Parker were drawing particularly close with each passing day, their time together at *Vanity Fair* forming the basis of a deep, lifelong friendship. The two were a splendidly complementary team, both as writers and personalities; Parker's writing displayed a darker, subtler, more acerbic spirit than Benchley's lighthearted flights of fancy, and his gregarious, gracious nature enabled the reticent, introverted Parker to break out of her protective shell.

Perhaps it was only fitting that their common ground was often sited where others neither cared nor dared to tread. Shortly after Benchley started working at *Vanity Fair,* the office's incoming mail began to include two publications he had sent away for. The magazines, both of the trade variety, were named *Sunnyside* and *The Casket,* and it's quite likely that Benchley was the only subscriber in the whole country who wasn't professionally concerned with the care and handling of dead bodies and bereaved families. Mrs. Parker quickly adopted Benchley's interest in the undertaker magazines. Together, the two would while away idle hours howling over the articles and photos, usually saving the best for last—a waltz through the *Sunnyside* joke column, "From Grave to Gay."

If either of the two arrived late for work on a morning when one of the magazines arrived, he or she would be sure to find some particularly gruesome illustration torn out of the issue and placed on the desk. They might also choose one for themselves. "I cut a picture out of one of them," Parker recalled, "in color, of how and where to inject embalming fluid, and hung it over my desk until Mr. Crowninshield asked if I could possibly take it down." She and Benchley also regularly exchanged ideas for epitaphs via memo sheets from one desk to another, with top honors going to "This is on me," "Excuse my dust," and "If you can read this, you're standing too close." (Time, as well as Parker's two suicide attempts later in life, would eventually prove her interest in the morbid a bit more than just passing.)

In July, after barely more than a month on the job, Benchley was left in complete charge of *Vanity Fair* as both Nast and Crowninshield sailed for an extended stay in Europe, and it didn't take long for the mice to start playing. Without any haughty supervision, Benchley and his colleagues were free to flex both their muscles and their imagination. The summer had brought to Broadway a bitter struggle between theater owners, producers, and managers and the Actors' Equity Association, leading to a strike which darkened most of the houses along the Great White Way. Parker wasted little time letting her opinions be known. Her column for the issue prepared that month, "The

New Plays—If Any," featured a graphic of a slickly dressed hoofer treading the boards, with the caption reading, "George M. Cohan, Strikebreaker." Benchley inserted a pictorial entitled "What They Did During the Strike" in which he was able to poke a few neat jabs at producer (and former Benchley employer) William M. Brady, who, it was noted, had taken up one of the roles in his own theater's production rather than allow the actors' union to close the show.

The October edition of the magazine, completed in August while Nast and Crowninshield were still away, was of special significance to Sherwood. Acting editor Benchley had chosen to publish an essay Sherwood had written, thus giving him his first official *Vanity Fair* byline, and, secondly, there was the matter of some uncredited writing he did for that particular issue—writing that very nearly got him fired.

One of Sherwood's many tasks at the magazine was to fill out any articles that ran short when laid out. That month, the regular author of the impenetrably foggy "For the Well Dressed Man" column had gone off on vacation, and when the art department informed editorial that another page of copy was needed, Sherwood gleefully sat down at the typewriter and pounded out the necessary verbiage. *"On dit,"* he mused, "that peg-topped pants and cloth-top shoes are coming back; also that the best dressed man's next year's waistcoats will glitter darkly with cut jade." The piece concluded with the theory that the burgeoning new Canadian sport of ice hockey could have serious effects on the sartorial look of U.S. citizenry in the near future. It was hardly surprising that the fashion writer returned from holiday enraged at what had been done to his column; nor were some of the clothing advertisers amused by what they read. When Nast and Crowninshield returned and got wind of what had happened, Sherwood knew he could kiss his expected raise and any chance of better job security goodbye. Just as in college, he was back on probation—another three-month trial period, and at the same $25-a-week salary.

It was at the end of this especially rollicking summer that Gertrude Benchley gave birth to her second son, Robert Jr., who was so named mainly because of his parents' utter confusion upon his arrival. They had only been prepared for a baby they were going to call Barbara, and were at a complete loss when the new addition to the Benchley household turned out to be male.

Benchley had taken the expectant mother to a Bronxville hospital the morning of August 26. After being told by the doctor that it was probably going to be a while, and being reassured by Gertrude that she would be fine if he wanted to go to the office and return later in the day, he took his commuter train into Manhattan. His primary reason for going into the city was to see Lincoln McVeagh, an editor at the publishing firm of Henry Holt, who had requested a meeting to discuss the possibility of Holt's bringing out, in book form, a collection of Benchley's articles. Benchley called the hospital repeatedly throughout the day. After his meeting with McVeagh, he called the hospital once more to find out if anything had happened yet (it hadn't), bought some flowers, and grabbed the next train back to Bronxville. Gertrude was asleep when he arrived at the hospital, so Benchley quietly sat down and began to read. Before long, a nurse came in, cradling a newborn baby in her arms. Benchley peered at the little boy, gave it the proverbial tweak under the chin, and asked the nurse whose baby boy it was.

"Why, it's yours!" exclaimed the nurse.

"*What?*" shrieked Benchley. "Well, I've never had a baby so easily in all my life!"

Nast and Crowninshield returned from Europe at the end of August, and even though the staff had an inkling that there might be a few rough moments ahead (Sherwood knew he was in for it, and, indeed, complaints were coming into the office almost daily on a variety of issues), they welcomed their editor back with a suitably ridiculous celebration—Crowninshield walked into his office and discovered the entire place strewn with outlandish banners, streamers, signs, crepe paper, and assorted parade paraphernalia. Nast, however, was given no such reception. Benchley, Parker, and Sherwood simply didn't like him very much, and the feelings apparently were mutual. The publisher, hearing about the staff's "exploits" while he and Crowninshield were out of the country, was quickly tiring of what he considered the immature and disrespectful activities of these subordinates, and it wasn't long before he made up his mind to whip the *Vanity Fair* team back into shape.

The first thing he did was to hire Francis Lewis Wurzburg for the position of office efficiency manager. Wurzburg, an austere disciplinarian, was soon dispensing periodic barrages of terse memos which attempted to set down authoritarian rules and regulations regarding office policies and employee behavior. One day in October, the editors arrived at work only to find this "greeting" placed at each individual desk:

POLICY MEMORANDUM
*Forbidding Discussion Among
Employees of Salary Received*

It has been the policy of the organization to base salaries on the value of the service rendered. We have, therefore, a long established rule that the salary question is a confidential matter between the employer and the individual.

It is obviously important that employees carefully live up to this rule in order to avoid invidious comparison and dissatisfaction. Recently several cases have come to the notice of the management where employees have discussed the salary question among themselves.

This memorandum should serve as a warning that anyone who breaks this rule in the future will be instantly discharged.

It didn't take very long for the staff to register its contempt for such repressive tactics. In no time, they'd answered the memo with one of their own, written by Benchley:

POLICY MEMORANDUM
*Concerning the Forbidding of
Discussion Among Employees*

We emphatically resent both the policy and wording of your memorandum of October 14. We resent being told what we may or may not discuss, and we protest against the spirit of petty regulation which has made possible the sending out of such an edict.

We especially call your attention to the wording of the last paragraph, regarding the "instant" discharge of employees violating this new regulation, and would eagerly inquire if *our* obligations under the contracts we have been asked to sign are as elastic as those of the management are here construed as being.

Later that day, the rest of the office workers were witnesses to a protest march conducted in complete silence by Benchley, Parker, and Sherwood. Although they didn't say one word, their message was loud and clear: Around their necks, each of them wore a sign, upon which was printed, in large block letters, the exact amount of their weekly earnings.

No more memos about discussions of salaries were forthcoming.

Of course, a man as severe as Wurzburg was not one to let one small setback spoil the entire game plan. His next resourceful step was the introduction of the "tardy slip." Since the Nast organization stressed that all workers be in the office no later than 8:50 A.M. and at their desks, ready to work, precisely at 9:00, Wurzburg decided he could begin to bring the *Vanity Fair* staff in line by attacking them for their chronic lateness. The office manager had small, official pieces of paper printed up and announced that these "tardy slips" had to be filled out by all offending employees, explaining their lack of punctuality.

A few days after the tardy slips had been introduced, Benchley arrived some ten minutes late and found one of the slips waiting for him on his desk. Unfortunately for Wurzburg, Benchley was ready for the occasion. After sharpening his pencil to a fine point, he proceeded to fill, in the smallest handwriting he could muster, every millimeter of available empty space on both sides of the paper. He had been on his way down 44th Street, he wrote, when he noticed a large gathering of people outside the Hippodrome. After ascertaining that the famous Hippodrome elephants had just escaped, and that good and decent citizens everywhere were being called upon to pitch in and help prevent the random trampling of innocent women and children, he'd joined the posse in charge of bringing the elephants back home.

The search, Benchley went on, took him up Fifth Avenue, around the Plaza, through Central Park, and over to West End Avenue, where the elephants were finally spotted, apparently headed for the Hudson River. Taking charge, Benchley managed to shift the flow of the herd in a southward direction, moving the pack of pachyderms down Twelfth Avenue, and all was fine until he realized that the docks were nearby, and that the elephants were curiously eyeing a Fall River Line boat about to sail. Calling into use all of his intimate knowledge of elephants and their habits, Benchley continued, he narrowly managed to avert a terrible marine disaster, kept the herd headed south, moved them crosstown on 44th (which, luckily for all concerned, carried only eastbound traffic), and returned them to their stalls at the Hippodrome. By the time the last of the animals was safely tucked away, unfortunately, the hour of nine had come and gone, leading to his failure to arrive at his workspace at the required starting time.

So ended the tardy slip experiment.

As the winter of 1919 set in, the atmosphere at the *Vanity Fair* offices grew denser with ill will, even as the work done by the editors continued to improve and widen in scope and technique. Benchley printed another of Sherwood's essays, this one on the rather strange way that the film industry was affecting the youth of America. (This was the first piece of film criticism that Sherwood published; he would later, while working at *Life*, become the nation's first regular movie critic.) In the article, Sherwood voiced the opinion that films were damaging and warping many young minds. "Soon," he wrote, "every film-trained child will be able to disclose the following facts of geographical interest: A forest is something that catches fire in reel four . . . the Grand Canyon is that ditch which Douglas Fairbanks jumps across . . . a desert island is a spot of land which yachts run into and which are usually inhabited by Norma Talmadge." Sherwood also attacked the way in which moviemakers were depicting war—a subject not foreign to one who had seen its destruction firsthand: "Motion picture promoters hope that the next war will be staged in a more suitable location (as far as lighting is concerned); that hope is shared, to a certain extent, by the inhabitants of Northern France."

It was in that same February 1920 issue that one of Benchley's most ingenious early works appeared, a piece credited to *"Vanity Fair's* Book Reviewer."* Its title was "The Most Popular Book of the Month," and in it Benchley succeeded in performing an almost impossible task. While many claim that great actors can captivate audiences just reading it, and that one wouldn't mind hearing a top tenor sing it, how many humorists ever had either the confidence or the nerve to review the telephone book? Benchley wrote:

> The author has made no attempt to discriminate. He is a realist. Not as Samuel Butler was a realist. Not as Oliver Optic was a realist. Not as Arnold Bennett is a realist. (There are lots of other names that could be used to show that the present reviewer is well read. Maugham would be a good one, too.) Not as Maugham is a realist. . . .
>
> Perhaps we should stand by the character who opens this book and introduces us into the Kingdom of Make-Believe—Mr. V. Aargaard, the old "Impt. & Expt." How one seems to see him, impting and expting all the hot summer days through, year in and year out, always heading the list, but always modest and unassuming, always with a kindly word and a smile for passers by on Broadway. . . .
>
> It is the opinion of the reviewer that the weakness of plot is due to the great number of characters which clutter up the pages. The Russian school is responsible for this. . . .

By December, the situation at the *Vanity Fair* offices had deteriorated to the point that even the almost always chipper Benchley had begun to feel the strain. To him, Parker, and Sherwood, the place was now feeling like a "whited sepulcher"—the outside reflecting a glossy, opulent image, the inside filled with a stagnant air in which most things fresh or impulsive were viewed suspiciously as threats to the status quo. The three editors felt they were scornfully looked down upon as mere "employees," quite noticeably underpaid, and, ultimately, treated like misbehaving children. As December wore on, it was becoming painfully clear that Crowninshield's familial status was changing from fatherly ally to Dutch uncle, at least as far as Sherwood and Parker were concerned.

There were a number of reasons for Crowninshield's turnabout. He was, above all else, a company man, possessing no desire whatsoever to rock the boat that Nast commanded; if Nast had grown disenchanted with the *Vanity Fair* editors, then Crowninshield was forced to side with his employer. Secondly, there was Crowninshield's sense that although Benchley, Parker, and Sherwood all liked him, they were losing respect for him, especially since he'd allowed the often humiliating events of the preceding few months to transpire without a word of either protest or support.

Perhaps most important, it appeared as though Crowninshield had simply stopped caring about what was happening to his staff, and it was here that his personal philosophy about young writers and editors came into play. It was Crowninshield's firm belief that young talent was best utilized when exactly that—young. "I find it safest to deal with such felines when they are still cubs, to snare them, in traps, before their teeth have sharpened and their claws grown long." Benchley, Parker, and Sherwood had ceased to be either tamable or impressionable, and Crowninshield no longer was feeling safe in the same den with them.

The beginning of the end came shortly after the start of the new year. Sherwood, now well past the end of his second three-month trial period, and still in limbo as far as both salary and job status were concerned, asked for a meeting with Crowninshield to clarify where he stood. Mrs. Parker had herself just recently been denied a raise, so chances were slim of getting one; then again, Sherwood was making so little that it didn't seem automatically out of the question.

Sherwood came away from his January 8 conference with Crowninshield almost in a state of shock. He was politely informed—in what Benchley noted in his diary as "exquisite pussyfooting" by Crowninshield—not only that a raise would not be forthcoming but also that he should look around for something else to do, since his position at the magazine was going to be taken over soon by a Mrs. Strauss—at the time employed as Condé Nast's daughter's music teacher.

A mere three days later, on Sunday, January 11, the other shoe dropped, and with a particularly ignominious thud. Crowninshield had earlier in the week asked Mrs. Parker to meet him at the Plaza Hotel for a drink and "a discussion of her work," and had told her that P. G. Wodehouse's return as *Vanity Fair*'s theater critic was imminent, and so it was his unfortunate task to inform her that he couldn't keep her on salary anymore. He did express the hope, however, that Mrs. Parker would continue contributing to the magazine by "writing little things from home" and sending them in. Parker's angry response was to tell Crowninshield that she'd have her desk vacated in two weeks—and as for future articles by her, she was sure he'd soon find them everywhere but *Vanity Fair*.

At home in Westchester, Benchley waited by the telephone for the inevitable call from Parker, whom he'd tipped off on Friday as to what was going to happen. Crowninshield had, in fact, discussed the matter with Benchley during the week—if "discussed" could be deemed the appropriate word. Nast, Benchley was told, had had enough of all the complaints he was getting from Broadway producers and theater owners concerning Parker's reviews of their shows, and there appeared to be a more than passing threat that advertising revenues would be lost if she continued as the magazine's play reviewer. Benchley had violently objected, warning his editor in chief that he wouldn't be able to just sit idly by if such action were to take place. Crowninshield had just shaken his head sadly and repeated that Nast's orders were Nast's orders, and that all he could do was follow them.

The most severe damage, it turned out, had been done in Parker's January column, where she'd "fixed," or panned, a David Belasco play called *The Son-Daughter* and a show entitled *Caesar's Wife* which starred Florence Ziegfeld's wife, Billie Burke. *The Son-Daughter* had shown up on Broadway not long after another play with an Oriental theme, *East Is West*, had struck it big, and Parker couldn't resist noting the similarities:

"The producers have played it safe and followed 'East Is West' almost exactly, save for the introduction of a revolution into this plot.... If Samuel Shipman is in the house, I should be glad to have him observe me get down and crawl abjectly along the ground for anything I may have said about his brainchild, 'East Is West.' Last season, in the exuberance of youth, I used to think that no play along the same lines could possibly be worse; that was before the dying season brought us 'The Son-Daughter.' " As for *Caesar's Wife*, an ill-fated, regrettable Somerset Maugham endeavor about an Egyptian bride who almost, but ultimately does not, leave her elderly husband for his dashing young secretary, Parker wrote that leading lady Billie Burke "looks charmingly youthful. She is at her best in her more serious moments; in her desire to convey the girlishness of the character, she plays her lighter scenes rather as if she was giving an impersonation of Eva Tanguay"—a reference to an actress best known for her overly emotional, grossly uninhibited performing manner.

Parker called Benchley with the expected bad news around seven in the evening, and he immediately boarded the next train to the city, where the two commiserated over the recent developments. Benchley had, over the weekend, made up his mind that if Parker was actually fired, he would tender his own resignation forthwith, and he told Parker of this decision. The two then called Sherwood, who, although in effect on his way out as well, nonetheless said that as a matter of principle, he, too, would officially quit.

On Monday morning, Benchley told Crowninshield of his intention to resign. The editor listened quietly, then asked Benchley to think it over for a few days; perhaps he might reconsider. On Monday evening, Benchley, Parker, and Sherwood dined at the Algonquin with several friends and talked heatedly over what had happened at their magazine over the past few weeks. Among those present was *Times* theater critic Alexander Woollcott, and the next day, that newspaper's drama page featured this uncredited, Woollcott-authored item:

VANITY FAIR EDITORS OUT
Robert Benchley Follows Mrs. Parker
—Criticisms Under Fire

Frank Crowninshield, editor of Vanity Fair, is looking about him for a new staff as a result of a walkout which deprived him yesterday of two-thirds of his assistant editorial personnel. Only last week the monthly and one of its staff of three, Robert Sherwood, came to a parting of the ways. Yesterday, Mrs. Parker, who had been with Vanity Fair for four years and who had been concentrating in recent seasons on the theatres, abruptly tendered her resignation. This was no sooner accepted than Robert Benchley, chief wag and managing editor of the publication, served notice that he, too, was leaving. . . .

All these agitating circumstances began, said one of the departing editors last night, when, over a pleasantly decorated tea table at the Plaza, Mr. Crowninshield broke the news to Mrs. Parker that her days as dramatic critic of Vanity Fair were over. She was assured that her work in other ways would still be valued highly by the magazine. Mrs. Parker's reception of this news was complicated by the fact that she was well aware of a recent simultaneous fire of complaint on the part of offended subjects of her criticism.

Both she and Mr. Benchley resigned because they were under the impression that it was these coinciding protests which had led to her removal as dramatic critic.

By the afternoon, Benchley's "official" resignation, written on three small office memo sheets, was on Crowninshield's desk. In it, Benchley explained that Woollcott's article had forced the issue and he could not even consider remaining a member of the magazine's staff.

> I do not want you to think that the story in this morning's "Times" was inspired by either Mrs. Parker or myself. It came as a result of the conversation which took place at dinner last night at a table at which were present eight people, including Alexander Woollcott (in an entirely unprofessional capacity, as we have often eaten there together). . . . The subject of the conversation was, quite naturally, the recent events in the office, but, as Woollcott is in no way connected with the news end of his paper, we did not give the possibility of its being converted into a news story a moment's consideration. . . . I was extremely sorry to see it, and, as a matter of fact, I have told reporters from the "World" and "Tribune" who came up for stories on what they heard was a "walk-out" that there was absolutely nothing in it. . . . They got their tip, I presume, from the fact that I called Frank Adams to see if he had any suggestions for Mrs. Parker or myself, and he called up [publisher Herbert Bayard] Swope of the "World" to see if he had anything. . . .
>
> I cannot tell you how sorry I am that all this fuss should have arisen, but I really do not see how you could have expected to avoid it with the circumstances of the case as they were. . . . Wholly apart from the merits of the incredibly stupid and insincere action in Mrs. Parker's case, my own work is not, in itself, attractive enough to hold me in this office with both Mrs. Parker and Mr. Sherwood gone from it. I am therefore giving whatever notice I am bound, under my one-lunged contract, to give. . . .

It's difficult to estimate just how much real work—if any—was done by Benchley, Parker, and Sherwood during their last two weeks together on the magazine. It is known that the three of them, in one last grand gesture of irreverence, took to donning red chevrons—the kind worn by dishonorably discharged soldiers—and there was talk around the Algonquin of setting up picket lines outside the Nast offices. On the last day that the three editors worked together (Benchley had agreed to stick around until the end of January, to help close the next issue), Benchley escorted Parker and Sherwood, who were about to head off to Mamaroneck to see about jobs writing captions for filmmaker D. W. Griffith, down to the lobby. Under his arm was a sign that he'd made up earlier in the day and had kept hidden in his desk. When they got downstairs, Benchley hung it up for all to see. It read: "Contributions for Miss Billie Burke."

Many years later, in relating the story of her firing from *Vanity Fair*, Dorothy Parker spoke of her coworkers' loyalty. "It was all right for Mr. Sherwood [to resign]," she said, "but Mr. Benchley had a family—two children. It was the greatest act of friendship I'd known." For the second time in his life—and a scarce two years after he'd quit the *Tribune*—Benchley had left a desirable position because of matters of conscience. Though few of his chuckling readers had a clue to this side of his nature, he had once again demonstrated that he would not have his values compromised, even if it meant his job.

Nor was he the kind of man to forget easily. Several years later, while working as *Life*'s theater critic, Benchley was reviewing a play which starred none other than Miss Billie Burke. The review concluded this way:

> A few years ago, a young dramatic critic lost her job for saying, among other disrespectful things, that Billie Burke had a tendency to fling herself about like Eva Tanguay. Even in the face of this proof of divine vengeance, we apprehensively endorse the unfortunate reviewer's judgment and assert that even after having her attention called to it three years ago, Miss Burke *still* flings herself coyly about like Eva Tanguay.
>
> Applications for the job of dramatic reviewer on *Life* should be sent to the Managing Editor.

8

Appearing Knightly

"THESE ARE SOME OF THE PEASANT CLASS, I PRESUME?"

"*It would* have been nice to have had it last as it was, but it probably is better for all of us to do things by ourselves," Benchley told Parker and Sherwood as their whirlwind tenure at *Vanity Fair* was drawing to a close. And yet, as he walked out of the Nast offices and onto Madison Avenue after his last day's work on the magazine on the afternoon of January 31, 1920, it's doubtful that Benchley could have had any real idea of just what "things" were in store for him before even just the first year of the decade destined to be known as the Roaring Twenties had run its course. One thing was certain, however, and that was that the encouragement given to him by fellow writers and editors that he could indeed make a go of it as a freelance writer was not unwarranted.

"Aleck Woollcott took me aside and told me that Harold Ross, editor of *The Home Sector*, wants me to do six stories, at $200 a story, on homely subjects such as the dentist, barber, etc.," Benchley noted in his diary a week before his departure from *Vanity Fair*. Ross, Woollcott's crony from their *Stars and Stripes* days during World War I and future founder of *The New Yorker*, wasn't the only editor seeking Benchley's services, either. Within a week of the termination of Benchley's contract with the Nast organization, he was signing a brand-new one, for freelance work, with no less an employer than Herbert Bayard Swope, publisher of the *New York World*. "You are to supply three articles a week for use in *The World*," stated the contract, dated February 4, 1920, and signed by Ralph Pulitzer, the paper's editor. "*The World* agrees to pay you one hundred dollars weekly for these articles, [which] are to treat of books or related subjects, and are to be signed with your name. . . ."

At the dawn of the 1920s, New York's newspaper field was a crowded and thriving one. With radio still in its infancy, newspapers were the primary and often sole source for most people to acquire information about global, national, and local events, and no less than a dozen publications, tailored to fit virtually every political stripe, economic level, and cultural station, competed for circulation. Most people regularly bought several papers each day—"serious" (i.e., news-heavy) morning papers like the *Times*, the *Tribune*, or the *Sun* to read on the way to work, lighter, more feature-oriented papers like the *Post* or the *Journal* to read on the way home from work, and up-start tabloids like the *Daily News* for titillating stories of gossip and scandals. The *World* was in the upper tier of the city's six major morning papers—more liberal than the *Times* and more populist than the *Tribune*. One of publisher Swope's innovations was the introduction of columns and essays on various topics on the page opposite the editorials and letters to the editor. "Nothing is more interesting than opinion when opinion is interesting," he often said, and it was here, on the *World*'s "op-ed" page (as it ultimately became known), that Robert C. Benchley made his debut as a book columnist on February 9. At the time, the only other bylined book reviewer was the *Tribune*'s highly respected journalist Heywood Broun, and, unflinchingly, Benchley quickly addressed the subject of his qualifications, as well as any possible comparisons to Broun, in his initial effort as author of the *World*'s "Books and Other Things" column:

It has been called to my attention that I am to write something about books three times a week on this editorial page. Just why I, out of 3,000,000 users of the Free Public Library in 1919 (2,573,691 of whom pencilled vitriolic comments in the margins of the books), should have been elected to do this work is still a great mystery to my family. (I have, by the way, a distinct advantage over Heywood Broun of the *Tribune* as a book reviewer in that I have two children, both boys, in both of whom rudimentary Freudian complexes are distinctly visible on a clear day.)

. . . A book reviewer ought at least be able to dash through a new book . . . in a month at the outside. I mean, the people for whom he is working have a right to expect that. With books piling up as they do, it is only fair that a reviewer should finish one before the sequel is published. . . . [Now] it isn't that I have so much trouble spelling through the words or figuring out what they mean. When my eye is on the page there isn't a man who can touch me for speed. But after I have read a sentence I grow contemplative and look out the window. I say to myself, "How true that is!" Perhaps I cry a little. I can make one sentence of H. G. Wells last me from the Grand Central Station on to the point where we stop to let the express go by.

For those who are in any way interested, I enclose a sample mentograph of my reading processes at work. Let us take the opening sentence in Hugh Walpole's "Fortitude" (printed in 1912 but finished by me only this morning). . . . Its opening sentence, with my concurrent mental reactions, might be summarized as follows:

" ' 'Tisn't life that matters. 'Tis the courage you bring to it. This from old frosted Moses, in the warm corner by the door.' That's right, it isn't life that matters. Why didn't I write that myself? But I never heard anyone say ' 'tis' except in books. Maybe that's the way they talk in Cornwall. That's where the Great Cornish Giant comes from. He was a Barnum feature, as I remember it. Frosted Moses—there's a name for you. Sounds like Frank Adams' frosted sassparilla—or it would if 'Moses' and 'sassparilla' sounded more alike. Frosted Moses sitting in a warm corner by the door. There's a funny one—good night! I forgot to get that weather stripping for our front door—too bad, too bad—and it's going to be a cold night, too. Well, I can say that I asked for it in the hardware shop and that they didn't have it. That's always good. Ho hum, where was I?"

Now anyone can see that a book reviewer will never get anywhere in his work if he reads at that rate. Either I have got to speed up or else the whole established system and convention of book reviewing has got to be upset to make room for what I am going to do. On the whole, I think that the latter would be simpler, because I am quite sure that I can't read any faster.

Anyway, we'll see how it works out.

"Books and Other Things" worked out for just about a year, with mixed results. Scarcely a week after its maiden appearance, Benchley confessed to his audience that a slow reading pace was not the only detrimental habit the *World's* new literary critic was encumbered with. He explained:

Reading plays demands just about four per cent more concentration than I personally have got. You have to watch all the stage directions and exits and entrances pretty closely or you will soon have a stage-full of people in your mind's eye who oughtn't be there at all. I have an impressive little way of skipping the italics in my hurry to get on to the next spoken line, and I am incapable of paying attention to the directions regarding entering from the right or the left. . . .

Consequently, I am afraid that my visualization of the scene is not always accurate. I picture doors where there are no doors and leave out windows entirely. I forget to take people off the stage and leave them hanging around with nothing to do while the rest of the act is being played. If I were to draw a diagram at any given point in a play that I am reading, showing the setting and position of the characters, the author would never recognize his little piece. He might get some novel ideas for another play entirely. . . .

You can now see why I am always surprised when I go to see a play that I have read. It is all so different.

Luckily for the paper's readership, the contracted request for articles pertaining to books or "other related subjects" was taken most liberally by Benchley, leading to reviews of such noteworthy publications as *Bricklaying in Modern Practice* ("It takes a book like this to make a man realize what he misses in his everyday life. For instance, who would think that right here in New York were people who specialized in corbeling?"), *American Anniversaries* ("I must confess that I turned to the date of the anniversary of my own birth with no little expectation. . . . It certainly was a big day for patents"), and *Scouting for Girls* ("This is not the kind of book you think it is. The verb 'to scout' is intransitive in this case"), not to mention the New York Central Railroad's Harlem Division's latest timetable:

> Of the text matter it is difficult to write about without passion. . . . In order to read the new time-table understandingly the following procedure is now necessary: Look at the time-table for a train that leaves about 2:45. Write down "2:45" on a piece of paper. Add 150. Subtract the number of stations that Valhalla is above White Plains. Subtract the first number you thought of, and the result will show the number of Presidents of the United States who have been assassinated while in office. Then go over to the Grand Central Terminal and ask one of the information clerks what you want to know.

The beginning of the "Books and Other Things" column was marked by another debut as well—that of the Robert Benchley–Dorothy Parker "office" on the third floor of the Metropolitan Opera House Studios at 1425 Broadway. There had been talk of their collaborating on a play, the plot of which, according to Benchley's diary, concerned "a man who has an affair with a domestically inclined woman in preference to his gay, outgoing wife"; perhaps the two felt that the outward appearance of responsibility in renting bona fide office space would help spur them on to actually get the work done. Whatever the motivation, the two writers decided to invest $15 apiece per month for the cubbyhole-sized room, which they furnished with nothing more than two tables, two typewriters, three chairs (one for a guest), and a hatrack. "It was so tiny," said Parker years later, "that an inch smaller and it would have constituted adultery."

It didn't, though. While many speculated then—and, indeed, were to speculate for the remainder of their lives—about the nature of their relationship, Benchley and Parker succeeded in keeping their platonic friendship platonic in the truest sense of the word: a spiritual love that transcended physical desire. And it would be the one unspoiled constant in lives that were to become incredibly complex and complicated. Not that they weren't soul mates, as anyone who ever saw them together could clearly see. Alexander Woollcott once took the visiting son of a friend to the opening of a Broadway play, and pointed out Benchley, who was deep in conversation with the woman next to him. "And that, I suppose, would be Mrs. Benchley?" said the young man. "So I have always understood," answered Woollcott, "but it *is* Mrs. Parker."

They were, of course, both married—even if Parker's marriage was already showing signs of unraveling. She didn't know how to handle Eddie Parker's drinking and drug use, which made him moody and prone to sudden fits of rage aimed at whoever was closest (and that was usually her), but she loved him nonetheless. World War I had broken his spirit, and she could not repair it, no matter how hard she tried. Benchley, having grown up with a father whose distant manner and predilection towards drinking had resulted from his exposure to the horrors of the Civil War, and with a mother whose answer to her husband's problems was simply to stonewall them, felt understanding of Eddie Parker's condition and sympathy for Dorothy's. And the more she confided in him, the more that confidence seemed a matter of almost familial trust. He felt like a brother toward her—and would continue to do so as long as he lived.

While very little worthwhile work seems to have emanated from their office, the experiment did lay the foundation for a number of jokes that survived long after the partnership was dissolved. There were rumors that the door to the office had been lettered "Utica Drop Forge and Tool Co.," but no hard evidence exists to support that claim. (After Benchley moved out, Parker retained the space, telling friends she'd changed the name on the door to read "Men" to "see if I could attract some new faces.") Nor did they apply for, or receive, a cable address of Parkbench. But the stories circulated, more often than not getting a start in the dining room of the Algonquin Hotel, where the "Round Table" that Benchley and Parker were founding members of was starting to assemble regularly for food, bon mots, and barbs—and not necessarily in that order.

"There they go," theater agent Herman Mankiewicz said to Hippodrome press agent Murdock Pemberton one day in the spring of 1920 as the remainder of their luncheon crowd—Robert Benchley, Dorothy Parker, Robert Sherwood, George Kaufman, Marc Connelly, and Laurence Stallings—headed toward the door of the Algonquin Hotel's Rose Room and out into the hustle and bustle of midday midtown Manhattan. "The greatest collection of unsalable wit in America."

First they were known as "the Board," and their meals together were dubbed "Board Meetings." Then, in honor of Luigi, the waiter deputized by hotel manager Frank Case to take care of them, and to poke some fun at the craze of psychic readings, they began calling themselves the "Luigi Board." But then a cartoonist for the *Brooklyn Eagle* named Duffy published a caricature of them hard at play, and the caption underneath referred to them as "the Algonquin Round Table." By that time, Case had moved them from their square-shaped table in the Pergola Room up near the front of the lobby back into the Rose Room, where the large round table reserved for them each day fast became the centerpiece not only of the hotel's restaurant, but of the high-spirited, carefree artistic community of the twenties as well. Duffy's name stuck, even though those who wound up on the wrong side of the skewering sentences and jabbing puns emanating from its ranks would usually use another one—"the Vicious Circle."

It was, legend has it, for want of an exquisite piece of angel cake that the adventures of the Round Tablers began. It was late spring 1919, and press agent John Peter Toohey, working for producer George C. Tyler, was seeking to coax some promise of publicity out of *Times* drama critic Woollcott. Mutual friend and fellow publicist Murdock Pemberton had suggested to Toohey that if he wished to get the always difficult Woollcott into as receptive a mood as possible, it would be a good idea to try to satisfy his prodigious sweet tooth (it was Woollcott who, in search of a way to make "harsh" liquor tolerable to his palate, had invented the brandy alexander). To that end Toohey brought Woollcott to the Algonquin, where a new pastry chef named Sarah Victor was known to be baking several heralded desserts.

Woollcott, as was his nature, got his angel cake and ate it, too. When they parted, all Toohey was sure of was one thing—that he'd just treated the man to lunch; he could, at best, only hope that a few lines of type might show up in a future *Times* theater page concerning some upcoming Tyler production. But Toohey's report to Pemberton about the meal, and of Woollcott's apparent approval of the hotel and its dining facilities, got Pemberton thinking. Woollcott's awestruck reports from the front for *Stars and Stripes* during the last year of World War I had glorified not just fighting doughboys but even hero dogs like "Verdun Belle," a mothering mutt who followed the Marines from battle to battle, pups in tow, and since his return from (in his words) "his seat in the theatre of war" he hadn't ceased "bestowing" endless war stories upon endless sets of tired, bored ears. Why not give him a mock "welcome home" luncheon to get the point across? And since the Algonquin, which opened in 1902, already had acquired a sizable reputation as a haven for actors, actresses, and other theater-related people, what better place to throw a party for the drama critic?

Over the next few weeks, Pemberton and Toohey gleefully made ready for the affair. Elaborate invitations were mailed out, including a typed agenda calling for numerous wartime reminiscence speeches—all to be delivered by Woollcott, of course—and, knowing (a) how much Woollcott hated having his name misspelled, and (b) the full extent of Woollcott's contempt for one S. Jay Kaufman, who wrote a snobbish column called "Around the Town" for the *Tribune* and whose pretentiousness greatly exacerbated the *Times* man, Pemberton availed on the Hippodrome wardrobe department to construct a huge felt banner, which, on the day of the big celebration, was hung from the rafters of the Pergola Room. In gold letters, it read

A W O L

cot

S. JAY KAUFMAN POST NO. 1

The cast assembled for that fateful first group luncheon included, besides the co-organizers and their guest of honor, such luminaries as Heywood Broun, Franklin P. Adams, *Harper's Bazaar* editor Arthur Samuels, music critics Deems Taylor and Bill Murray, assistant producer Brock Pemberton (Murdock's brother), and writer Laurence Stallings (who, having lost a leg fighting in the Great War, presumably lent some authenticity to the party's theme). As the hours drifted away in a sea of good-natured ribbing and healthy shop talk, Toohey, perhaps still looking for a way to turn that lost meal of a few weeks before to his advantage, suggested that this gathering of the intelligensia be turned into a regular—maybe even daily—event. Woollcott, always ripe to preside over an already captive audience, deemed it a perfect suggestion, and before long, the table reserved each day for the party of Woollcott, Adams, Toohey, et al. began to grow in both size and stature.

So much so that, in time, the "charter members" of the Algonquin crew eventually numbered better than two dozen, and among its regular members were represented, if not arguably the cream, then certainly at least those at the Jazz Age's literary cutting edge. According to Margaret Case Harriman, daughter of Frank Case and author of *The Vicious Circle*, the "official" Round Tablers were Alexander Woollcott, Franklin P. Adams, Heywood Broun, Brock and Murdock Pemberton, John Peter Toohey, Deems Taylor, Bill Murray, Laurence Stallings, and Arthur Samuels, all from the AWOL cot party; *Home Sector* editor Harold Ross; *Times* drama editor George S. Kaufman; former *Telegraph* theater reporter and budding playwright Marc Connelly; theatrical agents Herman Mankiewiecz and David Wallace; writer John Weaver; and, dating from their *Vanity Fair* days, Sherwood, Parker, and Benchley. Joining Parker on the Round Table women's team were Jane Grant, wife of Harold Ross and, like Woollcott and Kaufman, a *Times* writer; Ruth Hale, press agent and wife of Heywood Broun; Beatrice Kaufman, wife of George Kaufman and reader for publisher Horace Liveright; author Edna Ferber; artist Neysa McMein; actresses Peggy Wood and Margalo Gillmore; and young writing hopeful Peggy Leach.

Herman Mankiewicz may well have found them an "unsalable" lot in 1920, but before long, not only were most of the individual members of the Round Table proving that their various artistic skills were, indeed, quite salable, but they were also proving themselves to be collective celebrities. The Algonquin crowd began to pass their hours together with such amusements as the "I can give you a sentence" game, whence sprung Parker's "You can lead a horticulture, but you can't make her think." (Other classics included Adams's "We wish you a meretricious and a happy new year" and Kaufman's "I know a man who has two daughters, Lizzie and Tillie; Lizzie is all right, but you have no idea how punctilious.") Their table talk began to get repeated in ever-widening circles. Sometimes it was through word of mouth, as those seated at nearby tables would eavesdrop, and then regale their friends at dinner parties with what they'd heard. Sometimes it was through print, as Adams would regularly appropriate some of the better one-liners for his "Conning Tower" column. In no time, the group acquired an almost fearsome reputation as fast-thinking, fast-living urban sophisticates, and to be accepted into their company meant being considered part of a new—and distinctly American—"in" crowd.

To hold one's own with this crowd, one had to be both sharp-witted and, if not actually thick-skinned, then at least highly resilient. Noel Coward, for example, was invited to lunch at the Round Table and was taken aback when he entered the room and saw that Edna Ferber was wearing, like him, a new double-breasted suit.

"Why, Miss Ferber," said Coward, "you look almost like a man."

"Yes," Ferber answered, "and so do you."

Trying to match them in one-liners could clearly be most dangerous. A visitor to the table once moved behind Marc Connelly's seat and began stroking Connelly's bald pate.

"You know," the man said after he'd gotten everyone's undivided attention, "this feels as soft as my wife's behind."

"So it does, sir," Connelly answered devilishly. "So it does."

Sometimes, just showing up could be a big mistake. One time, Margalo Gillmore came to lunch escorting a young actor who had expressed a great desire to meet Woollcott. Coming to the table and seeing a new, untested face, Woollcott first glared at the man, then deliberately seated himself as far away as possible. When, at last, Gillmore brought the fellow over to be introduced, she gingerly said, "Aleck, this young man is a great admirer of everything you've written."

"Oh?" said Woollcott, his eyes never coming off of the menu in front of him. "Can he read?"

Those whose behavior the Round Tablers considered fatuous or self-aggrandizing were usually headed for a swift-comeuppance. Once an Algonquin guest bragged at length about his supposedly distinctive lineage. "Did you know," he proudly announced, "that I can trace my family all the way back to the Crusades?"

This time it was Kaufman who matter-of-factly delivered the *coup de grâce*. "I had an ancestor, Sir Roderick Kaufman, who went on the Crusades, too," the Jewish writer said. "As a spy, of course."

As a rule, Woollcott's generally hostile remarks ("Hello, ugly" was one of his more endearing ways of greeting friends) were accompanied by grandiose physical gestures, with the favorite Woollcottian prop being a poised forkful of food, which would get gobbled swiftly and with self-satisfaction after the latest insult had been delivered. Once, however, even the generally impenetrable Kaufman found Woollcott's words a bit too much to take. The two had been arguing heatedly over some literary point, when Woollcott, tiring of a debate which, it seemed to all present, he was well on his way to losing, suddenly snapped at Kaufman, "Who cares what you have to say anyway, you Christ-killer?"

An uncharacteristic silence befell the Round Table, and then, ever so slowly, Kaufman rose from his seat and addressed his companions in calm, measured tones. "This," he said, "is the last time I will tolerate any slur upon my race. I have had enough from Mr. Woollcott. I am now going to walk away from this table, out of this dining room, and out of this hotel."

With that, Kaufman put down his napkin, pushed back his chair, and began to leave. Then he suddenly stopped and looked at Dorothy Parker—Dorothy *Rothschild* Parker, who was Jewish on her father's side. "And I sincerely hope," he said, "that Mrs. Parker will accompany me—*halfway*." With that, everyone began laughing, and seeing that the now silent Woollcott had been sufficiently upstaged, Kaufman triumphantly reclaimed his seat.

Had most of the Round Tablers not achieved a fair amount of success or fame on their own, it's highly unlikely that their collective antics would have drawn much notice. But as the pace of the twenties quickened, successful and famous they did become—Kaufman, Connelly, Sherwood, and Stallings as playwrights, Ferber as a novelist, Parker as a poet and short-story writer, Wood and Gillmore as leading ladies of the stage, McMein as a magazine cover artist, Hale and Grant as vocal sufragettes and women's rights crusaders, and Broun, Woollcott, Adams, Taylor, and Benchley as "personality" columnists and critics.

With the fame, predictably, came charges of smugness, "logrolling," and favoritism from those who felt a chill in the Round Tablers' air. Writer Gertrude Atherton, herself a longtime Algonquin patron, sarcastically spoke about a group she called "the Sophisticates" in a best-selling 1923 novel titled *Black Oxen:*

> They met at the Sign of the Indian Chief where the cleverest of them—and those who were so excitedly sure of their cleverness that for the moment they convinced others as well as themselves—foregathered daily. There was a great deal of scintillating talk in this group of the significant books and tendencies of the day. . . . They appraised, debated, rejected, finally placed the seal of their august approval upon a favored few.

That much of the criticism leveled against the Round Table came from older writers and theatrical personalities—call this period America's first cultural generation gap—only served to make the Round Tablers even more attractive in the free-spirited, no-holds-barred creative atmosphere of the times. That "seal of approval" did indeed help many an aspiring thespian and scribe. There was Tallulah

Bankhead, who, wearing the same black dress almost every day, scavenged among the leavings on plates at the end of Algonquin lunches until she finally started to get regular work on Broadway stages; and there was Donald Ogden Stewart, who came to New York from Columbus, Ohio, in 1920, penniless and starry-eyed, and, through the contacts he made as an accepted addition to the Round Table, began to make good as a budding humorist.

Yet it was, when everything else was stripped away, shared sensibilities and a shared view of what could be considered good and worthwhile work that gave the charter Round Tablers and their ultimately rather lengthy list of auxiliary members both a collective identity and a true *raison d'être*. Adams succinctly stated in his "Diary of Our Own Samuel Pepys," a lighthearted "about town" record of weekly activities among the see-and-be-seen-with crowd: "About Log-Rolling, there is this to be said: that friendships are first formed through admiration of work, rather than the other way around."

That Robert Benchley would fit squarely into the Round Table pegs was hardly surprising. He not only met whatever unstated personal and intellectual "standards" existed for acceptance by the group as a whole, but he quickly established himself as a perfect companion because he was probably the easiest audience of any of the group. "He has one gift possessed by few humorists," Adams wrote of Benchley. "In fact possessed by few human beings. He is not only a wonderful listener, but a flattering one. It doesn't matter what your yarn happens to be, how old or how shopworn. Benchley will burst into laughter and you will go away from him thinking that you must be a witty dog."

Of the many Benchley friendships either founded or solidified by way of the Round Table, two stood out in conveying not only the truth of Adams's assertion about how these relationships were formed but also the very real delight in frivolity that was a hallmark of Benchley's nature.

When Benchley first met Marc Connelly, what probably struck them both was that they'd each survived decidedly lackluster and unsatisfying experiences as newspaper reporters in New York City. Connelly hailed from McKeesport, Pennsylvania, his first newspaper work coming when the *Pittsburgh Press* gave him a job collecting money owed for classified ads. After stints as a cub reporter for first the Associated Press and then the *Pittsburgh Gazette Times*, Connelly came to New York in 1917, where he first lived in a two-room unheated apartment shared by six other fellow struggling city newcomers (among them artist John Held, Jr.)—a place not-so-affectionately dubbed "Cockroach Glades." He eventually landed a job reporting on theater news for the *Morning Telegraph*, whose roster included a sports editor named Bat Masterson, a motion picture news editor named Louella Parsons, and a Sunday columnist named Broun. Connelly's term of employment there ultimately proved fruitful mostly because of a fellow theater reporter he kept running into on his beat—the *Times'* Kaufman. As the two grew friendly enough to confide in each other, they began contemplating the possibility of trying, as a team, to make real their shared desire of writing for the stage—dreams that were soon to be fulfilled through such successful 1920s collaborations as *Dulcy*, *To the Ladies*, and *Merton of the Movies*.

Introduced through the circle of friends inhabiting the Round Table, Benchley found Connelly to be a kindred spirit—intent on enjoying life and also intent on not taking it, or himself, too seriously. Soon the two were regular companions, and with that companionship came opportunities for spontaneous madcap behavior such as the episode fondly remembered by Connelly in his autobiography, *Voices Offstage*.

It was the spring of 1920, and Robert Sherwood had enlisted the help of Benchley, Connelly, Parker, and Margalo Gillmore (Connelly's girlfriend at the time) in a rather extravagant attempt to impress both actress Mary Brandon, whom he was then courting, and movie director Rex Ingram, to whom Sherwood was hoping to sell a film script. The plan called for everyone to attend a dinner party, hosted by Sherwood, in one of the private rooms at the posh Delmonico's on Fifth Avenue so that Ingram would believe Sherwood was a wealthy man and, as such, likely to command a fairly high price for any possible screenplays. At the same time, the wooing of Miss Brandon could be abetted by a touch of class.

At the designated hour, everyone gathered in formal evening attire, but, according to Connelly, the dinner was doomed from the moment it started. "Alice Terry, Ingram's movie-star wife, wobbly from cocktail parties she'd attended all afternoon, had decided to limit her drinking to pousse-cafés. Within five minutes, Dotty Parker solicitously made the first of several trips with Miss Terry to the ladies' room. Each time they returned, Miss Terry, at Dotty's hair-of-the-dog recommendation, had another pousse-café. In a moment, she and Florence Nightingale Parker would withdraw, Dotty's gentle smile indicating her relish for being of service."

Meanwhile, a nervous Sherwood tried to engage Ingram in conversation about his latest film, but the director brusquely told him that his contract with the studio he'd been working for had expired, and that he and Alice were about to leave the United States for a lengthy stay on the French Riviera. He said he didn't care if he never saw a movie again, and he certainly didn't want to waste the evening discussing motion pictures. What he did want to discuss, though, was his new tweed suit, which he'd gotten for a very reasonable price and whose fabric he insisted everyone personally examine. Recalled Connelly:

Sherwood concealed his chagrin and assured Mary that we were not going to talk all night about men's clothes. [Her] audible comments on her suitor's inadequacy in organizing dinner parties caused Margalo to leave the table to see what was causing the latest, protracted absense of Dotty and her patient. As Ingram's head lowered, indicating he had fallen asleep, Benchley and I discreetly left Sherwood to soothe Mary and stepped through one of the dining room's French windows onto a balcony overlooking Fifth Avenue. It was still daylight. Bob and I looked down on the traffic along Fifth Avenue. Conscious of the gentlemanly appearance of our black ties and dinner jackets, Bob took a patrician puff on his cigarette and remarked, "These are some of the peasant class, I presume?"

That was enough to prime the pump of gaiety. Traffic below us was moving slowly. I stepped to the balcony rail, and raising a commanding hand, shouted, "People, people!" Benchley looked at me with only mild curiosity as pedestrians, motorists, and bus passengers all craned their necks upwards. I cried out, "Here he is—your new prince!"

Without a flicker of hesitation, Benchley stepped forward to the balustrade. He lifted his hands to silence unshouted cheers, then, as smoothly as though he had gone over his speech with an equerry, he assured his listeners—in broken German—that he did not want them as a conquered people to feel like slaves under a yoke but as chastened human beings aware that their future depended on the acceptance of a regime which they might resent but that would do its best to govern them in a kindly fashion. Benchley promised that as soon as they evidenced self-restraint he would order curfews lifted, begin freeing political prisoners, and, in time, restore to qualified Americans the right to vote for local officials.

"And now," he concluded, "my prime minister and I will retire to discuss matters of state. And you have all been so cute, next Saturday night I will permit fireworks and dancing in the streets."

[As] many appreciative listeners below us applauded vigorously . . . we rejoined our host and reported that the streets had been cleared, and that it was now safe to proceed home.

While Connelly had entered into his friendship with Benchley as an Algonquin equal, Donald Ogden Stewart was one of the literary new kids on the block. Though on paper he didn't have much to recommend himself by, he was quickly deemed up to snuff by Benchley and Parker. A Yalie from Columbus, Ohio, Stewart came to New York in 1921 after being fired by a business firm in Dayton. Although unpublished, Stewart hoped to be a professional writer, and, armed with a parody of novelist Theodore Dreiser and a letter of introduction from F. Scott Fitzgerald, whom he'd known briefly in Minneapolis in 1919, Stewart went up to *Vanity Fair*, the magazine in which he most wanted to appear. There he met, and was encouraged by, Edmund Wilson, who, along with fellow Princetonian John Peale Bishop, had taken Benchley's and Sherwood's places as the monthly's main editors. It was Wilson who first introduced Stewart to Benchley when he brought the aspiring humorist over to the Algonquin one day. Having taken an immediate liking to Stewart, Benchley several days later invited him to lunch at the Plaza with the old *Vanity Fair* trio. It was a day Stewart never forgot.

"After our meal, Bob Sherwood returned to work and Benchley, Mrs. Parker and I wandered down Fifth Avenue in the June sunshine," Stewart wrote many years later. "It was an enchanted afternoon. I felt I had found two people who understood me completely. I didn't need to explain my ideas, or even to finish my sentences. Benchley was the soul, the essence of humor, and Mrs. Parker that of wit. And they were warm, friendly, sympathetic. I fell in love with both of them, and remained so the rest of my life."

Of course, even as early as 1920, Benchley didn't need to look to his own fertile imagination to get the idea that simply living, working, and raising a family was enough to try one's belief in any kind of sense-making natural order. The year had begun with the *Vanity Fair* catastrophe, but by the beginning of May, Benchley had not one but two new jobs (in addition to the *World* column, he had just been recruited by *Life* to become its regular theater critic), and a new home as well, in the town of Scarsdale, New York. The Crestwood house the Benchleys were renting had been sold, and the new owners had notified them that they intended to move in by May 1. Robert and Gertrude took a look at a house being built in Scarsdale, and finding out that the mortgage terms made it possible for the $17,500 house to be purchased for just $4,200 down, and with his income now suddenly greatly increased, Benchley signed all the necessary papers—even though he had no idea where all that cash was going to come from.

According to Nathaniel Benchley, the steps leading to his father's acquiring the necessary amount of money went, in rather typical Benchley fashion where finances were concerned, as follows: Ernest Greuning, his old friend, lent him six New York City municipal bonds to put up as collateral, while Mrs. Parker lent him $200 in cash. Taking the $200, Benchley went to the Lincoln Trust Company and opened an account. Now possessing an account, he had the bank lend him $4,000 on the bonds and deposited that into the new account. Then he withdrew the $200 that Parker had given him, returned it to her (total time of possession—thirty minutes), and made arrangements to get an advance for some freelance writing to cover the remaining $200 in down-payment money. These lightning-fast transactions had two far-reaching results: The Benchleys now owned the home that would be theirs throughout their lives, and Benchley was firmly back into the limbo world of debt, a world he would escape from all too rarely for the remainder of his days.

Unfortunately for Robert Benchley and bankers throughout the country—and, given his extensive travels, quite possibly all around the globe—money management was not one of his strong suits. Indeed, many an official of the Scarsdale branch of Bankers Trust would, over the years, find the back of a check made out to a restaurant or night-club personally addressed with the inscription "Dear So-and-So, Having a wonderful time, wish you were here—Robert Benchley." And so regularly were the Benchley finances in a muddled state that on more than one occasion bank officers took pity on him and actually deposited funds into his accounts rather than face what could turn into an eternity of convoluted paperwork. Benchley once became in-censed when he found out that the bank had squared his balance after he'd apparently bounced a sizable check. "How credible an institu-tion can this be which deposits and withdraws funds willy-nilly from one account to another without proper procedure?" he complained. Errors, after all, were only human, and completely excusable. Deco-rum, however, dictated that at least bankers should knowingly go by the rules.

In a piece called "Turning Over a New Ledger Leaf," Benchley ex-amined the difficult task of trying to balance that ever-slippery indi-vidual or home budget:

> New Year's morning approximately ninety-two million people in these United States will make another stab at keeping personal and house-hold accounts for the coming year.
>
> One month from New Year's there will be approximately seventy-three of these accountants still in the race. Of these, sixty will be groggy but still game and willing to lump the difference between the actual balance in their pockets and the theoretical balance in the books. . . . The remaining thirteen, who came out even, will be either professors of accounting in business schools or out and out unreliable. . . .
>
> The high mortality rate among amateur accountants is one of the big problems of modern household efficiency, and is exceeded in magnitude only by the number of schemes devised to simplify house-hold accounting. Every domestic magazine, in the midst of its autobi-ographical accounts of unhappy marriages, must need run a chart showing how far a family with an income of $1,500 a year can go with-out getting caught and still put something aside for a canary. Every in-surance company has had prepared by experts a table of figures explaining how, by lumping everything except Rent and Incidentals

under Luxuries and doing without them, you can save enough from the wreckage of $1,200 a year to get in on their special Forty-Year Adjournment Policy.

The trouble with all these vicarious budgets is that they presuppose, on the part of the user, an ability to add and subtract. . . . As for me, there is no sense in becoming a slave to numerical signs which in themselves are not worth the paper they are printed on. It is the imagination which one puts into accounting that makes it fascinating. If free verse, why not free arithmetic?

It is for the honest ones, who admit that they can't work one of the budget systems for the mentally alert, that the accompanying one has been devised.

Let us take, for instance, a family whose income is $750,000 a year, exclusive of tips. In the family are a father, a mother and a fox terrier. The expenses for such a family come under the head of Liabilities and are distributed among six accounts: Food, Lodging, Extras, Extras, Incidentals and Extras. For this couple I would advise the following system:

Take the contents of the weekly pay envelope, $14,423.08 (if any one is mean enough to go and divide $750,000 into fifty-two parts to see if I have got it right, he will find that it doesn't quite come to eight cents, but you certainly wouldn't have me carry it out to any more places. It took me from three yesterday afternoon until after dinner to do what I did). Take the contents of the envelope and lay them on the kitchen table in little piles, so much for meat, so much for eggs, so much for adhesive plaster, until the kitchen table is covered. Then sweep it all into a bag and balance your books. . . .

There is one little technical point that the amateur accountant will do well to remember. It gives a distinction to the page and shows that you are acquainted with bookkeeping lore. It is this: Label your debit column "credits" and your credits column "debits." You might think that what you receive into the exchequer would be credited and your expenses debited, but this is where you miss the whole theory of practical accounting. That would be too simple to be efficient. You must wax transcendental, and say, "I, as an individuated entity, am nothing. Everything is all; all is everything."

. . . The advantage of keeping family accounts is clear. If you do not keep them you are uneasily aware of the fact that you are spending more than you are earning. If you do keep them, you *know* it.

So, knowing that he was spending more than he was earning, Robert Benchley, along with wife, Gertrude, and sons, Nat and Robert Jr., moved into his new home at 2 Lynwood Road in Scarsdale. The immediate financial situation may have appeared a bit rocky, and Benchley may very well have gone to bed on the night of May 1, 1920, wondering if the ceiling above his head was really there. But all doubts were surely erased by the end of that first month. On May 30, he was awakened at three in the morning by not only strange noises, but the strange feeling of being pelted from above. That ceiling was real, all right. Only real ceilings caved in.

9
The Program's the Thing!

"SHOW ME *ABIE'S IRISH ROSE* OR LEAVE ME ALONE"

$The\ very\ first$ issue of *Life* to feature a Robert Benchley theater review was dated April 29, 1920, and it's interesting to note that
a number of the humor/commentary magazine's articles that week
were devoted to satirizing Ouija boards, séances, and explorations of
the paranormal that were fascinating the leisure classes during this
period. Interesting because when *Life* managing editor Thomas Masson offered the position of drama critic to Benchley, whose experience in this area was limited to the handful of reviews he'd done for
the *Boston Traveler* and his fill-in columns at *Vanity Fair*, he must
have heard some voices from the great beyond assuring him that this
risky experiment would succeed. It did, all right; Benchley's last theater page for the weekly didn't come until some nine years later, and
when he did leave *Life* at the end of March 1929, it was to become
The New Yorker's chief theater critic, and he held *that* post for almost eleven years.

  Life was a publication with roots dating back to the late 1800s, and
it showed it. Filled mainly with genteel light verse, mildly humorous
essays, and droll captioned drawings, the magazine looked woefully
out of step after the emotional wake of the World War—a national loss
of innocence—had ushered in a flashier, more urgent American
lifestyle. Clearly, *Life* was in dire need of a transfusion. As it happened,
it was Robert Sherwood who first helped pull the stodgy old magazine into the twenties. Edward S. Martin, the weekly's kindly sixty-
four-year-old editor, was an old friend of Sherwood's father, and
when the younger Sherwood found himself unemployed after being
let go by *Vanity Fair*, Martin had quickly hired him as assistant editor, and Masson had allowed Sherwood to start a regular movie review column, "The Silent Drama."

  When James S. Metcalfe, *Life*'s theater critic for the previous thirty-
one years, announced his departure in early April, Masson (perhaps
urged on by Sherwood) asked Benchley if he was interested, and
Benchley told him that he certainly was. The only hitch, Masson explained, was that Martin apparently had some years before made
mention of someone else being "in line" for the job if Metcalfe ever
left, but this proved to be not too big a problem. First Masson arranged
for Benchley to come and meet Martin, and so Benchley spent an

hour talking into the hard-of-hearing Martin's speaking tube, discussing his great love of the theater and his eagerness to try to be a fitting critic for the magazine. Then, as insurance, Masson had Benchley also talk to Charles Dana Gibson, *Life*'s publisher. The next day, Masson told Benchley that Martin had agreed to give him an audition and that if whatever he turned in for his first piece was acceptable, the $100-per-thousand-words weekly job was his.

On April 16, Benchley went down to the Fulton Theatre to attend the premiere of an entertainment entitled *The Bonehead*—the play that would form the basis of the review that would determine his fate as prospective *Life* theater critic. He watched as much of the play as he deemed necessary to formulate his opinions, dashed over to the Opera House office, wrote until 12:15 a.m., caught the last train back to Westchester, and presented his finished opus to Martin the next morning. What Martin quietly read, and then published, was the following:

The Bonehead may or may not be at the Fulton when this appears. It was announced a day or two after its opening that the producer was sailing for England shortly to arrange for its production there. This announcement usually means much the same thing as the announcement of a defeated political candidate who states that he is about to demand a recount, or that of a suspected assemblyman who gives it out that he will insist on a thorough investigation of the charges made against him.

Whether or not *The Bonehead* is still running matters very little, however, in the sweep of the world's affairs. Probably nothing could matter less. No one should have been deceived in *The Bonehead*. It was clear from the start that it was going to be about Greenwich Village, free love and free verse; so you knew right away that it was going to be dull. A burlesque cannot be burlesqued.

This much having been decided in the first ten minutes, there remained nothing else to do but look at the program. And, as a review of *The Bonehead* would be of practically no historic or documentary value (and it was the sole offering of that notable week), the program is really all there is to talk about.

And what a most fascinating program it was, too. Did you know, for instance, that London is leaning toward the shorter garments, the blunter lapels, the natural sleeve-head which is neither square nor puffed, the skirt which drapes and ripples but does not flare? No, I thought not. And how do you ever expect to know things like that if, when you go to theatres, you pay all of your attention to the acting? Had *The Bonehead* been a different sort of play, I might never have had it brought home to me that I could get a knitted waistcoat for golf which, because of its being a five-buttoned affair with a waist-seam and two lower flapped pockets, is snug and yet, at the same time, so elastic withal that it will follow my every posture like a shadow.

(At this point I was interrupted by someone on the stage making a joke about Flatbush. I counted four more Flatbush jokes at intervals when I was turning the pages of the program. I have no idea how many more I missed.)

But to return to our review.

A certain racy international flavor is given to the program by the insertion of French phrases in an advertisement. The following appeal, of course, is delicate and yet irresistible:

"Madam, Mademoiselle, le secret de votre beauté et de votre grace, n'est-il pas l'usage de ma poudre?"

Then, in order that no one may go wrong and read something into the French that is not there, a literal translation in idiomatic English is furnished directly beneath, and what is our surprise to learn that all that it means is this:

"Translation: Madam, Mademoiselle, the secret of your beauty and charm, is it not my face powder?"

Surely a fair enough question and deserving of a fair answer. And surely two minutes well spent reading the native language of Voltaire (and Victor Hugo, too, for that matter). One feels refreshed, as on returning from a stroll in the Bois.

The annoyance is therefore doubly poignant at this juncture to hear Mr. Nicamber, who is playing the title role in *The Bonehead*, pronouncing "Epicurean" with the accent on the "cure." He is telling someone in a loud voice that he's an Epi*cure*an. Someone ought to speak to him about that. At any rate, he ought to use a lower voice. How do they expect anyone in the audience to read if the people on the stage are going to run about talking stridently and mispronouncing words?

A discussion of economics follows on the next page. I here learn that, although it is commonly believed that high quality means high prices, such is not the case in buying flowers at our shop. No, indeed. Our flowers (believe it or not) are the finest, most beautiful and longest lasting, AND are most moderately priced. Thus, in so many words, is another popular superstition demolished, although I personally have never been under any particular delusion that high prices had anything to do with high quality. Isn't that a rather old-fashioned idea?

(That sounds like John Daly Murphy's voice on the stage. John Daly Murphy here, and in a part like this! My, my! It only goes to show that you never can tell.)

The theatre management announces reassuringly at the top of the page that it takes only three minutes to empty the house "under normal conditions with every seat occupied." It seems a bit optimistic to speak of every seat being occupied at the Fulton as representing normal conditions. But, of course, that is none of my business. And I can say this much for *The Bonehead*. Two Bolshevists are introduced into the play, and neither of them has long hair or whiskers, and they both wear clean white collars. Furthermore, the bomb which they carry looks like a bomb, and not like a medicine ball with a spluttering fuse. For these original departures from convention due recognition should be given.

But, after all, the program's the thing! I would especially recommend to all audiences a careful perusal of the advertisement for cough drops. Don't miss it!

Life had its new theater critic.

The New York theater world of the twenties teemed with new activity virtually every night of the week. With more than seventy-five legitimate theaters, as well as a host of burlesque houses, vying for business, even the most grizzled veterans of the reviewing corps had their hands full simply keeping up with the openings and closings, let alone keeping their critical acumen up as well. For Benchley, operating a weekly column, the difficulties were different, though no less confounding. The newspaper reviewers could at least take the two-hundred-odd plays which would open every year one at a time, deal with each as it came by, and be on their way. Benchley, in any given week, was faced with a multitude of opening nights, any number of which—perhaps one, perhaps all—could prove deserving of notice, whether favorable or damning; with limited space, he always had to weigh carefully his choice of which plays to write about and how much to say about each of them. Moreover, *Life*'s "Confidential Guide," a precursor of *The New Yorker*'s "Goings On About Town," required that, week in and week out, Benchley not only list but offer capsule commentary on every one of the fifty or so attractions, on the average, currently on display. To his credit, he ran his small department conscientiously and fairly for, by his own count, 468 weeks, with few complaints—other than about the enormous number of dreadful plays he was forced to encounter.

"We took this job with the understanding that it was to be only for a few weeks . . . until they could get a regular man," Benchley would later joke in his farewell *Life* column on March 29, 1929.

> We knew nothing about the theatre at the time and have religiously tried to keep to that standard ever since. . . . [Thinking that we'd] been so tentatively assigned to the Drama, we have never thought it worth while to read any books on the subject or to take seriously the movement as a whole. We know nothing of the history of the theatre and have given practically no thought to its future other than to look in the paper to see what plays were opening Monday night. All of this tells in the long run and we find ourself, at the end of nine years of play reviewing, even more inexpert than we were at the start. We hope that none of you have ever been taking this page seriously.

Of course, one could very well take much of Benchley's theater criticism quite seriously, especially because, although by reputation he was a generally benign and optimistic reviewer ("This may be *it*," he'd always say as the curtain rose for each new premiere), he often spent much of his column space thinking up creative ways to pan the often all too forgettable "entertainments" thrust before his kindly eyes.

Take the case of *Love Birds* and *The Right Girl*, two musical comedies that opened on the same night in 1921 at adjacent theaters, thereby giving Benchley an idea of how to get each out of harm's way, and fast:

> The Apollo and the Times Square Theatres, with their adjoining lobbies, are so close together that when you go out in front of one be-

tween the acts, you are quite likely to saunter back into the other. In fact, your correspondent did.

The first act of "Love Birds" is just about what you would expect the first act of a musical comedy named "Love Birds" to be. It always has been. There is a song in which the hero complains that girls aren't like they used to be when Grandma was a girl, during the second chorus of which a young lady comes on dressed as—what do you think? Grandma! Yes, sir, that's what she comes on dressed as, crinoline, parasol, and all. It is a riot. On this particular night, the parasol refused to open at the crucial point in the song, a feature which lent just the right touch of novelty to the thing.

There is also a charming scene in which a large lady in red becomes intoxicated. . . .

Something better may have come in the second act, but it was during the intermission that the big transfer scene was staged. By a peculiar coincidence (it seems now as if there almost must have been some mysterious force at work in the affair) the audience from "The Right Girl" were standing in excited groups in front of the Times Square Theatre, just as the inmates of the Apollo came out to get a breath of sea air right off the Forty Second St. meadows. One thing led to another and your correspondent aimed a little too far to the left, with the result that when the doorman to the Times Square cried "Curtain!" we dashed impetuously in there.

It was decided that it would be better to stand up back during this act, near an exit, in case the drunken lady took it into her head to come on again. This did away with whatever scene there might have been had we attempted to occupy by force seat M-2.

Aside from the fact that there wasn't so much of Pat Rooney and Marion Bent (the "Love Birds" stars), there was really no way of telling that this was not the second act of the same show we had started out with. It might have been the second act of any musical show. They sang a song about an oriental serenade, and one in which Love was graphically shown as a steam engine, with the chorus-men taking hold of hands and giving a lovely imitation of a piston-rod. You could half shut your eyes and almost kid yourself into believing that it was a real engine right there on the stage. You could entirely shut your eyes and almost kid yourself into believing that all men were created free and equal.

It seemed rather odd that Rooney and Bent didn't come on, and once in a while there was something that sounded just a trifle out of keeping with the plot of "Love Birds" as it had been unfolded in the first act. But, on the whole, the thing hung together as well as most musical shows, and what few suspicious moments there were could easily be laid to first night nervousness.

So it really doesn't make much difference whether you see "Love Birds" and "The Right Girl" on the same night or on separate nights— or at all.

For the long-suffering audiences of endlessly red-herringed murder mystery plays, for which Benchley had little patience, he offered this appraisal in August 1923 of a "thriller" called *Thumbs Down:*

Owing to a little engine trouble just north of Albany, this department reached the opening performance of "Thumbs Down" along about nine-forty-five. As we entered the foyer we heard a shot fired on stage. Rushing hurriedly to our seat, we tried to catch up with the plot and figure out who had been killed and by whom, and, if possible, why. Following is the evidence. Do with it as you see fit, Mr. District Attorney.

Our first view of the stage disclosed a young man embracing some girl-friend of his, just as a policeman entered the room. "I killed Sheridan," said the young man quietly, handing a gun to the officer. Then the curtain came down and everyone went into the lobby.

Conclusive as this sounded, the author evidently thought that something more was needed, for there was another act scheduled. It was a very hot night, and since the young man had said that *he* killed Sheridan, it seemed as if they might have taken him at his word and called the show off. But, as there had as yet been no scene in the office of the District Attorney, they naturally couldn't stop. The next scene was in the office of the District Attorney.

We gathered from the conversation between the Public Prosecutor and a gentleman in a Court of Appeals cutaway who seemed to be somebody's father that "Larry is high-strung, quick-tempered, and loyal to the core." So far, so good.

Then a young lady came in and cried a good deal. She didn't seem to know exactly what it was that she wanted, and we certainly were in no position to help her decide. Once she said that *she* killed Sheridan. Then they brought *Larry* in and he repeated his statement that *he* killed Sheridan. Once the District Attorney seemed on the verge of confessing that *he* had killed Sheridan, but that evidently would have been too silly. Sheridan, however, was evidently dead.

Things went on and on, with strange names being introduced into the conversation and an occasional character coming in to say that another bullet had been found embedded somewhere. The District Attorney's answer to all this was to open his mouth very wide and say nothing.

Then in came a lady whom we had never seen before, who said: "Don't call her Queenie Sheridan, call her Jane Ward," surely a reasonable enough request to make. But it threw Somebody's Father into a terrible state of nerves and he cried: "What—your daughter?" "Yes—and *yours!*" came the reply.

This brought the curtain down, and as the whole thing seemed to be satisfactorily explained, we thought the show was over and went home. Imagine our surprise to read in the papers the next morning that there was still another act. It probably had something to do with the question of who killed Sheridan, but we expect never to know.

With hundreds of productions surfacing each season, the theater critics of Benchley's era had the ill fortune to confront, over and over, shows with identical or nearly identical plots, character types, and even dialogue. Successful plays, then as now, came in all shapes and forms, but the considerably lower overheads enabled shows of the twenties to turn profits much quicker. A "successful" play often meant anything that ran past one-hundred-and-fifty or so performances, and the giant turnover rate usually prompted numerous imitations of even moderate hits. One quite popular plotline, Benchley discovered, was the one involving seemingly "pure" women who, it would turn out, had had a moment or two of, shall we say, *weakness* before falling in love with the upstanding, virtuous hero, leading, naturally, to great moral dilemmas. By 1924's *Hurricane*, he had seen enough variations of the same theme to adopt a new strategy for surviving them:

After a season or two devoted almost entirely to plays in which fallen women have been falling with the monotonous patter of rain on a tin roof, we refuse to struggle against sleep during those scenes in which the woman confesses her past to the man she really loves. . . . This sleeping during annunciation and denunciaton scenes in the theatre is an art of which this department is justly proud. When we see a scene coming in which the heroine is obviously going to take ten minutes to point out to her doubting lover that if he will only trust her until the third act she can explain everything, we brace our elbows against the arms of the chair, clasp our hands directly in front of the diaphragm and drift off in Baby's Boat to Sleepy Land.

The only precaution that is necessary is to ask the person sitting next to us to keep us from lurching, and now that we have discovered a dress-collar with sharp tabs which automatically arouse us when we tilt forward beyond a certain angle, we are practically independent of any assistant. The uncanny feature of our talent in this field is that, once the scene is through and they begin talking of something new on the stage, a sixth sense in us operates to send the blood pounding through our temples and we awake with a start, rosy-cheeked and refreshed.

Other equally shopworn plot devices and characterizations inspired more explicit comment, as was the case with 1926's *The Half-Caste:*

When, in the first act, kindly Dr. Holden confided to Mrs. Farham that "after all, men are just animals," we began reaching for that old gray hat of ours. At the entrance of a native girl named Tauna who gave every indication of talking as every native girl has talked since Fay Bainter in "East Is West," with special emphasis on the "damn"s and "hell"s, we put away our program. . . . And long before the hero had stopped kissing this child of nature we were a tiny figure in the distance, running up Forty-first Street. So we never did hear the announcement of the fact which we had suspected from the first, namely, that the hero and the half-caste were half-brother and half-sister.

We are getting to be an old man now, and our temper isn't what it was when Rutherford B. Hayes used to kid us. And we hereby serve notice that whenever we see that a playwright is re-hashing someone else's stuff, with no prospect of contributing anything of his own, up the street we go again, like a startled, albeit aged, fawn.

Benchley's threat, it turned out, was not an idle one. On November 11 of that year, a play called *The Squall* opened at the 48th Street Theatre, and the next day, Alex Woollcott's review in the *World* (where he was now working) centered around the vibrant performance by a rather unlikely member of the opening-night assemblage:

> The scene is a farmhouse on the vineclad hills not far from Granada. The good people of the play—pious, gentle, loving, rustic—are gathered for the evening meal. Up the valley comes a storm, a tornado, and in out of the tempest, drenched, cowering, terrified—a mad creature in search of shelter—the wild girl enters. She is a half-clad, sweet-blooded, tawny-skinned gypsy girl. She crawls to the feet of the good mother of the household and kisses the hem of her garment.
>
> "Me Nubi. Nubi good girl. Nubi stay here."
>
> At which point in the premiere of "The Squall" last night, the dramatic critic of "Life" rose and started for the open air.
>
> On his way towards the exits, he was heard by his scandalized confreres to murmur: "Me Bobby. Bobby bad boy. Bobby go away."

During his years with *Life*, Benchley waged a number of campaigns against what he deemed to be especially deserving targets. One was audience coughers: "Laurels for the evening must go to the gentleman sitting in the neighborhood of G-115. Not only was he in excellent voice, but he picked his pauses with great cleverness, coughing only when impressive silences were being indulged in on the stage.... Good work was also done by the people sitting in C-111, M1-3, G-7, and L-114. The rest of the house was adequate." Another was "The Great Lilliputian Terror," a 1924 group of visiting Russian dwarf pantomimists driven out of their motherland by the Communist revolution: "What a night that must have been in Red Russia! Lenin, at the height of his strength and power . . . whispering nervously, for he is about to undertake a coup on which hangs the success or failure of the Red Regime. 'Tonight, men,' he says, 'Soviet Russia meets her test. Tonight we drive Mr. Ratoucheff's famous troupe of Lilliputians out of the country or we ourselves go under, for they constitute the sole remaining menace to the Red government!' "

Still another target was none other than William Shakespeare.

Benchley found Shakespeare's works a wonder to read, but torture to watch.

Shakespeare is all right bound in limp leather, pocket-size, for personal use under a reading lamp, where you can skip or go back and re-read," he wrote in a review of a production of *Macbeth* in 1921. "But when recited by a company of players for hours at a stretch, most of the spoken words of the Immortal Bard are like so many drops of rain on a tin roof to this particular member of the intelligentsia. "Macbeth" [is] one of the few Shakespearean plays which we *can* sit through . . . but there is one scene in this otherwise robust murder-melodrama which typifies all that is unactable, and, to us, unbearable in Shakespeare when presented on the stage.

We are in the middle of a perfectly bully bloodletting scene, with the murderer sneaking out from the victim's chamber, covered with gore and trembling with apprehension. He runs into his wife, who wants to know how tricks are. And, in the midst of this terrific mental upheaval and the nervousness which is always attendant on the consummation of one's first murder, what does the terror stricken thane reply? He clears his throat and declares that Macbeth has murdered sleep, "sleep that knits up the ravell'd sleeve of care, the death of each day's life, sore labor's bath, balm of hurt minds, great Nature's second course, chief nourisher in life's feast." This panicky fugitive stops in the midst of his flight and turns thesaurus, while Lady Macbeth has to stand by until he has thought up all the literary synonyms for sleep and act as if she really were excited. No actor in God's world would make a scene like that anything but plaster-of-Paris, for it is bad psychology, bad human-nature, and perfectly rotten theatre. And to any one sending in a stamped, self-addressed envelope we will specify a dozen important scenes equally bad for acting purposes from every one of Shakespeare's plays.

Additionally, Benchley believed, "If there is a streak of ham anywhere in an actor, Shakespeare will bring it out. It makes them roll their 'r's' and their eyes. It makes them say 'me heart' and 'me life,' and stretch out the right hand with the fingers fixed like those of the lady in the advertisement who is showing her new washing machine to her visitors. It makes them sonorous, and forces them to laugh in a hollow manner as they leave the stage to cover up the impossible rhymed couplet exits which the author has given them. Next to Robert Hichens, Shakespeare has probably been just as bad an influence in the English speaking stage as there is today."

Benchley's battles with the Bard were little more than harmless skirmishes, however, when compared to the all-out war which he single-handedly conducted against *Abie's Irish Rose*. It began simply enough in May of 1922, when Benchley joined the rest of his fellow critics in turning thumbs down on author Anne Nichols's corny piece of sentimental fluff about the family-related problems that often accompany interfaith marriages; it didn't finish until the play concluded its run—an improbable five years later.

Abie's Irish Rose had its New York debut the night after the premiere of a debacle called *The Rotters* which Benchley had dismissed as "just about the worst show of the season." Then he saw *Abie's*, and reconsidered. In *Life*'s June 8 issue he wrote:

> On the night following "The Rotters," residents of Broadway were startled by the sound of horses' hoofs clattering up the famous thoroughfare. Rushing to their windows they saw a man, in Colonial costume, riding a bay mare from whose eyes flashed fire. The man was shouting as he rode, and his message was: " 'The Rotters' is no longer the worst play in town! 'Abie's Irish Rose' has just opened!"
>
> "Abie's Irish Rose" is the kind of play in which a Jewish boy, wanting to marry an Irish girl named Rosemary Murphy, tells his orthodox father that her name is Rosie Murphesky, and the wedding proceeds.
>
> Any further information, if such could possibly be necessary, will be furnished at the old offices of "Puck," the comic weekly which flourished in the '90's. Although that paper is no longer in existence, there must be some old retainer still about the premises who could tell you everything that is in "Abie's Irish Rose."

As noted before, one of Benchley's duties at *Life* was to provide a "Confidential Guide," a listing of all current theatrical attractions, with brief comments about each one. The week after *Abie's Irish Rose* first appeared at the Fulton Theatre, Benchley described it as "something awful." Seven days later, the play still hadn't closed, and Benchley's words were even more direct: "among the season's worst." The weeks passed . . . and passed . . . and passed. Despite the unanimity of critical disdain, audiences kept flocking to see the play, and instead of withering and dying, *Abie's Irish Rose* bloomed quickly into not just *a* hit show, but *the* hit show of the year—and, ultimately, the decade to boot. And week in and week out, right at the top of the alphabetically listed "Confidential Guide," Benchley looked for the right words to express his ongoing consternation at its inexplicable and unavoidable success.

At first, Benchley tried the direct route, with comments like "eighty-ton fun," "all right if you never went beyond the fourth grade," and "denounced continuously by this department but apparently unconscious of the fact." Eventually, though, as the play settled in for an obviously extended run, Benchley changed his tactics, with the result that the first thing many *Life* readers would turn to in each week's issue would be the "Confidential Guide," where they'd look for, and laugh over, the latest Benchley one-liner about *Abie's Irish Rose*. Among them were the following:

We refuse to answer on advice of counsel.

The Phoenicians were among the earliest settlers of Britain.

People laugh at this every night, which proves why a democracy can never be a success.

The management sent us some pencils for Christmas; so maybe it isn't so bad after all.

There is no letter "w" in the French language.

This department will not be printed next week, owing to the second birthday of this comedy, on which occasion we plan to become ossified.

We, the people of the United States, in order to form a more perfect union (to be cont'd).

For the best comment to go in this space, we will give two tickets to the play.

Contest for best line closes at midnight on Jan. 8. At present, Mr. Arthur Marx is leading with "No worse than a bad cold."

One good thing about this contest is that no matter how long it takes the judges to decide, the two tickets will still be good.

This space reserved; compliments of a friend.

They have leased the theatre for another year; applications for the job of Confidential Guide editor will be considered in order of their receipt.

We see that earthquakes are predicted in these parts some time in the next seven years. Could it be that———.

Closing soon. (Only fooling!)

Stop me if you've heard this one.

The movie people who have just bought the rights to this are now making overtures to this department to influence our bitter opposition to the picture. It ought to be worth at least $250,000 to them and that is our asking price. We will oppose it half-heartedly for $100,000.

See Hebrews 13:8.

Stet.

As the summer of 1927 approached and *Abie's Irish Rose* celebrated its fifth anniversary (Benchley noted its passing by thanking the show's management for giving him a birthday cake as a "token of appreciation for continuous service"), word came that attendance had, finally, begun to dwindle enough so that the show's closing appeared imminent. "We are panic-stricken over the possibility of this closing soon," Benchley wrote in his "Confidential Guide" in late June. "What will we have to write about?" By July, his emotions were running high. "Are we, the drama lovers of America, going to sit idly by and let this great epic of the People die for lack of patronage?" Benchley pleaded. "Write your Congressman today and send contributions to the 'Save Abie's Irish Rose' Fund to this office—in new bills, if possible."

At last the final week was approaching, and, to honor the event, Benchley used a full quarter of his theater page for the following elaborately scripted proclamation:

The Dramatic Department of "Life" takes great pleasure in announcing the successful culmination of its campaign to close "Abie's Irish Rose." On August 6th this comedy will end a nominal run of two hundred and seventy-one weeks.

We rest on our sword and await the tocsin for a fresh crusade.

Unfortunately for Benchley, August 6 came and went, and *Abie's* was still breathing; the show's producers had decided to hang in for a few more gasping weeks. Benchley was irate:

Whether someone in the office where "Life" is printed played turn-coat and informed the Anne Nichols management that we were appearing in print with a broadside of victory, or whether the advertisements run by that management for over a month announcing its closing on August 6th were just vicious decoys leading us into a trap, we'll probably never know. There was dirty work somewhere. Whatever the cause, it is certain that on the very day when this department declared itself victor, the management of "Abie's Irish Rose" announced that it had reconsidered its advertised decision to close and would continue for some time longer, possibly until Labor Day. If the idea was to make this department look like a sap, a straw vote would probably indicate some degree of success.

From now on we refuse to commit ourselves about this play. It can run forever for all we care. We have lost interest in it. We will play safe and run it in the Guide not only until it has really closed but for six months thereafter, but as for wasting any more time boosting it, we are through.

True to his word, Benchley continued to list the show until the end of the year ("According to the newspapers, this closed on October 22," he noted in mid-November. "We are taking no chances.") Its final "Confidential Guide" appearance was saved for *Life*'s Christmas issue of 1927: *"Abie's Irish Rose*—Always in our hearts."

Benchley's final words on the subject came when the author responsible for *Abie's* presented another play. He wrote:

And now along comes Miss Anne Nichols, who (some years ago) placed the gypsy's curse on us with "Abie's Irish Rose," and sponsors a new play called "Howdy King." It is a sterling comedy, full of honest fun and deep insight into human nature, and kept us laughing from start to finish.

You don't catch us again, Miss Nichols.

Beneath the good humor of Benchley's crusade against *Abie's Irish Rose*, however, there was a somewhat serious subtext—a subtext which Benchley wrote about only once, in a February 1927 column commemorating the play's 2000th performance. The passing of that milestone had elicited comments from Nichols regarding the show's popularity in which she said that "people like it because it preaches tolerance and brotherly love," but Benchley begged to differ, voicing the opinion that "exactly the opposite is true." Since most of the play found Abie and Rosemary's ethnically stereotyped fathers continually at each other's throats, Benchley believed that

> up until its final act, *Abie's Irish Rose* is teeming with racial hatred and intolerance. . . . If there is one character in a play who hates everybody else . . . who flies into a rage the minute an object of his hate enters, that character is a sure-fire comedy hit. . . . *Abie's* has not only one such character, it was two—Mr. Cohen and Mr. Murphy. . . . It is quite possible that the tolerance motif in the [play's] last act serves to flatter the audience into an emotional confidence that their hearts are in the right place and sends them home in a glow of righteousness, but the show is a hit long before the last act.

Indeed, throughout his career as a theater critic, both at *Life* and, later, at *The New Yorker*, Benchley regularly used his column to speak out against racial hatred and intolerance, especially when it came to the depiction and treatment of blacks in the theater. In 1921, when black actor Charles Gilpin, the star of Eugene O'Neill's *The Emperor Jones*, was denied an invitation to the New York Drama League's annual dinner, Benchley wrote that

> Negroes are always an embarrassment to a dinner committee, for there seems to be a feeling that if a Negro is present, some of the diners will get up and leave the room. It is not clear just how valuable to the success of the dinner these sensitive souls themselves are, or how much of a loss it would be if they *did* leave the room. . . . Mr. Gilpin does not need the honor of being asked to dine with the New York Drama League, but it is doubtful if the New York Drama League can well dispense with the prestige which Mr. Gilpin's presence would have given to its head table.

In 1924, when a storm of protest greeted the announcement that the production of O'Neill's *All God's Chillun Got Wings* would feature white actress Mary Blair playing the wife of black actor Paul Robeson, Benchley again spoke out about this "threatened insult to

Nordic purity," and used the occasion to attack what he felt was the root cause of racial prejudice. He found it puzzling that "no protests are ever received against a white actress' playing on the stage with a white actor who may be degenerate, criminal, or unclean. If there is such a jealous watch to be kept over the honor of our white woman-hood, we should not limit it to the cases of diverse pigmentation." And, recalling what had happened at the *New York Tribune* to his friend and colleague Ernest Greuning during the First World War, Bench-ley noted that

> there is some sort of parallel to be drawn between the type of mind which reads an insult to his race in social contact with other races, and the type of mind which refused to eat sauerkraut during the war until it had been renamed "Liberty cabbage." It usually occurs in those whose sole activity in behalf of the honor of their country or the integrity of their womanhood consists of just such agitations. It must spring from some subconscious sense of inferiority which calls for a loud booming on a bassdrum which has no relation to the band.

"But come, come," concluded Benchley. "This is the Drama page."

Fortunately for Benchley the theater critic, as well as Bench-ley the theatergoer, there was an abundance of great talent and ex-ceptional work to marvel at throughout the 1920s. Each Broadway season brought to the stage new works from such distinguished play-wrights as George Bernard Shaw, the aforementioned Eugene O'Neill, Philip Barry, August Strindberg, and Luigi Pirandello, as well as those of friends Kaufman, Connelly, Stewart, and Sherwood, the last of whom left *Life* in 1928 to begin a new career as a playwright and screenwriter. And among the performers appearing in the flurry of productions each year were some of the finest actors and actresses ever seen on the American stage: Maude Adams, the Barrymores, Fay Bainter, Jane Cowl, Katherine Cornell, James Cagney, Spencer Tracy, George M. Cohan, Leslie Howard, Humphrey Bogart, Ruth Gordon, Helen Hayes, Roland Young, John Drew, Estelle Winwood, Florence Reed, Alfred Lunt, Lynne Fontanne, Edward G. Robinson, James Gleason, and June Walker.

Still, it was the variety show—the revues, follies, and burlesque programs that threw together everything from juggling circus performers to jiggling chorus girls, and from blackfaced minstrel singers to blackout sketches—that often drew the heartiest responses from Benchley, primarily because of the multitude of comedians he so enjoyed watching. Benchley loved to laugh, and laugh he did, to the antics of budding stars like Ed Wynn, W. C. Fields, the Marx Brothers, Joe Cook, Fred Stone, Gallagher and Sheen, Smith and Dale, Willie Howard, Mae West, Jimmy Durante, and Al Jolson. "First night audiences in Manhattan include one heroic laugher," wrote Brooks Atkinson. "Mr. Benchley explodes like a dynamite pit. It is not helpless laughter; it is none of your brief snorts or casual chuckles, but a bellow of merriment, instantaneous and unguarded. Nothing can drown it out. The Benchley crescendo dominates the house with the natural gusto of the man amused. Mr. Benchley is the God of Laughter and the bellwether of any audience he inhabits."

That Benchley should himself become a performer, eliciting those hearty fits of laughter from audiences filled with strangers each and every night of the week, was probably the farthest thing from his mind when he assumed the role of theater critic for *Life* magazine. And it probably still was the farthest thing from his mind when he stepped in front of a curtain at the 49th Street Theatre in 1922 to make good on a promise to take part in a portion of a show written and performed as a lark before an invitation-only audience by the members of the Algonquin Round Table and delivered the ten-minute "speech" that was ultimately to alter the course of his life forever—"The Treasurer's Report."

10
No Sirree, Bob

"MR. ROSSITER, UNFORTUNATELY OUR TREASURER"

It was rather ironic that the program for the one and only performance of the *No Sirree!* revue—billed by its creators as "An Anonymous Entertainment by the Vicious Circle of the Hotel Algonquin"—made no mention whatsoever of Robert Benchley's "Treasurer's Report," since not only did his monologue get the biggest laughs of any of the skits and sketches essayed by the novice Algonquinite thespians, but also because, were it not for his performance in this one show, it's unlikely that Benchley would ever have taken seriously the notion of becoming a "professional" actor. But the truth of the matter is that almost right up until the show was staged, no one was quite sure just *what* Benchley was going to do, which no doubt left program writer Marc Connelly reluctant to put any extra pressure on his friend by actually announcing an act that, from all indications, was subject to change without notice.

The impetus for *No Sirree!* (the name was a pun on the highly successful Russian revue *Le Chauve Souris*) came when actor J. M. Kerrigan, joining the Algonquin crowd for lunch and growing weary of all the Vicious Circle grousing about the current theater season, half-jokingly dared them to get out there on the other side of the footlights and see if they could do better. "Since you don't like the plays you go to see," he said, "why don't you write one yourself and see if we actors like it?" The challenge seemed like too much fun to pass up, and soon nascent impresario Woollcott, after arranging for the group to rent out the 49th Street Theatre for the night of Sunday, April 30, 1922, was recruiting a troupe of would-be performers from the ranks of the Round Table—with a few outer Vicious Circle "ringers" like Helen Hayes, Ruth Gillmore, Tallulah Bankhead, Sidney Blackmer, June Walker, and Kerrigan himself asked in to give the production some professionalism.

The logical place to rehearse was the 57th Street studio of Neysa McMein, magazine cover artist and unofficial hostess of most post-daytime Algonquinite gatherings. Born Marjorie Moran, and originally from Quincy, Illinois, she had come to New York in 1917 from Chicago after honing her painting skills as a student at the Art Institute of Chicago and changing her name on the advice of a numerologist. She quickly captivated almost all who met her, and her entrance into the world of the Round Tablers came early. Soon after moving to New York, she showed up at the *Tribune* office unannounced, seeking an audience with F.P.A., and see him she did—even a semi-grouch like Adams could hardly refuse a strikingly lovely young woman, her long blond hair braided in two buns over her ears, holding a nosegay of sweet peas, which, she explained, was a gift for the man whose column she enjoyed so much. The utterly disarmed Adams took her to lunch at the Algonquin, and next day the columnist's "Diary of Our Own Samuel Pepys" reported: "Mistress Neysa McMein [came] to see me, and we talked of Quincy and Chicago and Art and Literature and the war, and I was regretful that she went away so soon. . . ."

McMein was always inviting people she met to drop by her art studio whenever they felt like it, and as more and more of these acquaintances took her up on her offer, the McMein salon, like the Round Table at the Algonquin Hotel, began to acquire its own reputation as the place where the Vicious Circle and their cronies would congregate to unwind at the end of their busy days. For in all of New York, there was no single place as filled with the unending, undemanding party atmosphere to be found at Neysa's. Musician Jascha Heifetz, after meeting McMein and being asked over, arrived with his violin and an accompanist in tow, assuming that he'd been invited to come and entertain. But one of the Algonquin group word games was in progress, so Heifetz was simply asked to join in with the others, and McMein never did get around to asking him to play—treatment which surprised and delighted the famous violinst, who quickly became a regular.

In a magazine profile of her, longtime friend and part-time suitor Woollcott described a typical McMein gathering:

The population is widely variegated. Over at the piano Jascha Heifetz and Arthur Samuels may be trying to find what four hands can do in the syncopation of a composition never thus desecrated before. Irving Berlin is encouraging them. Squatted uncomfortably around an ottoman, Franklin P. Adams, Marc Connelly and Dorothy Parker will be playing cold hands to see who will buy the dinner that evening. At the bookshelf Robert C. Benchley and Edna Ferber are amusing themselves vastly by thoughtfully autographing her set of Mark Twain for her. . . . Chaplin or Chaliapin, Alice Duer Miller or Wild Bill Donovan, Father Duffy or Mary Pickford—any or all of them may be here. In Paris, they say of the terrasse of the Café de la Paix that if you sit there long enough you will see everyone you know. If you loiter in Neysa McMein's studio, the world will drift in and out. . . .

Standing at the easel itself, oblivious of all the ructions, incredibly serene and intent on her work, is the artist herself. She is beautiful, grave and slightly soiled. Her apron is a shabby, streaked remnant of a once neat garment. Her fair hair, all awry, is discolored from an endless drizzle of pastel dust. . . . [And when] the daylight has dwindled to dusk, she finally comes wandering around the easel and drops into a chair, dog-tired but sociable. . . .

What would surprise the people to whom the word studio has faint connotations of debauchery, is the homely, neighborly flavor which circumstances and the quality of this woman have imparted to this crazy one of hers. In its casualness and its informality, it has the accent of one of those ugly, roomy, hospitable homes on the edge of a small town, where the young folk are always running in and out. You can almost hear voices calling across the fence, almost catch the aroma of fresh bread sifting in from the kitchen. Neysa McMein has made a small town of New York.

Benchley was a virtual fixture at the McMein studio throughout the early twenties, and for a number of reasons. First was the fact that Benchley was in his element at *any* party, and since the core of the crowd at McMein's was composed mainly of his closest friends, here was perhaps the ideal party, and one which was taking place almost every day. Moreover, it took place at the ideal time of day. Most weekdays, Benchley's schedule followed the same pattern. He'd take a midmorning train in from Scarsdale, spend some time at the *Life* office reading the morning papers and going through his mail, then go to the Algonquin for a Round Table lunch, and then spend the remainder of the afternoon back at his *Life* desk, working either on his theater page or a freelance piece. And since most curtain times fell between eight and nine, a non-city-resident drama critic's early evening usually consisted of a longish dinner that still left him quite a bit of time to kill. The McMein studio gave Benchley a comfortable spot to relax, a place to meet Gertrude on the increasingly rare evenings that she came into town to join him in his critic's seats, or, on the increasingly frequent evenings when a projected long night of theater-hopping was compounded by an early deadline to be met the following day, a place to figure out who was free for dinner, who was interested in seeing a new show, and whether it was Connelly's, Stewart's, or Sherwood's turn to put him up for the night.

As at the Round Table, the amusements at Neysa McMein's studio were provided primarily by those who were inhabiting the domain. There were, naturally, spillovers from lunch like the "I can give you a sentence" game and, with room for people to get up and move around, charade contests, with teams, team captains, and probably the most (on purpose, of course) mind-bending and (even more on purpose) degrading titles, sayings, and phrases ever acted out in mixed company. Card playing at McMein's was tolerated, but not particularly encouraged, since the Vicious Circle had its own official poker auxiliary—the Toohey-inspired and Adams-named Thanatopsis Literary and Inside Straight Club, which dated from the *Stars and Stripes* days of the Round Table World War vets, and which held regular meetings on Saturday nights in a room at the Algonquin made available to the players by Frank Case.

Benchley wasn't much of a card player or gambler—about the only thing he was good for in his rare appearances at Thanatopsis marathons was kibbitzing. Weak player that he was, he wisely tended to stay clear of the uncommonly serious and often cutthroat competition at the poker table between sharks like Kaufman, Harpo Marx, and Herbert Swope and marks like Broun, Ross, and Connelly. Nor did he care much for charades. "Benchley loathed parlor games, especially the charades the Algonquin people called 'The Game,' " recalled George Oppenheimer. "One night, however, he encountered a hostess more resolute than he and rather than seem impolite, he capitulated. He was then given to act out the name of a Hungarian playwright, 'Ladislaus Bus-Fekete.' Nothing daunted, Benchley glanced briefly at the paper on which the name was inscribed, promptly dropped down to his hands and knees, circled the floor twice, and disappeared through a French door. They waited and waited, but to no avail. Benchley had gone out, hailed a cab, and headed off."

What Benchley could, and often did, contribute to the McMein get-togethers by way of entertainment were those always popular parodies of speakers, speechmakers, and lecturers that he'd been concocting since Harvard days. So, when the Round Tablers gathered one evening at McMein's to organize the prospective acts and sketches that were to make up the *No Sirree!* show, Benchley was promptly volunteered to work up one of his little "talks" for the occasion.

Although the *No Sirree!* "extravaganza" was neither conceived nor planned as anything too serious, the Algonquinites rehearsed faithfully as they worked on the various parts of the program. The "acts" began to take shape. "He Who Gets Flapped" was a musical number starring elongated Robert Sherwood, in straw hat and cane, leading a surrounding bevy of "chorus girls" (actually, nine actresses, including Tallulah Bankhead, Helen Hayes, Ruth Gillmore, June Walker, and Lenore Ulric, as well as the future Mrs. Sherwood, Mary Brandon) in a rendition of Dorothy Parker's less than classic musical composition "The Everlastin' Ingenue Blues" (sample lyric: "We are little flappers, never growing up / And we've all of us been flapping since Belasco was a pup"). "Zowie, or the Curse of an Akins Heart" was a spoof of Zoe Akins's high-society tragedies in which the decidedly not theatrically inclined Harold Ross, after failing auditions for all other available parts in the sketch, was finally awarded the much-coveted role of "Lemuel Pip (An Old Taxi Driver)," who never appears onstage. Also worked up were lampoons such as "The Greasy Hag, an O'Neill Play in One Act," featuring Kaufman, Connelly, and Woollcott as, respectively, "First Agitated Seaman," "Second Agitated Seaman," and "Third Agitated Seaman," and "Mr. Whim Passes By—An A. A. Milne Play" ("The scene is a morning room at the Acacias, Wipney-cum-Chiselickwick," read Connelly's program notes), and such "diversions" as an "Opening Chorus," in which Woollcott, Toohey, Kaufman, Connelly, Adams, and Benchley all would come out dressed only in bathrobes and sing a song explaining that they had written the show to suit themselves, and several serenades from Heifetz—performed, appropriately enough, both offstage and off-key.

All in all, everything being done in preparation for the show went quite well throughout the several weeks of rehearsal—with one notable exception. "The only doubtful number seemed to be Bob's speech," recounted Donald Ogden Stewart. "With characteristic modesty, he was most reluctant to attempt it during rehearsals." It turned out, though, that it wasn't merely modesty that was preventing Benchley from running through his number. The truth was that he didn't have anything written up to run through. The only time Benchley ever actually wrote down his speeches was when he was working an engagement as a paid after-dinner speaker; his parodies and imitations, done primarily for friends or at parties, most often were impromptu flights of fancy, and he never took the time to set them to paper afterward because there simply was no reason to do so. Besides, the whole formality of acting out his speech seemed wrong, for it implied an importance to the thing much greater than he believed it should have.

Still, he knew that he wanted to do something a bit different. After all, most everyone else involved in the writing of the show was contributing fresh material, and Benchley certainly didn't want to fail to do his part in providing a special-for-this-show-only spot. According to Stewart, the first inkling anyone had about what was ultimately to form the basis of his "act" came when Benchley, sharing a taxi with Stewart roughly a week before the show was due to take place, "began to scribble some notes on the back of an envelope." He had finally hit upon an idea that he thought might work. "Bob read me the opening of what he described as a 'sort of treasurer's annual report.' 'Do you think something like this will be all right?' he asked. I encouragingly said I thought it would be just fine. What an understatement *that* turned out to be. When our *No Sirree!* revue was finally presented to a packed theatre, Bob's 'Treasurer's Report' stole the show."

Imagine a highly nervous and disorganized person, unaccustomed to making any kind of "speech" in public, suddenly thrust into the limelight to deliver a report on his town's financial situation. And, since it is any public speaker's nightmare to be addressing an audience that isn't paying attention, imagine further that the group listening to the speech hasn't the faintest notion of what the person making the speech is talking about. The poor soul at the podium valiantly tries to make the best of an utterly disastrous situation.

So it was that in the middle of the show, without any announcement or introduction, Benchley sheepishly walked to the front of the stage of the 49th Street Theatre and began talking:

I shall take but a very few moments of your time this evening, for I realize that you would much rather be listening to this interesting entertainment than to a dry financial statement . . . but there are one or two points which Dr. Murnie wanted brought up in connection with it, and he has asked me to bring them up in connec—to bring them up.

In the first place, there is the question of the work which we are trying to do up there at our little place at Silver Lake, a work which we feel not only fills a very definite need in the community but also fills a very definite need—er—in the community. I don't think that many members of the Society realize just how big the work is that we are trying to do up there. For instance, I don't think that it is generally known that most of our boys are between the age of fourteen. We feel that, by taking the boy at this age, we can get closer to his real nature—for a boy *has* a very real nature, you may be sure—and bring him into closer touch not only with the school, the parents, and with each other, but also with the town in which they live, the country to whose flag they pay allegiance, and to the—ah—town in which they live.

Those of you who contributed so generously last year to the floating hospital have probably wondered what became of the money. I was speaking on this subject only last week at our uptown branch, and, after the meeting, a dear little old lady, dressed all in lavender, came up on the platform, and, laying her hand on my arm, said: "Mr. So-and-so, what the hell did you do with all the money we gave you last year?" Well, I just laughed and pushed her off the platform—but it has occurred to the committee that perhaps some of you, like that little old lady, would be interested in knowing the disposition of the funds.

Now, Mr. Rossiter, unfortunately our treasurer—or rather Mr. Rossiter our *treasurer, unfortunately*—is confined at his home tonight with a bad head-cold and I have been asked if I would fill in for him. Following, then, is a summary of the Treasurer's Report:

During the year 1929—and by that is meant 1928—the Choral Society received the following in donations: B.L.G., $500. G.K.M., $500. Lottie and Nellie W., $500. In memory of a happy summer at Rye Beach, $10. Proceeds of a sale of coats and hats left in the boat-house, $14.55. And then the Junior League gave a performance of "Pinafore" for the benefit of the Fund which, unfortunately, resulted in a deficit of $300. Then, from dues and charges, $2,354.75. . . . Making a total of receipts amounting to $3,645.75. . . . This is all, of course, reckoned as of June.

Now, in the matter of expenditures, the Club has not been so fortunate. There was the unsettled condition of business, and the late Spring, to contend with, resulting in the following—er—rather discouraging figures, I am afraid:

Expenditures, $23,574.85. Then there was a loss, owing to—several things—of $3,326.70. Car-fare, $4,452.25. And then, Mrs. Rawlins' expense account, when she went down to see the work they are doing in Baltimore, came to $256.50, but I am sure that you will all agree that it was worth it to find out—er—what they are doing in Baltimore. And then, under the general head of Odds and Ends, $2,537.50 . . . making a total disbursement of . . . $416,546.75—or a net deficit of several thousand dollars.

Now, these figures bring us down only to October. In October my sister was married, and the house was all torn up, and in the general confusion we lost track of the figures for May and August. All those wishing the *approximate* figures for May and August, however, may obtain them from me in the vestry after the dinner, where I will be with pledge cards for those of you who wish to subscribe over and above your annual dues, and I hope that each and every one of you here tonight will look deep into his heart and into his pocketbook, and see if he can not find it there to help us to put this thing over with a bang and to help and make this just the biggest and best year the Armenians have ever had! I thank you.

It wasn't until 1930 that the above-quoted version of "The Treasurer's Report" was finally committed to print by Benchley, and even then he still seemed diffident about it. "To sit down and put the threadbare words on paper has always seemed just a little too much to bear," he remarked in an introduction to the piece when it was finally published. "I am writing it out now more as a release than anything else. Perhaps, in accordance with Freudian theories, if I rid myself of this thing which has been skulking in the back of my mind for eight years, I shall be a normal man again. No one has to read it. I hope that no one does, for it doesn't read at all well." At varying points in those eight years, Benchley noted, he had "inflicted it on the public in every conceivable way except over the radio and dropping it from airplanes" (a limitation eventually eliminated by his performances of the piece over the air during the course of a highly successful radio career and by World War II, when air cargo shipments including copies of his books were parachuted to GIs overseas).

Benchley wasn't really looking to "inflict" "The Treasurer's Report" on anyone ever again after *No Sirree!* came and went. He'd simply done his bit for the show, and was both surprised and a bit embarrassed that it had gone over so well, and that he was being lauded by theater people from both sides of the footlights for his "performance." He didn't feel that any degree of acting skill had been involved in doing the sketch, since he wasn't following any strict script and was only winging it for a lark, as he had back at Harvard or for those Curtis dinners. Furthermore, he hadn't put that much effort into the monologue—except perhaps spending an inordinate amount of time worrying about it. Certainly, he was delighted that the reception had been so warm; who knew if people would even get it, let alone laugh at it? But this was much too easy to be classified as "acting." Every night in his seat in the audience as a working theater critic, he saw *real* actors who worked extremely hard at their craft. This was just a bit of fun, that was all.

Still, "The Treasurer's Report" stayed in people's minds. In early fall of 1922, after Woollcott, Ross and his wife Jane Grant, and Woollcott's college chum Hawley Truax had begun sharing a house at 412 West 47th Street, a celebrity-studded housewarming party was held, and the festivities included a much-requested reprise by Benchley of his act from *No Sirree!* In November, when Kaufman and Connelly attempted to stage an "official" Round Table–authored revue, open to the general public, the sketches solicited included Benchley's "Treasurer's Report." (This particular show, called *The 49ers*, in honor of the theater that once again was housing a Vicious Circle theatrical venture, was backed financially by producer George Tyler, who insisted on using "real" actors for the sketches in the hope that a well-known and professional cast would attract a paying audience. It didn't; the show, filled with endless inside jokes, non sequiturs, and nonsense sketches, lasted but fifteen poorly attended performances. For the record, an actor named Denman Maley gave what reviewer Woollcott—for once not personally involved in an Algonquin affair—deemed a "tolerably well delivered" rendition of the Benchley piece.)

At the beginning of 1923, Irving Berlin, who had watched the *No*

Sirree! show from a seat in the orchestra pit as conductor of the program's music, approached Benchley about the possibility of his performing "The Treasurer's Report" in Berlin's *Music Box Revue*, an annual collection of music, dance, and comedy numbers that would be starting its third season the following fall. Benchley, who knew and greatly admired Berlin, told the songwriter that he was genuinely flattered that he really thought enough of the sketch to want to put it in one of his shows, but that taking part in a production himself was sure to pose too much of a potential conflict with his duties as a theater critic. "Nonsense," replied Berlin, arguing that Benchley was simply delivering a monologue that he'd written himself, that it in no way meant any kind of connection to the rest of the show, and that everything would be done to make sure that appearing in the revue wouldn't interfere with his play reviewing; it would be guaranteed that he could be offstage and out the door in time to see whatever plays were opening, for the entire run of the revue. No problem whatsoever.

This all seemed slightly ridiculous, Benchley thought. It wasn't that he was particularly frightened by the thought of being on a stage. It just didn't feel *correct* to do something like this. Then again, George Kaufman had begun to write plays with Marc Connelly, and Kaufman still held, with unquestioned integrity, his position as drama editor of the *New York Times*. In fact, stories abounded concerning Kaufman's bending over backward to make sure no one could accuse him of any publicity-mongering for his own shows. One time the press agent for the Kaufman-Connelly comedy *To the Ladies*, at wit's end because Kaufman had flatly refused to print a feature story about the play's star, Helen Hayes, exasperatedly demanded to know what on earth he had to do to get Miss Hayes's name in the paper. "Shoot her," suggested Kaufman.

As the excuses for bowing out gracefully continued to vanish, Benchley played what he was sure was going to be his ace in the hole: money. If he asked for an inordinate amount of it, Berlin and his producer Sam Harris would surely refuse and that would be that. No hard feelings; just a business deal that fell through. Benchley called Harris and told him his price, his *nonnegotiable* price—$500 a week. There were a few moments of silence at the other end of the line, and

Benchley smugly waited for Harris to tell him that a salary that high, for a person who was, after all, little more than an untested amateur, was clearly out of the question. What a relief this was going to be.

Instead, Benchley very nearly fainted dead away when Harris again spoke. "All right, Bob," said the producer. "Five hundred a week it is. But for that much money, you'd better be awfully good. I'll talk to you when the contracts are ready." And with that, Harris cordially hung up, leaving the flabbergasted Benchley staring at the phone, trying to figure out where exactly he'd gone wrong.

Prior to his appearance in Irving Berlin's *Music Box Revue*, the only evidence that Benchley might have seen to support the suggestion that he was any kind of "celebrity" most likely would have been the two volumes of collected pieces which Henry Holt & Company had published, to both glowing reviews and good sales, in 1921 and 1922. The first, *Of All Things*—including among its twenty-five essays the aforementioned "Call for Mr. Kenworthy," "Turning Over a New Ledger Leaf," and "The Most Popular Book of the Month" phone book review—was praised on both sides of the Atlantic. Reviewing it in the *World*, social crusader Broun, while expressing his personal belief that "even the lightest of humorists is under obligation to start at a definite point and head for a given point, [lest] these journeys are to be nothing more than joy rides," commented, "Benchley begins with such an unusual equipment in himself that almost anything will do for a springboard. . . . He begins with the telephone book, with a piece of roast beef, with the Saturday Evening Post, or any other commonplace commodity and with no more than a few yards' run he is up in the clouds and zooming along. It is not enough to emphasize his facility. It is gorgeous as well as easy humor." And in England, Stephen Leacock, himself an immensely gifted humorist, wryly proclaimed Benchley's first book to be "an event in the history of literature not equalled since Milton produced his 'Paradise Lost.' More than that," he added, "I will go so far as to say that if Shakespeare was only alive he would recognize in Bob Benchley a friend and an equal."

Of All Things and its follow-up, *Love Conquers All*, each went through numerous printings, and their success established Benchley not only as a popular national writer but also as one of the chief architects of a new brand of humor. "Crazy humor," Donald Stewart called it; stuff that just sprang from a fertile, open-ended imagination and was, indeed, as Broun had categorized it, sometimes nothing more—or less—than mental joy-riding. But America itself was on a joy ride in the twenties, careening along, as fast as it could travel, with no particular place to go, and writers like Benchley were serving as merry tour guides on the dizzying road to nowhere.

From "A Romance in Encyclopedia Land":

"Well," he sighed, as he gazed upon the broad area of subsidence, "if I were now an exarch, whose dignity was, at one time, intermediate between the Patriarchal and the Metropolitan and from whose name has come that of the politico-religious party, the Exarchists, I should not be here day-dreaming. I should be far away in Footscray, a city of Bourke County, Victoria, Australia, pop. (1901) 18,301." And as he said this his eyes filled with tears, and under his skin, brown as fustic, there spread a faint flush, such as is often formed by citrocyde, or by pyrochloric acid when acting on uncured leather.

From "Opera Synopses," a summary of *Die Meister-Genossenschaft,* Act I:

Immergluck has grown weary of always sitting on the same rock and with the same fishes swimming by every day, and sends for Schwul to suggest something to do. Schwul asks her how she would like to have pass before her all the wonders of the world fashioned by the hand of man. She says, rotten. He then suggests that Ringblattz, son of Pflucht, be made to appear before her and fight a mortal combat with the Iron Duck. This pleases Immergluck and she summons to her the four dwarfs: Hot Water, Cold Water, Cool, and Cloudy. She bids them bring Ringblattz to her. They refuse, because Pflucht has at one time rescued them from being buried alive by acorns, and, in a rage, Immergluck strikes them all dead with a thunderbolt.

Benchley was at once displaying the inner workings of a mind running delightfully amok and turning the supposedly ordered world of "convention" upside down and shaking the change out of its pockets.

By juxtaposing one set of standards with another—in the case of the encyclopedia piece taking the dense tone and forbidding haughtiness of the universally accepted "book of knowledge" and transplanting it into the guided-by-emotions setting of a romantic novel, or in the case of "Opera Synopses" exposing the fact that folk myths from one culture don't necessarily add up to anything even remotely comprehensible to differing cultures—Benchley was neatly underscoring the fact that our methods of communication were predicated by endless sets of rules and regulations that perhaps were useless except to the rules and regulation makers themselves, leaving the rest of us to fend for ourselves in a world apparently determined not to make sense. In which case, Benchley's articles implied, we'd *better* have a sense of humor.

In the brave new world of postwar America, people and events moved fast, and society fairly demanded that one either keep up or get out of the way. The "modern" man, America told itself, was equally at home with matters of business and pleasure. He grasped the intricacies of the national economy just as easily as he grasped the workings of the engine of his new automobile. He was as suavely comfortable with a deck of cards in his hands as he was on the deck of a sailing boat. He could weed his backyard plot of land until not a single blade of crabgrass sullied his immaculate lawn, and he could canvas his territory better than any other salesman in the region. He was the strong-minded, strong-armed American man, and he could do anything he set his mind to.

Benchley, on the other hand, didn't know a steam pipe from a corncob pipe, and crabgrass was usually the only thing that *would* come out of the earth around his home, regardless of what he'd planted. His coal furnace ran out of fuel in the middle of the coldest nights of the year, and all he could say with absolute certainty about economic matters was that money was something that showed up and was gone before he could even count it. You could just as soon ask him to build a bridge as play a hand of it, for the good it would do you, and authority was something other people displayed airs of, and he constantly cringed from.

As Benchley chronicled his own simple fears, frustrations, and foibles, readers everywhere saw, in the mirror of his work, the reflection of their own quiet struggles and defeats at the hands of an uncaring, impervious universe. When *Of All Things* sold what seemed to Benchley to be quite an unexpectedly large number of copies, he had to admit to himself that here was indeed tangible evidence supporting the proposition that he was a writer whom people would pay to read. Not that this state of affairs necessarily made sense to him. "I find that if I try to evolve gags, they always fall flat," he told an interviewer. "Yet, if I select some incident that I am sure has happened to only me, it seems to make a great hit. I am of the opinion that simple everyday things are what make humor, at least as far as the public is concerned. People are tickled to realize that, after all, their experiences happen, in just the same way, to everyone else."

As for suggesting that he was a *good* writer as well as a popular one, well, that was quite a different thing, and one was not likely to win *that* argument with Benchley. Asked not long after the publication of *Love Conquers All* to contribute an essay to a book devoted to successful writers' views on English composition, Benchley declined. He explained:

> I do not think of myself as a writer in the technical sense of the word. I know practically nothing of the craft, and am constantly in dread of violating some elementary rule which every pupil of English A ought to know. The only technique which I ever remember trying to master was that which was impressed on me in my first job—writing advertising copy. God knows I do not recommend writing advertising copy as a training for writing, but there is one thing that you do learn in that business, and that is that if you don't interest the reader right away, he isn't going to read beyond the first paragraph. For the rest I have no feeling in the matter at all. I am usually late with my copy and in a great hurry. I slap it down and hope to God that it is spelled correctly. (God is not always on the job, either.)
>
> Dean Briggs once told me that I had the "fatal facility" which would always lead me into writing passable stuff easily when I might do good stuff with care. Perhaps as a protection against ever having to take pains, I have evolved a purely private theory that the way for me to write is to put things down just as they come into my mind and

let it go at that. This, of course, is no kind of advice to give, and is probably bad advice for me to give myself, but, with the printers in the rush that they usually are, it is just what I need as a practical theory. I *do* think that as far as humor goes, it is a good plan to put down your first flash, just as it comes out of the oven, without fussing much over it or using your good judgment. But for style, it is probably terrible.

On a Saturday night in the fall of 1923, Robert Benchley—author of two best-selling humor books and drama critic of *Life* magazine—did his first professional rendition of "The Treasurer's Report." He went onstage at precisely 8:50 PM. and went offstage, to a noticeably rousing round of applause, at precisely 8:58 P.M. When the entire cast of the *Music Box Revue*—including singers Grace Moore and John Steel, comedians Frank Tiney, Hugh Cameron, and Solly Ward, dancers Florence O'Denishawn and Dorothy Diller, and lead model Ivy Sawyer—came onstage together for the grand finale, Benchley was conspicuously absent. Had one been backstage between 8:58 and 9:05, one might have been able to see him frantically racing into his dressing room, removing his makeup, changing his suit, and then dashing out the stage door, on his way to a new play opening a few blocks away on Broadway.

Since the *Music Box Revue* gave eight performances a week, (six nighttime shows and two matinees), and since there were, as noted previously, premieres of new shows almost every night, the physical strain on Benchley soon began to show. Shortly before the start of 1924, he developed a fever and an accompanying ache in the knees that he assumed was simply a bad cold, but, as days and eventually several weeks wore on without either subsiding, he knew there might be something seriously wrong. And, he confessed later in life, he might have gone to a doctor earlier but for the actor's phenomenon known as "audience healing," which helped him get through the evenings. "The first night that I really felt badly, I limped to the theatre scarcely able to bend my knee and very uncomfortable with fever. As I stood waiting to go on I wondered just how I could make the distance between the entrance and my position on the stage. And yet the moment I stepped out and began to get the charge from the audience, I actually forgot everything and when I was through walked briskly off and was halfway home before the effects of my treatment wore off and my knee tightened up again. Had I been able to have kept the audience seated for the rest of the night and have stayed on the stage, I would undoubtedly have avoided a very painful twelve hours—whatever it might have been for them."

Benchley finally did see a doctor, who diagnosed his sudden affliction as arthritis and told him that if he was interested in preserving his health, he had better choose between working at night and commuting to and from Scarsdale. At least that's what Benchley told Gertrude the doctor had said. As it was, Benchley was barely spending any time at home anymore with his wife and his sons; Sunday dinner was the only evening meal they were having together as a family. But as far as Gertrude could see, it wasn't just being in a show that had further separated them. Ever since he'd become a theater critic— ever since he'd begun living the night life that he so clearly took to, and that she had such little interest in—their worlds were growing apart.

At Crestwood and while he worked for the Liberty Loan program and at *Vanity Fair*, he'd seemed perfectly content—a good husband and a good father. He wrote a very funny article about giving Robert Jr. a bath. "What should the parent wear while bathing the child?" he'd written. "A rubber loin-cloth will usually be sufficient, with perhaps a pair of elbow-guards and anti-skid gloves." But in the three years they'd been in Scarsdale, he'd begun to change. He was becoming increasingly distanced from her and the boys, and she saw that it was only during July and August, when the Broadway season closed down and they vacationed in Siasconset on Nantucket Island, where they'd begun renting a summer home in 1921, that the Benchley she'd grown up caring for seemed to fully reappear. True, he called her from the *Life* office in New York every afternoon, like clockwork. But she knew the crowd he ran with. Oh, they were all quite modern and smart and cosmopolitan. She remembered the first time she'd ever gone with Benchley to Neysa McMein's studio, and Dorothy Parker, seeing that she wore no makeup, had handed her a compact. "Have some powder on your nose," she said. So Gertrude began to put it on, looked in the mirror, and saw that her nose had turned red. It was rouge! She felt like a country bumpkin. Parker, and Donald Stewart, and, really, just about all of the Algonquin crowd drank alcohol—and not just a little, either. And they talked about sex— in public! In their company, who knew what kinds of things Benchley might be getting himself into?

Still, she felt powerless to do anything about it. He was providing for her and the boys, and they had a lovely home—even if he was hardly ever in it. And now, on the doctor's advice, he was going to have to take a room in the city if he was to keep working and stay healthy. She couldn't argue with the facts of the matter, not the way he presented them to her. She knew how many jobs he'd been through before *Life*, and how fearful he was about losing work. So she would adapt.

For his part, Benchley prayed that Gertrude would believe that he was moving to Manhattan on the orders of his doctor. It was the truth— if only part of the truth. The arthritis was real, all right; his knees were killing him. But no doctor would have examined a man with a wife, two little boys, and a house in the suburbs and prescribed that he take up a separate residence in New York City so that he could have a safe haven in which to drink bootleg whiskey and conduct an affair. Which was precisely what Robert Benchley had already begun to do.

11
Wet—and Wild

UNCLE ALBERT, FONDLY REMEMBERED

In the summer of 1923, Carol Goodner was a striking nineteen-year-old blonde who daydreamed about being a Broadway actress while working as a telephone operator at the Western Union office in the Biltmore Hotel near Grand Central Station. Cutting through the hotel lobby on the way to his train, Benchley kept seeing her, and one day he stopped to talk. Before long, they'd struck up a friendship that progressed to the point where she became his protégé—and mistress. Benchley got Goodner's stage career off the ground by securing her a spot in the *Music Box Revue* that fall as a showgirl; she appeared as "Miss November" during the program's "Calendar" number. From there, the ambitious Goodner was to make the most of her opportunities: By 1925, when she ended her relationship with Benchley via a letter from England, she was performing in the London production of George Kaufman's *The Butter and Egg Man*. (Interestingly, she was to return to the United States several years later to appear on Broadway in another Kaufman hit, *The Man Who Came to Dinner*—the title character of which was based on another Round Tabler, Alexander Woollcott.)

Benchley handled his affair with Goodner with appropriate discretion—they were seen together in public almost exclusively at speakeasies, where the dark, smoky atmosphere lent itself to illicit, conspiratorial activities. Of course, that meant that nearly all his Algonquin friends, who frequented those speakeasies, knew about it. Their responses varied—bemusement from Kaufman and Heywood Broun (the former was in a loveless marriage, and had a particular fondness for call girls; the latter was in an open marriage, and had a particular fondness for young actresses), chagrin from Dorothy Parker and Edmund Wilson. In his diaries, Wilson described Goodner as "quite a pretty blonde with thick ankles who I thought had something of that hard-eyed prostitute stare" and noted that Mrs. Parker had found Goodner "very inferior." (Of course, considering her own mostly disastrous romantic entanglements after Eddie Parker left her in the early 1920s—most notably, a tumultuous affair with Charles MacArthur that included an aborted pregnancy and a wrist-slashing suicide attempt—Parker was hardly in a position to offer much more than understanding to Benchley about his predicament.) Suffice it to say that in the blasé, morally emancipated crowd Benchley ran with, more people wondered why it took him so long to finally have an affair than wondered why it was Goodner with whom he was having it. "She enters the room like a duchess," Benchley told Parker early on, as if trying to convince himself that Goodner was more than what met the eye. As it was, she was pretty, young, and willing—and for Benchley, the temptation proved too much to resist.

If nothing else, the affair with Goodner resulted in the nearly complete division of Benchley's life into two separate entities. The line between Benchley the responsible suburban homeowner with a wife and two children and Benchley the carousing big-city boulevardier with a showgirl at his side was now irrevocably demarcated. Still, the thought of a divorce seems to have never seriously entered his mind. Benchley once remarked to James Thurber that "a man had his wife, whatever their relationship might be, and that was that. The rest was his own business." In the prim environment that he and Gertrude had grown up in, appearances defined one's character in the eyes of the community. So long as scandal was avoided, and so long as both parties understood their positions (whatever those positions might actually be), affairs were best kept under lock and key along with all the other skeletons in the family closet. (From all the evidence, Gertrude Benchley didn't dispute that philosophy. In 1970, some twenty-five years after her husband's death, she told Babette Rosmond, "People asked me if we were going to be divorced—how absurd! Except for the times he was in Hollywood, he called me once, sometimes twice a day. . . . Do you know, in all the years we were married, we never had a cross word!")

A part of Benchley still clung to Gertrude, to his children, to at least the appearance of a proper, respectable existence. Scarsdale became mostly an insurance policy, a safety net against his life's getting completely out of control—and though his affair with Goodner was but the first of many extramarital relationships for Benchley, he held on to that policy. Whatever he did, no matter how bad a boy he was, he believed he could still go home, and that everything there would remain as it was supposed to be. And, thanks to Gertrude's own sense of responsibility, it did. Benchley never told anyone he stopped loving her, and in his own way, he probably didn't. He continued to call her every day, and later in life, when he spent more and more time in California, he wrote her with remarkable regularity—even if his letters, in time, took on the this-is-what-I've-been-doing narrative tone of a son dutifully writing to his mother.

Also contributing—and in an increasingly major way by the mid-1920s—to the new "bad" Benchley was an ingredient that no doubt helped provide at least part of the stimulus for behavior that the old Benchley would never have tolerated. It was found in a bottle, and it was illegal throughout the 1920s. Its name was alcohol.

The Eighteenth Amendment to the Constitution of the United States—the Volstead Act—which prohibited the sale and distribution of beer, wine, and all distilled spirits, had gone into effect at midnight on January 15, 1920. And no sooner did it become law than drinking became the number one participatory sport in the country. Virtually overnight, most major American cities started sprouting basement and back-alley establishments in which otherwise upstanding citizens congregated to take part in an activity for which, technically, they could be arrested. As the temperance unions and religious organizations that had applied the necessary pressure on Congress to get the law passed soon found out, outlawing what they perceived as perhaps the chief cause of society's ills not only failed to alleviate those ills (the rise of the organized crime syndicates might very well never have happened had it not been for the creation of the new and lucrative crime of bootlegging), but also was directly responsible for introducing a whole new segment of America to the world of taverns, as going out for drinks at a speakeasy became a fashionable and "exciting" social event.

Before Prohibition, the old drinking house, the saloon, was a public place frequented by an almost exclusively male, working-class clientele who went there primarily to drink cheap beer and whiskey and secondarily to fraternize. The rich and refined usually did most of their drinking in the privacy of the home, where a well-stocked liquor cabinet was a symbol of affluence and success. Prohibition turned this whole class system inside out. The new drinking house, the speakeasy, was a private place where a mixed clientele of men and women came to drink ridiculously expensive beer and whiskey, and they came as much to socialize with friends and meet new people as they did to sample the bootlegger's goods. It was now mostly the poor and working class who were home drinking gin—gin that came from a bathtub, not some fancy bottle. The well-to-do dressed up and showed off their connections with "the right people" by saying the designated password or flashing the proper card to the man guarding the bolted door, thereby gaining entrance to dimly lit cellars where the unventilated air reeked of cigarette and cigar smoke and the alcohol was distributed in paper cups or inexpensive teacups, which could easily be disposed of in the event of a raid by the authorities.

Not that such a thing was really ever likely to occur at most "better" speakeasies, though, since the proprietors of those well-frequented establishments made certain that the local constabulary was nicely compensated for leaving their "joints" alone to operate in peace. Besides, few big-city law enforcement agencies spent much time actively trying to close down speakeasies. True, the federal government sought to crack down on the large-scale smugglers and bootleggers, but to the average cop on the beat, the speakeasy was just a place where regular folks—often his very own friends and neighbors—were coming together to "commit a crime" in which no one was really going to get hurt, at least not until the hangovers kicked in the next morning. If there were signs of some actual trouble, like a full-scale riot breaking out, then, sure, there might be a raid, but that would be the only time you'd ever catch most policemen stepping inside. At least in uniform. Once a shift was over, one might well spot the off-duty patrolman right there at the bar among the other customers, downing a few free drinks, courtesy of the management, before heading home.

Still, it was that very illusion of danger, that possibility, however faint, of "getting caught," that helped make the speakeasy such a tempting place to so many people. A person went there and felt like part of the scene, part of the "in" crowd, part of that portion of America that was standing up to an unjust law and was determined to enjoy itself, even if that meant a trip inside a paddy wagon—and wouldn't *that* be something to tell your friends about! If you were a person with anything on the ball, you *had* to know a few good places in town that would let you in and serve you a drink.

For almost a year into Prohibition, Robert Benchley, a man with plenty on the ball, went into speakeasies freely, but not one drop of liquor passed his lips. He had, after all, grown up under the hawk-like eye of a mother who was appalled by other people's drinking, and who never failed to reprimand his father whenever she harbored even the slightest suspicion that he might have stopped to sip a beer downtown before coming home from work. The research paper Benchley had done at Harvard documenting the decreased crime rate in Worcester after the town had voted to go dry well before the Volstead Act had been written into the nation's Constitution—hadn't that helped confirm his feelings? Alcohol made a man behave unpredictably; it caused him to lose his sense of decency, his self-respect. Those drunks one saw every now and then lying on the streets of New York—there was the proof of what alcohol did to you.

At least that's what he believed until he started accompanying Parker and Stewart and his other Algonquin friends to these speakeasies that were fast becoming all the rage. First of all, he couldn't believe just how many of these places there were around town. No matter what kind of crowd one ran with, there seemed to be a particular speakeasy catering to it. There were collegiate joints like the Pre Catalan and Matt Winkle's; the latter was such a favorite with the Ivy Leaguers that both the Yale and Harvard campus newspapers openly recommended it to students headed off for a weekend in New York. Or Jack Bleeck's Artists and Writers next to the *Tribune* building, which teemed with newspaper types—though its men-only policy (shared by a few "traditional" places along the speakeasy circuit) usually left the Vicious Circle women's rights advocates, Ruth Hale and Jane Grant, fuming whenever it was patronized by their husbands, Broun and Ross.

Eventually, the Round Tablers settled in at two places. Jack Kriendler and Charlie Berns's Puncheon Club on West 49th Street, a "fancy" speakeasy which served not only authentic, imported whiskey but also good food dished out by an authentic, salaried chef, was always the first choice, as long as someone in the crowd could cover the steep prices. Then, if the evening wore on and the money started to run out, it was time to move across the street to Tony Soma's, where cheaper booze and "humble"—i.e., barely edible—Italian food was available to keep the party going a bit longer.

For months, Benchley simply sat at the red-and-white-checked tables at Jack and Charlie's or stood at the cramped bar at Tony's nursing a soft drink or a cup of orange juice while the rest of his friends casually drowned their martinis, manhattans, and pink ladies. But as the hours he spent in speakeasies increased—and it was virtually impossible *not* to wind up in one, be it for dinner or just to kill time, since almost all of his friends preferred to at least go somewhere where they could get a drink if they wanted one without having to resort to a hip flask brought from home—he began to see that great numbers of people were indeed drinking alcohol and remaining very much themselves.

Perhaps their tongues might be a bit looser after a few cocktails—Stewart, in particular, could get a bit crude at times when he'd had a few—but Stewart was also often quite hilarious when he was drinking. There was the time, for example, that Benchley and Stewart had come out of Tony's only to find themselves caught in an unexpected downpour, and Stewart did something Benchley himself never would have had the nerve to do—he nonchalantly jumped under the first umbrella he spotted, grabbed its surprised owner by the arm, officiously announced, "Yale Club, if you please," and merrily took off down the street with his newfound friend. Drinking, it seemed, just brought him out a bit more, took away some of his shyness.

Benchley's feelings about the subject had once been quite strong. He had, after all, proudly voted for the Prohibition candidate in the Massachusetts gubernatorial election in 1915, and on the day that the Eighteenth Amendment was ratified by the last state necessary, he'd confided to his diary, "I never thought I'd live to see this . . . it is almost too good to be true." But the experience of seeing his closest friends hanging out in bars and drinking liquor while continuing to remain nice, hardworking, functioning people—people whose lifestyle he otherwise both respected and admired—was changing him, and he knew it. Of the entire Algonquin crowd, only he was a teetotaler, and while none of them made fun of him because of it—they all liked him too much to do that—he began to worry about the perception, however unfounded, that he somehow sat on a higher moral plane, judging them. The more he went to speakeasies, the more he came to feel that perhaps it was *he* who had a problem, that he'd allowed himself to become a typically prudish New Englander without ever seeing for himself how the "other half" lived. And life, the twenties were fairly screaming in his ear, was for living.

One night in the fall of 1920, Benchley stood at the bar at Tony's, flanked on one side by Dorothy Parker and on the other by Donald Stewart. Stewart, about to order their drinks, laughingly asked Benchley if he wanted "the usual"—namely, orange juice. "No, I don't think so," he answered. "Why don't *you* order me something?"

Stewart and Parker looked first at each other, then at Benchley. "You mean, you wish us to order you a *drink*, Mr. Benchley?" asked Parker.

"Er, um, yes—I believe I do," he said. "Let's find out what all the fuss is about."

Soon an orange blossom was staring him in the face, and for a while, Benchley just stared right back. Then, with great deliberation, he lifted the cup to his lips, leaned back, swallowed, made a sour face, and ceremoniously put the drink back on the bar and shoved it away.

"Well, Bob, what do you think?" asked Stewart.

"I think," Benchley answered, "that this place ought be closed down by the law."

Parker and Stewart cracked up, and soon all of the Algonquin Round Table had heard the news: Teetotaling Robert Benchley, at the tender age of thirty-one, had had his first social drink. Few of them had any idea, however, just how quickly—and prodigiously—he would make up for lost time.

Benchley soon developed a taste for several types of alcohol—especially scotch, gin, and rye. The first time he drank rye, the smell of it suddenly evoked a childhood memory of his uncle Albert Prentice, who, he realized, had smelled just like that. So that's why Uncle Albert was always heading out to the barn to take care of assorted "chores" all day long, and always smelled stronger when he returned. Another thing Benchley quickly developed was an impressive tolerance to alcohol—a tolerance that almost always enabled him to function in a stimulated state without appearing drunk, even to his closest friends. According to Marc Connelly, the outward appearance of a drinking problem "would never have been accepted at the Algonquin. . . . One day Bob came to lunch really drunk, and the contrast was remarkable. We realized then that Benchley had been reasonably sober all the years we'd known him, when, knowing how funny he always was, we assumed otherwise."

Right around the time Benchley was making ready to find a residence in Manhattan, he found a kindred soul, and drinking partner, in the form of Charles MacArthur.

According to his close friend and collaborator Ben Hecht, MacArthur's first encounter with Robert Benchley occurred, prophetically enough, over the punch bowl at a congested, snobbish affair at which both were seeking refuge from the stuffed shirts surrounding them. When MacArthur casually remarked to another guest that the party's hostess was acting, in his opinion, just a bit too "enthroned," Benchley, overhearing what he later admiringly recalled as "the first actual language I'd ever heard at a Social Party," sauntered over and introduced himself. In no time they were inseparable—and, all too often, insufferable.

Benchley and MacArthur shared an apartment on Madison Avenue for almost three years—years which midtown Manhattan had a tough time surviving. The heights of frivolity to which these two were able to inspire each other were perhaps best summed up by the eventual Mrs. MacArthur, Helen Hayes, who finally captured this most elusive good-time Charlie and somewhat settled him down in 1926, thus ending the duo's reign of mayhem. "Singly," Miss Hayes wrote in her autobiography, *On Reflection*, "each was an urbane and witty man; together they became a menace to society."

Charles MacArthur had ventured to New York in the early twenties from Chicago, where he'd made a moderate name for himself as an all-purpose reporter on the *Examiner*, a tabloid with a penchant for scandal, murder, and assorted outrages. (He would later, together with fellow ex-reporter Hecht, fashion the hit play, and subsequent movie, *The Front Page*, out of his experiences there.) He had had a stern upbringing. His father, an evangelist from Pennsylvania, ruled with a Bible-thumping iron hand. When Charlie was seven, his father had refused to let his mother lance a giant boil which had sprung up on the boy's neck, believing it to be the manifestation of the devil's presence in his soul; when, after a week, the boil finally broke, he claimed a victory in God's name.

MacArthur's schooling was equally harsh. Though he showed absolutely no inclination to follow in his father's footsteps, he was nonetheless sent off to an austere missionary training academy near the family's home in Nyack, New York, where he was continually warned about the evils of such "heathen" activities as movie watching, dancing, and even unauthorized reading. Small wonder, then, that as soon as he was old enough, he "escaped" to the battlefields of first Mexico and then Europe. He landed in Chicago at the end of World War I, hooked up with a newspaper, and never looked back. He arrived in New York City with little cash, an estranged wife, and shaky job prospects, but his good looks, intelligence, easy manner, and joie-de-vivre were so winning that in no time he became both an always welcome guest at Algonquinite gatherings and a dependable feature player in many Benchley-related shenanigans.

To the mirthmaking firm of Benchley and MacArthur, no stunt was too outlandish, no prank too childish, no practical joke too complicated; if there was even the slightest possibility of some fun to be had, they'd spring into action. And, professionals that they were in the jollity business, they often pulled off their capers strictly for each other's amusement. There was, for example, the time when Benchley and MacArthur, cavorting down Fifth Avenue, happened to recognize Charles Even Hughes, the former Supreme Court justice who was currently serving as the country's Secretary of State. Within seconds, they were fast on the diplomat's trail, shouting out, "Mr. Secretary of State! Mr. Secretary of State!" Hughes, more than a tad surprised at being recognized, turned to face the strangers calling after him. "Yes, gentlemen?" he asked. "Mr. Secretary of State! Mr. Secretary of State!" they kept shouting. *"Why aren't you down in Washington doing your job?"* Hughes, his face flushed, spun around and hurriedly took off down the avenue, but that didn't stop the catcalls, jeers, and raspberries. "Yoo hoo! Mr. Secretary! We know it's you!" called the voices. Finally, the besieged Hughes bolted from the street, flagged down a taxi, and sped away—leaving behind his tormentors, who by this time were collapsed on the curb, doubled over with laughter.

Running into famous people and then doing something to disrupt their day apparently was a particular speciality of the Benchley-MacArthur team, as Theodore Roosevelt's son Teddy found out. One very early Sunday morning Benchley and MacArthur were walking home after picking up the Sunday papers when they spied the young Roosevelt coming down the street. They hailed him down and proceeded to engage the young army colonel in a lengthy conversation concerning military protocol. That is, Benchley proceeded to engage Roosevelt in conversation. MacArthur, moving behind the colonel, quietly placed his stack of newspapers in a neat pile behind Roosevelt's feet, took out a match, and started a fire. "Somewhat chilly for this time of year, isn't it, Colonel?" mused Benchley as the flames crept up toward the seat of Roosevelt's pants. "Well, actually, it seems to be getting a bit warmer," answered Roosevelt. "In fact, it's quite . . . quite . . . *my God, I'm on fire!*" Trying desperately to keep straight faces, Benchley and MacArthur furiously waved their hats at Roosevelt's behind while the befuddled victim stamped out the fire on the ground and started down the deserted street for signs of the street urchins that MacArthur swore he saw running away just as the fire began.

According to Nathaniel Benchley, the most elaborate practical joke came about when MacArthur somehow talked the owners of a mausoleum in Union, New Jersey, into letting him serve as their public relations representative. MacArthur, like Benchley, was constantly in debt, and he had somehow pried loose $1,000 from the mausoleum's owners by convincing them to open a "Poet's Corner" in which would be entombed the remains of famous scribes. His advance, he explained, was necessary to fund a campaign to try to get the bones of Henry Wadsworth Longfellow unearthed from a simple grave in Boston and moved to the New Jersey resting place. Even if they failed, MacArthur told his employers, the publicity generated would be invaluable, and certain to attract plenty of new business.

To get things under way, MacArthur wrote a letter to the mayor of Boston, James M. Curley, asking him to use the power of his office to have Longfellow's skeleton dug up and shipped to Union. The city of Boston, he explained, had shown itself not worthy of housing the great poet's remains, since it was not honoring his express wishes. Had not one of Longfellow's poems stated that "Life is real! Life is earnest! And the grave is not its goal"? And didn't that mean that burying him in a grave, as the city of Boston had done, had deprived him of what he'd really hoped for after his death—namely, entombment in a crypt, such as the most famous "Poet's Corner" in Union, New Jersey?

The letter, sent on mausoleum stationery and signed by one of the staff's clergy (having the signature of a man of the cloth attached to the request would, MacArthur asserted, give it more weight), received a speedy—and bewildered—response from Mayor Curley. Henry Wadsworth Longfellow wasn't buried in Boston, but in Cambridge, Curley explained, and since that town was outside his jurisdiction, the matter was out of his hands. Cambridge's mayor, he suggested, would be the proper person to discuss this matter with—although he didn't understand why, so long after his death, Longfellow's remains were suddenly a pressing issue. Benchley, after reading Curley's reply, came up with an idea. Why not turn this into a *very* pressing issue, perhaps even a *national* one?

Immediately, Benchley and MacArthur began sending out scores of telegrams to Curley, all demanding that he relinquish Longfellow's body, or face (pardon the expression) grave political consequences. The messages poured into the mayor's office, signed with the names of whatever fictitious organizations Benchley and MacArthur could think of. Soon the Boston papers picked up on the story, chronicling the efforts of "The Longfellow Lovers of America," "The Longfellow Society of Union, New Jersey," and "The Parochial Students' League for Longfellow"—all of which were apparently reachable through the mausoleum's public relations consultant, Charles MacArthur. Curley finally put two and two together and contacted the mausoleum owners, who, after apologizing profusely for any trouble they might have caused either the mayor or the city of Boston, promptly informed MacArthur that his "services" were no longer required.

That Benchley and MacArthur made such an ideal pair was hardly surprising, since the two had much in common. MacArthur, like Benchley, was a talented writer who worked hard but didn't find it hard to work—the facile manner that Benchley brought to his essays, reviews, and now acting was matched by MacArthur in his newspaper work and short stories, and soon in his writings for the theater—

and their respective strict upbringings had left them with similar, almost limitless, energies for instigating devilishly good times on the streets and in the speakeasies of 1920s New York.

If it is ironic that Benchley might never have begun to drink had it not been for Prohibition and speakeasies, it is also ironic that had it not been for Prohibition and speakeasies, Benchley might never have begun to bend elbows and rub shoulders with some of the country's richest and most socially influential people. With economic good times abounding, a new breed of young and wealthy Americans saw the speakeasies as part of a vibrant and different scene—*their* scene, marked by bobbed hairdos, jazz music, and bootleg whiskey. They flocked to the speakeasies to feel fashionable and adventurous, to celebrate themselves and the new age they were a part of. They were the emerging members of high society, and when they went to the speakeasies and bumped—literally—into Benchley, Parker, Stewart, and the rest of the Algonquin crowd, they were smitten. "The speakeasy was a kind of club where what counted was not social position, but whether the people one met there were fun to be with," noted Donald Stewart. And, as young bon vivants like Averell Harriman, Robert Lovett, and John Hay Whitney soon discovered, the Round Tablers were nothing if not fun to be with—as long as they liked you, of course. And, by and large, the Smart Set hit it off quite well with the Society Set.

Before the era of the speakeasies helped, in Stewart's words, to "merge [the borders] together in the interests of having a good time," the closest glimpse that Benchley's crowd had ever really caught of the world of high society came though the goodwill of *World* publisher Herbert Swope, who often invited his op-ed "boys" (as he called them) and their friends out to his Great Neck, Long Island, estate for weekend-long parties that were sufficiently opulent to whet everyone's appetite for the "good life." At the Swope home, visitors would come and go irrespective of the hour, so much so that guests sitting down in the immense dining room were always offered the choice of breakfast, lunch, or dinner, and even the simplest request would be met with an extravagant response—as when a guest who innocently inquired about the possibility of there being a stick of chewing gum in the house soon found himself gazing at a servant holding a silver tray upon which rested six full packs of various-flavored gums.

It was also primarily through trips to the Swope estate that the Round Table's decade-long affair with the upscale game of croquet was promoted and nurtured, as Swope's manicured lawns were the stage for marathon matches (often with stakes running into the thousands) which often extended beyond sunset and were completed only after cars were moved into position around the course and their headlights switched on to provide the obsessed players with sufficient light. In fact, the Algonquinites became so enthralled with the sport that in October 1923, an F.P.A. "Samuel Pepys" column documented the Round Tablers actually going to the trouble of getting a permit to play croquet in Central Park. "We tried to find a name for the club," wrote Adams, "and Dot [Parker] said the Jolly Rovers, but that, we said, was deceiving, forasmuch as we were not rovers until we had gone through the last wickets, so Rob [Benchley] said the West Side La Cross Club, and that, quoth I, shall be." It is unknown just how many 1924 Sheep Meadow passersby realized that the rotund man gleefully smashing his opponent's ball clear off the course and into the woods was Alexander Woollcott, that the gruff, gap-toothed man heading off into the woods after that ball and screaming at the laughing fat man was Harold Ross, or that the demure-looking little woman with the big hat holding a tiny dog in one hand and a mallet in the other was Dorothy Parker, but such scenes apparently prevailed whenever the Round Tablers found themselves up for a few rounds but lacking more exclusive facilities. Before long, though, those more exclusive facilities began to become progressively more available to the Algonquinites as they increased their contact with high society, much of it stemming initially from the speakeasies and their close cousins the entertainment-filled after-hours clubs—like the Durant Club, presided over by the irrepressible Jimmy Durante, and the Club Trocadero, where a brother-and-sister team named Fred and Adele Astaire performed their dazzling dance routines before thrilled audiences.

As Donald Stewart noted, the new "Elite" were different in that they actively sought the friendship of people like him and Parker and

Benchley—people who, in earlier, more snobbish times, would have been dismissed as unacceptable companions. "They hated the stuffiness of Newport and all that pre–World War I pretentiousness," wrote Stewart, and were delighted to be able to share with the Round Tablers some of the accouterments of their wealth and social status. This extended, it turned out, considerably farther than the townhouses on Manhattan's East Side or the mansions of Long Island's Great Neck, Manhasset, and Syosset. Come to Europe, the Algonquinites' new rich acquaintances told them, and let us show you around. The offers, made earnestly and genuinely, were quickly taken up, and soon a good number of the Round Table were setting up summer headquarters on the French Riviera; the chance to spend one's days languishing on glistening beaches and one's nights enjoying good food and wholly *legal* drink seemed much too good to pass up.

Benchley had followed his nine-month stint with the *Music Box Revue* with a ten-week engagement performing "The Treasurer's Report" on the Keith traveling vaudeville circuit, and toward the end of the tour, in the spring of 1925, he telephoned Gertrude and told her that since he desperately needed a vacation, since he'd hardly seen his family for much of the previous year and a half, and since the Broadway season was coming to its usual late-spring close (as a rule, new shows never opened during the summer months), he thought it would be a good idea for all of them to take off on a trip to Europe. (His guilt over his affair with Goodner, who was now in England and had notified him that she was ending their relationship, most likely also contributed to the offer.) Stewart, who seemed to have quite a knack for meeting the right kind of people wherever he went, had been making regular sojourns to Paris ever since 1921, and he set Benchley up with two of the swing members of the literary-social set, playwright Philip Barry and his socialite wife, Ellen, who had a house in Cannes and promised to find the Benchleys something they could rent in nearby Cap d'Antibes, which was fast becoming the "in" spot for well-to-do Americans.

Until the twenties, the south of France had always been considered almost exclusively a winter resort, but the early part of the decade saw such an influx of wealthy tourists into the region during all parts of the year that by 1925 such places as the Grand Hôtel du

Cap and the Villa des Violettes, which previously had been closed for the summer season because of lack of business, were now doing a booming one. Arriving in France via a Holland-America Line cruiser in April, the Benchleys soon found themselves in familiar company— Stewart, Woollcott (who, according to Gertrude Benchley, "would swim out to a raft on the water, roll his one-piece French maillot swim-suit down to his waist, and sit there cross-legged, looking just like a Buddha, surrounded by a group of interested listeners"), English actor Roland Young (who had been one of the headlining stars on the Keith vaudeville tour Benchley had taken part in), Scott and Zelda Fitzgerald, Archibald and Ada MacLeish, and the unofficial host and hostess for the American literati in France, Gerald and Sara Murphy.

"Gerald Murphy was intelligent, perceptive, gracious, and one of the most attractive men I have ever known, and his wife Sara was the perfect complement to these virtues," wrote Stewart in remembrance of the Murphys, whom he first met in Paris in 1923. "If this sounds like a child's fable beginning, 'Once upon a time there was a prince and princess . . . ,' that's exactly how a description of the Murphys should begin. They were both rich; he was handsome; she was beautiful; they had three golden children. They loved each other, they enjoyed their own company, and they had the gift of making life enchantingly pleasurable for those who were fortunate enough to be their friends." Murphy's father had left him the Mark Cross leather goods company, but the Yale graduate, not interested in running the day-to-day affairs of the business, had simply gone off with his bride, Sara, to live a life of leisure in France. Murphy continually expressed a desire to paint, but guests of the Murphys at their home in Paris or their villa on the Riviera rarely saw the "artist" at work. Instead, Stewart believed, "Gerald's primary concern was to live as he and Sara wanted to live, and their money gave them the opportunity."

The Murphys' way of life, it turned out, was simply to have as good a time as possible all of the time, and the couples' unending hospitality was not wasted on Cole Porter (a Murphy classmate at Yale), John Dos Passos, Douglas Fairbanks, Pablo Picasso, and the incredible array of actors, dancers, writers, musicians, and artists who helped keep the Murphy household filled with a gaiety and glitter that reminded most of the Algonquin visitors of a Neysa McMein studio gath-

ering all done up in evening clothes and whisked off to a fantasy setting by the sea. And, best of all, the Murphys never acted as though
they sought to impress with their obviously great riches—they wanted
solely to entertain and be entertained.

The summer of 1925 proved to be a splendidly gay—and refresh-
ingly uneventful—one for Benchley, who watched as nine-year-old
Nathaniel and five-year-old Bobby frolicked in the sand with the Murphy children or helped the eternally juvenile Fitzgerald set up his vast
collection of lead toy soldiers for afternoon-long battles conducted
on the parlor floor of the Fitzgeralds' rented house in Cannes. Outside of a Stewart-accompanied excursion to Munich, Vienna, and
Budapest in order to conduct a survey of foreign theater for his *Life*
drama page—a trip recalled by Stewart as "a joyful progress through
the museums and vineyards of Austria and Hungary interrupted only
once or twice by touches of reality"—Benchley's three-month stay in
Europe was highlighted primarily by the fact that it was on this vacation that Robert Benchley, bon vivant and boulevardier extraordi-
naire, made his one and only known contribution to the world of male
fashion, serving as the motivating force behind the creation of an
oversized briefcase known as the "Noah" bag.

The idea of the bag came about when Gerald Murphy took Benchley to several horse races at Paris's Longchamps racetrack, where
Benchley became so captivated by a large feedbag that one of the
jockeys was toting over his arm that Murphy, in a characteristic move,
personally designed, and had his company manufacture, a line of
natural-grain-leather tote bags. The first one produced was bestowed
upon Benchley as a gift for inspiring its conception. Upon receiving
the spacious satchel, Benchley promptly dubbed it the "Noah" bag,
because of its capacity to hold "two of everything," and not only did
he carry one wherever he went, but he also gave away scores of them
throughout the years as presents to favorite friends.

From 1925 until the mid-thirties, when escalating tensions brought
on by the rise to power of Hitler in Germany, the establishment of
the Rome-Berlin axis, and civil war in Spain cost Europe most of its
allure for American tourists, scarcely a year went by without some sort
of Benchley expedition overseas. In the winter of 1926, Ernest Hemingway made a much-ballyhooed trip to New York in order to break

his publishing contract with Boni & Liveright and sign a more lucrative one with Scribner's. After being introduced by Stewart, who'd made Hemingway's acquaintance in Paris several years earlier and had gotten to know him well enough to serve as his sidekick when he went to Spain in 1924 for the celebrated "run of the bulls" through the streets of Pamplona, Benchley and Parker helped usher the author of the newly published *The Sun Also Rises* around town for several weeks of carousing. When it came time for him to leave New York, the appreciative Hemingway, seeking to reciprocate for the fine time Benchley and Parker had shown him, invited the two of them to join him on the voyage back to France aboard the S.S. *Roosevelt*. On literally just a moment's notice, they accepted—leading to a short but apparently rollicking Atlantic crossing and week-long holiday with Hemingway, and the ever-present Murphys, seeing the sights in Paris, Cherbourg, and Montana Vermala, a Swiss skiing village where Benchley, assisted by head cheerleader Parker, late one night serenaded the darkened and deserted Alpine streets with a homesick boy's medley of Harvard football fight songs.

In 1928, Benchley took off for what he thought was going to be just a short visit to Great Britain at the insistence of John Hay ("Jock") Whitney, a wealthy young man whom Benchley had become friendly with as they continually ran into each other along the speakeasy/society circuit. Whitney, who would later in life own the *New York Herald Tribune* and be chief benefactor of the New York museum that bears his name, was known at the time mainly as the footloose playboy son of millionaire Payne Whitney and an avid follower of the racehorses that the family raised at its upstate New York stables in Saratoga. This particular year, a Whitney-owned thoroughbred was competing in England's prestigious Grand National race, and Jock was deputized to represent the family—which he did, accompanied by his old Philadelphia school chum Jimmie Altemus and his new New York speakeasy chum Robert Benchley. (Actually, few people ever heard Whitney call Benchley anything but "Gramps," a nickname that Whitney tagged him with in mock deference to the fifteen years' difference in age that separated them. The name stuck so well that, before long, most of Benchley's own family started using it.)

Benchley later claimed to have missed the race entirely because of his inability to manipulate a pair of binoculars. In a piece called "They're off!" he wrote, "I can swing them jauntily by my side before the race starts, and I can hold them up to my eyes (until my arms get tired—then to hell with them), but I can't seem to see anything except an indistinct blur of grass and an object which later turns out to be the back of the head of one of the officials. The last time I used field glasses at a horse race I thought I saw a rowboat in the distance manned by a suspiciously large number of oarsmen; with my naked eye I can at least see the surrounding country, and without the complication of strange rowboats." Afterward, Whitney suggested that the threesome take a few side trips on the continent. Considering himself something of a veteran of foreign travel, Benchley spent the last night in London dutifully examining his collection of train schedules, and got up the next morning ready to show off his perfectly arranged itinerary—only to have Whitney tell him that he'd decided to charter a private plane, complete with pilot *and* mechanic, to take them over to Paris. And Benchley soon found out that familiarity with Europe's intricate rail system was superfluous while traveling with a Whitney.

"Jock intended to use the plane only on the trip to Paris," Benchley wrote to Gertrude from Germany on March 21, "but he's kept it ever since and we have flown everywhere without ever getting on a train. We stayed in Paris until Sunday, chiefly going to theatres and night clubs. Then we flew to Berlin. Then, on Friday, we flew to Vienna, stopping at Prague along the way. Monday to Budapest and today here to Munich. Friday we hope to return to Paris—making about twelve or thirteen hundred miles of flying so far."

Equally superfluous on this particular trip, Benchley noted, was a knowledge of hotel room rates. "Needless to say," he continued in his letter, "I am travelling in a style that is pretty new to me. We have a sitting room and two bedrooms and baths in each hotel and there is a general rush among the help to do things for us. Jock has so far insisted on paying the hotel bills, saying that I wouldn't be getting such layouts if I were alone, but I don't like that exactly and intend to pay some arranged fee per day according to what I would have paid myself.

"The only drawback [in flying] as a party affair is that you can't talk unless you scream—the motors are so noisy—and you have to keep running up and down the length of the plane to keep warm because there's no heat."

Benchley ended his account of this journey by apologizing to Gertrude for his belated correspondence. "I am terribly sorry to have been so lax in writing," he wrote, "but there is something about flying which makes it hard to concentrate when you are on the ground." Despite all the dizzying changes in altitude, his wit didn't desert him. When the chartered plane landed back in Paris at the conclusion of the country-hopping trip, Benchley allegedly emerged from the cabin, removed his helmet, stood at attention, and shouted out, "I am Charles Lindbergh!"

In 1929, Benchley again took his family to France for the summer, with accommodations this time provided by the Murphys, who had transformed several structures in the middle of the orange grove on their Cap d'Antibes villa into cottages and were "renting" them out to friends at modest fees. (The cottages were christened "Ferme des Orangers" by the Murphys; Benchley renamed them "La Ferme Dérangée.") It was during this three-month stay that Benchley, not the world's most physically active person to begin with, swore off swimming, which was, by this point in his life, the only actual exercise except walking that he even sporadically took. The reason was sunstroke, which Benchley suffered one afternoon when he fell asleep on the Antibes beach after a two-mile swim with Gerald Murphy. The attack didn't come on at once; no one knew anything was wrong with him until much later that day, when the Benchleys and Murphys went to dinner at the Colombe d'Or in Saint-Paul, an old walled city renowned because the Romans used to send signal fires from atop its ramparts to announce battlefield victories. When Benchley suddenly rose from his seat in the restaurant and insisted that he could see a Roman centurion running along a nearby wall, everyone assumed he was joking. When he persisted and then said he was feeling faint, everyone knew he wasn't. The next day, his family was unable to rouse him, and his fever remained quite high for several days, finally subsiding just before the local doctor called in to attend him was about to administer the rather severe French cure-all known as *ventouses*— heavy glass cups, into which cotton balls dipped in alcohol are placed, then ignited, are inverted and applied to the patient's back, causing a suction and thus bringing about a rising of the blood to the surface and, presumably, the desired effect of increased circulation.

"I shall be applying some *ventouses* now," the doctor told Benchley.

"Not unless you make sure they're blondes," responded Benchley, pretending that the physician had said *vendeuses*—salesladies. At that point it was apparent that Benchley was well on the road to recovery, and he was spared the unorthodox treatment. But he never did do much swimming or sunbathing after this episode.

Benchley took his mother to France in 1930 so that the then almost eighty-year-old Jennie could visit her niece Dot Goddard, who was living in Paris at the time, and on this particular trip Benchley managed to do the unthinkable: he actually consumed alcohol in his mother's presence. On the very first night aboard ship, Benchley, accustomed by this time to capping off his meals with at least one after-dinner drink, unthinkingly asked the waiter to bring him a white crème de menthe. Between the time he ordered it and the time it arrived, he figured out what to tell Jennie—namely, that he was having problems with his digestion and had been directed by his physician to take a peppermint drink after dinner every night. Jennie simply nodded understandingly, and each evening thereafter, Benchley sampled a different colorless drink, from kirsch to Cointreau, and, dutiful mother that she was, the one night that Benchley forgot to ask for a drink, she reminded him that it was time to take his medicine.

(It's possible that by this time, Jennie Benchley's attitude toward drinking had softened, at least slightly. In the midst of the voyage, she accidentally wandered into the bar one afternoon and thought the whole thing was quite funny. "I was staggering, too," she joked to her son afterward. "I suppose it will be all over Worcester by the time I get home.")

Perhaps best remembered about Benchley's travels abroad are the bon voyage parties that preceded them. There was, for example, the time that Benchley, leaving on short notice and assured in the midst of predeparture revelries that his friends would see to all the packing that needed to be done, set sail with a suitcase filled entirely with assorted New York metropolitan area telephone directories. (Not that Benchley was in any condition, or position, to complain—he and Marc

Connelly once left a stack of flapjacks and a one-hundred-pound bust of Beethoven in the Europe-bound Alexander Woollcott's cabin as "parting gifts.") Or the time that Benchley, in the role of seer-off to Jock Whitney and Nicholas Luddington, participated in so many toasts in their stateroom aboard the docked ship that he never did hear the departure whistle and wound up going with them to Paris—with $7 in his pocket, no passport, and no change of clothes. How did he survive? Whitney paid for the room, the ship steward took his clothes away every night and returned them, washed, each morning, and a U.S. consul in Bremen who had attended Harvard with him smuggled him through customs without the official documents.

"Traveling in a style that is pretty new to me" indeed.

12
A Funny Face and Some Sound Advice

"I LIKE IT BEST WITH THE ROPE IN THE MIDDLE"

S_{everal} $days$ before his wedding to Beatrice Ames in July 1926, Donald Stewart took his best man, Benchley, to see the Church of All Angels by the Sea, the Montecito, California, chapel where the ceremony was to take place. As the two peered out at the bright ribbon of white sands and the calm blue waters of the Pacific, Benchley pointed a skeptical finger toward the horizon. "I don't trust that ocean," he said to Stewart. "It's just pretending to be peaceful, waiting for the right time to sweep up and in and over everything."

Benchley's initial impressions of California in general and Hollywood in particular on this, his first ever venture west, could probably best be characterized as bewildering. Stewart had been in Hollywood for better than half a year working as a scriptwriter for the fledgling Metro-Goldwyn-Mayer movie company, and from everything he'd told Benchley about his experiences so far, it seemed an utterly bizarre place in which to work or live. Stewart's long-standing desire to break into the motion picture business had intensified ever since a 1924 women's club lecture tour brought him to Los Angeles and into contact with the wives of several Hollywood producers and directors, who, in turn, introduced the starstruck writer to their influential husbands. His big chance came in 1925 when his book publisher, Boni & Liveright, notified him that MGM had purchased the rights to his novel *The Crazy Fool*, and that he'd been invited to go to Hollywood to write the script for the film.

Stewart arrived in Hollywood and immediately sought an audience with MGM's production chief, Irving Thalberg, since he'd learned that it was the celebrated wunderkind himself who'd personally purchased the book for the film studio. Thalberg, however, proved too elusive to pin down, so it was arranged that Stewart would meet with the prospective director, King Vidor, who, as it happened, had been the one to bring *The Crazy Fool* to Thalberg's attention. Stewart had spent most of his time on the train going cross-country filling notebooks with ideas and suggestions for the transformation of the book into a motion picture, and when he arrived at Vidor's office, he excitedly deposited on the director's desk not only the notebooks, but also several new scenes that he'd recently written in hopes that they could be incorporated into the script. Before long, however, Stewart sensed that Vidor didn't seem to be sharing his enthusiasm; as a matter of fact, he hardly seemed to be paying attention to anything that Stewart was saying, but just sat staring silently at the notebooks set before him. Finally, the puzzled Stewart asked Vidor if there was anything wrong.

"Well, you see, Don," said Vidor, "I got Irving interested in your book by reading him bits of it one weekend out at Catalina. He was crazy about it."

"Oh, I understand," said Stewart. "Mr. Thalberg doesn't want anything in the book *changed*. That's all right, I suppose. Although I do think that—"

"No, I'm afraid you *don't* understand," interrupted Vidor. "I have a rather embarrassing confession to make. What I read Thalberg was part of your book *Perfect Behavior*, and it wasn't until it was too late that I found out that he thought I was reading from *The Crazy Fool*."

"You mean he bought *the wrong book?*" cried Stewart.

"Yes," Vidor laughed, "I'm afraid so. I suppose we'll just have to make the best of it. It *is* a pretty good joke on Irving, though, don't you think?"

At $250 a week, with a guaranteed contract for six months of employment—*Crazy Fool* or no *Crazy Fool*—Stewart wasn't about to argue. Besides, the jokes kept coming. No sooner had Stewart begun to report for work at the Metro offices in Culver City than Vidor was switched over to a different picture, leaving Stewart "free" to try his hand at other scripts while *Crazy Fool* remained in limbo. Not anything of his own, however. "MGM decided that as a Yale graduate I was just the right boy to write the script for an old-time play called *Brown of Harvard*," he later recalled. Stewart tried as hard as he could to make something of the dusty old melodrama, but, he remembered, his struggles to "bring truth and light to the problems of Brown at Harvard were received with pronounced apathy by producer Harry Rapf, who called in two title writers to apply their expertise at what was called 'continuity.' " By June, Stewart had more than a sneaking suspicion that his six-month contract would not be renewed, but there was no doubt that the experience, on the whole, had been more than worthwhile, if not especially on a professional level, then at least on a personal one. Stewart was now friends with stars like Jack

Gilbert and Charlie Chaplin, and, through Marion Davies's invitations, he was even spending weekends at William Randolph Hearst's gargantuan San Simeon estate. Moreover, he'd fallen in love, and was about to be married.

In March, it was announced that Donald Stewart had become betrothed to one Beatrice Ames, a pretty Santa Barbara resident who'd first caught Stewart's eye a year before in Paris. At the time, she was the fiancée of actor Harry Crocker—yet another of Stewart's Yale chums—but that romance had fizzled by the time of Stewart's arrival in Hollywood, and before long it was the writer, not the actor, to whom the eager-to-be-wed Ames was engaged. A July date was set for the nuptials, and Stewart happily wired Benchley, asking him to come to California and serve as best man.

As it happened, Benchley had for several months been doggedly ducking another invitation to come west—that of movie producer Jesse L. Lasky. Unlike Stewart, Benchley had no burning ambitions for a career in screenwriting, but the terms of the contract offered him by Walter Wanger, the Lasky Corporation's general manager, were so good that it seemed foolish to turn down such a profitable way of attending Stewart's wedding. According to an agreement dated June 8, 1926, Benchley would be hired by the Lasky Corporation to work as a writer for a period of six weeks, at a salary of $500 a week. During this time, he would be expected to write "an original story suitable for reproduction as a motion picture screenplay," which, if accepted, would net him an additional payment of $3,500. Moreover, he could be assigned to help out on any films in production requiring captions and titles, with an extra sum of $750 to be paid to him for each film worked on in that capacity.

Benchley's attitude toward the job is apparent in a letter he wrote to Gertrude, vacationing with Nat and Bobby in Nantucket, shortly after his arrival in California. "The most important part," he explained, "is that, whether I do any work or not, I am getting $500 a week. If, and when, I finally hand in a story which they take, I get the $3,500. I am on salary from the day I reached here, which was July 7th. And you can bet your life that at the end of those six weeks I duck—story or no story." Hollywood, after all, was the last place in the world where a theater critic would want to try to make a living. But as a short diversion—as what he was sure wasn't going to be much more than a paid vacation—there seemed little harm in the venture. Besides, he wasn't the only one using the Stewart-Ames wedding as an excuse to grab some easy Hollywood money. Both Marc Connelly and Herman Mankiewicz had finagled similar filmwriting deals to pay for their trips west to attend the wedding. (In fact, for a few weeks in July, the lobby of the Mark Twain Hotel on Hollywood's North Wilcox Avenue could very well have been mistaken for a road show of the Algonquin Vicious Circle, with Benchley, Connelly, Mankiewicz, Stewart, and playwright-turned-scenarist Laurence Stallings all traipsing about.)

Benchley had been hired by Wanger in the hopes that he could furnish a vehicle for silent comedy star Raymond Griffith, and to that end, Benchley spent most of his days sitting quietly in an office at Paramount Pictures tinkering with a story he titled *Ship Ahoy*. The high-seas farce featured Griffith as a well-heeled boulevardier who accidentally becomes a moneyless stowaway on an ocean liner and spends the entire voyage dressed in evening clothes and top hat pretending to be a cruise line official—that is, until he and the girl whose good looks lured him aboard the cruiser in the first place get shipwrecked on an island that ultimately turns out to be the one called Staten. But Benchley never quite completed the script, and the Lasky Corporation passed on the unfinished eight-page outline he submitted at the end of the six-week term.

For the record, Benchley did emerge from his stint as a Famous Players–Lasky Corporation employee with his very first film credit—the titles for a Griffith picture called *You'd Be Surprised*. At the time, though, the Hollywood community was much more impressed by his emergence from the wings at the Stewart-Ames nuptials on crutches, his left leg in a plaster cast—the result of a tumble down some stairs in the dark at one of the many Santa Barbara parties held in Stewart's honor prior to the wedding. That the cast had been profusely autographed with lewd comments by most of the guests at the bridegroom's bachelor party only added to Benchley's embarrassing popularity at the ceremonies.

(Of course, in case anyone wasn't sufficiently amused by the commentary adorning the cast, Stewart was quick to point out the teeth marks etched into Benchley's cane and make sure that everyone knew just how they got there. "A friend of Bea's named Chris Holmes had an interesting hobby that we somehow neglected to warn Bobby about," Stewart recalled. "When he called at the Holmes residence for the first time and the butler showed him into the study, he found all of the seven chairs occupied by Great Danes who growled ominously each time Bobby moved. Then through the window leaped a small monkey who jumped playfully onto his shoulders and chattered in a language which he didn't recognize. After a bit of this the door opened and in came a medium-sized orangutan who proceeded to search eagerly through Bob's pockets." "He liked my cane almost as much as my crème de menthes," Benchley noted in a letter to Gertrude shortly after the wedding.)

True to his word, Benchley did abandon the Lasky people the minute his contract was up, even though Griffith, whom Benchley found to be "quite a nice man," had asked him along on a trip to Honolulu so that perhaps together the two could work up a new scenario that might prove more appealing to the producers than *Ship Ahoy*. By mid-August, a relieved Benchley was back in New York City; Hollywood, he'd concluded, was simply too strange a place for a sane person to stay in for very long. When Wanger approached him during the winter about the possibility of his returning to California on another writing assignment, Benchley, figuring that the six weeks he'd spent on his first trip west was about twice as long as he felt he could reasonably handle without going batty, responded that he could only come out for three weeks, in July, and that he couldn't agree to do anything more than straight titling. Much to his amazement, Wanger agreed to the terms. So Benchley went out, titled *A Social Celebrity* (starring Adolphe Menjou) and *The American Venus*, and came home feeling as if he'd just robbed a bank and gotten away with it. *Anyone* could do this work (and probably do it better than he, he suspected), and these sunbaked motion picture people were only too happy to keep throwing piles of money at him to come clear across the country to do it. Hollywood, he was now firmly convinced, was not just a place for strange people—it was a place for foolish ones, too.

Upon his return to New York, Benchley received a writing offer from people he didn't consider either strange or foolish. In fact, it may have seemed at first as if he were being rewarded from above for just surviving Hollywood. Broadway producers Alex Aarons and Vinton Freedley were working on a new show called *Smarty*, starring Fred and Adele Astaire, with a score being prepared by George and Ira Gershwin, and they asked Benchley if he was interested in collaborating with Fred Thompson on the book for the musical. They didn't have to ask twice.

Unfortunately for Benchley, what on paper looked like a dream assignment turned out to be anything but. The Astaires hadn't performed in New York in over two years; their show *Lady, Be Good!* had been a bit hit in New York, and when they took it over to England, it became an even bigger one. By the time the dance team returned to the United States in the summer of 1927, they had become full-fledged international stars. No wonder, then, that Aarons and Freedley felt great pressure to come up with a surefire smash to mark the Astaires' return to the Broadway stage—a pressure only magnified by the fact that the two impresarios were using *Smarty* to launch their own newly built theater on 52nd Street, the Alvin (whose name was derived from a combination of the first syllables of the two producers' first names).

Confounding matters further were the problems besetting the script for *Smarty*. Early in their careers, the Astaires often played opposite each other as romantic leads so that they could dance together, but once they'd become famous as real-life siblings, they stopped performing in such roles. And since *Lady, Be Good!* was a show that cast them as brother and sister, they were leery of repeating themselves. In thinking up the framework for their new play, the Astaires and their producers had hit upon the notion of making Fred the protective legal guardian of three girls, one of them Adele. "This seemed to be a good idea," Astaire recalled in his autobiography, *Steps in Time*, "but we had no thought whatsoever about what would happen from there on." Fred Thompson, who'd worked with the Astaires in 1922 on a show called *Stop Flirting*, was put in charge of fleshing out the plot and dialogue, but the producers soon discovered that Thompson, who was known primarily as a rewrite man, was in need of one himself. Which was where Benchley came onto the scene.

It is possible that the excitement he felt about finally getting a chance to do some "real" writing, for the medium he cared about above all others, the theater, clouded Benchley's judgment of what he was getting himself into when he agreed to help coauthor the book for *Smarty*. He may have believed that in the company of such proven talents as the Astaires and the Gershwins, there was little chance that things could go wrong. However, construction setbacks at the Alvin delayed the beginning of official rehearsals for the show, and when they did finally begin, it was evident that the production needed work, and lots of it. The batch of songs which the Gershwins had furnished for the show—including " 'S Wonderful," "My One and Only," "The Babbitt and the Bromide," and "High Hat"—were among the best they'd ever composed, and the Astaires and their dance director, Bobby Connolly, had developed several new routines the Broadway audiences were sure to enjoy. But the songs and dances just weren't fitting in with the book; the comedy, as written, was coming across flat and stodgy. It was the script, everyone agreed, that needed the revamping.

Perhaps under a different set of circumstances, Benchley might have been able to handle the task of whipping up satisfactory new scenes on virtually no notice. But before he could really get his bearings and a grasp on what the frazzled producers wanted from him, it was already time for the show to head off to Philadelphia for the beginning of its out-of-town tryouts. Commuting back and forth between Philadelphia and New York, spending his nights attending shows that he was reviewing for *Life* and his days scrambling around at rehearsals and rewrite sessions with Thompson, Benchley felt a strain and pressure he'd never encountered before. The Philadelphia run went so poorly that ticket brokers in New York refused to make any deals until the show got better notices. When Aarons announced that the New York premiere of the production was being delayed until late November and that he felt almost two-thirds of the show would have to be completely redone, Benchley found himself stuck in a woefully untenable position. Taking their cues from audience reactions each night, Aarons and Freedley were insisting that various scenes be overhauled or completely reconstructed literally on a daily basis, and this naturally required that the writers be continually on call. But Benchley's *Life* duties, as well as other magazine commitments, precluded his accompanying the show to its next preview stops in Washington, D.C., and Wilmington, Delaware. He had no choice. Reluctantly, the disheartened Benchley dropped out of the production.

According to Nathaniel Benchley, one of the last things that Benchley was asked to do before officially leaving the show was to watch the run-through of a particularly troublesome scene that had been through numerous rewrites and was being rehearsed amid a chaotic rearranging of scenery by the stagehands. "Throughout the playing of the scene," wrote Nathaniel, "a rope dangled from the flies, first in the center of the stage, then over to the left, and then across right, and there were times when the actors had to duck to get out of the way. Ladders were moved about, men called to each other from the wings, and idle actors spilled coffee and crumpled sandwich bags. Finally, when the scene was over, Freedley asked Robert what he thought of the new version. 'I like it best with the rope in the middle,' Robert said, and drifted out of the theatre."

By the time the show finally arrived on Broadway in late November 1927, it had a new name, *Funny Face*, and new authors' credits—"Book by Fred Thompson and Paul Gerard Smith." (The producers had offered to leave Benchley's name in, but since virtually everything he'd contributed had eventually been taken out of the script, he declined.) That it also arrived as a hit only served to increase Benchley's embarrassment about the entire project. From all of his years as a critic, he knew that everything that precedes the curtain's going up on opening night is merely prologue; the show, after all, doesn't really exist until then. But here he'd been given the opportunity to be the coauthor of a Broadway-bound show, and he'd simply fumbled it away. That there were a multitude of excuses available ultimately did not matter. Connelly, Kaufman, Ferber, Stallings, Sherwood—they'd all written plays, *original* plays, which had made it to the stage and had been hits. He, on the other hand, had been given the chance to take part in a can't-miss proposition that, after all was said and done, had not missed. It didn't matter that there were troubles along the way; all new shows have kinks and knots that have to be worked out. He'd underestimated the amount of time and work that would be involved in such an undertaking, and had wound up over his head. Even the most loyal of his friends, like Dorothy Parker, who'd been telling everyone for weeks that "Bob wrote a fine musical comedy, and they massacred it so that he wouldn't go near it," couldn't say very much (except perhaps about the public's taste) after the show began playing to sold-out houses at the Alvin. And neither could he. *Smarty* left Benchley smarting.

On an early morning in January 1928, less than two months after *Funny Face* premiered on the Broadway stage, Benchley stood on a movie set in Astoria, Queens, most likely wondering to himself if the new film he was working on was going to be an even bigger personal disaster than the play he was still trying to forget. It certainly had the potential. Back in Hollywood the previous summer, a William Fox executive named Thomas Chalmers had begun hounding Benchley about the possiblity of getting him to do some work for the Fox studios—as an actor! Benchley would hear nothing of it at first, but eventually Chalmers cornered him long enough to explain the proposition.

Like many of the other motion picture companies at the time, Fox was experimenting with the use of sound in its films, and the company was looking for the proper vehicle to showcase its new Movietone talking picture process. Chalmers had seen Benchley perform "The Treasurer's Report" on stage several years before, and was positive that the monologue was an ideal choice for such a picture. There had been dozens of films during the previous year which had employed some sound—mostly bits of music, snatches of dialogue, and sound effects—but never for more than a minute or two; "The Treasurer's Report" would be the first continuous sound picture ever attempted by a major studio. Moreover, shooting could be done in New York, thus sparing Benchley any unwanted travel or major upset in what Chalmers knew was an already busy schedule. Reluctant as ever when it came to working in the movie business, Benchley found it impossible to say no. For $2,000, he would go to Queens and let Fox try to make a talking film out of "The Treasurer's Report."

In terms of timing, the January shoot that had been agreed upon back in the summer now seemed like a a terrible idea, but a contract was a contract, and so, while admitting later that he felt "pretty tired out and mentally depleted," Benchley went out to Astoria and, with

Chalmers directing, had his eight-minute piece recorded by the Movietone cameras. Though Chalmers and the three other performers used in the sketch congratulated him when the alarmingly fast shooting was finished, Benchley was positive that he had looked and sounded awful. What little solace he felt stemmed from knowing two things—at least he knew the material well enough not to stumble over it and mess up the filming, and he probably would never have to do anything like this again.

The Treasurer's Report was released by Fox in March 1928, and to nobody's surprise—except maybe Benchley's—it was an instant success. Benchley *did* look flushed and weary, that was true, but his appearance only helped make the character of the beleaguered assistant treasurer that much more comical. And his vocal delivery, which displayed no stagebound affectedness or self-conscious mannerisms, was perfect. The notices the short received were uniformly excellent, most of them praising Benchley for his "smart and intelligent" acting, and for a wit that was "vastly pleasing to his audience." (Oddly enough, one of the few discordant notes came from Robert Sherwood, who complained in his *Life* review that audience laughter during the screening of the film had drowned out almost half the speech, and that the makers of sound pictures needed to figure out how to time comedic pauses so that jokes wouldn't get buried.)

After *The Treasurer's Report* had established itself as a money-maker, Chalmers was anxious to get Benchley in front of the cameras again, and, according to a *Variety* report, Fox offered Benchley a contract that called for him to make twenty additional shorts for $2,000 each. Benchley, wanting neither that much film work—he couldn't possibly give the movies that much of his time—nor that little money—if he got that salary as an untested novice and had made a picture that turned a profit, surely he was in line for a sizable increase were he to do any more of them—turned it down categorically. So categorically, in fact, that Fox came back with another one of those Hollywood deals that Benchley couldn't really believe, and couldn't really turn down, either: five shorts, at $5,000 apiece, to be filmed during two three-week stretches in California, for which Benchley would receive an additional $500 a week to cover living expenses.

The second Fox short, *The Sex Life of the Polyp*, was filmed in Hollywood in the spring of 1928 and, like its predecessor, was structured as a straightforward monologue. Right there, however, all similarities to *The Treasurer's Report* ended. Based on one of Benchley's old *Vanity Fair* pieces, "The Social Life of the Newt," the short features Benchley giving a talk to a women's club about the mating habits of the mature polyp. Whereas the Benchley of *The Treasurer's Report* had been a nervous, uncomfortable speaker given to stumbling over his words and forgetting the direction in which his sentences were heading, the Benchley of *The Sex Life of the Polyp* is a perfectly engaging lecturer, dapper-looking in his tie and tails, and erudite-sounding in his discourse and exposition. And, outside of some subtle touches that hilariously register the lecturer's unavoidable embarrassment at having to go into detail about such "delicate" matters before a group of women (Benchley's eyes dart sideways, and his voice drops precipitously, whenever he gets to words like "reproduce" or "sex"), it isn't so the manner in which the speech is being delivered that provides most of the humor here, but rather the speech itself. "Dr." Benchley—as he is introduced by the appropriately matronly head of the women's group—arrives at the podium with a relaxed, confident air about him; one immediately senses that this is a man who knows what he is talking about. He clears his throat, gives his audience an acknowledging smile, and begins his dissertation:

> If you will remember, in our last lecture we took up the subject of emotional crises in sponge life, and we saw how wonderfully nature takes care of the thousand and one things which a sponge must think of before it can [pause] *reproduce* other sponges. We also saw, if you remember, that a positive sponge, if mated with a negative sponge, will reproduce positive sponges—and vice versa. We also saw that this phenomenon is known as Liscombe's Law, so-called after Professor Liscombe, who discovered it quite by accident one day in the bathtub. This afternoon, we will take up certain phases of the emotional and physical reaction of the polyp as expressed in its [pause] *sex life*. If you can call it a sex life. . . .
>
> Now, the only way in which a polyp resembles other animals at all is that at certain periods during its growth, it does display a sentimental interest in polyps of the opposite sex. Now, this presents a very complicated situation, as the polyp has no definite sex itself. That is, it is

neither one thing nor another. By that, I mean the same polyp may be either a boy or a girl, according to what—or how—it happens to feel like being. As Dr. Achenholz says in his valuable book, *Der Werchmeltz Des Polypismus*, [opens book and reads] "Mit ein ander conder shu benicht su geiden, und das geholden machen nicht du michde angushdelt"—and this, mark you, from a man who's given his whole life to a study of the subject!

Now this tendency to change sex at any moment, while it does save the polyp a great deal of time, and expense, nonetheless makes difficult any definite analysis of its sex behavior. However, Dr. Rasmussen and I made some interesting experiments along this line, and it is the result of these experiments that I wish to bring before you this afternoon.

In order to study the polyp at close range, which is about the only way you can study a polyp, after all, we took one of the tiny creatures home with us to live. It was, at the time, a girl polyp, so we named her Mary—after Ethel Barrymore. She was at first naturally shy but soon grew accustomed to our mannish ways and became more like a child of our own than like a polyp, although of course she looked more like a polyp than a child of our own. It was in this way that we were able to tell the difference. . . .

Before long, Benchley lowers a screen. On it are animated renderings of Mary and a male polyp that he and Dr. Rasmussen have provided for her after an extensive search in Bermuda—"Bermuda being a great hangout for polyps."

We placed the two polyps in an open space behind the Princess Hotel and proceeded to await developments. Here is a picture taken just before the gong sounded. The one on the right is the male and on the left the female, unless I am mistaken. I *am* mistaken! The one on the right is the male—er, the female—and on the left the male. What a mistake!

As you can see, the entire courtship is carried on with an open space between the male and female of perhaps fifteen paces, polyp measure, which in a way makes it difficult for the male to be anything much more than a pal. Now the male has a rather unusual way of attracting the opposite sex—female. It was Dr. Rasmussen who discovered that during the courting season—the courting season begins on the 10th of

March and extends on through the following February, leaving about ten days for general overhauling and repairs—during the courting season the male gives forth a strange phosphorescent glow, something like a diamond scarf pin. Now, this glow is supposed to be very attractive to the female and it is by dazzling her with his appearance of elegance that the male is able to bring the lady around to, er, his point of view.

In order to test the powers of observation of the male during these maneuvers, we played a rather mean trick on the little fellow. We took away the original female for whom he was so frantically flashing his gleamer, and put in her place another but less attractive female. This seemed to make no difference at all to the male, who continued to flash on and off just the same. We then took away the second female and put in her place a small button, something the color of a polyp, following this with a crumb of cornbread.

Now, so far as we were able to detect, this change in personnel made no difference at all to the male, who continued to exert himself, still under the impression that he was making a conquest—even with the crumb of cornbread. Now this little ruse of ours, while it proved that the male polyp is not particularly clear as to just what it is he is after, rather put an end to our experiment as a whole, for the male, evidently frustrated at his inability to excite the button or the crumb of cornbread, suddenly gave up the whole thing as a bad job and turned into a female.

Now, this left us practically where we were in the first place, with no male at all, so Dr. Rasmussen and I, after going back to Bermuda and finding a good home for what were now our two *girl* polyps, returned to America still marveling at nature's wonderful accomplishments in the realm of sex, but rather inclined to complete our experiments with some animal which takes its sex life a little more seriously.

Released theatrically in July 1928, *The Sex Life of the Polyp* turned out to be a worthy, and profitable, successor to *The Treasurers's Report* (everywhere but Detroit, that is, where the picture was banned, sight unseen, for its "risqué subject matter"), and it also proved conclusively that Benchley's acting success was certainly no fluke. Although few would have objected had he simply reprised his character from the first film—as, indeed, many fledgling "comedians" might have done in similar circumstances—he had taken a chance and introduced a completely different type of character, and a completely different type of humor, and had made it work. When a third Chalmers-directed short, *The Spellbinder*, came out in the winter and found Benchley doing a wicked satirization of a hot-air-filled buffoon of a political speaker, still another facet of his talent was revealed, and he was soon being heralded in the press as the motion picture medium's leading "talking comedian."

Though still a bit befuddled by his fame, Benchley clearly enjoyed it, as well as the money that came with appearing in films. Hollywood, however, continued to annoy him; though he, personally, was doing well there, many of his friends were not. "I still hate this dump as much as ever," he wrote Gertrude in a letter dated December 7, soon after he'd arrived in California to shoot his next three Fox shorts.

There are some really nice people here [from the East], all of whom are miserable. . . . Dottie is living at the Ambassador and can't get out until she pays her bill, which she can't do until she gets her first pay check. Then she is going to a cheaper hotel. She hates her job at Metro and is trying to get out of it. After they hurried her out here and fussed because she hadn't left New York, when she finally got here and saw the Big Boss—Mr. Thalberg—he said: "Now let's see . . . what is it you wanted to do for us?" Then they put her on a job writing dialogue for a tragedy, "Madame X." Gerald Murphy is up at Metro, too, working on a Negro picture with King Vidor [*Hallelujah*], and he and Sarah are both disgusted with the place. . . . No matter where you live you are ten miles from anywhere else. My hotel is actually eight miles from Dottie's, six miles from the studio where I work—and it isn't considered out of the way.

The three shorts made that December at the Fox studios were all adaptations of magazine pieces which, like "The Social Life of the Newt," had appeared in Benchley's first book collection, *Of All Things*. But they differed from Benchley's first trio of films in that these longer two-reelers were not set up as simple monologues, but rather as more visually oriented and theatrically plotted situation comedies. *Lesson Number One* features a mechanically frustrated Benchley confounding a friend who is trying valiantly to help him learn how to drive a car. *Furnace Trouble* (taken from "Thoughts on Fuel Saving") features a technically frustrated Benchley unable to figure out how to keep enough coal burning in the temperamental basement furnace to keep his family and his snobbish guests sufficiently warmed. And *Stewed, Fried and Boiled* (based on "Gardening Notes") features a physically frustrated Benchley trying to make a fertile garden out of an ungiving and barren patch of earth behind the house.

Released in close order in the spring of 1929, the three new films, while significant historically because they represent the first hints of the Benchley "everyman" screen character later to be known as "Joe Doakes," didn't fare quite as well as the earlier ones either artistically or commercially. The often surreal atmosphere of the earlier monologues gives way to a staid and somewhat forced tone, with too much reliance on physical bits of humor that don't play particularly well, and with the simple novelty factor of "talkers" wearing off quickly, the box-office figures for the shorts fell somewhat short of Fox's expectations. At the end of March, not long after the release of *Stewed, Fried and Boiled*, Benchley and Fox amicably parted company. "Let me take this opportunity to thank you for the time you have given us," wrote studio executive Courtland Smith in a letter accompanying Benchley's final paycheck from Fox, "and for the splendid cooperation you have shown at all times. Some of the pictures were outstanding successes, and I think that *The Treasurer's Report* was one of the reasons why sound was generally accepted."

The studio had expressed interest in continuing the series, but by this time, Benchley simply wanted out. Being a movie short star had upset both his professional writing career and his personal life. Because of Fox's failure to finish the shorts in the designated three-week period back in December, it was necessary for him to either renege on or reschedule a host of writing assignments, and the prolonged shooting schedule forced him to remain in Hollywood throughout the entire holiday season, which he found singularly depressing. "They have Christmas trees all over the place here," he noted wearily in a note home, "and they look quite silly with the hot sun beating down on them." The movies had become what he didn't want them to be—an impingement on his "real" life.

"I fought going into pictures as long as possible," Benchley told the *New York World* in an interview dated April 28, 1929. "But they made it financially impossible for me to refuse to go into picture work. So here I am, now, considered an actor. Or am I? I've never felt stage fright once while making talking films; maybe my lack of self-consciousness shows that I'm not a real actor. Regular artists are very nervous about their work. Maybe I'm just a human being after all. That suits me. I'd clutch at straws rather than be known as an actor."

Still, it was clear that Benchley could have made a go of it as an actor right then, had he so desired. But the movies were still perceived as a risky—albeit immediately lucrative—business, and his closest friends and colleagues knew where his deepest allegiances still lay. "If he so wishes, Mr. Benchley would appear to be all set now as a vocal film star," Robert Sherwood had written in a review in *Life* back in the summer of 1928. "But I hope the money and fame won't go to his head. There are plenty of good actors in this world, but all too few good dramatic critics."

At the end of March 1929, though, when Benchley left his reviewing post at *Life* and the periodical announced his departure by saying that "Mr. Benchley has given up Dramatic Criticism for the Talking Movies," it seemed that Sherwood's cautionary words of advice hadn't been heeded. But apparently Benchley had only used his film work as a convenient excuse to leave *Life* for the theater critic position at a different, up-and-coming weekly publication. It was a magazine with which his name would be associated even to this day—a magazine called *The New Yorker*.

13
Look Wayward, Pressman

OF HOBO ROSS, GUY FAWKES, AND JESUS

On $October$ $3,$ $1930,$ Jim Moriarty's speakeasy on East 61st Street was the setting for a lively gathering of many of the Algonquin Round Tablers. Marc Connelly, fresh off the resounding success of his Broadway play *The Green Pastures*, was about to marry former Mack Sennett girl Madeleine Hurlock, and he'd arranged with Moriarty to keep the speakeasy open all night for a prenuptial party. It was somewhere around three in the morning when, during a slight lull in the festivities, humorist Frank Sullivan overheard Harold Ross, editor of *The New Yorker*, in the middle of a heated discussion with his theater critic, Robert Benchley. "Dammit, Bob," blurted Ross, just loud enough for all assembled to hear, "I don't want you to think I'm not incoherent!"

It wasn't just that, because of his penchant for talking only in short, profane bursts, and invariably fidgeting (if he was sitting), pacing (if he was standing), and jangling the loose change in his pockets while he spoke, Harold Ross often sounded incoherent. (Writer Samuel Hoffenstein once observed that talking with Ross was like drinking a glass of water without the water.) With a three-inch-high pompadour, a sizable gap between his front teeth, a tongue that often dangled over his lower lip, and oversized ears, hands, and feet, he often looked incoherent, too. So one could imagine how difficult it must have been for Benchley and the rest of the Algonquinites to take the brilliant but peculiar Ross seriously when, in 1924, he first began talking about the new weekly magazine he intended to start publishing as soon as he could find enough of someone else's money to finance it. To begin with, it sounded—both from Ross's typically spare description and the slim, dog-eared dummy copy he carried in his coat pocket in case a prospective investor happened by—as if this magazine of his was going to be devoted primarily to humor and the arts, which meant immediate competition with both *Life* and *Vanity Fair*, two firmly entrenched, successful periodicals. And while Ross vowed that his publication would be vastly different from those magazines, or any other, even his oldest and dearest friends at the Round Table—Woollcott, Adams, and Broun—had trouble believing him. True, they'd been in Paris with Ross during the World War and had seen him, more by sheer force of will than anything else, almost single-handedly mold a fledgling serviceman's publication, the *Stars and Stripes,* into a professional and popular newspaper. But Ross's track record after the war consisted only of editorial stewardships of veterans' magazines (the *Home Sector* and the *American Legion Weekly*) and a short stint at the humor publication *Judge*—hardly the kind of credentials to put a scare into the Frank Crowninshields of the publishing world.

Ross, however, was determined. As a charter member of the Round Table, he'd seen the group grow in stature and notoriety in the postwar gaiety of the early 1920s, and he correctly sensed that the group was serving as a symbolic focal point for the intelligent and creative people from all over the country who were continually streaming to New York hoping to catch, and possibly become part of, the city's unique magic. There wasn't any magazine geared specifically to those people, he thought. There were "smart" magazines like *Life,* and cultured magazines like *Vanity Fair,* but their national slant precluded too much trumpeting of an authentic New York aesthetic. And Ross was convinced that a magazine that radiated the flavor of New York life would appeal to cosmopolitan types everywhere.

Still, it seemed as if his "dream" magazine was destined to remain just that—a dream—until Ross found his "angel" in the person of Raoul Fleischmann, heir to his family's baking fortune and a semi-regular at the Round Table's cardplaying auxiliary, the Thanatopsis Poker and Inside Straight Club. Fleischmann was an active gambler who enjoyed the Algonquin crowd (his skill at the poker table led George Kaufman to dub him "Royal Flushman"), and Ross's offer of half-ownership in the new magazine provided Fleischmann an opportunity to combine gambling and good company.

With his financing in place—Ross sank his and Jane Grant's life savings of $25,000 into the pot, and Fleischmann matched it—Ross enlisted the Round Table's help in coming up with a suitable name for the magazine. Whoever came up with the name, he vowed, would be awarded several shares of as yet nonexistent stock in the F-R Publishing Company. Since the only magazine title Ross ever professed liking was *Life,* finding one he'd go for proved difficult. *Our Town, New York Weekly, Manhattan,* and *Truth* were several of the titles that came close, but it turned out to be the no-nonsense publicist John Peter Toohey who finally won Ross over. If it was to be a magazine about New York, Toohey told Ross, then why not just call it *The New Yorker?* And that was that.

The new magazine, whose February 21, 1925, debut issue featured the now classic Rea Irvin cover drawing of the fictional character of high-hatted boulevardier Eustace Tilley, snootily eyeing a passing butterfly, was anything but an instant success. Ross disliked mastheads, so *The New Yorker* didn't have one, and that confused some people. In its stead, Ross printed a list of "Advisory Editors" at the top of the first page of copy during the early months of the magazine's existence. But of the seven writers and illustrators named—Ralph Barton, Marc Connelly, Rea Irvin, George Kaufman, Alice Duer Miller, Dorothy Parker, and Alexander Woollcott—only Irvin was actively involved with the magazine. That confused even more people. (Ross had grudgingly agreed to try to help the business department attract advertisers by printing the names of some "famous" people who supposedly were to contribute to the magazine. It was, he later stated, "the only dishonest thing I ever did in my life.") Eventually, though, *The New Yorker* began to catch on, and within two years not only did the stock Ross kept handing out as payment to freelances start to be worth more than the paper it was printed on, but actual cash began to get disbursed to the magazine's contributors.

During the magazine's infancy, most of the Round Tablers took a wait-and-see attitude before committing themselves to do regular work for Ross—an attitude that was best summed up by Dorothy Parker, who said that she had gone up to the office once to write something, but "someone was using the pencil." Benchley was no exception; there were enough magazines around that wanted his byline and paid him well, and, especially in *The New Yorker*'s earliest days, he knew that his *Life* employers wouldn't like his helping to establish a rival publication. Still, Benchley liked Ross quite a bit, and Ross never stopped asking him for contributions. Eventually, his name did begin to appear under short pieces in the front of the book—"casuals," as they were called around the office. Benchley wrote just two articles for the magazine in 1925 (both in December, at that), but the number increased to fifteen in 1926, and in 1927, when it looked as if the magazine was finally going to survive and prosper, Ross made him an intriguing offer: Morris Markey, who was pulling double duty as the magazine's chief "Reporter at Large" and also its newspaper critic ("The Press in Review"), had expressed a desire to abandon the latter column; was Benchley interested?

Ross knew just how voraciously and thoroughly Benchley read the daily newspapers. In fact, onlookers often marveled at his methodical system of "perusing" the *New York Times*: Starting at the top left-hand corner of the front page, Benchley would read straight down to the end of the column, move to the top of the next column, again proceed straight down, and continue thusly through each and every page of the paper. Reading this way—skimming and skipping, to be sure, but never jumping around—enabled Benchley the humorist to make sure that no possible topic for a funny piece would go unnoticed. In the process, though, it also made the onetime *Tribune* employee something of a lay expert on the various ways newspapers chose to report the news to the public. Ross himself was a newspaper obsessive. He'd crisscrossed the country in his late teens and early twenties as what was at the time called a "hobo" reporter—someone who'd work at a big-city paper just long enough to save enough money to travel to the next big city. In fact, he worked at so many papers, ranging from the *Brooklyn Eagle* to the *Denver Post* to the *San Francisco Call*, that his professional nickname was "Hobo Ross." Ross knew newspapers from the inside out, and in Benchley he believed he'd found someone equipped to assess them from the outside in.

The idea for Benchley's becoming *The New Yorker*'s newspaper critic may well have originated with the very first article Benchley contributed to the magazine. In the December 19, 1925, issue, there appeared a front-of-the-book piece titled "Up the Dark Stairs," in which Benchley satirized the growing trend of newspapers to dress up even the most mundane news items with either flowery prose or some far-fetched feature-oriented angle, or—worse—both:

> Among the major menaces to American Journalism today (and there are so many that it hardly seems worth while even beginning this article) is the O. Henry–Irvin Cobb tradition. According to this belief, every reporter is potentially a master of the short story, and because of it we find human interest raising its ugly head in seven out of every eight news columns and a Human Document being turned out every

time Henry H. Mackle of 1356 Grand Boulevard finds a robin or Mrs. Rasher Feiman of 425 W. Forty-Ninth Street attacks the scissors grinder.

Copy readers in the old days used to insist that all the facts in the story be bunched together in the opening paragraph. This never made for a very moving chronicle, but at least you got the idea of what was going on. Under the new system, where every reporter has his eye on George Horace Lorimer, you first establish your atmosphere, then shake a pair of doves out of your handkerchief, round off your lead with a couple of bars from a Chopin étude, and finally, in the next to last paragraph, dialogue the names and addresses and what it was that happened.

A story which, under the canons of old journalism, would have read as follows:

"Mary J. Markezan, of 1728 Ocean Parkway, was found early this morning by Officer Charles Norbey of the Third Precinct in a fainting condition from lack of gin, etc." now appeals to our hearts and literary sensibilities as follows:

"Up the dark stairs in a shabby house on Ocean Parkway plodded a bent, weary figure. An aroma of cooking cabbage filled the hall. Somebody's mother was coming home. Somebody's mother was bringing in an arm-full of wood for the meagre fire at 1857 Ocean Parkway. Soon the tired woman would be at the top of the shadowy stairs. But fate, in the person of Officer Norbey, was present, etc."

A fine bit of imaginative writing, perhaps, satisfying everybody except the reader who wants to know what happened at 1857 Ocean Parkway.

Most of the trouble began about ten years ago when the Columbia School of Journalism began unloading its graduates on what was then the N.Y. *Tribune* (retaining the best features of neither). Every one of the boys had the O. Henry light in their eyes, and before long the market report was the only thing in the paper that didn't lead off with "Up the dark stairs at—"

Fine writing in news stories was actually encouraged by the management and daily prizes were offered for the best concealed facts. The writer of this article was a reporter at the time—"the worst reporter in New York City" the editors affectionately called him—and one day he won the prize with a couple of sticks on the funeral of Ada Rehan. This story consisted of two paragraphs of sentimental contemplation of old-time English comedy with a bitterly satirical comparison with modern movie comedy, and a short paragraph at the end saying that Ada Rehan was buried yesterday. Unfortunately the exigencies of make-up necessitated the cutting of the last paragraph; so the readers of the *Tribune* the next morning never did find out what had inspired this really beautiful tribute to somebody.

From the *Tribune* the scourge of fine news writing has spread to all the other papers with the exception of the *Times*. Your Monday morning copy of the *World* reads like something you find on the table by the guest room bed—"Twenty Tales of Danger and Daring" or "My Favorite Ghost Story: An Anthology." The news of the day is dished up like *Comedie Humaine* with leads running from "Up the dark stairs at—" to "This is the story of a little boy who lost his kitty." A picture of the city room of the *World,* by one who has never been there, would disclose a dozen or so nervous word artists, each sitting in a cubicle furnished to represent an attic, sipping at black coffee, with now and then a dab of cocaine, writing and tearing up, pacing back and forth in what the French call (in French) *le travail du style.* There must be a little hidden music, too, to make the boys write as they do. One feels that back copies of the *World* should be bound and saved for perusal on rainy days when the volumes of "Harper's Round Table" have begun to pall.

Soon it will creep into the foreign dispatches, hitherto held somewhat in check by cable rates. From a debt conference in London, we may have something like this:

"Up the dark stairs at 10 Downing Street trudged a tired figure in a silk hat. Under his arm he carried a brief case. Outside, the unheeding swirl of London swept by, but in the heart of the tired man there was peace. Austen Chamberlain had brought to a conclusion the negotiations for the day."

Or:

"The twilight falls quickly on the left bank of the Seine, and yesterday it fell even more quickly than usual. At a table on the sidewalk of a little café on Montparnasse, a pale man sat figuring on the back of an envelope. Not a man that you would look at a second time, perhaps, but, as Kipling says, that is another story. This man was Jules Delatour and he ran a little shop on the Boulevard Raspail. And Jules Delatour was sad last evening as the quick twilight fell over Montparnasse. For yesterday the franc dropped again, to twenty-six to the dollar."

When this has happened, we can have newstickers installed in our home and let the newspapers give themselves over entirely to the *belles lettres.*

Writing under the pseudonym "Guy Fawkes," the sixteenth-century English Gunpowder Plot conspirator, Benchley made his debut as *The New Yorker*'s newspaper critic in the magazine's July 23, 1927, issue. In December, the title of the column was changed, at his request, from "The Press in Review" to "The Wayward Press," and over the course of the next twelve years, in a total of nearly eighty pieces, he deftly jabbed away at the foibles of the fourth estate. With no less than twelve daily New York newspapers to choose from, Benchley never found himself wanting for material with which to fill "The Wayward Press." From the lofty *Times* to the lowly *Graphic*, he found all of them worthy of comment—and spared none of them in his criticisms of their assorted journalistic transgressions, both great and small.

Benchley the newspaper reader had several long-standing pet peeves. As demonstrated by "Up the Dark Stairs," he disdained overwrought prose masquerading as news reporting, and he had little tolerance for any news story in which any of the basic "Five W's"—the who, what, where, when, and why's—was either missing or inacurately reported. He abhorred what he perceived as public-relations-driven news stories—from his experiences as a theater critic, he always suspected bribery of some sort or other was at the bottom of it. And he was often both bemused and annoyed by the way in which newspapers subtly (and sometimes not so subtly) slanted news stories to fit their editorial bent simply through subjective description.

Sometimes it would take as little as one careless word to get Benchley's attention. When, for example, a 1927 *Times* story noted that during a birthday celebration in Washington, President Calvin Coolidge "smiled expansively," Benchley quipped that "any reporter who would designate the Coolidge smile as 'expansive' must be in the pay of the Government." And when the *World*, announcing the death of a big-time gangster's mother in 1929, reported, "She had seen her son rise from drug-clerk to bootleg king," Benchley angrily noted, "When one of our better newspapers considers that one *rises* from anything to be a bootleg king, what are we to tell our children? After all, Keats was a drug-clerk."

Other times, Benchley simply quoted from a newspaper verbatim to make his point—as in this short item that ended a 1932 column:

> The old newspaper rule of getting all the facts into the first paragraph of a story, in case the copy desk gets fresh and starts cutting from the bottom up, is exemplified for use in schools of journalism in the following lead of a *Times* reporter:
>
> "Samuel C. Chainowitz, who lives with his parents at 545 West 158th Street, felt worried last night when he remembered a conversation he had Monday night with Constantine Gregoroff, his 19-year-old chum, who only two weeks ago moved into a rooming house at 519 West 157th Street to be near his friend and to forget the quarrel which had caused his mother and Andrew Gregoroff, his father, a singer in a chorus, to separate."
>
> You could really cut the story right there.

One of Benchley's favorite practices in "The Wayward Press" was to match up the coverage by different newspapers of the same story and see where the facts fell. In January 1928, after a scandalous trial in which a Queens woman named Ruth Snyder and her lover, corset salesman Henry Gray, were convicted of premeditated murder in the brutal death of Mrs. Snyder's husband, the two were electrocuted at Sing Sing Prison. The execution made the front pages of every paper in town. Using the event as "an indication of the unreliability of individual witnesses' testimony, even though they are trained reporters," Benchley presented "a few statistics culled from the news-stories of the electrocutions":

> Twenty reporters witnessed the executions. They agreed that Mrs. Snyder and Mr. Gray were dead, but on practically no other point. The Associated Press set the time of the two deaths as 11:09 and 11:15 respectively. The *Herald Tribune* set them at 11:06 and 11:14; the *Times*, at 11:05 and 11:16. The *Post* rushed them through at 11:01 and 11:08. . . .
>
> As to the dress of the victims: the *Evening World* had Mrs. Snyder wearing a light brown dressing-gown, with a sheer silk stocking on her left leg. The United Press man saw her in a green smock with white stockings. The *Journal* said that she wore a calico skirt and one black

cotton stocking, while the *Sun* insisted that she had on a white shirt-waist and dark gray stockings. The Associated Press summarized the costume as "a black dress, a tan smock, black cotton stockings and gray felt slippers. . . ."

Some of the papers said that Mrs. Snyder was silent, only mumbling a prayer at the end. The *Post* said that her voice ranged from a high shriek to a hiccough. The *Post* also saw Gray in "deadly fear" at the last, while the others found him "strong," "game" and "emotionless." . . . The *American* described the "deathlike stillness" in the corridors, while the *Herald Tribune* said that the prisoners uttered "noisy good-byes. . . ."

Mr. Andrew McClean Parker, who is Managing Editor of the *Bridgeport Herald*, tells a story of an execution he witnessed as a reporter some years ago, when, on the way out, the question came up of the color of the rug in the death chamber. One reporter said it was gray, another brown. The matter was finally put up to the warden who settled it by informing them that there was no rug at all in the room.

While "The Wayward Press" often touched on issues of national and global import, ranging from the Sacco-Vanzetti case in the 1920s to the Lindbergh kidnapping and the rise of fascism in Europe in the 1930s, the columns that stirred up the most controversy were those that dealt with the apparently very touchy subject of advertising dollars dictating editorial concerns. Several newspapers objected to Benchley's assertions that the ample coverage allotted to, say, a new model Ford or the latest Ziegfeld production was the result of pressure by those newspapers' advertising salesmen on the editorial department to get enough "free" publicity—i.e., news stories—to ensure major advertising commitments from Ford and Ziegfeld.

Fortunately for Benchley, *New Yorker* editor Ross not only shared his contempt for such backroom policies but relished the idea of his upstart magazine thumbing its nose at such supposed bastions of propriety as the *New York Times*. Such an opportunity came in the fall of 1931, when the opening of the refurbished Waldorf-Astoria Hotel drew what seemed to Benchley to be an inordinate amount of publicity-type news coverage from the *Times*. Benchley noted that the paper had devoted "almost a whole section of its rotogravure department (possibly paid for, but with no mention of the fact) to a pictorial representation of the charms of our new hostelry." Shortly after the column appeared in print, Ross received a phone call from *Times* executive Arthur Hays Sulzberger, son-in-law (and future successor) to the paper's publisher Adolph Ochs, the contents of which he relayed in a memo to Benchley:

> Bob:
> A Mr. Soltzberger of the New York Times called on the telephone this morning and after several young men and ladies had said "Wait a moment" and "Mr. Seltzberger will be on in a moment" and things like that, Mr. Sultzberger got on the telephone personally and talked at some length about your mention of the Waldorf pictures in the Times, saying they looked like advertising but weren't labelled such. He said the Times had gone to the Waldorf people after advt. and the Waldorf had said yes, they'd advt. ($6000 worth) if the Times would agree to publish pictures on the Waldorf. The Times advt. man was duly appalled. He was shocked. The Times ran the pictures anyhow, the news dept. being independent of the advt. . . . Mr. S. said he wouldn't have bothered us about it but he wanted to tell us the circumstances, wanted you to know. So I'm telling you. . . . I told him the Times was above reproach. He said he didn't want anything done about it. Just wanted to tell us. I can't think of anything we could do about it except print a line or two saying the Times has assured you that they didn't get pd. for the pictures and that you didn't actually think they had received money for them. I leave this entirely up to you. I don't care. I write this note because I told Mr. S. I'd tell you, and to show that I do have a little bit of fun in life at that.

Officially, the column drew a curt response from *Times* business manager Louis Wiley, who fired off a letter to Ross stating, "The New York Times would never publish anything in its news or rotogravure picture columns for payment," and reciting chapter and verse of the federal postal laws prohibiting "the publication of reading matter not marked as advertising when such publication is paid for or is supplementary to an advertisement. . . . The Times is careful to separate advertising from reading matter so that no one can possibly be misled." He continued, "It is inaccurate and unfair for your commentator to hint anything to the contrary. The Times further never consents, as some other newspapers do, to publish a special section for one advertiser."

Benchley printed the letter in his next column, with this response: "Now we know that the *Times* wasn't paid for anything, the thing is less understandable than ever. The *Herald Tribune* at least got a great big advertisement for its pains."

Ironically, while Benchley the newspaper critic remained steadfastly apolitical in his handling of "The Wayward Press," Benchley the private citizen found himself—as, indeed, did many other writers and intellectuals of the era—unable to remain uninvolved in the Sacco-Vanzetti affair. In 1921, Nicola Sacco, a shoemaker, and Bartolomeo Vanzetti, a fish peddler, were arrested for the shooting deaths of two men during a payroll robbery in Braintree, Massachusetts. The pair, Italian immigrants who were acknowledged anarchists, pleaded their innocence from the day they were arrested, and the trial, presided over by Judge Webster Thayer, was long and controversial. The evidence against the two was largely circumstantial, and it appeared to many observers both inside and outside the courtroom (the trial received enormous publicity all across the United States and throughout Europe as well) that the two were being tried more for being foreign-born anarchists than as possible killers. Nonetheless, they were found guilty, and were sentenced to death by Thayer in July 1921.

While Sacco and Vanzetti sat on death row awaiting their execution, world sentiment on their behalf swung into action. Famous people ranging from dancer Isadora Duncan to scientist Albert Einstein spoke out on their behalf, and the Sacco-Vanzetti Defense Committee, operating out of Boston, began filing appeals seeking everything from a mistrial to a complete overturning of their convictions. The grounds, as argued by Harvard law professor (and future Supreme Court justice) Felix Frankfurter in an article in the *Atlantic*, was clear prejudicial conduct on the part of nearly everyone involved in the trial—especially Judge Thayer.

Benchley wasn't surprised when he read Frankfurter's comments. Back in June, while the trial was in progress, he and Gertrude had been visiting friends in Worcester. While they were there they traveled one day to the Worcester Golf Club to pick up their host, Loring Coes. Coes emerged from the locker room and told them he'd overheard some interesting remarks made by Judge Thayer, who'd just finished a round of golf at the club. Thayer, Coes said, had referred to Sacco and Vanzetti as "those bastards down there," and had said that even though they were "trying to intimidate him," he "would get them good and proper." Furthermore, Coes continued, Thayer had told the others that "a bunch of parlor radicals were trying to get these guys off and trying to bring pressure to bear on the bench," and he would "show them and would get those guys hanged," and "would also like to hang a few dozen of the radicals."

Benchley relayed those statements in a sworn affidavit that was sent, along with four other affidavits of prejudice, by Bartolomeo Vanzetti to Massachusetts Governor Alvan Fuller on May 4, 1927, in an appeal for a new trial. Why it took six years for Benchley to come forward isn't known. Many of his Round Table friends had gotten involved in the Sacco-Vanzetti cause—most notably, Heywood Broun, who used his "It Seems to Me" column in the *World* to champion Sacco and Vanzetti's plight throughout their many years on death row, and Dorothy Parker, who was arrested in a demonstration on their behalf in Boston. Perhaps Benchley had hoped that Coes, husband of one of Gertrude's dearest friends, Katherine, would eventually break his silence, or that some other person who'd heard Thayer's remarks at the Worcester Golf Club that day would do so. Nevertheless, Benchley did finally come forward with his testimony. Unfortunately, when his statement was made public—it was published in the *Boston Evening Transcript* on May 5, 1927, the day after the affidavit was filed—Coes categorically denied every word of it in an interview with the *Boston Traveler*.

By the early summer of 1927, Governor Fuller attempted to alleviate some of the pressure on his office by appointing a three-man "advisory committee," headed by Harvard President Abbott Lawrence Lowell, to examine all aspects of the case. Benchley went to Boston and gave his testimony before the panel, but all the members did was stare at him as he talked and then thank him for coming. Benchley was so incensed—they hadn't even asked him one question!—that he made an appointment to see Fuller himself. That meeting, however, proved equally fruitless. Fuller listened to Benchley's statement, then said to him, "Mr. Benchley, when I hear a good story, and then when I go back and tell it to my wife, Mrs. Fuller often says to me, 'Alvan, haven't you fixed it up just a little?' And sometimes I have, just to make it better telling. Now doesn't that happen with you, too, Mr. Benchley? Don't you think we all sometimes improve a story with the telling?"

Fuller went on to suggest to Benchley that if he really thought Judge Thayer had acted with prejudice, perhaps he could go through some of the court testimony and see if he could find anything in the transcripts that would back up his claims. Since the Massachusetts supreme court had already cleared Thayer of any prejudicial conduct during the trial, Benchley knew there wasn't much point in doing so, but he took the transcripts home with him anyway. In mid-July, he wrote Fuller a three-page, single-spaced letter in which he asked the governor to consider his statements "as a layman who wants to see justice done, even justice at the expense of the judiciary—if such a paradox is possible, and I am afraid that it is." The letter went on to cite several of Thayer's remarks from the transcripts in which, Benchley charged, there indeed was prejudicial conduct such as heckling the defense and taking the defendants' statements out of context in reiterating them for the jury.

"It is too bad the Supreme Court did not have an opportunity to pass upon his remarks *outside* the court-room," Benchley wrote, "for he is distinctly censurable for those. The same cold legal code which allowed his actions in court is equally inflexible in its prohibition of even *conversation* concerning a case on the part of a judge outside the court. . . ." Benchley concluded, "I am afraid that this has been rather a long letter. I hope that you have had time to read some of it. I have no personal interest in the case and have, in fact, tried not to think about it any more than I could help because I get so sore when I do. . . . But Massachusetts is my home state . . . and, although I am technically a New Yorker now, I find that I have more than an outsider's interest in this and a very deep sense of shame at this contribution my home city of Worcester has made to the legal history of the state."

The Lowell panel published its findings in July. Leafing through it, Benchley found this reference to his testimony: "The Judge may have been indiscreet in his conversation with outsiders during the trial, but we do not believe that he used some of the expressions attributed to him, and we think that there is exaggeration in what the persons to whom he spoke remember." The panel's conclusion was that the trial had been wholly legal and fair—and that conclusion finally sealed Sacco and Vanzetti's fate. "Governor Fuller never had any intention in all his investigation but to put a new and higher polish upon the proceedings," charged Broun in the *World*. "The justice of the business was not his concern. He hoped to make it respectable. . . . What more can these immigrants from Italy expect? It is not every prisoner who has a president of Harvard University throw on the switch for him."

On August 23, 1927, amid demonstrations, labor strikes, and even riots in some places around the world, Sacco and Vanzetti died in the electric chair. In his "The Press in Review" column in the September 3 issue of *The New Yorker*, Benchley discussed the end of the case, but without alluding to his own role in it. Instead, he wrote mostly about Broun, who'd been warned by the *World*'s editor, Ralph Pulitzer, not to submit any more columns about the case, and who found himself censored by his own paper when he refused to do so. (The action led Broun to leave the *World* for the rival *Telegram*.) Commenting on the incident, Benchley noted, "The *World* contributed what was the most startling editorial somersault when, after leading the field in the fight for the two men, it suddenly prostrated itself in front of the august report signed by Abbott Lawrence Lowell and developed a serious streak of yellow. . . . Mr. Broun . . . not having been informed of the editorial shift . . . found himself standing alone in the middle of the field with the ball and his interference in a huddle conference fifty yards away. Although the *World* maintained that Mr. Broun was still on the team, when last seen he was in the locker building and in street clothes."

Benchley did reserve one terse paragraph for Judge Thayer, though. "The prize editorial coup in the case was pulled by the *Sun*," he observed, "when it came forth with a eulogy of Judge Webster Thayer, a thing which not even the Lowell Board could bring itself to indulge in. The *Sun* discovered that Judge Thayer had been 'by inheritance and education incapable of entering into a controversy with the persons who have most maliciously assailed him' and closed its disclosure by referring to the high ideals of the Massachusetts judiciary which 'this upright and faithful gentleman has maintained in so distinguished a manner.' We recommend the writer of this *Sun* editorial for the Pulitzer Prize for the best satirical editorial written during 1927."

By 1929, *The New Yorker* was well on its way to becoming everything Harold Ross had always envisioned it to be—an impeccably written and edited magazine brimming with civility and humor. With even such early doubting Thomases as Woollcott and Parker regularly appearing in its pages—Woollcott with a frothy column of pontifications and whimsy called "Shouts and Murmurs," and Parker with poems, short stories, and semiregular book reviews written under the pseudonym "Constant Reader"—*The New Yorker* began to attract not only the best established writers, but scores of young literary hopefuls as well. Ross took the best of those—Katherine Angell, E. B. White, Wolcott Gibbs, James Thurber, and others—and put them to work as fact checkers, copy editors, manuscript readers, and local reporters. This combination of youthful élan and even-keeled professionalism provided a lively mix, and made *The New Yorker*'s pages—as well as its offices—the place to be in the magazine world as the decade turned.

Benchley's relationship with *The New Yorker* also intensified during this period. Delighted with Benchley's work on "The Wayward Press," Ross sought to get as much of Benchley as he could into his magazine. In 1929, Benchley left *Life* and succeeded Charles Brackett as *The New Yorker*'s theater critic, and, between theater reviews, the "Wayward Press" column, and assorted humor pieces, Benchley's presence in the magazine was quite pronounced. In 1930, for example, *The New Yorker* published eight of his casuals, eleven "Wayward Press" columns, and forty-five theater reviews—some sixty-four pieces in all—and during the next four years (1931–34), the magazine published an average of better than forty-eight Benchley pieces annually.

Quite pronounced as well was Benchley's influence at *The New Yorker*, most notably on White, Thurber, and Gibbs. Each of the three had begun his association with the magazine during its first few years of existence. Elwyn Brooks White, son of a Mount Vernon, New York, piano manufacturer, was a Cornell graduate who had come to Ross's attention via an unsolicited piece entitled "Defense of the Bronx River" the *The New Yorker* ran in a May 1925 issue. White was hired a short time later to write punch lines for the magazine's "Newsbreaks"—filler copy used whenever an article ended before the bottom of the column—and his poems and casuals began to appear with great regularity in the magazine. His writing, warm and optimistic, attracted Benchley's attention as well. He pressed Ross to encourage White as much as possible, and White, who was always a bit in awe of Benchley, later noted, "The day Ross told me Benchley had praised something I had written was one of the big days of the Twenties for me." (Benchley even went so far as to ask Ross to have White fill in for him as theater critic during several of Benchley's vacations and sabbaticals during the early thirties—even though White had no previous experience as a play reviewer.)

Thurber, a native of Columbus, Ohio, worked on several newspapers in his home state as well as in Paris, before joining *The New Yorker* in 1927. Like White's, his first contributions were unsolicited; unlike White's, many of them were rejected. Thurber had had but a few published when White (whose sister had, via a chance meeting in France, become friends with Thurber and his wife) arranged for him to be interviewed by Ross for an editorial position. Ross hired Thurber as one of his endless string of administrative managing editors ("Jesuses," as Ross called them); eventually Thurber settled in as one of the magazine's chief editors, and as a contributor of both written and illustrated satires and musings.

Like White, Thurber viewed Benchley as part idol, part role model, and part teacher. In a 1949 *New York Times Book Review* article, Thurber recalled how he first came to meet Benchley, after Ross had sent him over to the Algonquin to pick up an overdue casual. "I was a proud young Western Conference spy on the New Yorker, and I wouldn't have chased down just any Ivy Leaguer's copy, but for Benchley's I would have gone anywhere—to the Harvard Club, if necessary. I read and admired everything he wrote, and I knew how hard it was to do the way he did it—usually in fewer than 1,500 words. . . .

I was a little breathless that day when I first saw Benchley plain. He eased me into a chair, with that warm laugh, and gave me a glass of Moxie. When the New Yorker phoned [for me] he answered, and explained that he was having the devil's own time with a cognate accusative. I had had his copy in my pocket for nearly two hours."

Both White and Thurber worried aloud at their *New Yorker* desks about covering comic turf previously claimed by Benchley. "He had written about practically everything," wrote Thurber, "and his comic devices were easy to fall into. White once showed me something he'd written and asked anxiously, 'Did Benchley say that?'" And in the preface to his 1933 collection *My Life and Hard Times*, Thurber described himself as someone who "is aware that billions of dollars are stolen every year by bankers and politicians, and that thousands of people are out of work, but these conditions do not worry him a tenth as much as the conviction that he has wasted three months on a stupid psychoanalyst or the suspicion that a piece he has been working on for two long days was done much better and probably more quickly by Robert Benchley in 1924."

Native New Yorker Wolcott Gibbs was thrust into the journalistic life by a cousin, Round Tabler Alice Duer Miller, after his wealthy family decided that his job as a brakeman for the Long Island Railroad was perhaps a bit beneath his station. After a brief fling at a suburban weekly, Gibbs found himself at *The New Yorker*—at Miller's urging, Ross hired him as a proofreader. Through hard work and diligence, Gibbs rose to become one of *The New Yorker*'s most indispensable hands—as copy editor, rewrite man (he was capable of subsuming himself so fully in another author's style that he often was called upon to pen literary satires for the magazine), even art editor. He also was one of its jumpiest employees, forever spilling drinks, fighting an upset stomach, and worrying that people were following him down the street. (When Katherine Angell once expressed concern over Gibbs's behavior, Ross pointed out that all of it just proved what a bona fide staff member he was.)

In a letter to Nathaniel Benchley in the 1950s, Gibbs recounted the difficulty Benchley's pieces presented to the copy desk at *The New Yorker*. "The single-spaced stuff drove the proof and checking departments crazy because they couldn't write between the lines, which

I'm sure was his object. And the fact that it was not only single-spaced but also crowded off to one side of the page made it almost impossible to get a word count without actually counting the words. It always came out shorter than I thought it was going to, and it was hell working out last minute fillers. . . . There was one time he called up on Sunday and said he was in Philadelphia (a fact he couldn't account for) and also that nobody there seemed to have a typewriter. The copy got in somehow because it always did, but things looked bad for a while. It was a hard way to work but I guess stimulating. If it hadn't been for the fact that it was such wonderful copy (everybody always wanted to read it before it went off to [the printers in] Greenwich) I might not have found it quite so stimulating."

For Ross, the problem wasn't Benchley's copy as much as Benchley's finances. Once he began writing regularly for the magazine, Benchley often leaned on Ross for advances against his articles, and Ross quickly discovered that Benchley's habit of always being out of money was impacting on *The New Yorker*'s bookkeeping department. Ross's solution was to try to get Benchley to write more, especially humor pieces. "Damn it," Ross wrote in a note to Benchley in the early thirties, "if you'll write pieces for us instead of the Cunard Line *Deckchair*, the Smith College *Hairpin*, and the Rivet and Bolt Manufacturer's Club *Quarterly News*, you'll make more money, have your stuff displayed more satisfactorily and conspicuously and—oh, you know. For instance, you could sell us a piece and pay for an ocean passage with the proceeds instead of making a dicker to pay for a passage by doing a piece for the ship's newspaper. Also, we would have the piece."

Unfortunately, the cycle became such that as Benchley wrote more, he made more, and as he made more, he borrowed more—and before long, *The New Yorker*'s accounting department found him as "stimulating" as the copy department. Eventually, one of Ross's "Jesuses," Bernard Bergman, tried to figure out a solution. At the beginning of 1932, Bergman sent Ross a note proposing that Benchley simply be guaranteed $300 a week all year round, applied against his earnings and including vacation pay, so long as he contributed a minimum sum of theater pieces, "Wayward Press" columns, and casuals. "If he approaches anywhere near the suggested program," wrote Bergman, "he'd have a sizable amount coming due at the end of the year—around $3,000." In relaying the proposal to Benchley, Ross sweetened the pot by suggesting that there could be a settlement of surpluses over the weekly guarantee every three months. "The $300 a week arrangement would mean merely that we did the bookkeeping instead of you, but personally it would put you in a position of making it easier for me to help you in emergencies (Ah, those emergencies!) such as being stuck in France," noted Ross. Benchley would thus be assured "a certain regular income, rain or shine, and considerable time off for vacations, other work, and indoor activities. It might help you with your budget, and I know how meticulous you are about your budget."

Benchley found the proposal acceptable—and within a month was asking Ross if his vacation pay for the following summer could be put toward wiping out the $875 in advances he still owed from the previous year. In time, neither Ross, Bergman, nor any of the succeeding "Jesuses" who tracked Benchley's work for *The New Yorker* until he stopped writing for the magazine in early 1940 were able to discern which Benchley payment was corresponding to which Benchley article. And that probably was all for the best. After all, as far as his personal finances were concerned, Benchley didn't want anyone to think he wasn't incoherent.

14
The Little Rose Bower
on 44th Street

MR. MACGREGOR, PLEASE

O*ne night* in the late 1920s, Robert Benchley sat down at the typewriter in the room he was keeping at the Algonquin Hotel to begin work on a magazine piece that was due in a few days. He knew a poker game was in progress down the hall, but he had put the evening aside to write, and was determined not to let anything interfere with the mission at hand. After staring for some time at the blank piece of paper in front of him, he decided it must be curiosity about the poker game that was at fault for his failure to make any progress. If he just saw who was there, simply observed the proceedings for a short time, his curiosity would be satisfied, and he could then return to work with an unencumbered, unfettered mind. Leaving the paper in the typewriter, he ventured down the corridor, surveyed the proceedings for a brief period, and, proud of his resolve, returned to his room with a renewed sense of purpose.

Within seconds, the word "The" appeared on the page. Unfortunately, inspiration came to an immediate halt following the appearance of that lone word. Benchley then decided it must be his curiosity about whether any of the Round Table crowd might be convening in the downstairs lobby that was now impeding his progress. We'll take care of *that* just like the poker game, he told himself. Again leaving the paper in the typewriter, he went downstairs, bade hello to his friends, eyed the clock, and conscientiously excused himself before he got caught up in any lengthy conversations. Back in his room, he again sat down confidently at the typewriter. The word "The" stared him in the face. For a while, he just stared back. Finally, he began to peck away furiously at the keys. "The . . . hell with it," he wrote—and took off for a night on the town.

The Royalton Hotel on the south side of West 44th Street in midtown Manhattan was just about everything the Algonquin Hotel on the north side of West 44th Street was not. If the Algonquin, with its elegant decor and meticulous service, was a hotel whose ambience both reflected and promoted the ongoing presence of the leading writers, actors, and bon vivants of the day, then the Royalton, with its drab furnishings and undistinguished service, was a hotel whose lack of atmosphere both reflected and promoted its simple function as a residence for bachelors looking neither to see nor to be seen. Devoid of a restaurant, and with a small, uninviting lobby area usually inhabited only by the man at the front desk, the Royalton was a place where people roomed, not congregated—and after too many years of fighting a losing battle against his own extroverted impulses, Benchley figured the Royalton was the right place for him to room, too.

When Benchley informed Algonquin owner Frank Case that he intended to leave the Algonquin for a room at the Royalton, Case tried in vain to talk him out of it. If it was privacy that Benchley needed, Case promised, privacy he would have; the owner pledged to ensure personally that Benchley was not disturbed whenever he so desired. Benchley, however, had already made up his mind. "You might be able to keep them from coming up," he told Case, "but you can't keep me from coming down." So over to the Royalton he went near the end of 1929, convinced that, from both a professional and a personal standpoint, the move would prove productive. Before long, visitors to Benchley's rooms realized that the move was indeed proving to be undeniably productive—though not quite in the way he, or anyone else, might have anticipated.

What Benchley's Royalton suite produced was an accumulation of clutter—clutter of such astonishing proportions that the accommodations quickly became a sort of midtown literary landmark. (The first time Noel Coward saw it, he remarked to Benchley, "So *this* is your little rose bower. I must say, it does look rather *lived* in.") When he first moved into the half-furnished two-room suite, Benchley looked at the living room's pale walls, mahogany baseboards and trim, and diamond-shaped windowpanes and decided that the place exuded a certain Victorian mood. To enhance that mood, he acquired a dark red rug, dark red drapes, a tasseled red velvet cover for the table, and three pictures of Queen Victoria herself for the walls between the windows. Beyond that, Benchley told friends he was open to suggestions—and the result was a never-ending stream of bizarre donations to the Benchley suite. He noted in a reminiscence:

> I invited contributions from my friends, but what I meant was contributions I could use. I didn't mean that I was starting a whaling museum or that I planned to build more rooms on. I had more or less in mind a mid-Victorian study of the "what not" variety. Well, I got my

"what nots." It began with little articles to line up on top of a book-case—miniature geese, little men with baskets, shells with eggs in them and broken stags. Everybody had fun but the lady who dusted.

Then people began looking around town for heavier gifts. Trucks began arriving with old busts of Sir Walter Scott, four-foot statues of men whose shirt fronts lit up when attached to an electric connection, stuffed owls and fox terriers that had lain too long at the taxidermist's. This phase ended with the gift of a small two-headed calf in a mod-erate state of preservation. From then on the slogan became "Send it to Benchley." Chipped cornices from the old post office, detached flights of stairs, hitching posts and railings began pouring in. Every day was like Christmas in Pompeii. The overflow went into the bed-room and I started sleeping under an old spinet cover with a set of bead curtains which had been brought back to me from a bordello in Marseilles.

The friendly mood in which the game started changed gradually to one of persecution. Once the Missing Persons Bureau took a hand in it and searched my rooms for a runaway college girl. They found noth-ing, however, but three Chinese laborers, who had been smuggled into the country and delivered to my place in a caterer's wagon.

Benchley wasn't exaggerating very much. As Nathaniel Benchley recalled, the ambience of the Royalton suite was established as soon as you opened the front door, revealing a square-shaped hall

filled with trunks, stacks of old newspapers and foreign magazines, overcoats, canes, a sword . . . and a deer skull. . . . Just inside the liv-ing room, on the left, was a blue couch, sometimes called "The Track," because when he wanted to take a nap on it he would say, "Well, I guess I'll do a couple of laps around the track," and then lie down. . . . Be-yond the couch was a small desk, on which was an old battered type-writer, and over the desk was a five-foot shelf of books that were collected for their titles alone. Over the years, he acquired such items as *Forty Thousand Sublime and Beautiful Thoughts, Success with Small Fruits, Talks on Manure, Keeping a Single Cow, In and Out with Mary Ann.* . . . In one corner was a cello and a music stand, gifts of a friend to whom he once remarked that he would like to play the cello. The music on the stand was dedicated to him, but he never got around to playing it.

... In the corner beyond the windows were two more bookcases, which reached to the ceiling, and in one of which were drama books and the programs for most of the plays he had seen. The next wall was taken up pretty much by his desk, over which were reference books, four small Breughel prints, and two signs, one reading "We All Speak English," and the other, "Why Can't You Write?" To the right of the desk was the door to the bedroom, [over which] hung four beer mugs ... and a sign saying "MR. Benchley, please"—a gift from Frank Adams. ... A closet was sandwiched between two bookcases and it contained, among other things, clothes, a banjo mandolin, glasses, a fire chief's hat from Worcester, a hot plate, several empty flasks and decanters, a three-foot cocktail shaker in the form of a lighthouse, a couple of suitcases, and a large jar of New England boiled dressing with which Gertrude always kept him supplied. Also, hidden in the closet were his most erudite books—books in German, books on philosophy, books on music—which he didn't especially want people to know that he was reading."

The rooms faced onto 43rd Street, almost directly over a fire station—meaning that alarms, sirens, and whistles were always sounding unexpectedly at all hours of the day and night. Suffice it to say that the Royalton suite seemed to Benchley's friends to be the perfect physical manifestation of the inner workings of his brain.

Ironically, one of the places where Benchley sometimes went for his own peculiar kind of rest before he moved into the Royalton was an old building at the corner of 59th Street and Madison Avenue where Polly Adler, "America's most famous madam," conducted business. Throughout the latter half of the Roaring Twenties, Adler's house of prostitution was a favorite haunt of New York's late-night crowd. Aside from the obvious, it served as a convenient all-night speakeasy, and its clientele, like that of the more "respectable" speaks, was a curious mix of both the famous and the infamous. Pearl "Polly" Adler was a diminutive Polish immigrant who had stumbled into the prostitution business when a bootlegging friend offered to pay the rent on her apartment if she would let him use it to conduct extramarital affairs. For a while, Adler tried to "go legit," but after investing—and losing—all her money in a lingerie shop, she returned to the oldest profession, and within a few short years she'd established herself as

New York's most fashionable madam. Notwithstanding a few stray gangsters like George McManus and Frank Costello, the high-spirited, high-profile Adler drew her customers primarily from the upper brackets of the social, financial, literary, and theatrical worlds, and a goodly number of the Round Tablers—including Benchley—were among them.

In her autobiography, *A House Is Not a Home*, Adler recounts her friendship with "Bob the writer," as he's called in the book. "Every so often Bob would arrive and inquire if I had a room to spare—an empty one. He would say he was in need of a good night's sleep before tackling a magazine piece. Sometimes, when he had a deadline to meet, he'd stay right there to do his writing." For Benchley, Adler's place represented a sort of strange haven. Unlike any standard hotel, Adler's establishment operated on a schedule very much like his—activity of some sort or other virtually all night, and little movement before noon of any given day. There's no evidence of Benchley's having had any particular affinity for Adler's working girls. In fact, outside of Polly Adler (or, as he called her, "Pawly"), with whom he remained friendly for the rest of his life, Benchley's favorite person at the Adler house was the madam's personal maid, known affectionately as Lion. A four-foot-ten-inch black woman around forty years old, Lion had acquired her nickname when one of Adler's customers dubbed her "a regular female Richard the Lion-hearted" because of her fierce loyalty to her boss. According to Adler, Lion worshiped Benchley. "You could always tell when he was in the house just from the increased candle power of her smile," wrote Adler, "and she would never let any of the other maids serve him." Whenever Benchley stayed the night, Lion would routinely launder his clothing and press his suit, and when he awoke, she'd cook breakfast for him. "That terrific smile!" Adler recalled Benchley saying about Lion. "It lights up a room like the sun."

Often, Benchley came to Polly Adler's simply because it was the last place still open and serving drinks—by the end of the 1920s, Benchley was rarely making it through a night without consuming something alcoholic—and at those times he usually brought a small entourage with him. Dorothy Parker (herself now fast becoming a heavy drinker) and whoever she happened to be seeing at the time could be counted upon to join him, as could a tall, dark-haired beauty named Betty Starbuck, a Brooklyn-born comedienne whom Benchley began seeing not long after Carol Goodner broke off their affair. Benchley's relationship with Starbuck lasted until the early 1930s, when she quit show business to become a stockbroker's wife—the first of many of Benchley's "protégées" that he was to later claim he "placed well." Benchley had learned one valuable lesson from his affair with Goodner—that he needed any woman he was going to take on as a lover to also be a friend. That Starbuck indeed was, to such an extent that after she married, she eventually got to know the entire Benchley family, including Gertrude, quite well.

Another key to the safe conduct of his extramarital affairs was Benchley's aforementioned sense of discretion. Benchley made no great secret of his friendship with Starbuck—after all, there was nothing unusual about a theater critic's being seen in the company of an actress—but he went out of his way to make sure that his name never popped up in the gossip columns in connection with other women.

One incident in particular stands out as an example of the lengths Benchley would go to in order to keep his name out of the columns. In June 1929, Betty Starbuck was appearing in a show called *Hello Daddy* at the Erlanger Theatre, and most nights Benchley would pick her up at the end of the show. One night, Benchley went backstage to the wardrobe room, changed into some women's evening clothes, donned a fright mask, and waited for Starbuck on the fire escape outside her dressing room. When Starbuck entered the room after the final curtain and looked outside, she first let out a howl, and then, realizing it was Benchley pulling a prank, promptly pulled one of her own by locking the window shut and leaving. Benchley made such a racket out on the fire escape that someone from an adjoining building called the police, who showed up and rescued the suitably embarrassed Benchley.

While none of the New York papers reported the incident, someone from the *Mirror* sold the story to the *Philadelphia Daily News*, which printed it. A furious Benchley not only wrote the paper to deny the story, but even went so far as to engage the law firm of Kohlman and Austrian to threaten a suit unless the story was retracted. The paper agreed only to print Benchley's letter, and it was all the lawyers could do to convince Benchley that a full-fledged lawsuit was likely to be far too damaging to his reputation.

By the time he moved into the Royalton, both Benchley's professional and personal life had grown so complicated that he began to contemplate hiring a secretary to help keep track of everything. Then one day a friend he was meeting in front of the Public Library on Fifth Avenue showed up with a small man who was introduced to Benchley as, simply, MacGregor. Benchley noticed that MacGregor had some flowers with him, and, looking to make conversation, he asked the man who they might be for. "Actually," replied MacGregor, "these are for a sick shirt I'm visiting at the shirt hospital. It's in for a minor operation—cuff-turning." Suitably impressed, Benchley asked MacGregor if he might be interested in escorting any of Benchley's own shirts to their annual checkups—and when MacGregor replied by inquiring about his shirt doctor's education, Benchley knew he'd found his man.

Ostensibly, MacGregor was hired as a secretary, but he quickly settled into the role of personal assistant with a surprising ease—surprising because much of the time Benchley would simply throw him his checkbook or his calendar and ask him to somehow see to it that it all made sense. That MacGregor proved uniquely capable of doing, and Benchley soon came to regard him as an ally as well as an employee. When, for example, Benchley was late for a deadline, MacGregor would often run interference. He'd take editors over to a speakeasy like Tony's, assuring them that Benchley would be arriving shortly with his copy. After several rounds of drinks, and not a sign of Benchley, MacGregor would suggest that perhaps he'd misunderstood his boss, and that it was the 21 Club where they were supposed to rendezvous. Eventually, they'd wind up taxiing back to the Royalton—"perhaps Benchley left a message at the front desk," he'd say, leaving the poor, now semi-inebriated soul in the back of the cab—where MacGregor would, with luck, find Benchley frantically finishing his piece. He'd then rush back down to the street, deliver it into the hands of the editor with an apologetic "I must have misunderstood him; the man at the desk says he left this envelope here hours ago," instruct the driver to take the man back to his office, jump out of the cab—and disappear into thin air.

Actually, disappearing into thin air was one of MacGregor's best talents. Each year, as winter approached, he would anxiously await the season's first snowfall, and the confirmed sighting of the first flakes would result in his not being seen or heard from for several days. Then he'd suddenly reappear at the Royalton to resume his duties, without ever mentioning where he'd gone or what he'd been doing. (Skiing in New England, it turned out.) Gertrude Benchley also got a taste of the inscrutable MacGregor style when Benchley made his famous unintended cruise to Europe with Jock Whitney and Nicholas Luddington. He'd already purchased tickets for the Harvard-Yale game, which was being played in a few days at the Yale Bowl in New Haven, and he wired Gertrude from the ship that if she wanted to attend the game, MacGregor was holding the tickets for her. Unfortunately, Gertrude had no success tracking down the elusive assistant. No one at the Royalton had seen him, and even MacGregor's wife had no idea of his whereabouts. Gertrude knew enough about MacGregor, though, to anticipate what might happen. When the day of the game arrived, she went to Grand Central Terminal and stood by the entrance to the platform for the train to New Haven. Sure enough, just moments before the train was scheduled to depart, a breathless MacGregor materialized from out of nowhere, gave her the tickets, and, saying nothing more than "I have no more home than a rabbit," toddled off.

At various times during the six years that MacGregor worked for him, Benchley had his assistant accompany him on trips to California. This proved to be a mixed blessing, though, since MacGregor was not the ideal traveling companion. Possessed of a weak heart, and with a tendency to worry himself sick even when he was technically healthy, MacGregor found both train and air travel uncomfortable—on trains he dreaded taking ill in the middle of nowhere, and on planes he fretted over the effect of high altitudes on his heart. On the other hand, he was remarkably comfortable aboard any boat; he had served in the Navy in the World War and was utterly immune to seasickness. Since Benchley never suffered from seasickness either, the two of them handled stormy seas with particular relish. They sailed to Bermuda one early-1930s summer to hook up with the vacationing Gertrude. While nearly all the other passengers on board took ill when the boat had to push through a terrible storm, Benchley and MacGregor amused themselves by smoking big black cigars and performing dance routines in the ship's main ballroom. When the ship finally arrived safely at its destination, they were just about the only inhabitants sorry to see the voyage end. After all, how often do you get to have a cruise ship all to yourself?

That Benchley got a special kick out of having MacGregor around is evidenced by the many appearances that his assistant began making in Benchley's prose. In fact, it was mostly through MacGregor's repartee with him that Benchley was able to revive in his writing his sense of the absurd. A sample, from the early 1930s:

"If we had a goat," I said to Mr. MacGregor, "it would solve all our problems."

"A what?" he asked without looking up.

"A goat," I repeated.

"It would solve what?" he asked again, still marking down figures.

"All our problems." (He apparently hadn't heard anything I said the first time except the words "would solve.")

There was quite a long silence during which Mr. MacGregor went out and bought some sport shirts. I tended shop.

When he came back he walked straight through the office with his bundle and into the planetarium.

"Who would take care of the goat?" he finally asked.

"Well," I replied, "technically it would come under your department—Public Works . . . [but] you would find me very willing to help, I assure you."

He said no more, but I heard a sound of clicking once, like suitcase snaps being snapped. . . . Hearing nothing for several hours after that, I went into the planetarium. On the table was a note.

"I am running away from home," it read, "to go to sea." The old Navy urge had been too strong for him.

I was a little hurt, but disgust was predominant in my mind. Loyalty to me, the amassing of a great fortune from the business, his brown hat (which he had left in the front office), all these meant nothing to him. Obviously the man was incompetent.

Within two hours private detectives (paid out of my own pocket) had him back in the office. They had found him just as he was enlisting. I thought it best not to say anything about his escapade. He seemed a little subdued.

"About that goat," I said. "When we get it—"

"I bought a goat on the way home from the recruiting station," said Mr. MacGregor. "He's out in the car."

So everything worked out all right.

In March 1931, after several years of successfully avoiding the lure of Hollywood, Benchley traveled to California for a four-week job writing dialogue for a film being produced by Howard Hughes for Radio Pictures. In typical Hollywood fashion, Benchley arrived to begin work and discovered that the genesis of the film was simply that the studio had shot a tremendous amount of aerial footage for another picture, *Hell's Angels*, and was trying to figure out a way to use the excess film. "They have a lot of shots left over," Benchley wrote Gertrude, "and are trying to make a comedy out of them. One of the shots shows a plane crashing, which makes it a little difficult to be funny, even though it turns out that the pilot isn't hurt. They don't even know who is going to be in it." In the letter, Benchley mentioned going to several teas, one at Gloria Swanson's, and another at P. G. Wodehouse's. "He says that he writes stuff which is never heard from again, so he doesn't see why they pay him," Benchley wrote of Wodehouse. "But he'll soon get over worrying about that." Several times in the letter, Benchley noted that he was finding himself with almost nothing to do: "Everyone eats at the Brown Derby (not the one down by the Ambassador, but an uptown one which, thank God, isn't shaped like a derby). I find it simpler just not to eat. . . . Will keep in touch as things happen—but as nothing much seems to be happening—it won't make very exciting reading. I wish, for my sake, that you were all out here, but not for yours."

Luckily for Benchley on a psychological level—though perhaps not a financial one—his guaranteed four-week minimum contract was, after four weeks, reevaluated as a four-week *maximum* contract, as Radio Pictures decided to put the still-untitled comedy on hold. Benchley headed back to New York after his sixth trip to California feeling in his mouth the usual bad taste he experienced whenever he was exposed to too much time in the California sunshine. This time, though, he tried to exorcise some of those feelings by way of an article which was published by the *Yale Review* in its autumn 1931 edition. Entitled "A Possible Revolution in Hollywood," the piece found Benchley endeavoring to explain the difference between life in Hollywood as perceived from the outside by the general public, and life in Hollywood as perceived by someone viewing it from the inside:

> Hollywood is to the rest of the United States what America is to England . . . and yet more is written about Hollywood than about any other section of the country, and what is even more to be wondered at, most of what is written is actually read. There seems to be no limit to the curiosity of the cultured classes in the East concerning the affairs, public and private, of these movie people of Southern California. Considering their low position in the public esteem, they rate an enormous amount of space in contemporary history as it is being written from day to day. In fact, they run second only to the gunmen of the country in agate lines of publicity. . . .
>
> Hollywood is simply a flat, unlovely plain, inhabited by a group of highly ordinary people, all of them quite at sea and usually in a mild state of panic in their chosen work, turning out a product which, except for certain mechanical excellencies, is as unimportant and undistinguished as the mass product of any plant grinding out rubber novelties or automobile accessories. . . .
>
> But there *is* news of Hollywood, news which is just breaking, and it may be that . . . the beginnings of a revolution may have taken place. The Hollywood of 1932 may be as different from the Hollywood of 1931 as the present-day Hollywood is from that of 1910. We can only wait and see. . . . For, after laying waste the rest of the land, the Depression has hit the movies. . . . Wall Street has taken away the check book. Within the past six months the moving picture concerns have, for the first time, been brought face to face with the horticultural fact that money does not grow on the same trees with those California oranges.
>
> . . . In the first place, you must know that everything that has been said about the waste of money in the motion picture business has been an understatement. . . . The comedy "Once in a Lifetime," in which two thousand airplanes were bought for no purpose whatsoever, Mr. P. G. Wodehouse's disclosure that he had received $104,000 a year for

not one line of dialogue that was used, the tales of wide-eyed travellers who have returned from seeing thousands of dollars thrown in the scrap heap daily, all these have been but faint wisps of smoke curling out from a raging subterranean blaze. One can never realize how little money has meant to the motion picture producers until one has helped them actually to throw it away.

All of this went smoothly so long as there was novelty enough in talking motions to bring the public into the theatres merely to hear a voice, albeit indistinct, coming from the mouth, or approximately the mouth, of an image on the screen. Talking pictures were turned out by the hundreds, and there is no genius on earth which could turn out hundreds of good talking pictures. Most of them were simply terrible. But, so long as the public paid to see them, who cared?

Then suddenly somebody began to care, and, of all people, it turned out to be the public. Lay it to a shortage of money or to an unnatural acquisition of taste, whatever the reason, people began to stop going to dull pictures, and, as most pictures were dull, the result was that most pictures lost money. Spending a million dollars on a picture, even if it could have been made for a hundred thousand, was considered good business so long as the picture was going to take in a million and a half or two million. But spending a million dollars on a picture which turned out to gross something under eighteen dollars was almost universally recognized (by the bankers who were furnishing the million) to be uneconomical. . . .

With all of Wall Street's money at its disposal, Hollywood has been able to get actors and actresses from the legitimate stage and writers and directors from all over the world who have been unable to resist the dream-offers made them by men whose judgment in such matters they must, of necessity, hold in low esteem. But with the reduction in such offers which must inevitably follow the resignation of the Goose Who Laid the Golden Egg, Hollywood will discover just how much the California sunlight, the orange juice, and the Art of the Motion Picture have really meant to those who have been flocking out there for the past five years. Just as soon as the scale of salaries in the studios reaches a low enough level to approximate that of the legitimate stage or legitimate writing, the "Menace of the Movies" to the Theatre will vanish into thin air. For most good actors and most good writers would much prefer working on Broadway at five hundred a week to working in Hollywood for seven hundred. It is only when the sum gets up into fifteen hundred or two thousand that the sunlight and orange juice and the Art of the Motion Picture seem to be important.

For Hollywood is not only a dull place in which to live. It is an uncomfortable one. There is the constant realization of espionage, resulting in even the bravest spirits becoming careful, afraid to speak their own minds or laugh at things they want to laugh at. Fifteen hundred dollars a week is too good a sum to throw away just for speaking your mind or laughing in someone's face. And so everyone tiptoes about, making sure just who he is talking to and what he is saying, and going to bed at eleven o'clock. It is safer. Time enough to talk and laugh and be yourself when you have garnered in all that there is to be had and have gone back to New York.

So we find that, just as Hollywood is at its heights as a center for the world's curiosity, it is on the verge of turning into something different. No one can tell what it will change to, if it changes at all. It will either go back to the old days, inhabited by people who are willing to work there at comparatively small salaries and will again justify its old description as "a mining camp with service from the Ritz," or some new producers will come along who can convince Wall Street that they have the secret of the Perfect, or Money-Making, Movie. In the latter event, the flood of gold will begin all over again (as soon as Wall Street finds the gold) and Hollywood will stay as it is.

Deep down, Benchley probably knew his "possible revolution" was a fantasy. While the "flood of gold" didn't begin all over again in 1932, the motion picture business did start to pick up significantly. With the Great Depression now impacting on nearly every American's life, people sought what inexpensive pleasures they could find, and the motion picture house became a place where the common man, after saving up just a little change, could check his troubles at the ticket window and, for a few hours in a darkened theater, allow himself to get good and lost in the make-believe world of Hollywood's (as Benchley often called them) "papier-mâché mountains." Even when times are hard, Wall Street was finding out quickly, entertainment sells, and, in no time, investors and their money started returning to the film business.

Benchley returned as well. In the summer of 1932, he was finishing up the theater season (from January through July, he'd written reviews in twenty-seven straight issues of *The New Yorker*) when Radio Pictures asked him to come out and complete the air comedy, now officially titled *Sky Devils*. He was as reluctant as ever, but the studio offered him dialogue work on several other films, with a fee for each picture added on to a base salary, and Benchley succumbed. He arrived in August and soon found himself at work on a melodrama starring Joel McCrea and William Gargan as a pair of college football heroes. At first Benchley was just rewriting Corey Ford and Francis Cockrell's script, but at some point, executive producer David O. Selznick and director Dudley Murphy talked him into taking a role in the film as well. So it was that Benchley, who hadn't been in front of a motion picture camera since the last of the Fox shorts in 1929, made his feature film debut in a movie called *The Sport Parade*. He appeared in five scenes as an inept sportscaster bumbling his way through several football games, wrestling matches, and a six-day bicycle race. His monologues, while brief, carried the unmistakable Benchley touch. "Birdie seems to be still in the lead—unless he's last," Benchley notes after falling asleep at the microphone during the bike race, and he delivers this hilarious commentary during one of the football games: "Quite a wind blowing today across the diamond— I mean the gridiron . . . the ball is in Harvard—Princeton—Dartmouth's possession on their own, that is, Columbia—*Yale*'s twenty, er, thirty. As I said before, there's quite a wind blowing across the, er, um, *field*. . . ."

"Things are just as terrible out here as ever, and I shall be glad to duck in two weeks," Benchley wrote to Gertrude on August 20 during the filming of *The Sport Parade*. "If they want to keep me another four, I might possibly do it just to get a little more of that money (*what money?*), but I am sure that these two jobs will be finished then and probably shows will be coming into New York." As it happened, RKO kept him working under contract for a total of ten weeks, and he didn't get back to New York until mid-October. He hadn't missed the opening of a theater season since 1921 (E. B. White substituted for him on *The New Yorker*'s theater page), and in his first column back, Benchley expressed his customary embarrassment for once again partaking of the motion picture business's easy money. "If, from now on," he wrote, "there seems to be creeping into the weekly *causeries* a soft note of leniency, an Old World tolerance for the little indiscretions of the Drama, it is because Teacher has been working in Hollywood for three months and is so goddamn glad to see actors on a real stage and in real plays again that practically anything on which a curtain goes up and down is an event of almost insupportable excitement."

"There seems to have been some critical talk about a play called 'I Loved You Wednesday' being too clever," he wrote later on in the column. "It was good, they said, but not as good as it should have been. Listen, my brethren! If a play is good at all, it is so much velvet. This I tell you out of a heart battered from having gone into the writing of dialogue so much more inexcusable than that in 'I Loved You Wednesday' that the authors [of it] tower like so many (two) Whistlers in a group of gag-men."

Just a few weeks after those words were written, *The Sport Parade* was released. The picture received fair reviews and was a meager success financially—and everyone who saw it thought Benchley was just about the best thing in it. One of them was David Selznick, who told Benchley that RKO wanted him under contract again—as a writer *and* an actor—and that the studio was prepared to pay him much more than he was getting as a "mere" writer. The following summer, Benchley once again headed off for California. And, though he may not have realized it at the time, he was firmly on his way toward becoming as much a part of the "Menace of the Movies" as those dreaded papier-mâché mountains.

15
The Kitten Coil, the Leaping Jitters, and the Two-O'Clock Bounce

HOW TO SLEEP—AND WIN AN OSCAR—WITHOUT
REALLY TRYING

C*orey Ford,* the writer responsible for naming *The New Yorker*'s perennial cover boy, Eustace Tilley, was working for RKO Pictures in Hollywood when he looked out the window of his cell-like office one morning in the early 1930s and spied fellow scribe Robert Benchley toddling toward his own cubbyhole at the far end of the long, one-story stucco building known by its inhabitants as the RKO "writers' block." As Ford recalled in his memoir *The Time of Laughter,* Benchley that day seemed to be suffering from "the grandfather of all hangovers, his hands shaky, his face a ghastly gray." Ford asked him if he'd had breakfast. "Had it?" shuddered Benchley. "I've thrown it up." "A garden hose was lying on the grass, parallel to the walk," Ford remembered. And as Benchley made his way painfully towards his office, the gardener gave it an absent-minded flip, sending a snakelike ripple down its length past him. Benchley cast one horrified look, turned on his heel, and drove back to the Garden of Allah and went to bed.

For Robert Benchley, as for nearly all of the film colony denizens who made it their home during the thirties and forties, the Garden of Allah, located on Sunset Boulevard near North Crescent Heights in West Hollywood, was part sanctuary and part sanitarium. The Garden of Allah Hotel and Villas (as it was described on its stationery) had once been the home of Alla Nazimova, the Russian-born silent film star who, along with Mary Pickford, Douglas Fairbanks, Charlie Chaplin, and D. W. Griffith, had formed the United Artists studio in 1921. Nazimova had made her name playing *femmes fatales*—most notably, Camille, opposite her onetime protégé Rudolph Valentino—but by 1925, with her screen career beginning to wane, she was talked by her manager into converting her three-and-a-half-acre estate into a hotel. Twenty-five Spanish-styled two-story bungalows were constructed around the old, odd-shaped swimming pool (supposedly, it had been designed to remind Nazimova of the Black Sea), and the main house was remodeled to include eight more guest rooms, as well as a separate apartment for Nazimova to use for the remainder of her life.

In January 1927, the Garden of Allah—the "h" was added, over Nazimova's objections, to give the hotel a faintly Arabian air—officially opened with a gala all-night party. The guests included John Barrymore, Sam Goldwyn, Marlene Dietrich, and Francis X. Bushman. During its first year, business was slow—most stars preferred the more established Beverly Hills and Ambassador hotels—and the hotel ran up such huge operating debts that Nazimova abruptly sold the property back to its previous owner in 1928. In time, though, the Garden began to acquire a regular clientele with a distinct profile. Because of its many entrances—besides the parking lot on Sunset, one could get inside the grounds from various paths along the neighboring streets on all sides of the property—the Garden was ideally suited to celebrities looking for a kind of privacy and informality that they couldn't find at other Hollywood hotels. Ronald Colman and John Barrymore found the Garden a perfect hideout during messy divorce proceedings. Gilbert Roland found it the perfect place to pursue the onetime "It" girl, Clara Bow. And Tallulah Bankhead found it the perfect place to end a party, jumping into the hotel pool in full evening clothes—and emerging, moments later, stark naked. "People went to the Garden because it was a deluxe hotel without the inconveniences," producer Jed Harris recalled in Hollywood gossip columnist Sheilah Graham's book *The Garden of Allah*. "The anonymity of the place was its chief virtue. It was a short distance, a short drive, from the studios, the restaurants—anywhere you wanted to go. It was an informal place where you could always arrive and be accommodated. It was made for people like Benchley."

It is significant that, for all the ensconced feeling of his suite at the Royalton in New York, Benchley, while he was to spend parts of nearly fifteen years at the Garden of Allah starting in the early 1930s, never once sought to reserve a particular Garden bungalow for his stays in Hollywood; he'd simply arrive in town and rent whichever one was available. Nonetheless, he came to be so closely associated with the Garden of Allah that Graham, one of his closest friends in Hollywood, regarded him as the hotel's patron saint. Whether by inviting fellow writers and actors over to his bungalow for late-afternoon "tea"—martinis served in cups and saucers from a glass teapot—or rounding up a group of friends to take to dinner at the nearby Players Club or Brown Derby, Benchley usually had a crowd around him, day or night, during his time at the Garden. "Every party needs a host, and Bob was the host of hosts at the Garden of Allah," noted Graham. "He would have resented the title, but if a leaf is a photograph of the tree, then Mr. Benchley was the reflection and the heart of the Garden."

Of course, part of the reason for Benchley's dinnertime roundups, especially when the objective was the Players Club, was his own sense of self-preservation. The restaurant was directly across from the Garden of Allah, but rested in a bend on Sunset Boulevard, and the corner where one crossed the street to get there was a blind spot. Since there was no traffic light, the walk was always something of an adventure, and Benchley was terrified of it. Graham recalled that when she went to dinner with Benchley at the Players, she'd usually insist that they walk. "Bob would reluctantly agree, and, taking a fierce grip on my arm, we'd wait and wait for the rare moment when there was no traffic coming. When we reached the other side, Bob would raise his head triumphantly as though he were Washington and had just crossed the Delaware." More often than not, though, Benchley would get a group together and then, according to actress Natalie Schafer, "He'd call for a taxi. We'd have the cab drive about a half a mile down Sunset to where he'd have the driver stop, tell him to wait while he went into any old store on the block, then he'd come back a minute later, and tell the driver to turn around and take us to the Players. All because he couldn't bear to cross the street on foot."

The motion picture industry that Benchley encountered in his first full summer in Hollywood in 1933 was one that was simultaneously both thriving and changing. The talkies, which Benchley himself had helped usher in just five years before with the filming of *The Treasurer's Report*, had eliminated the silent movie, and the major movie studios were forced to recruit a great many theater-based actors and writers to meet the heavy production schedules needed to keep up with both the competition and the demand for new product from the ever-growing audience. Writer and actor Albert Hackett, who first came to Hollywood in the early thirties to serve as a dialogue director for the filming of his hit Broadway play *Up Pops the Devil*, and who was to become, together with his wife and collaborator, Frances Goodrich, one of the most successful screenwriters in Hollywood (their credits include the Thin Man series, *Naughty Marietta, Easter Parade*, and *The Diary of Anne Frank*), recalled that in his early days in Hollywood, few of his colleagues from the stage really believed the movie business was going to continue flourishing. "Once a week, a bunch of us would go over to Jimmy Cagney's house," said Hackett. "Jimmy was already a big star, but he'd want us to put on a play with him—the first act of some melodrama—just so we'd stay fresh. Jimmy'd say, 'Look, when this picture stuff is over, we're going to have to go back to New York and *work*, so we'd better be ready.'"

For their part, the studio executives regarded most of the newly arrived stage-bred actors (especially those whose names fell below the marquee), as well as virtually all the playwrights and novelists hired to work on scripts, as completely replaceable parts on the dream factory assembly line. This was especially true when it came to screenplay writers. It was not uncommon for a studio such as Metro-Goldwyn-Mayer to use up to ten different writers on a screenplay, and for the final, filmed version to bear little if any resemblance to the original story the studio claimed it was intending to shoot. Then again, sometimes a screenplay could go full circle. Hackett remembered the first script he and Goodrich were put to work on when they were under contract to MGM.

> The day we arrived we were shown a "sick" picture which everyone in the studio was working on. After we had seen it in a projection room, we were called into a meeting and asked what we thought of it. Of course we said we thought it was terrible. The production was bad; the writing was bad; the direction was bad; the acting was awful. I guess we must have offended about fifteen different people right then and there, and before we had really landed in the place we were in the doghouse.
>
> They threw the story in to keep us company, and said that since we didn't like it, maybe we could fix it. We worked like badgers and when we had fixed it up we took it to the only friendly person we knew out there at the time, Zelda Sears. When she read it, she burst out laughing. "Why," she said, "you've written it back into just what it was to begin with. And do you know why I know that? Because I wrote the original story!"

Having been placed under contract to RKO Radio Pictures as both a writer and an actor, Benchley no sooner arrived in Hollywood in mid-May than he was immediately thrust into a frantic production pace both in front of and behind the camera lens. In a letter to Gertrude dated June 28, 1933, he noted, "I am so dead when I get home from the studio that I can't keep out of bed," and, reading the list of all the projects he'd already been involved in just in the space of six weeks, it was easy for Gertrude to understand his weariness. "The pictures I have worked on so far," he wrote, "have been 'The Headline Shooter' with William Gargan, in which I do a bit as a radio announcer (I am the stock radio announcer, I guess); 'In the Fog' (which will be changed in name) with Roland Young and Laura Hope Crews in it; 'Flaming Gold' with Pat O'Brien and someone else; 'Rafter Romance' with Ginger Rogers and Norman Foster (Laura Crews was in that, too, and she and I had a scene together); and 'Frivolous Sal' with Irene Dunne. I haven't done anything on 'The Glory Command' yet, although I am supposed to play a bit in it, and John Cromwell asked me if I would play a part in 'Ann Vickers' with Dunne when it gets under way." Benchley said that he'd spent most of the last week "hectic with acting" in *Rafter Romance*, and that, while he was doing his best to avoid having to act in the first place, "they do take me off any writing assignment I may be on when I have to act. At any rate, I am not on one picture long enough to get sick of it."

While acting in *Rafter Romance*, Benchley, playing the role of a zealous sales manager for the "Icy Air Refrigerator Company," got to see firsthand one humbling aspect of the changes that the advent of talkies had caused among the Hollywood acting community. "All day Friday and Saturday we were out at a park, shooting an employees' picnic scene at which I had to lead songs and cheers," he wrote. "Some of the extras are people who used to be featured players in the old days, and are now out working for $7.50 a day—and glad to get it."

Actually, Benchley was "hectic" with a lot of things during the summer of 1933. For one thing, David Selznick, who'd contracted Benchley for the work he was doing for RKO, had just moved over to MGM (he'd assumed the position of studio production manager after marrying the daughter of MGM president Louis B. Mayer), and Selznick approached Benchley about making a new series of shorts for Metro—"one short a month on various news subjects"—and, knowing how much Benchley disliked Hollywood, he went so far as to intimate that

Benchley could probably film the shorts in New York. "He's offering a thousand dollars down for each one and a quarter of the profits," Benchley wrote Gertrude. "It sounds like a good proposition—if there are any profits." (Benchley was already mistrusting the studio accounts of profits and losses. Just a few months previous, he'd allowed Universal Studios to talk him into doing a two-reeler entitled *Your Technocracy or Mine*—a lecture parody of the popular new "theories of technocracy" going around at the time—and, supposedly, Benchley was going to receive a percentage of the profits. None were ever forthcoming, even though the film was a great success and ran for months all across the country.)

As if this weren't enough for him to handle, June 1933 also marked the beginning of his thrice-weekly humor column for the Hearst syndicate. It's not surprising, then, that he was soon turning out pieces like "A Writer's Code," on the difficulties of meeting deadlines and working to word counts. "I once heard of a man who, when asked to fill out a column with a few words, made up an anecdote about a man who made up an anecdote in order to fill a column, and was later sued for libel by another author who claimed that he was unmistakably the one referred to and that his professional standing with editors had been irreparably damaged. Both writers were fired and later married each other. (One of the writers was a woman.)"

By August, Benchley's schedule was turning (as he wrote Gertrude, who was in Siasconset with Nat and Bobby and hoping that Benchley could join them for at least part of the summer) from hectic to "frantic," because of his being "loaned" to MGM to work on *Dancing Lady*, a movie starring Joan Crawford and Clark Gable.

When I was called over to MGM, it was to write on the picture, which was going into production almost immediately. Then they found a part in it which they thought I could play (that of a newspaper columnist) and, as a favor to Dave (and also because I have to, according to my contract), I agreed. So several shots were made of me, thereby establishing me irrevocably in the picture. . . . In the meantime, Gable, with whom I have three or four scenes, came down with appendicitis and had to have an operation. So the whole picture is waiting for him to come back, and I have to wait until those shots are made before I can leave. There is no other way, except for them to spend a lot of money and re-take the scenes which have already been made with me in them, and that would involve hiring a whole party-scene full of extras in one shot. They think Gable will be back a week from Monday and then nobody knows when they will get around to the scenes with me in them. I knew I shouldn't get mixed up with acting. But Dave is the one who is going to let me make shorts in the East during the winter, and that would be something worth keeping in with him for.

As it turned out, Gable didn't get back to working on *Dancing Lady* until mid-September, and Benchley spent most of the ensuing time at RKO fixing up scripts during the week, working on syndicate pieces during the weekends, and trying (without much success) to stay on a diet that depended on his staying on the wagon. As in the previous year, Benchley was stuck in Hollywood just as the theater season in New York was beginning, and the frustration became increasingly evident in a series of cables he sent Gertrude. On September 13, he wired, "It looks as if the governor is going to pardon me soon," but on September 21, he sent word that "MGM has got me hooked, and can't leave until October 4. At least I'm actually acting for first time." October 4 came and went, and Benchley was still on call. "They didn't get around at all to me today," he complained. "It'll probably be the end of the week before I can get away." Even that estimate proved woefully optimistic, though. By the time Benchley— playing the role of Ward King, a world-weary Broadway gossip columnist hanging around the theater where beleaguered stage director Patch Gallagher (Gable) is trying to save a faltering musical starring "Dancing Lady" Joan Crawford—completed filming his three ninety-second scenes with Gable and was paroled from the set, it was October 15. And, adding insult to injury, RKO balked at paying Benchley's train fare back east, telling him he should take up the matter with MGM. Finally, on October 20, Benchley arrived back in New York—and, under the somewhat disdainful eye of Harold Ross, was back in his *New Yorker* theater critic's seat for the opening of a show the very next evening.

Still, a guaranteed weekly salary some three to four times greater than his *New Yorker* pay was more than Benchley could afford to turn down—especially for what he still considered just "a summer job" while Broadway was preparing for its new season. So, while his relationship with RKO had been considerably strained by the events of the previous summer, Benchley nonetheless was back at work for the studio in 1934, albeit for a shorter contract and with a decidedly less taxing schedule of both writing and acting. He and Marc Connelly were asked to try to work up a screenplay based on P. G. Wodehouse's novel *Piccadilly Jim,* an assignment Benchley wrote that he found "very pleasant—although a bit difficult, as there is nothing in the book (written in 1916) to make a picture from."

Sharing one of the Garden's two-bedroom bungalows with Connelly helped brighten Benchley's spirits considerably, as did the presence of a number of other old friends. Donald Stewart, fast evolving into one of MGM's top writers (in 1933 alone, he'd received onscreen credits for four films, including *Dinner at Eight*), was working on *The Barretts of Wimpole Street,* and he and his wife, Bea, spent a great deal of time with them. Later that summer, Dorothy Parker and her dashingly handsome new husband, former stage actor Alan Campbell, showed up to work as dialogue writers for Paramount, and Benchley found Hollywood in 1934 not quite so dreary and humorless a place to be. (It also hadn't hurt that, back in December, the Eighteenth Amendment had finally been repealed, and liquor was back on everyone's shelf, rather than under it.) He even got a quiet sense of vindication when, years after the *Funny Face* fiasco, he was asked to collaborate on the screen adaptation of Fred Astaire's Broadway hit *The Gay Divorcée* and saw the film end up with many of his lines intact—albeit uncredited. (Actually, Benchley was to receive his first official screenplay credit for a film he worked on during this trip—the 1935 RKO release *Murder on a Honeymoon*.)

That summer Benchley also filmed a short for RKO, entitled *How to Break 90 at Croquet.* Like *Your Technocracy or Mine,* it was intended as a parody of a topical subject—in this case, a popular series of instructional shorts that had been made by golf professional Bobby Jones under the title *How to Break 90.* Benchley had recently addressed the subject of croquet in a magazine piece for the *Detroit Athletic Club News,* explaining, "The idea of the game is to knock a wooden ball through the wickets with a wooden mallet in such a manner as to make a loud clicking noise," and advising, "A good rule to remember is 'Never push the ball through the wicket—unless you can do it on the sly with your foot.' " Directed by Leigh Jason, who'd recently come to RKO from the Hal Roach studios, the film uses a number of slapstick sight gags—for example, while an off-camera Benchley describes the intricacies of assuming the correct stance for properly hitting the croquet ball, a contortionist is shown following the instructions until he is, literally, tied up in knots—and, additionally, the old habit of having Benchley appear to be lecturing at some luncheon or assembly is dropped; Benchley simply looks straight into the camera and talks directly to the movie audience. At one point, he says to another character, "I just want to make it clear to these people out front." "What people?" says the other man, looking quite confused. "I don't see any people!" To which Benchley laughingly responds, "You'll just have to take my word for it. There are people out there. At least I hope so."

There indeed were, and in the winter of 1935, not long after RKO released *How to Break 90 at Croquet*, Benchley was notified by his Hollywood agent, David Selznick's older brother, Myron, that the younger Selznick wanted Benchley to come and work for him at MGM. There was a particular film, about to go into production, that Selznick wanted Benchley to appear in—a big-budget action-adventure movie called *China Seas*, starring Gable, Jean Harlow, Wallace Beery, and Rosalind Russell. Benchley was interested, but with filming set to begin in late March, he knew he'd have to run it by Ross. Not that there was much Ross could do about it; he wanted Benchley in the magazine as much as possible, but he also knew he simply didn't have the money to compete with the movie business for Benchley's services. With his usual grumblings, Ross gave Benchley his blessing and left coverage of the remainder of the Broadway season to Wolcott Gibbs, who had replaced E. B. White as the designated Benchley substitute.

On the transcontinental train ride out to California, Benchley got to witness firsthand the terrible dust storms that were crippling much of the western half of the country. "That sandstorm we came through in Kansas was a honey," Benchley wrote Gertrude on March 25. "They had to take our engineer and fireman to the hospital for their eyes, and two trains ahead of us came together. They were going so slow, however, that nobody was hurt. The people on the California Limited (which was one of them) had to wrap wet towels around their heads when they went back to flag other trains, and all the towns that we went through had water flushing through the streets all night to prevent drifts from forming."

Benchley knew his acting assignment on *China Seas* was going to be a bit different from his previous roles when he reported for wardrobe and was told he would need "three of everything—one set of clothes for the water sequence, one for the mud sequence, and one for dress-up." In the film, Benchley plays an American writer named McCaleb, providing comic relief for a story centering around a Gable-captained ship that sails from Hong Kong to Singapore and survives both a typhoon and an attack by Chinese pirates—events that Benchley's character, who is drunk during the entire picture, remains blissfully unaware of. Along the way, Benchley performs a number of sight gags—he plays chopsticks on a piano as it rolls across a room, lights a cigarette on deck in the middle of a typhoon, and, at the end of the film, falls off the ship entirely. "I had to float around in the water for half an hour this morning," Benchley wrote on April 16. "Don [Stewart] came down just to watch me flounder around, and threw orange peels and bits of lettuce in at me."

Though stand-ins were used for many of the rougher sequences, it was determined that the cigarette-lighting scene needed to look authentic, and so Benchley spent all of May 9, his last day of work on the film, "being hit by a ton of water from over the side of the ship eleven times. Someone had to lie down and hold my legs, to keep me from being toppled over by the force of it. Gable and the others who were supposed to be on deck in the storm were knocked clean off their feet each time, but the point of the gag was that I, the drunk, was the only one who stood up under it, still trying to light my cigarette with a lighter when the wave had passed. They, however, were in oil skins and I was in a tuxedo. . . . The water came onto the deck just like a regular wave, and I'm here to tell you that it did. Thanks to a pint of rye furnished by the company, I was warmer when I finished than when I started."

Benchley had never been on one film for such a long period of time, and in his letters to Gertrude throughout the shooting of *China Seas*, he kept noting how surprised he was to be actually enjoying the work. At one point, he even felt comfortable enough to pull a practical joke on director Tay Garnett, who got married during the filming of the movie. "We all chipped in and gave him a pair of fine steamer blankets for his new sail boat," wrote Benchley. "They asked me to present them to him, and, as I had a scene where I was supposed to make a speech at the Captain's table, I ran the presentation speech right into my regular lines. He was sitting in front of me, directing, and when I got into the presentation part, they say he almost went crazy trying to figure out what was happening." Benchley also received an enormous ego boost his final day on the set when Harlow, then the country's leading sex goddess, approached him with a request. "I suppose you'll hit me," she said, "but could I have your autograph?" "That's news all right—man bites dog," Benchley wrote to Nathaniel, now a freshman at Harvard. "If you want, Nat, I'll give you an autographed picture of myself—one with all *my* clothes off."

After finishing *China Seas*, Benchley was put to work by MGM on a writing and acting assignment that was to alter his relationship not only with the studio and the Hollywood community as a whole, but with the film-going public as well. In the early 1930s, a former MGM publicity and advertising executive named Pete Smith began to produce a variety of shorts for the studio that, straddling the line between educational and comic films, proved quite popular. (Typical of Smith's work were his early-1930s "MGM Oddities," such as *Motorcycle Cossacks*, showing the Mexico City Police Department's motorcycle corps in synchronized action, and *Vital Victuals*, a cooking demonstration aimed at budding homemakers.) Reportedly at the request of the Simmons Mattress Company, which had funded a six-year study of the mysteries of sleep by the Mellon Institute of Pittsburgh and was now seeking publicity of that study's results, Smith scheduled production for a 1935 short about people's sleeping habits. When the time came to start preparing the script, however, Smith took ill, and it was suggested (probably by David Selznick) that Benchley take a try at it. Jack Chertok, the production head of MGM's short-subject department, was at first dubious about using Benchley. He knew little about Benchley's previous experience as either a writer or an actor—so little, in fact, that at their first meeting he bluntly told Benchley that "he didn't look like a comedian" and asked him just what he did that was funny. Benchley explained as best he could, and, upon this rocky foundation, work commenced on the MGM short, *How to Sleep.*

Benchley worked on the script for the film during the latter part of May, and the film was shot in two days in early June. ("The acting was not much of a strain," Benchley later recalled, "as I was in bed most of the time.") Directed by Nick Grinde, *How to Sleep* effectively brought together several facets of Benchley's humor. The film opens with Benchley, dressed in a three-piece suit, sitting behind a desk and looking cheerfully officious. "If you remember, in our last lecture," he begins, "we took up the subject of how to keep awake. And, on looking about me, I notice that many of you did not seem quite to catch the idea. Today, therefore, we are taking up the subject of how to sleep—and I am hoping for a better response."

After establishing the character of the narrator/lecturer, Benchley begins to describe the ways in which one can facilitate a good night's sleep, and at each juncture, while the offscreen Benchley offers the theoretical wisdom of each activity, the on-screen Benchley demonstrates the often diametrically opposed practical results of such undertakings. "There are several methods of drawing the blood sufficiently from the brain to induce sleep," he notes. "For example, the hot pine bath. . . ." Benchley is shown preparing his bath and eagerly stepping in—that is, until his toe comes in contact with the scaldingly hot water, and he runs from the room. "Of course, there is always the alternative method of *not* taking the hot pine bath," muses the narrator. "In this case, the man has succeeded only in putting his left foot to sleep, but that's something. A little more each night and he will soon be cured of his insomnia."

Once set, the pattern continues: Benchley goes to the kitchen to warm up a glass of milk, but when he returns the bottle to the ice box, he discovers some leftover cold lobster—and coleslaw, and chicken, and pie—and soon is gorging himself silly. "This will fix up that insomnia, all right," notes Benchley. "But, on the whole, when using the hot-milk method, it's better to have the milk brought to you by someone else after you have gotten into bed." Once in bed (and wearing some hilarious loud-print pajamas), Benchley is prevented from falling asleep by an assortment of distractions ranging from dripping faucets to flapping window shades to flying insects. Even counting sheep doesn't help, because of that other great sleep preventive—worry. "Worry can be caused by putting your mind on any one thing," he notes. "No matter what it is, you'll find it easy enough to worry about it in the middle of the night. There is a theory that if you count imaginary sheep jumping over a fence you will induce sleep. This has proven to be a fallacy, as the patient is likely to start worrying about one of the sheep not quite making it."

At one point, Benchley is shown bolting upright in bed, then wandering around the room aimlessly. "This form of sleeplessness," he explains, "is known as the leaping jitters, or the two-o'clock bounce." While Benchley sits down on the edge of the bed, looking ghastly and agitatedly clutching at himself, the offscreen Benchley describes the illness. "This condition is induced by alcoholic excesses and manifests itself by a pounding of the heart, a tightening of the throat causing suffocation, and a cold moisture appearing on the forehead. If the patient had not indulged in his appetite to the detriment of his health, he would not be in this condition," admonishes Benchley. "And this is a lesson all of us should take to heart.." As he says this, the onscreen Benchley suddenly looks up toward the direction of the voice and snaps, "Oh, shut up and mind your business!" "You see?" continues the narrator. "He's in a state of nervous irritability as well as sleeplessness."

The next part of the film is devoted to an examination of how people move around in bed while they're asleep. "We have here a pamphlet issued by the Mellon Institute of Pittsburgh," says Benchley, holding up a copy of "Bodily Positions in Restful Sleep." The actual booklet, written by H. M. Johnson, Ph.D., who had headed up the Mellon Institute's investigation of sleep, featured a photographic record of all the positions the average person takes over the course of a normal eight-hour sleep cycle, with names for each one ("Supine Curl," "Right Ventro-Lateral Sprawl," and so on)—and Benchley, simultaneously echoing and parodying the study, describes shots of a man lying in bed in various outrageous positions. ("Our patient then dropped off into the Kitten Coil, which he held for twenty minutes—practically a record for the course! . . . The best way to get into *this* position is to fall into it from above. This is a great favorite with drunks.")

In the final segment of the short, Benchley returns to the "poor sleeper," who's now lying in bed trying to decide what to do about the sudden thirst that's taken hold of him. "He's running three courses over in his mind: to get up and get a drink, to lie there and die of thirst, or to go back to sleep. The last is out of the question, the second would take too long—oh, he might as well get the drink of water." Benchley gets out of bed and stumbles toward the bathroom, where, in typical Benchley "Bumbler" fashion, he does battle with the medicine cabinet (reaching for a glass, he knocks just about everything *except* the glass off the shelf and into the sink) and his old nemesis, the faucet (first, with his eyes barely open, he misses the glass entirely; then he turns the faucet on too much and spills most of the water). When, at last, he's finally quenched his thirst, he tries to feel his way back to the bed without really opening his eyes—and, naturally, trips over a pair of shoes lying by the side of the bed. The last shot of Benchley in bed shows him finally drifting off, a peaceful smile spread across his face. The clock on the night table reads 7:20. "There's no sense in trying to go to sleep now; that clock is going to ring," warns the narrator, who is starting to sound as if *he's* nodding off. The camera returns to Benchley at his desk for a closing statement—and finds him propped up on one elbow, barely awake. "Well," he says, groggily, "I guess that [yawn] will be all [yawn] for today."

How to Sleep tested so well in previews that MGM decided to put a significant promotional push behind its official release, which was scheduled for mid-September 1935. The Simmons Mattress Company was delighted as well—so much so that it made arrangements to use a still from the short in a Macy's bedding ad. In fact, about the only people who didn't think much of the short when they saw it in previews were the folks at the Mellon Institute, who weren't amused by Benchley's poking fun at their six-year study. Representatives of Mellon wrote Fred Quimby, the executive head of MGM's short-subjects department, and requested that the film be withdrawn from circulation. "This short subject uses copyrighted material that is being used without our permission," they asserted, "and the reference to the Mellon Institute in conjunction with this picture might be deemed libelous." MGM's always jittery legal department began to put pressure on Quimby to do something to placate the Mellon people, and Quimby went so far as to have Jack Chertok look into the cost of reshooting some scenes with Benchley so as to eliminate the specific references to Mellon and the display of the "Bodily Positions in Restful Sleep" pamphlet.

In late October, the Simmons Company put an end to all the bickering by telling the Mellon Institute that since Simmons had provided all of the funding for the sleep study, and, indeed, had paid for the printing of the results in book form, "Bodily Positions in Restful Sleep" was, technically, its property. Therefore, as Simmons had no problem whatsoever with the use of the material, Mellon had no legal right to complain about its use. Finally, at the very end of October, *How to Sleep* was formally released to theaters nationwide—and proved to be an instant hit.

Since it had already tested so well with audiences in previews, MGM had gone ahead and quickly put Benchley to work in September on two more "How to" shorts—*How to Train a Dog* and *How to Behave*. Benchley wasn't particularly enthusiastic about either of them, mainly because of an MGM official named Harry Rapf, who had been the executive producer of *How to Sleep*. "Rapf," Benchley wrote Gertrude, "who hadn't liked it up until the successful previews and had made a point of saying so, is now convinced he must get credit for all future ones (he had nothing to do with *How to Sleep* except to crab) and has decided that we must do the next two at once. He has transferred the man who really worked with me [Chertok], and is taking the whole thing over himself, now that he thinks he has a good thing, and the result is that I am working night and day on some things that I know won't pan out as well as *How to Sleep.*"

Benchley's assessment was accurate, to a degree. *How to Train a Dog*, another Pete Smith–intended film which Benchley had no hand in scripting, is a slow-paced spoof of dog-training techniques that is mostly a collection of quite predictable sight gags. (Benchley, with whip in hand, tries to teach a tiny puppy how to roll over; before long, it's he who's rolling over, to the great amusement of the dog.) *How to Behave*, on the other hand, which Benchley *did* write, features a number of very funny scenes all concerning matters of etiquette.

(The best one deals with introductions at social gatherings. While narrator Benchley explains the intricacies of properly introducing people to each other in regard to age, gender, and position, the on-screen Benchley is shown fumbling his way through the presentation of a priest to six women of varying ages, and growing progressively flustered—until he just throws up his hands and yells, "Oh, figure it out for yourselves!") Whatever the shortcomings of these two films, however, the speed with which MGM got them made was a clear indication that it believed Benchley to be a marketable screen personality—and its instincts were proved correct when *How to Sleep* went on to win an Oscar as the best comedic short subject of 1935.

It was around this time that Benchley's instincts were to consult professional help to determine the exact state of his personal health. The previous summer, his faithful secretary, MacGregor, who had always feared that his heart would give out on him, had collapsed and died while on vacation in Bermuda. The shock, as well as his own mounting weight problem (after having spent most of the 1920s at around 150 pounds, Benchley had, from the time he turned forty, begun gaining an average of five pounds a year), motivated Benchley to have a complete physical. Enlisting the companionship of Donald Stewart, who himself had been complaining of stomach cramps that he was afraid might be ulcers, Benchley and Stewart went to see Cecil Jones, a doctor who'd been recommended to Benchley by Lewis Milestone. After preliminary examinations, Jones checked both of them into Wilshire Hospital for a week of tests.

Writing to Gertrude from the hospital, Benchley reported on the doctor's findings, which included an assessment of what his now habitual drinking was doing to his system:

Instead of being sub-thyroid, which I'd always suspected, my basal was plus eighteen, which is on the high side. However, the reason I am not getting the benefit of this thyroid, in the way of consuming fat and giving off energy, is that my liver is sluggish and is giving off toxins (uric acid) into the blood stream (I may not be getting this right, but the idea is there) which is occupying all the thyroid's time to get rid of. As soon as this toxic condition is remedied, all that plus eighteen will be free to make me beautiful and vital. This is absolutely the only thing wrong with me, and wait until you hear what is right! He said I was the luckiest guy in the world, in that, for every flaw in my system I seem to have some compensatory thing which takes care of it—no thanks to me. My hemoglobin is 100 percent. I have a lovely assortment of red corpuscles . . . and my stools—you could sell them at a bazaar for favors! (He did say that a possible shortage in gonads would explain my inability to open letters or answer the telephone, or in other ways to face the little realities of life.) Also, negative Wassermann!"

Apparently, spending a week in the hospital alongside Stewart (the two had adjoining rooms) helped rekindle some of the old practical joke spirit with which the two had once terrorized Manhattan. After returning to the Garden of Allah, Benchley was receiving regular visits from Dr. Jones, who, Benchley wrote, "was coming by every other day to shoot something or other into me." Jones kept telling Benchley the injections were "just to make sure we're on the right track," and that gave Benchley an idea. One day when Jones came to his bungalow, he was met at the door by Stewart, who with a look of grave concern pointed him toward Benchley's bedroom. Benchley was lying in bed with the covers drawn up to his neck and a look of helplessness spread across his face.

"Now, now," said the doctor, trying to be cheerful. "What seems to be the trouble? Aren't we feeling well today?"

"Well, *we're* not sure," replied Benchley, pulling down the covers and turning over on his stomach to reveal a growth of feathers and fur extending from the back of his neck all the way down to his rear end. "Is this what you meant by the right track?"

16
A Confused Liberal in King Louis B.'s Court

INGENUE OR OTHERWISE, THE EYES HAVE IT

In June 1938, Robert Benchley stood in line at the Culver City council chamber to cast his vote in the Hollywood screenwriters' affiliation election. Mandated by the National Labor Relations Board, the election pitted the writer-backed Screen Writers Guild against the producer-supported Screen Playwrights and signaled the culmination of a pitched battle that had raged between the writers and the studios for nearly five years. The Screen Writers Guild had been formed in July 1933, as a response to a pay cut that MGM had imposed on all of its employees, and though those wages were restored the following year, the guild, under the stewardship of such leaders as John Howard Lawson and Nunnally Johnson, continued to work to protect writers from being indiscriminately trampled, both economically and artistically, by the movie studios. (Not that the writers were the only studio employees who needed protecting: When a new Motion Picture Code was in the process of being incorporated into Franklin Delano Roosevelt's National Industrial Recovery Act in October 1933, the studios lobbied for a provision that would have prevented any writer, actor, or director from earning more than $100,000 a year. It took a personal visit by Screen Actors Guild president Eddie Cantor and writers Fannie Hurst and Robert Sherwood to persuade President Roosevelt to have the provision eliminated.)

Benchley had joined the Screen Writers Guild in 1936, when, among other affronts, the studio-run Academy of Motion Picture Arts and Sciences issued an edict giving producers the sole right to allocate writing credits "based on an assessment of substantial contributions"—in other words, pretty much as they pleased. By 1938, the guild, trying to force a showdown, was petitioning the National Labor Relations Board for certification as the official bargaining representative of motion picture screenwriters, and the June 28, 1938, election gave writers the opportunity to choose between the guild and the studio's Screen Playwrights organization.

Three polling places were set up, with the Culver City site used for the MGM writers, and, to ensure that no fraudulent votes were cast, "checkers" from each side were on hand to verify that each person taking part in the election was certified. "The studios were running all sorts of people in, claiming they were writers," recalled Albert

Hackett, whose wife, Frances, was the Guild's assigned checker for MGM writers. "Jean Harlow's mother showed up, and when Frances challenged, she said Louis B. Mayer had contracted her to writing dialogue for her daughter's pictures!" When it was Benchley's turn to vote, Howard Emmett Rogers, the Screen Playwrights checker, challenged *him*, claiming he was an actor, not a writer. Rogers, an MGM suspense film scenarist who'd been a producer's darling since the early thirties, was so conservative he was usually categorized as a reactionary—and so, lifting a page from the Revolutionary War history book, Benchley looked Rogers square in the eye and snapped, "Get away from me, you Knickerbocker Grey!" As the cringing Rogers retreated, Benchley cast his vote for the Screen Writers Guild, which went on to win the election by a better than four-to-one margin.

While Benchley supported the Screen Writers Guild, his physical involvement in it, or, for that matter, in any of the numerous political and humanitarian causes that were being spiritedly taken up by Hollywood's literary community in the mid and late 1930s, was fairly minimal—a sharp contrast to the tremendous amount of energy that was being expended by some of his oldest friends in the name of social change and justice. "Don [Stewart] is very much engrossed in the new liberal movement which is sweeping Hollywood," he wrote to Gertrude in the spring of 1936. "Everyone is on a committee to free the Scottsboro Boys, or help the Jews in Germany, or boost the Screen Writers Guild. Dottie and Alan are on *all* committees at once, and seem to be very happy about it. It is a new angle for Hollywood, and not a bad one. Last night I went to an anti-Nazi dinner at $20 a plate, at which $5,200 was raised for the Jewish refugees. It is all very laudable—and expensive."

Dorothy Parker and Donald Stewart had been instrumental in the creation of the Hollywood Anti-Nazi League, which sought to mobilize the film community in fighting Adolf Hitler's fascist regime and its persecution of German Jews. (By the end of the decade, the league counted a membership of nearly four thousand.) Stewart, the organization's chairman, had been leaning increasingly toward the left in his political views, and began to perceive himself as a socialist, even a Communist. "I had won all the money and status that America had to offer," he recalled decades later, "and it just hadn't been good enough." Socialism, he believed, was the answer to the world's problems—and to his own lack of spiritual fulfillment. In the Soviet Union, he found an example of "a country where the underdog had taken power into his own hands, and I wanted to be on the side of the underdog. . . . Over in the corner of my imagination, behind the worker, there crouched an image of a little man who needed my help—the oppressed, the unemployed, the hungry, the sharecropper, the Jew under Hitler, the Negro."

Stewart's sentiments were shared, to a great extent, by Parker, who during the latter part of the 1930s threw herself into "the good fights" with much the same blind passion that she'd always been famous for in her love affairs. Pivotal in Parker's transformation was the Spanish Civil War, a conflict that she witnessed firsthand during a ten-day visit in 1937. Writing for the left-wing weekly *The New Masses*, she reported on the struggles of the Soviet Union—backed Loyalist government against Francisco Franco's fascistic Falangist forces, and the terror etched into the faces of the children she saw in the streets of Valencia after several devastating raids by Franco's German-built warplanes. "The only group I have ever been affiliated with is that not particularly brave little band that hid its nakedness of heart and mind under the out-of-date garment of a sense of humor," she wrote. "I heard someone say, and so I said it, too, that ridicule is the most effective weapon. Well, now I know. I know that there are things that never have been funny, and never will be. And I know that ridicule may be a shield, but it is not a weapon."

Benchley, who, from his experiences with the *New York Tribune Graphic* and the Aircraft Board during the World War, had learned early in life that there were, indeed, many things that were not at all funny, often found himself squirming whenever Parker or Stewart tried to draw him into political discussions designed, he knew, to move him toward their points of view. Although he certainly preferred capitalism to communism, Benchley, a registered Republican who usually voted Democratic ("a confused liberal" was how he described himself), had an innate mistrust of governments—any governments. Like most Americans, he found the Spanish Civil War an unfortunate situation. Unlike most Americans, though, he'd lost his only sibling to a war that had involved Spain, and he had no desire to see the

United States take action for either side—although, if forced to choose, he certainly would come down on the side of the antifascists. People familiar with his brother's death knew not to press the matter; when, in July 1937, Ernest Hemingway arrived in Hollywood looking for help in the distribution of a documentary about the war that he'd partially financed and had written and narrated, Benchley attended the private screening at actor Frederic March's house, but no one was surprised when he declined to make a donation after an appeal was made to pay for ambulances needed by the Loyalist forces at the Spanish front.

(He had, however, helped end a war on the home front earlier in the day by arranging a small luncheon that included both Hemingway and new Garden of Allah resident F. Scott Fitzgerald, who was in Hollywood on a six-month writing contract with MGM. The two authors hadn't spoken in years, ever since Hemingway referred to Fitzgerald as "poor Scott" in his story "The Snows of Kilimanjaro." "It sounds like I'm dead," Fitzgerald had complained to Sheilah Graham, though, in point of fact, the descent of his wife, Zelda, into madness, his ongoing battles with alcoholism, and the paucity of fiction he'd produced in recent years had indeed made him an object of pity for those who knew him well. By not telling either one that the other would be present, Benchley managed to orchestrate what proved to be a friendly reunion. Hemingway altered the offending passage in the story in later printings of "The Snows of Kilimanjaro" to further smooth things over with Fitzgerald.)

As Stewart and Parker swung farther and farther to the left politically, they found their friendships with Benchley significantly strained. As far as Parker was concerned, a harbinger of things to come happened in New York in the spring of 1937, shortly before Benchley headed off to the West Coast to begin work on his series of MGM shorts for that year. There was a strike by the hotel employees at the Waldorf-Astoria, and many of the old Algonquin crowd, no longer in the habit of lunching together very often but still up for a good public nose-thumbing when the spirit moved them, had joined the picket line in a brief demonstration of solidarity with the strikers. After the demonstration, Parker and Heywood Broun decided to go for a drink at the 21 Club, where they walked right past a picket line that the 21 Club waiters had set up as a statement of support of the striking hotel workers.

Benchley, who'd passed on Alexander Woollcott's invitation to join the demonstration at the Waldorf, was at his regular booth at 21 when Broun and Parker arrived. At the time, Broun was helping to found the Newspaper Guild (he was to be its first president), and Benchley, already with a few drinks in him, went over to the corner banquette where they'd sat down and proceeded to berate Broun for fancying himself a labor leader when he'd just crossed a picket line—and for a cause he'd just been demonstrating for, no less! Finishing with Broun, Benchley turned to Parker, who was slinking down in her chair and trying to hide under a floppy black hat. "And you," snorted Benchley, "don't blink those ingenue eyes at me!"

"One of the minor feuds of the early summer season" was how Benchley described the consequence of his remark to Parker. "Dottie didn't mind my views on her labor activities," Benchley wrote to Gerald Murphy on July 1 from Hollywood, "but the 'ingenue' line (so I am told) cut her to the quick, and, during the month that she and Alan have been out here, they have refused to answer the telephone, although I have tried six or seven times. Finally, last Saturday, I paid a personal call at their hotel and left a note saying that I had just dropped by for a swim. (There was no pool at their hotel.) Mysterious underground forces have been at work since then, and tonight I am asked to dinner at the Wells Roots and, I understand, am to be seated at the same table as the Campbells. It almost seems as if I am back at Rosemary Hall, and I am sure that we will all end up making fudge in Alan's room later in the evening."

Outside of the fudge-making festivities, this was indeed what happened. After their not speaking to each other for several months, the first serious breach between Mr. Benchley and Mrs. Parker was closed as soon as the two caught sight of each other at the Roots' dinner party, and Benchley apologized.

Nonetheless, in Benchley's eyes, Parker was changing, and it was a change that he wasn't completely eager to accept. Her statements about the old Algonquin notion of humor being out of date, and in particular about ridicule being an effective weapon, underscored the differences in their perspectives on the human condition. Frank Sullivan wrote about Parker several years after her death in 1967, "She was at war with herself all her life. Maybe most of us are, and some negotiate ceasefires occasionally, which seldom last. All the digs she took at people, friend and foe alike, were really digs at herself." Parker's humor, while always clever, was usually belittling, and often cruel. There were things and people that needed to be ridiculed, and she could always be counted on to make sure they *were* ridiculed. The one element that her humor often lacked, though, was empathy—and empathy was central to Benchley's wit. Benchley saw humor in everything, most noticeably himself; after all, it was his self-deprecating reflection of the befuddled Everyman, constantly forced to cope with a world holding a deck stacked against him, that had helped make him so popular, both in print and now on the screen.

Between them, Parker and Benchley had represented humor's two poles. But in discovering in the 1930s just how hideous the world not only around her but around everyone could be, Dorothy Parker began to understand that the humor of ridicule could often indeed be "more a shield than a weapon." This, however, was not news to Benchley. He'd always perceived humor, in any form, as a shield, not a weapon. This difference was precisely what had made them such a complementary pair for so many years. In most surroundings, his humor warded things off, while hers attacked them. In a world gone haywire, though, a world whose admittedly minimal sense of order was being threatened by Mussolini and Hitler, Parker found her old weapons of little use, and sought new ones. Benchley, whose shield had barely moved from in front of his chest for over twenty years, simply sought cover.

In Donald Stewart's case, Benchley tried as best he could to bypass his friend's politics, even though many people around him warned Benchley that even if Stewart wasn't a card-carrying member of the newly organized Hollywood branch of the American Communist Party, many of the organizations he belonged to were known Communist fronts. In August 1939, though, when Russia signed the Nonaggression Pact with Germany, Benchley—one of the few non-leftist friends Stewart had left—could no longer keep silent. Stewart recalled:

Bob and I were finishing what had been a gay dinner, when unexpectedly Bobby began lecturing me about my hypocrisy as an anti-Nazi in not attacking Stalin's pact with Hitler. As his anger mounted, my fear grew that a dangerous can of tomatoes was at last being opened. There was good reason for my fears. All along, since my "conversion," I had been deeply sure Bobby respected me for my political activities, even though he wasn't at all interested in them, with the exception of rights for Negroes, about which he felt very strongly, and for which he had once or twice let me use his name on a committee. But now, as he kept pressing me with increasing scorn about the Stalin pact, I felt a horrible gulf opening between us; worse than that, I realized that my confident assumption that he had understood my "new life" and had sympathized with it had been an illusion. I couldn't answer his questions, other than to plead that Stalin must have had good reasons. "What reasons?" shouted Bobby, and his contempt for me was so violent that I couldn't answer. When the attack on me continued in Bobby's Garden of Allah rooms, I left without saying goodbye. But it was goodbye.

Indeed it was. For all intents and purposes, the argument that night ended the nearly-two-decade-long friendship between the two. Stewart, who went on to win an Oscar for the screenplay for *The Philadelphia Story*, was ultimately blacklisted by the film industry as a result of testimony against him before the House Un-American-Activities Committee during the post–World War II Communist witch-hunts. Before he could be called to testify himself, Stewart and his second wife, Ella Winter, the widow of writer Lincoln Steffens, moved to England, where he was to live the remainder of his life.

If it was politics that drove an unextractable wedge between Benchley and Stewart, it was alcohol that helped seal the bond of friendship between Benchley and actor Charles Butterworth. "Charlie has been practically living with me here," Benchley wrote to Gertrude in late May 1937, when Butterworth, in the midst of a divorce, moved into the Garden of Allah and, in the words of Sheilah Graham, "became Benchley's shadow."

Born in South Bend, Indiana, in 1897, Butterworth had come out to Hollywood in 1932 after a string of successful stints on Broadway. Benchley had known him casually since the late 1920s and had long been a fan of his work—in fact, he'd raved about him in his very first *New Yorker* theater column in 1929. "Mr. Butterworth is one comedian in a million," wrote Benchley in his review of Jerome Kern and Arthur Hammerstein's *Sweet Adeline*. "And I don't care whether I see the rest of the million or not." A balding, gaunt man who, both onstage and off, wore a perpetually blank expression and spoke in a monotonous, deadpan voice, Butterworth played shy, well-heeled bachelors in romantic comedies throughout the 1930s—a decade that he spent almost constantly inebriated, both offstage and on. Performing, whether in public or private arenas, frightened him to death. "I went on sober once, and I was lousy," Butterworth once said. "I never went to bed sober with a woman, either."

Typical of Butterworth's humor was the time he and actress Dusty Anderson went to eat at Romanoff's restaurant. "We had two drinks before dinner and not much to eat," Anderson recalled. "The bill came to fifty dollars. Charlie was horrified. He asked the waiter to review the bill because he was sure there'd been a mistake. The waiter came back and said, 'Yes, Mr. Butterworth, there is a mistake—it's sixty-five dollars.' Without blinking, Charlie replied, 'Ah, that's better.' "

In Butterworth, Benchley found not only a willing, dependable drinking partner, but the only person he'd ever met who loathed birds as much as he did. Although it's unclear exactly when Benchley began hating them, it's likely that his hostility was nurtured by the fact that he spent most of his adult life rarely going to bed before sunrise, and so was usually at odds with the feathered creatures that were noisily greeting the day just as he was trying to dispose of it quietly. According to Nathaniel Benchley, birds sensed his ill will toward them and often responded to it by (in Benchley's view, anyway) exhibiting openly aggressive behavior. It didn't matter whether they were pigeons on the ledge outside his room at the Royalton Hotel, terns on the sandy beaches of Nantucket, or catbirds amid the palm trees in Beverly Hills; they all conspired to make life miserable for him via noises, droppings, and, every now and then, an actual beak-first attack.

As proof of their scorn, Benchley once made a point of going to the fabled Piazza San Marco in Venice and standing in the spot where visitors to Italy are usually photographed feeding the friendly pigeons. Benchley took a bag of corn from his pocket and began tossing kernels in a circle around him. Within minutes, several dozen pigeons in the vicinity descended upon the piazza, landed on the ground around him—and pointedly turned their back on his offerings. To add insult to injury, they refused to fly off, opting instead to walk around the periphery of his corn-filled circle. When, at last, Benchley slunk away, the birds merrily started gobbling up the corn.

So while most residents found the songbirds that congregated in the shrubbery outside the Garden of Allah bungalows a delightful presence, Benchley and Butterworth viewed them as loathsome intruders. In fact, when the two of them would return to the Garden after a particularly long night of club-hopping, Butterworth would often roam the grounds outside their apartments methodically shaking every palm tree in search of winged occupants. "Wake me up, would you, you feathered bastards," he'd mutter. "Well, now it's my turn!"

Another friendship that solidified during the latter part of the 1930s was between Benchley and writer John McClain. The two had met in New York in 1930, when McClain, a native Ohioan who'd been a football star at Brown University, moved to New York and began working for the *New York Sun*. He covered the comings and goings of the society set, a job that allowed the strapping, good-looking McClain to ingratiate himself with both the rich and the famous, especially the female members of those two circles. Benchley got to know him during McClain's year-long love affair with Parker in 1931, a stormy relationship that ended when McClain, ten years her junior, left her for a young Long Island socialite—a move that prompted Parker to note angrily that "his body had gone to his head."

When McClain came out to Hollywood to try his hand at screenwriting in 1938, he fell in with Benchley, who was bemused by McClain's prodigious appetite for both women and drink, and the two of them wound up renting an apartment together that summer on South Rodeo Drive in Beverly Hills. Apparently, Benchley—or to be more accurate, Dr. Jones—had begun to be concerned over his drinking. Jones had suggested that perhaps a quieter home atmosphere would remove at least some of the impetus for indulging. ("I was getting into a kind of rut at the Garden," Benchley wrote to Gertrude, "and becoming a host to a lot of people who found themselves in the neighborhood around cocktail time.")

In 1939, Benchley and McClain spent part of the summer sharing a house with mutual friend Jock Whitney, who'd become involved in the movie business in the past few years, most notably as chairman of the board of Selznick International Pictures, the production company Whitney and David Selznick formed in 1935 when Selznick decided to leave MGM and strike out on his own. (As with most of his other investments, Whitney did quite well as a motion picture mogul, presiding over the making of such hit films as *A Star Is Born*, *Nothing Sacred*, and *Rebecca*, as well as the classic *Gone with the Wind*.)

That summer, Whitney managed to get both Benchley and McClain involved in another one of his lucrative businesses, horse racing, as proud owners—for three days, anyway—of the only thoroughbred ever to race under the colors of the Garden of Allah Stud Farms. Whitney, whose family owned Saratoga's Greentree Stables, had a number of horses racing at Santa Anita that year—so many, in fact, that he had decided to put one of them, named Sharpy, up for sale via a claiming race. Having always been asked by his less-moneyed friends exactly what it meant to own a horse, Whitney suggested that Benchley and McClain buy Sharpy for the three days between the time he was entered in the claiming race and the race itself. So between Monday and Wednesday, Benchley and McClain officially joined the California Racing Association, hired a jockey, and had an outfit hastily sewn together emblazoned with the registered colors of the Garden of Allah Stud Farm—a crimson shirt for Benchley's Harvard, with one brown sleeve for McClain's Brown and one blue sleeve for Whitney's Yale.

The day of the race, Benchley was in the midst of filming a short for MGM, and so couldn't attend, but McClain and Whitney did. After checking in with Sharpy and his jockey, the two went to Whitney's box in the owners' stand. They were awaiting the start of the race when McClain came to the sudden realization that if Sharpy didn't do well in the race, he probably would not be claimed—leaving McClain and Benchley stuck with the horse. "Don't worry," laughed Whitney. "Bob told me the horse can have his room at the Garden." Fortunately for all concerned—especially Sharpy—the horse won his race and was claimed for $1,500—$500 more than they'd paid Whitney. "After we had paid the jockey 10% and paid for the uniform and given the trainer his cut, we ended about $450 to the good," noted Benchley. "Not bad for turning a hand or, in my case, having no idea whatsoever of what it was all about."

Sharpy the horse wasn't the only thing to change hands between Benchley and Whitney during the 1930s. The two also had affairs, in some cases concurrent, with several of the same women, among them Louise "Louie" Macy and Tallulah Bankhead. Benchley had met Macy in the early thirties through her older sister Gertrude, who was actress Katherine Cornell's manager and who often brought Louie, then a salesgirl at the fashionable Hattie Carnegie clothing shop, along with her to Broadway openings. Tall and thin, with blue eyes and light brown hair, and always immaculately dressed, Macy was once described by an admirer (and there were many) as "an event." A native of Pasadena who'd gone to an exclusive girls' school in Virginia and then to Smith College, she had an intelligence and fashion sense that resulted in her becoming an editor at *Harper's Bazaar*, where, in 1937, she helped Nathaniel Benchley, then a junior at Harvard and beginning to follow in his father's writing footsteps, to place his first magazine article. ("That seventy-five is just twice what I got for my first piece," Benchley wrote his son that summer. "You may be supporting us yet.")

Benchley squired Macy around both New York and Hollywood, where she met two future suitors—James Forrestal, later the Secretary of the Navy, and Jock Whitney. Whitney's marriage to Liz Altemus had been shaky from the start, and by the late thirties, he was keeping regular company with Macy. Benchley, who often joked about "placing his women well," found it interesting that Whitney kept a picture of Macy in his bedroom at the house they shared in the summer of 1939. The next year, though, after the Whitneys divorced, Jock began seeing a lot of Betsey Cushing Roosevelt, the divorced former daughter-in-law of F.D.R., and he eventually married her in 1942. Not long thereafter, Macy herself got married—to F.D.R. adviser Harry Hopkins.

As for Bankhead, the Alabama-born actress, never the model of discretion in her private affairs, had long had "a great crush" on Jock Whitney. It was Whitney who arranged for Bankhead to star in the stage production of *Dark Victory* in 1934, and it was Whitney who lobbied hard for her to get the part of Scarlet O'Hara in *Gone with the Wind* (a move that backfired badly when influential gossip columnist Louella Parsons found out about it and wrote that if Bankhead got the role, "David Selznick will have to answer to every man, woman and child in America"). Long after their physical relationship ended, they remained friends; in fact, when Bankhead was the host of the hit radio program *The Big Show* in the early 1950s, Whitney was such an avid listener that he usually refused to make dinner plans for the Sunday evening hour when the show was aired.

In Whitney, Bankhead saw a rich, powerful young man. In the older Benchley, Bankhead saw something else: a good drinking partner—and a good bed partner. "She was always telling everyone what a terrific cocksman he was—always praising the size of his prick," Brendan Gill told Dorothy Parker biographer Marion Meade. Even Alexander Woollcott once commented on Benchley's "prominence" in the field. "Frankly," he once wrote Benchley, "I never did see (except once when you changed your bathing suit in my room) what women see in you, anyway."

In 1937, Benchley's contract with MGM was revised, making him officially the "property" of the short-subjects department—a change precipitated by Jack Chertok, who, after getting over his initial misgivings about Benchley, had taken over from Harry Rapf as Benchley's producer and was lobbying hard with the studio to keep Benchley out of features and concentrating on shorts. At first, MGM refused Chertok's request, casting Benchley in a small role in the revue-like *Broadway Melody of 1938*, and then, in July, putting him in a costarring role alongside Robert Montgomery and Rosalind Russell in the romantic comedy *Live, Love and Learn*. While the part was Benchley's largest to date in feature films, the plot and script were weak—so weak, in fact, that midway through production, Montgomery went to the front office at MGM and (as Benchley recalled) "told them they were crazy to keep on shooting with no story to shoot; so they stopped production and are re-writing the whole thing." Not that the rewrites helped much. In September, Benchley wrote to Gertrude, "They previewed it last Saturday and, as we all knew, it was so bad that they have had to re-take whole gobs of it. . . . I could kill them for their stupidity in putting me in the thing at all, when so much time has been wasted that might have [been] spent in making shorts." (Reviewing the film upon its release that November, Bosley Crowther of the *New York Times* wrote that its "principal distinction" was that "it has afforded a reasonably adequate vehicle for the graduation, out of very funny shorts into a not-so-funny feature-length production, of Robert Benchley.") The entire summer had gone by, and all producer Chertok had to show for it was one short, *How to Start the Day*, which had been shot back in June.

Hastily, Benchley and his new director, Roy Rowland, a former production assistant who'd been promoted to a directing job in the short-features department, went to work on a script that had been written by two of the department's staff writers, Robert Lees and Fred Rinaldo. The result was *A Night at the Movies*, a terribly funny film which, for the first time in a Benchley MGM short, forsook the familiar narrator/lecturer setup in favor of straight situational comedy. Playing a man taking his wife to the movies, Benchley is forced to confront one anxiety-provoking moment after another. His troubles start as soon as he enters the lobby: Confusing his movie tickets with raffle tickets being handed out for a drawing, Benchley mistakenly deposits his movie tickets into the raffle slot, and hands the usher the raffle tickets instead. The usher refuses to let him into the theater, and this necessitates several consultations with various management officials. (As other couples pass by and stare derisively, Benchley nervously tries to make small talk—"I remember when all this was just a skating rink!")

By the time they are finally allowed into the darkened theater, there are virtually no seats left, and when they do finally get situated, Benchley winds up not only unable to put his elbows down on either armrest, but sitting behind an enormous, obese man who completely blocks his view of the screen. Benchley tries to angle his head so he can see, but catches something out of the corner of his eye. He slowly turns his head to the left—and finds a little boy blankly staring him straight in the face. This is about all Benchley can take, and he tells his wife that he has to move—only at this point the only seats available are all the way down front and to the side of the screen.

Now it's not the people around him who are making him uncomfortable, but his view of the picture; he can see, all right, but everything is out of focus. In vain Benchley tries to distract himself by taking out a mint—which, of course, gets lodged in his throat. After a minute of coughing and choking as quietly as he can (all the while absorbing nasty looks from everyone on all sides of him, including his wife), Benchley nervously gets out of his seat and heads for the nearest exit door. Once on the other side, he finally clears his throat—and discovers that he's now out on the street. He finds another entrance door and walks through it, only to be blinded by a spotlight; somehow, he's landed onstage between features, at the end of a line of high-stepping chorus girls. As the entire theater bursts into laughter, and his wife hides her head, Benchley embarrassedly grins, shrugs his shoulders, and disappears behind the stage curtain.

A Night at the Movies proved to be Benchley's most popular short since *How to Sleep*. It was rushed into release less than a month after it was filmed, and its success (it went on to be nominated for an Academy Award) gave Chertok the ammunition he needed to get MGM to agree to keep Benchley working exclusively on shorts. Making good on the promise David Selznick had made to him years before, Chertok even saw to it that Benchley was able to film some of them in New York, dispatching Rowland eastward in the winter of 1938 to film *How to Figure Income Tax*, *Music Made Simple*, and *An Evening Alone*. When Benchley returned to Hollywood the next spring, Chertok set up a production schedule calling for nine shorts to be completed over a six-month period. And if the quota was met, Chertok said, Benchley could again shoot three of the following year's series back in New York over the winter.

It seemed like a doable task, not only because the threat of getting "loaned out" for features had been removed, but because once a script was written and approved, Benchley had rarely required more than a few days on the lot to shoot any of his previous shorts. (In fact, one of them, a 1936 *Treasurer's Report*–type monologue called *How to Vote*, was filmed, edited, and previewed in less than twelve hours.)

However, it took Benchley and Rowland nearly two entire weeks to complete filming on the very first short they tackled, *How to Raise a Baby*. The script, a primer for fathers seeking to "bond" with their little offspring, was drawn from several old Benchley humor pieces, one of which, a *Vanity Fair* article titled "The New Science of Father-Craft," went all the way back to 1916 and Benchley's experiences after Nathaniel's birth. It called for numerous interactions with infants, and while Benchley previously had never required more than two or three takes for any of his scenes on a short, such was not the case with *How to Raise a Baby*. He wrote Gertrude in late May:

> For days now we have been struggling with the entire infant population of Hollywood, and without much success, either. Our first was a five year old who went into a complete trance when the lights went on and couldn't remember anything. We had to make twenty-seven takes of one scene, and that didn't include twenty-five rehearsals. All that I had to do was hold him on my knee and ask him questions over and over that he didn't answer. One whole day was spent on that. . . . The next day we had a 16 month old. I had to feed him spinach, and he was supposed to refuse it. His mother claimed he hated spinach—well, he didn't. Every time I'd offer him a spoonful he'd grab at it with his mouth, thereby spoiling the plot, as I was supposed to have to eat it myself after he had turned it down. . . . Then I had to give a seven-month old baby his bath. He was the best of the bunch—although every time I squeezed water over my head with a sponge, he cried.

By the time *How to Raise a Baby* was finally finished (the shoots went so badly that it was ultimately decided to have Benchley simply narrate the entire short; only one scene was used with recorded dialogue—the one with the uncommunicative five-year-old), it was nearly the middle of June, and, in an attempt to catch up, Benchley decided to try to film his next short, *The Courtship of the Newt*—a reprise of 1928's *The Sex Life of the Polyp*—in one daylong shoot. He accomplished the task, but the format of the short required him to be standing for the entire film, and his old arthritic leg problems began to manifest themselves.

Dr. Jones sent him to Wilshire Hospital for tests, and it was suggested that he stay off his feet for a week. This he well might have done, except that just a few days later, on June 17, he went before the Columbia Broadcasting System microphones for a pilot broadcast of a possible weekly radio program that he'd been approached about starring in. The audition went well, but the next day Benchley was back in the hospital, where further tests revealed that his "sluggish" liver was again at the core of his medical problems. The upshot of all this was that Benchley, who, since April, had been guiltily implying in his letters to Gertrude that work might prevent him from flying back east at the end of June, missed the graduation ceremonies of both Robert Jr. from Phillips Exeter and Nathaniel from Harvard, where he gave the Ivy Oration just as his father had done twenty-six years before. "I am really disappointed, more than I can say and be believed," Benchley wrote his family on June 22. "Congratulations on the more virile members of the family, and again regrets (a weak word) that I wasn't there to witness it. I guess that I cried [wolf] once too many times to be believed when I really did have an excuse."

By mid-July, after he was scared enough to go on a (as he called it) "small wagon," Benchley's health stabilized, and he resumed work on the shorts *How to Read* and *How to Watch Football*. The latter was filmed at a stadium on two hot August days and required Benchley, his supporting cast, and over one hundred extras to sit in the stands with overcoats and mufflers on, watching an imaginary football game. ("I have no one to blame but myself," Benchley noted. "I wrote it.")

Meanwhile, negotiations heated up for sponsorship of the Benchley radio program. While his earliest experiences with radio in New York in the late twenties had always made him a bit nervous ("Everybody has a stopwatch, including the girl who checks your coat," he'd written in 1928), he was, a decade later, making frequent guest appearances on network variety shows hosted by Al Jolson, Louella Parsons, and Fred Allen. In fact, back in November 1936, Benchley had participated in the very first television entertainment program ever aired—a special demonstration cosponsored by commercial television's developers, the National Broadcasting Company and the Radio Corporation of America, which originated in the NBC studios and was broadcast, via an experimental transmitter atop the Empire State Building, to fifteen television receivers stationed in various places in the RCA building. The program, billed as "the first demonstration of television under practical working conditions rather than in the laboratory," was viewed by 250 members of the media and invited guests; Benchley's contribution (other performers included the Ink Spots and Hildegarde) was a lecture "explaining" the reasons for the Depression.

"I have been doing a lot of screaming lately, apparently much to everyone's amusement. That's what being a comic gets you," wrote a frustrated Benchley in August as the different parties involved squabbled over his prospective radio show. Benchley had been talked into doing the sample program by his radio agents, Lennen and Mitchell, and by the producer, Martin Gosch, who had gotten the Columbia Broadcasting System—and, in particular, CBS chairman William Paley, who just a few years before had made a radio star out of fellow Algonquinite Woollcott—interested in backing a Benchley show. Several sponsors, including Texaco and Old Gold cigarettes, wanted the show, but before anything could be finalized, MGM threatened legal action that would have pulled the rug out from under the entire enterprise. The studio had begun its own program, sponsored by Maxwell House coffee, and generally frowned on its contract players' making appearances on other shows, let alone starring in their own. Benchley knew MGM meant business—the previous April, it had blocked him from appearing on Louella Parsons's *Hollywood Hotel* hour—and the result was a three-way deal in which MGM received a small percentage of Benchley's weekly pay (insured by the fact that the paychecks had to go through the studio to get to him), as well as free advertisements for their Benchley shorts. Still, a salary of $2,000 a week—minus MGM's and his agents' cuts, that is—was nothing to sneeze at, especially since CBS was guaranteeing the show a twenty-six-week run, and was willing to let him broadcast from either Los Angeles or New York, depending on *his* schedule.

In early November, Benchley shot *An Hour for Lunch*, the eighth of the nine shorts he was supposed to get done in Hollywood, but, knowing that he was already in trouble with *The New Yorker* for once again missing the opening of the theater season, and with the radio show slated to debut within a month, Benchley got Chertok to let him leave town one short short, promising he'd make it up by getting an extra one done in New York over the winter. He arrived back east just in time to sneak his first theater column into *The New Yorker*'s November 19 issue, and to prepare hastily for his radio show's premiere.

The Robert Benchley program, *Melody and Madness*, debuted on November 20, 1938, in Columbia's Sunday-night 10:00–10:30 time slot. Sponsored by Old Gold (the company had sent Benchley a questionnaire inquiring whether he smoked cigarettes and, if so, what brand; "Marijuana, of course," was Benchley's response), the variety show's scripts were primarily written by two veteran radio gag men, Al Lewis and Hank Garson. Benchley rarely, if ever, contributed to the show's material. He simply showed up the afternoon of the airing, ran through rehearsals—at which the most he would do was ask that a joke be reworked, or, if it really fell flat, omitted—and returned for the broadcast. Utilizing the talents of clarinetist Artie Shaw and his orchestra, a small stock company of players including announcer Del Sharbutt, actress Grace Stafford (later to become famous as the voice of Woody Woodpecker), and an occasional guest star, the program was mildly entertaining. In a poll of radio program directors and critics conducted by *Radio Daily* at the beginning of 1939, Benchley placed sixth in a ranking of radio stars behind Jack Benny, Edgar Bergen, Bing Crosby, Fred Allen, and Bob Hope.

Nonetheless, the humor on display in *Melody and Madness* was at a level well below Benchley's self-written standards. (Representative of the show's comedic tone is this exchange between Benchley and frequent guest Jimmy Durante, taken from a 1939 broadcast. Durante: "I'm a reporter, you know. I've got a nose for the news!" Benchley: "And enough left over for the *Times* and the *Tribune*.") Producer Gosch told *Variety* that the "challenge" of putting Benchley on the air was to "unsmarten him. We realized that he had a reputation as a smart humorist that would appeal only to a few listeners, whereas we were aiming at a much larger audience. We began by making charts of the various gags, situations and jokes included in a dozen Benchley books. We found that seventy-five per cent of what he had written was based on what every person says, thinks and does under similar situations. Our conclusion was that his reputation as a 'smart' humorist was really a misnomer; we realized for the first time that Benchley was a down-to-earth humorist." Whether Benchley himself felt like a down-to-earth humorist in the role of a radio comedian or not, *Melody and Madness* failed to attract the "much larger" audience Gosch envisioned. Within three months of its going on the air, the ratings had slid—a fact which both the producer and the sponsor were quick to attribute to the late time slot. In February 1939, after CBS refused a request to move the program to a more advantageous spot on the network's schedule, Benchley wrote to William Paley asking if he could be released from his contract. Unfortunately, since word had already gotten out that NBC was interested in picking up the show were CBS to drop it, Paley decided to keep the program, rather than hand it over to the competition, for the remainder of its guaranteed run.

The following May, the program did indeed move to rival NBC, where it was aired at nine o'clock on Tuesday nights. The timing of the move, however, resulted in Benchley's missing yet another important family event—Nathaniel's May 19 marriage to his hometown sweetheart, Marjorie Bradford, at the Church of St. James the Less in Scarsdale. In all probability, Gertrude was already anticipating some sort of (as Benchley himself put it) "hitch" that would prevent her husband from showing up, and it came in the form of a scheduled appearance on a Screen Actors Guild radio program. "It seems that all movie actors who work for radio have to do a turn on the Guild program, in order to keep radio in right with the movies, and I knew that I should have to do my turn sooner or later," he wrote to his family on May 4, not long after returning to Hollywood to resume filming his shorts, "so as our last show for CBS is on Sunday the 14th and our first for NBC on Tuesday the 23rd, Old Gold decided that the best time for us to do our bit for the Guild was in between—on Sunday the 21st. On the same show are going to be Bert Lahr, Alice Faye, Bill Powell and others who are working in pictures, and they have to rehearse whenever these stars can get off, and nobody knows just what those hours will be. So we all have to stand by from Wednesday the 17th on. . . . Old Gold are insured against my getting sick, but not against a voluntary trip east. . . . So there is no way out that I can see—if I want to keep on with Old Gold—which I gather I do. . . . A Friday in the middle of May never was a good bet as a date on my schedule."

Having missed the two graduations and now his own son's wedding, Benchley was so racked with guilt that he actually invited Gertrude to come out and celebrate their 25th wedding anniversary with him in California. As he well knew, there was no end to what she had resigned herself to put up with as Mrs. Robert Benchley. In addition to having had to raise both Nat and Bobby by herself, she'd also spent most of her summers at the family's summer home in Siasconset playing reluctant host to Benchley's mother, Jennie. ("Don't worry about not sitting down and talking to her," Benchley once told Gertrude. "I can't, so why should you?") Significantly, the summer after Jennie's death at age eighty-five in December 1936, Gertrude traveled to Europe with Robert Jr.—but she'd long ago decided she would not go to Hollywood unless and until Benchley actually asked her to do so.

(Speaking of Jennie, it wasn't long after her death that Benchley received a letter from Lillian Duryea, whom he hadn't heard from in nearly twenty years, reminding him of the IOU she'd made him sign before entering Harvard. There were charities she was involved in, she wrote, which, now that he was such a famous and, she presumed, rich Hollywood actor, she believed he could easily help her to support. Benchley repaid her over the course of the year, and Albert Hackett recalled him telling everyone that summer that the real reason he was in Hollywood was that he was "working his way through college.")

In June 1939, when Gertrude came to visit, he was living in a house he was sharing with McClain and Whitney, and it was there, and not at the "sinful" Garden of Allah, that she stayed with Benchley for several weeks. He, of course, was on his best behavior, keeping his drinking to a minimum, and whenever possible out of her sight entirely. He took her shopping in Beverly Hills and Tijuana, to the races at Del Mar and Santa Anita, and to dinner at the Trocadero, the Brown Derby, Romanoff's, and Chasen's. They both knew he was masquerading for her, but she apparently appreciated the effort—just as she did whenever, in his letters, he would awkwardly try to refute gossip items that appeared in the newspapers about him and other women.

In August, also at his invitation, Nathaniel and his bride came for a visit. By then, Benchley was back at the Garden, back off the "small wagon" he'd tried to stay on following Gertrude's visit, and—with the help of the Benzedrine he'd begun to take with increasing frequency to help him "get going" in the mornings—working feverishly on several shorts that needed to be completed before fall, as well as the radio show. All went well with the newlyweds' visit, except for one incident, which occurred when Marjorie, relaxing with Benchley by the pool at the Garden, casually remarked that Los Angeles, with its sun-drenched climate, lush tropical greenery, and relaxed atmosphere, seemed a wonderful place to live and a terrific place to raise a family. Benchley knew that Nat, now working as a reporter for the *Herald Tribune,* was being told by everyone he met that he could do quite well if he wanted to make a go of it as a screenwriter. And he knew that one Benchley corrupted by Hollywood was more than enough. He looked at Marjorie sternly and, for an instant, dropped the mask he so scrupulously kept in place in front of his family. "Don't ever let me hear you say that again," he shouted at her. "There is nothing here for you, or for Nat, or for your children! You keep away from here!"

Marjorie Benchley wasn't the only one to see a mask drop that summer. One night at the Garden, Benchley was in his bungalow entertaining a crowd that included Scott Fitzgerald and Sheilah Graham, as well as both of his old *Vanity Fair* literary conspirators, Dorothy Parker and Robert Sherwood. Sherwood had become one of the country's most important playwrights in the 1930s, the author of such works as *The Petrified Forest, Idiot's Delight,* and *Tovarich;* his most recent play, *Abe Lincoln in Illinois,* had just garnered him his second Pulitzer Prize for drama. Benchley was drinking heavily, and, late in the evening, in the middle of a conversation with Graham, he suddenly began pointing at Sherwood, who was standing in another part of the room. "Those eyes," he exclaimed. "I can't stand those eyes looking at me!"

For a moment, everyone smiled, believing that Benchley was about to deliver one of his patented punch lines about Sherwood's six-foot-six-and-one-half-inch frame. After all, this was the man who, when once asked if he knew Sherwood, had responded by standing on a chair, reaching his arm up over his head, and saying, "Robert Sherwood? Why, I've known him since he was *this* high!" Instead, a look of genuine horror passed over Benchley's face as he backed away from Sherwood's gaze. "He's looking at me," cried Benchley, "and thinking of how he knew me when I was going to be a great writer—and he's thinking, *now* look at what I am!"

17
Shilling for Shostakovich

FINALLY, A CURE FOR DOPE'S DISEASE

They say that bad things often happen in threes, and during the fall of 1939, after finding out that (a) MGM had decided not to renew his contract with the studio and (b) his radio program was going to be canceled in the spring, Robert Benchley was nervously awaiting some further bad news when he received a call from Myron Selznick in California carrying what appeared to be, on the surface, very good news instead. Walter Wanger, the former Lasky Corporation general manager who, some fifteen years earlier, had hired Benchley to do his very first Hollywood film work, had told Selznick that director Alfred Hitchcock, long an admirer of Benchley's, was interested in having him work on dialogue for his next picture, *Foreign Correspondent*, which Wanger was producing for United Artists. The assignment, however, would require Benchley to be in California at the beginning of February, and that meant having to leave his *New Yorker* theater critic's post far earlier in the Broadway season than ever before.

Benchley knew he had already pushed his "leave of absence" arrangement with Harold Ross as far as it could go; in each of the two previous years, film commitments had caused him to miss not only all of October's, but most of November's shows as well. Moreover, outside of his theater reviews, Benchley was barely contributing to the magazine. Ross had counted on him for casuals, and for the "Wayward Press" columns he enjoyed so much. But Benchley hadn't submitted a humor piece to *The New Yorker* in nearly three years, and "The Wayward Press" had appeared only eight times over the previous five years. From Ross's point of view, it was all well and good that his friend Robert Benchley had become a successful motion picture and radio personality, but that wasn't much help to him in putting out a magazine every week.

When Benchley told him about his latest Hollywood offer, Ross told Benchley he'd try to figure something out, but Benchley came away from the awkward conversation sensing that the handwriting was on the wall. In mid-January, just weeks before Benchley was due to leave for California, Ross made his decision, and, as was his custom whenever anyone connected with *The New Yorker* was being let go, he left it to someone else to deliver the executioner's blow. When

Benchley received a call from managing editor St. Clair McKelway asking if he'd like to go out for a drink, Benchley knew precisely what was coming. Though word had already leaked out that Wolcott Gibbs, who'd been filling in for Benchley since 1934, was going to be officially designated the magazine's theater critic, McKelway, according to Brendan Gill, "found that he hadn't the heart to tell Benchley the bad news." Sensing McKelway's discomfort, "Benchley himself brought up the subject, said he understood perfectly—and ordered another round of drinks."

Benchley's final theater column appeared in *The New Yorker*'s January 27, 1940, issue. The news of his being dismissed by Ross had already spread around town, but Benchley made no statement of farewell in what was to be the last thing he ever wrote for the magazine. Instead, after reviewing a revival of Sean O'Casey's *Juno and the Paycock* and Elmer Harris's *The Man Who Killed Lincoln*, he wrote the following account of an incident that had taken place several weeks previous, when he had taken Nathaniel and Marjorie to the opening of a variety revue.

I attended the opening of Uncle Sam's Music Hall some weeks ago with my family, or as much of it as we could get at one table. It so turned out that the show was not only dull but extraordinarily offensive (a feature which I understand was eliminated the following night), and on my way out, slightly before the scheduled hour, I took occasion to deliver a short lecture to the producer on the sidewalk in front of his theatre. My argument that his show was not one which a father could take his children to was slightly vitiated by the fact that the child in question was at that moment towering over me from a height of six foot two and was accompanied by his wife, but my point was technically correct and I made the most of it. In fact, I lashed out.

Last week, in Danton Walker's column in the *Daily News*, appeared the following not-so-cryptic item:

"What litterateur, occasional radio comic and whilom dramatic critic was tossed bodily from [Music Hall producer] Harry Bannister's jernt for being drunk and disorderly?"

Both Mr. Bannister and Mr. Walker express pained surprise that anything personal should have been read into this innocent reference, and I would not bring the matter up except for that word "whilom." That's what hurt.

In many respects, Benchley had clung to his *New Yorker* theater critic post like a man overboard clutching a life preserver. Writing about the theater, especially during the thirties, had enabled Benchley to feel somehow above the soiled atmosphere of Hollywood. It was a window which, when opened each theater season, allowed enough fresh air to enter his lungs to undo six months of pernicious tinseltown smog. It also made him feel he was still contributing something as a writer. The mid-thirties humor column for Hearst, which, like his radio show, was a job he took solely for the money, had drained him of inspiration—so much so that, to his surprise, he found himself feeling relieved when his contract with the syndicate ran out after a few years and was not renewed. Benchley worked quite hard on the scripts for his shorts, but he knew that in adapting many of his old articles for material, he was on ground both familiar and safe. Moreover, he looked admiringly, and rather wistfully, at the work of younger humorists like S. J. Perelman, the Providence, Rhode Island, native whose crackling wit was a brilliant combination of New England breeding and New York chutzpah. In 1937, Benchley wrote the introduction to a Perelman collection called *Strictly from Hunger*, and alluded—only half in jest, as it turned out—to the effect that upstarts like Perelman were having on their satirical mentors:

Together with several others of my ilk, most of whom are now on movie relief, thanks to Mr. Perelman, I was making a decent living writing fugitive pieces for the magazines . . . which sprang from a congenital insanity which . . . several psychiatrists were good enough to refer to as "free association," or Dope's Disease. Then, from the Baptist precincts of Brown University wafted a cloud no bigger than a man's hams, which was S. J. Perelman. . . . Here was the real Magoo, a natural son of the Prophet Da-Da, and he was only an undergraduate. From then on, it was only a matter of time before Perelman took over the dementia praecox field and drove us all to writing articles on economics for the *Commentator*. Any further attempts to garble thought processes sounded like imitation Perelman. He did to our weak little efforts at "crazy stuff" what Benny Goodman had done to middle period jazz. He swung it . . . took it "out of the world." And there he remains, all by himself.

That Benchley was becoming increasingly dissatisfied with his own printed humor pieces was evident a year later, when he confided to Gertrude his disappointment, and embarrassment, over the publication of his tenth collection of essays, *After 1903—What?* "They're trying to get it out for Christmas," he'd written Gertrude after reviewing the galleys prior to its publication in 1938. "I wish they would *never* get it out. I haven't seen Gluyas's [Gluyas Williams's] drawings yet, but they have got to carry it, I'm afraid."

In light of Benchley's growing disatisfaction with his humor writing, it was perhaps not so surprising that the turn of the decade found him deciding that it was high time he made an attempt to write something of serious import. Benchley had always had a great interest in English history, and in particular the early part of the eighteenth century, when Queen Anne presided over the dawning of the Age of Enlightenment, and it struck him that a new, analytical history of the era would be a fitting enterprise. For several years, New York's Holliday bookshop had a standing order from Benchley; whenever any work on the Queen Anne period showed up, it was immediately dispatched to Benchley's suite at the Royalton. All told, Benchley accumulated nearly one hundred such books, and according to Nathaniel Benchley, he "read each one as it came in and then filed his notes on index cards using his own secret coding system."

Jeanette "Muggsie" Messurier, who left her job as a hatcheck girl at New York's Barclay Hotel to become Benchley's secretary in 1939, told Sheilah Graham that, especially when he was working on films in California and had time off from the lot, Benchley "was always saying, 'Let's lock the door, close the blinds and work on Queen Anne today.' At those times, if anyone knocked or the doorbell rang, he pretended he wasn't there." One morning at the Garden of Allah, Benchley received word that a film he was working on was being rescheduled, and that he didn't have to report to the studio until the following day. "He called and told me to be at his bungalow at 8:30 A.M., sharp, to work on Queen Anne. We'd have lunch sent in, and no drinking until 6:00 P.M. By nine, Mr. Benchley was dictating, and I was busy with the card file, when we heard a key being turned in the lock. Mr. Benchley swore, jumped up, grabbed me, and pulled me with him into the coat closet. We heard the valet—I had forgotten to cancel him—going from room to room." As the man approached the closet, Benchley realized he might be coming for the vacuum cleaner inside, and so he grabbed the door handle just as the man was trying to open it. They both pulled on it until the valet won the tug-of-war, and, as the door flung open, two things happened: the valet fell backward on the floor, and Benchley went barreling into the room. Benchley helped the man to his feet and began to explain why he was hiding in the closet with his secretary. Then he thought better of it; after all, this was the Garden of Allah.

Unfortunately, while it stayed on his mind for years (as late as 1944, he was still mentioning the project in letters to friends), the Queen Anne book never got past the note-taking stage—in part because Benchley simply couldn't stop himself from following every available informational lead wherever it might go. Nathaniel Benchley recalled that one night at the Royalton, Benchley was in bed reading one of his Queen Anne books when he happened upon a footnote that referred him to another book on the era. Finding that book on the shelf, he went to the page in question and started to read—only to find a footnote in that book referring to a third volume. He also had that one in his bookcase, and when he found yet another footnote, Benchley declared war. At dawn he was still awake, the floor littered with books, determinedly reading some passage in a volume totally unrelated to the Queen Anne era. Such obsessive behavior also kept Benchley from having to confront the fear that often gnaws at those who find themselves bearing the mantle of humorist—that, when the chips were down, he would find himself unable to write adequately on a serious topic.

Perhaps if he had felt differently about the relative worthiness—literary or otherwise—of motion pictures, Benchley might have regarded his work on *Foreign Correspondent* as being of importance. Here, after all, was a movie dealing with as serious a topic as there was in 1940—the war in Europe—and a plot involving undercover Axis operatives being exposed by an American journalist. Originally contracted (along with James Hilton) to hone the dialogue for Charles Bennett and Joan Harrison's screenplay, Benchley made such a strong impression on Hitchcock at story meetings that, just a week into the production, the director told Benchley he wanted to give him a part in the film as well. ("I had no intention of acting in the picture," Benchley said after the film was released. "But Hitch decided that anyone who looked as funny as I did should appear on the screen and had me write a part in for myself.")

The result was the role of "Plunger" Stebbins, manager of the London office of the *New York Globe*. "Twenty-five years and they haven't got on to me yet," the derby-hatted Stebbins says to the film's star, Joel McCrea, when McCrea arrives in England—and, true to character, Benchley, over the course of his first three scenes, is shown at a bar (on the wagon, though), squiring a young woman around town, and betting on the horses. On hand to provide a whimsical tonic to the movie's overall tension-filled atmosphere, Benchley more than holds his own alongside McCrea and costars George Sanders and Laraine Day—a notable achievement, considering that his only previous experience in a noncomedic picture had been *China Seas* back in 1935, a film in which, as a perpetual drunk, he'd been a complete caricature. Of course, it helped to have the exacting Hitchcock in the director's chair. At one point in the production, Hitchcock stopped a scene to prod Benchley into a better reaction shot. "Come now, Bob," he said, "Let's open those *naughty* little eyes a bit, shall we?"

While his contract called for him to be on salary for the length of the production, Benchley's work on *Foreign Correspondent* was finished about a month before completion of the shooting—a situation that, considering his usual economic befuddlement, should have been a pleasant one. It wasn't, however. "I find myself in a rather uncomfortable position, for the first time on the money end of a Selznick deal," he wrote Gertrude in the middle of April. "I am going to be drawing down my pay (which is almost the largest on the picture) for doing nothing. . . . I personally would rather be off the payroll, but Myron says 'The hell with them; don't worry about producers money,' and refuses to let me get off. Aside from the fact that I like Wanger and don't feel comfortable with Hitchcock and all knowing what I am getting, I don't think that it is good policy."

One of the reasons Myron Selznick wanted Benchley to sit tight was that he was talking to several of the studios about taking over the distribution of Benchley's shorts. The last of his MGM shorts, *Home Movies*, had been released in February, and, with the help of David

Selznick, who was now working as an independent producer, Myron was trying to swing a deal that would enable Benchley to get additional profits from each short by having his own to-be-formed production company make them and then selling them to a studio. It seemed like a feasible plan—the Selznicks had several meetings with Warner Brothers about it, and Benchley went so far as to talk to director Basil Wrangell, who'd worked on his last four MGM shorts, about being involved—but it never came to fruition. Benchley had told Myron that, all things being equal, he'd be satisfied with letting a studio "do the dirty work" of physically producing the shorts, and when Warner Brothers passed on the proposal, Selznick shelved the idea and instead signed Benchley to a contract with Paramount in early May to write and star in a designated number of shorts for a fixed payment per short. To sweeten the deal, Paramount agreed to give Benchley a 25 percent share of gross receipts for rental billings in excess of $30,000 for each short—and the studio also agreed to let him shoot all of them in New York. Moreover, the contract was only for Benchley's work on short films; as far as features were concerned, he was free to pursue any work he desired with any studio he chose, so long as it didn't interfere with the production of the shorts.

May 1940 also saw Benchley finally live up to Jock Whitney's name for him: Gramps. On May 8, Marjorie Benchley gave birth to Bradford Goddard, later renamed Peter Bradford Benchley. As usual with family events, Benchley found out via long distance: "The room here was full of people when you called," Benchley wrote Gertrude from the Garden of Allah on May 9, "so I didn't get an awfully clear idea of what had happened. . . . As soon as I get my next job lined up (which may be any minute) I will make plans to take a flying trip East—unless whatever I do has to be done right away. . . . I had yellow flowers sent to the hospital."

As it turned out, Benchley the new "freelance actor" got his next job lined up as soon as he was finished with *Foreign Correspondent*, and, while he was able to make a brief visit to New York in June to see his new grandson, he returned quickly to Hollywood to appear in *Hired Wife*, a film starring Rosalind Russell and Brian Aherne and directed by William Seiter, whom he'd worked with on *Rafter Romance* back in 1934. (Benchley's best scene occurs late in the film.

Playing Aherne's lawyer, Roger Van Horn, Benchley is shown trying to keep a cement company's expenses properly tracked. Going through a wad of receipts, he suddenly stops at one of them. "Twelve bottles of Old Remorse rye?" he reads indignantly, then abruptly cuts himself off. "Oh, that's mine!" he realizes—and quickly stuffs the paper in his pocket.)

Before the year was over, Benchley had begun his new series of shorts for Paramount. It began on a promising note with a short Benchley originally titled *The Woman's Angle* but that was released as *The Trouble with Husbands*. With the considerable help of actress Ruth Lee, who'd played the slow-burning, long-suffering Mrs. Joseph H. Doakes in most of his later MGM shorts, the film details a number of those familiar domestic situations in which (in the words of the smiling Benchley lecturer) "husbands irritate wives to the point of whatever that point is just before a woman kills a man." Those situations include disappearing into the bathroom for a wash and shave just as dinner is being served ("Ah, clam chowder!" Benchley says cheerfully as, with his wife glaring at him, he finally sits down at the table. He quickly eats a spoonful of his soup, then looks up surprised. "A bit cold, though!"); going to the store to pick up half a pound of butter and returning with a bagful of impulsively bought delicacies—and, of course, no butter; and demolishing a perfectly good wall while putting up a two-foot shelf, which, once installed and proudly shown off to the ever-dubious woman, naturally crashes immediately to the floor. (As it turned out, *The Trouble with Husbands* was to be far and away the best of the nine shorts Benchley made for Paramount over the course of the next two years. Under the undistinguished, slow-paced direction of Leslie Roush, the films were markedly inferior to the MGM shorts. They reached their low point with 1942's *Keeping in Shape*, in which a markedly overweight Benchley, wearing ill-fitting sweatshirt and shorts, attempts to work out at a health club.)

In August 1940, during a lull between acting assignments, Benchley again came east, joining the family in Nantucket to help celebrate Bobby's twenty-first birthday. The two visits so close together, right on top of the trips that both Gertrude and Nat and Marjorie had made to California the previous year—at his invitation—were surprises that none of them expected, but they nonetheless welcomed. Gertrude, especially, had long abandoned trying to understand Benchley's actions, but it was clear that he was much more comfortable being the father of two adult sons than he'd ever been as the father of two growing children. He'd certainly not been there for them throughout their adolescences, but if he wanted to be a closer friend now to his boys, well, that was certainly more than she'd come to believe would ever be possible for her "bachelor" husband.

After returning to Hollywood in the fall of 1940, Benchley worked on two additional feature films. The first was Walt Disney's *The Reluctant Dragon*, a combination live action/animated picture that Benchley agreed to do primarily because not only was he going to receive his first star billing in a feature film, but he was going to play himself. Unfortunately, the "himself" that Disney's writers created called for Benchley, while on a guided tour of the cartoonist's studios, to be involved in a great number of pratfalls and physical gags, such as learning to imitate Donald Duck, crawling around on all fours, and falling into a swimming pool. "I don't know what it will look like when it's all finished," Benchley noted at the conclusion of shooting in early November, "but I do know that I had to do a lot of stuff I didn't like personally. . . . Disney wants to make another picture with me to use his new sound equipment, but they play too comical in cartoons." In fact, the only truly Benchleyesque moment in the entire film comes when he gives a brief talk on the subject of elephants—a talk for which, at least, he did receive a screen credit for additional dialogue.

The second film was *Nice Girl?* starring the nineteen-year-old singing and acting sensation Deanna Durbin. Director William Seiter asked Benchley to play the role of Oliver Wendell Holmes Dana, a widowed science professor trying to raise Durbin and her two sisters in a small-town setting, and Benchley responded with what was unquestionably the finest straight acting performance of his entire film career. His Professor Dana is a gentle, supportive father who, even when confronted by substantial evidence that his beloved middle daughter, Durbin, has spent the night with big-city sophisticate Franchot Tone, simply trusts that the "nice girl" he's raised is telling him the truth when she says nothing happened. Throughout the film, Benchley plays against type. In one scene, he picks up a mandolin and accompanies Durbin in a song, and in another scene, during a Fourth of July celebration where he's supposed to make a speech (audiences were no doubt expecting a bumbling Benchley monologue), he declines. Overall, he exhibits in this film a tenderness and subtle depth of character that is revelatory, especially when one considers how little Benchley thought of his own acting skills. For a man who had been an absentee father to his own children for much of their lives, he was certainly able to project the exact opposite image in this quietly affecting film.

Work on *Nice Girl?* carried into the holiday season, and while Benchley dreaded having to spend Christmas in Southern California, there was little he could do about it. "Remember," he wrote Gertrude, "that I left here Christmas eve in 1928 choosing to spend the day on the train rather than on 'Santa Claus Lane,' as they call Hollywood Boulevard during the season." The result was that Benchley was in town for two terrible events that took place just one day apart—the death of F. Scott Fitzgerald from a heart attack on December 21, and the deaths of writer Nathanael West and his wife, Eileen, in an automobile accident on December 22. "They all had had dinner together on Friday the 13th," Benchley wrote to Gertrude on the 29th. "Alan Campbell was the fourth at dinner, and he is hiding under the bed. . . . Scott had had a heart attack three months before, but seemed to be all right. He was looking over some Christmas cards at Sheilah Graham's house and she thought he was stooping over to pick up a couple that had dropped, but he was dead." The deaths of West and Fitzgerald—the former a horrible, unexpected tragedy, the latter perhaps unsurprising (given Fitzgerald's acute alcoholism) but still shocking—turned the Christmas season into a period of mourning for the Hollywood writing community, and for none more so than Benchley.

As a good friend both of S. J. Perelman, who had been close to West since college and was married to West's sister, Laura, and of Sheilah Graham, Fitzgerald's lover and companion during his final years (he'd introduced them back in 1937), Benchley not only shared their grief but was struck by unavoidable feelings about his own mortality and that of those closest to him. With a war raging in Europe, it seemed only a matter of time before the United States would be involved and would have to start sending troops overseas. Young men like his own two sons might one day leave their homes and, like his own brother, Edmund, never be seen alive again. "With the young men of the country in the spot they are in right now, it doesn't make much difference what they do with their minds," he'd written Gertrude when Bobby's asthma prevented him from finishing one course during the fall term at Harvard in 1940. "Nobody is going to be very well educated for the next few years, except in ordnance and gunnery and sterling Americanism and horsecock, so it doesn't make much difference what happens to a college course. That is one advantage in belonging to a generation which can never get ahead—everyone else has the same Indian sign on him."

As for Fitzgerald, while he and Benchley had known each other for many years, there was always a bit of an uncomfortable undercurrent to their relationship. Fitzgerald's habit of carrying around a notepad and jotting down other people's conversations always bothered Benchley, while Benchley's courtly manner and geniality irked the socially awkward Fitzgerald. But a large part of the tension between them was probably attributable to the one major thing they had in common—problems with alcohol. When Fitzgerald died, Corey Ford remembered a late afternoon at Benchley's bungalow about a year before when the three of them, along with actor Roland Young, were sitting around talking. Benchley looked at his watch and, noting that the "small wagon" he was on at the time stipulated that he not drink before five o'clock, and that it was now a few minutes past five, began to mix a pitcher of martinis. Fitzgerald, who was going through one of his many drying-out periods, tried to talk Benchley out of his cocktail. "Listen, Bob—don't you know drinking is slow death?" said Fitzgerald, shaking his head in mock disapproval. Benchley took a sip, then looked at Fitzgerald and smiled wanly. "So who's in a hurry?" he said.

While working as a freelance feature film actor implied independence from the studio system, Benchley soon discovered that since the Paramount deal wasn't paying him enough to get by, he needed to take his work as he could find it. The result was a string of largely interchangeable character parts in mild romantic comedies in which he seemed to be on hand primarily to lend (as he was told by one director) "good taste" to such roles as that of the lecherous theater owner trying to score with chorus girl Rita Hayworth in 1941's *You'll Never Get Rich*. Not that Benchley felt much flattered by such "compliments," as evidenced by his comments to Gertrude about the next film he acted in, *Three Girls About Town:*

> I was told I was going to be going into *Bedtime Story* with Cary Grant. I knew this to be a reputable piece of work and asked no more questions. As the time grew near, my Selznick representative assured me that they were waiting for me with great eagerness. He said nothing of the fact that *Bedtime Story* had been postponed until fall. So, when I got the first twenty pages of the new script, and saw that the title was *Three Girls About Town*, I thought they were pretty silly to have dropped such a good title as *Bedtime Story* but said nothing—being glad that I was going on earning money anyway. Then I got some more pages of the script, and found that I am playing a character called "Puddle," the manager of a hotel, who spends his time carrying a corpse in and out of rooms trying to dispose of it. On my complaining of bad taste, they said, "Oh, but it isn't a real corpse—he's only hypnotized!" I finally got so mad at having been eased into such a cheap thing without a chance to turn it down that I told the Selznick office to take my name off their list of prospects unless they could get me a respectable writing job—and that I was through with acting (except for the shorts) and that I was going to get a New York writing job again and go back to where I started from with white folks.
>
> "At the age of 51, it is not very pleasant to find yourself on the edge of a career playing Edward Everett Horton roles just because your agent thinks that ten percent of any job is as good as ten percent of any other job. I would just as soon take on a writing job out here (but Selznick doesn't try for those, as they don't pay as much as acting), or would even go into a respectable acting job, if such a thing exists. . . . I was no fool when I clung onto the *New Yorker* job so long at a comparatively small wage for six months a year. This year I got no wage at all for almost six months, and now find myself carrying a cadaver all over the Columbia lot to make up for it. Faugh!

After the *Three Girls About Town* debacle, Selznick promised to be more attentive to Benchley's wishes, but there really wasn't much Selznick, or Benchley, could do about the kind of motion pictures

Hollywood was making—or looking to cast him in. Between 1941 and 1943, Benchley acted in twelve feature films, portraying (in the better ones) such characters as Frederic March's best friend and lawyer in *I Married a Witch*, Rosalind Russell's business partner in *Take a Letter, Darling*, photographer Joan Leslie's publisher boss in *The Sky's the Limit*, and orchestra conductor Robert Taylor's manager in *Song of Russia*. (While making that last-named film, Benchley went to lunch one day on the MGM lot in full costume; before anyone had a chance to comment on his fur hat and long Russian coat, Benchley proudly announced, "I'm a shill for Shostakovich.") While some of these films were better than average—*Take a Letter, Darling* and *Bedtime Story* (which was eventually made, starring Frederic March and Loretta Young) were both fairly intelligent, sophisticated comedies—Benchley found few opportunities to do much more than lend that air of "good taste" to his various surroundings. A prime example: In Billy Wilder's 1942 comedy *The Major and the Minor*, scripted by Wilder and Charles Brackett, Benchley plays a bored husband trying to throw passes at Ginger Rogers and delivers the one line that's always been most closely associated with him. Seeking to loosen up Rogers, who's come in from the rain, Benchley goes over to his bar and asks, "Why don't you get out of that wet coat and into a dry martini?" Actually, the follow-up line isn't bad, either. "I'd offer you a whiskey sour," he says, "but that would mean thinking up a new joke."

Was it Benchley's joke, though? In 1985, Wilder wrote *Los Angeles Times* columnist Jack Smith, "Brackett and I gave the joke to Benchley under the impression that he had originated it. When it came to the shooting, he modestly disclaimed credit, informing me that it had actually, indubitably and in fact been said by his friend Charles Butterworth." Sure enough, in a 1937 Mae West picture called *Every Day's a Holiday*, actor Charles Winninger, sweltering in a turn-of-the-century evening suit, complains to Butterworth that he's "hot—soaked all over." With his trademark deadpan, Butterworth flatly advises him that he "ought to get out of those wet clothes and into a dry martini."

Rarely, then, did Benchley get to display the kind of humor found in his shorts—with one glorious exception. In the aforementioned *The Sky's the Limit*, Benchley delivers a hilarious five-minute "report" on aircraft manufacturing that, clearly, he wrote himself. Staring at a completely indecipherable chart, Benchley clears his throat and announces, "By 1936, we of course mean 1934—and this is all per capita, mind you!" Significantly, the sheer zaniness of the scene seems very much out of context with the remainder of film.

In the spring of 1943, having fulfilled his contract for shorts with Paramount, and weary of freelancing, Benchley went back under an exclusive contract to MGM for a forty-week period. Although Selznick promised him that the studio wouldn't "mishandle" him, the deal, which called for him to make several new shorts as well as appear in features, went sour for Benchley very quickly. Between the shorts, their own features, and those features being made by other studios that they lent him out for, Metro ran Benchley ragged. In a July 30, 1943, letter to Gertrude, he complained about it:

> Please don't ask me what I am doing, or when it is going to be done. I don't know *anything* anymore. . . . Last week I was over at Universal (that's how Metro makes money on me—selling me to other companies for more than they're paying me); I did one day's acting on a Charles Boyer picture [*Flesh and Fantasy*], then worked on a turkey called *For All We Know* which they've had in the can for fifteen months and felt it needed a commentation to explain it to the audience. . . . This week I have been working on the script for several shorts that we had hoped to start shooting in August. In the meantime, today to be exact, they have decided that they want me for a three-day job in *See Here, Private Hargrove* next week, so the shorts are put off that much further.

It wasn't just the dizzying schedule that was making it hard on Benchley, either. Metro's accounting department was doing its fair share to confound him as well:

> I also just found out that no checks have been coming through the last three weeks. . . . I asked why, and they said they didn't know which department to charge me to—shorts, Universal, or just plain Overhead. They said they were in a dither about what to do, so they didn't put through any checks. So I called their head man and told him I wasn't going to do any more work until some money came through.

I told them when they got out of their dither I would get out of mine. . . . Now you know that if I, or any other writer or actor or dreamer, had given that as an excuse for not fulfilling a contract—that we "were in a dither" about something—we would be out on our asses. J'adore less hommes des affaires. They are so businesslike.

Benchley's contract with MGM ended in November, and it was no surprise to him that it was not renewed. He hadn't particularly endeared himself to the studio by complaining, and the studio became further annoyed with him when, deciding that it was high time he finally attend at least one important family function, he sent word he was going on unpaid leave, and attended his son Robert Jr.'s September 25, 1943, marriage to Detroit native Elizabeth Dickinson in Gross Pointe, Michigan. (The highlight of the wedding festivities, according to Nathaniel Benchley, came the morning after the ceremonies when, aboard a train from Michigan to New York, Benchley remained in his berth on the sleeping car because, as he put it when he finally stuck his head out from inside the tightly clutched curtains, "I think my clothes got off at Schenectady.") Even the four shorts he made for Metro during this second stint with the studio had turned out well below expectations. Only *No News Is Good News*, a parody of know-it-all commentators that Benchley's old friend Frank Sullivan had a hand in writing, showed any inspiration. The others, all built around various humiliating situations befalling Benchley's weary Joe Doakes—a frustrated "victory garden" grower in *My Tomato*, an inept executive going to Washington for *Important Business*, and, most regrettably, a nervous radio quiz show contestant beaten by a child in *Why Daddy?*—were painfully obvious, and none too funny.

The fact that Benchley had labored over the scripts only heightened his sense of futility. Indeed, just about any time he had sat down at a typewriter during the last few years, it had been hard, draining work. When Harper & Brothers, having purchased the plates of Benchley's 1920s books from Henry Holt, prepared his eleventh book, *Inside Benchley*, for publication in 1942, he'd agreed to furnish four new pieces for the collection of old essays. As he read over some of his most famous essays that were to be included—"Coffee, Megg and Ilk, please" "The Social Life of the Newt," "Shakespeare Explained," "Kiddie Kar Travel," "Ask That Man"—Benchley's despair only deepened. He remembered how quickly, and easily, he'd written those pieces. Some of them were over twenty years old, and they still read well—better, in fact, *much* better, than the forced paragraphs he was now slaving over. When he finally did finish the new pieces, he told James Thurber that they were "written in blood, I can tell you that." Ironically, *Inside Benchley* fared so well commercially (according to his tax return in 1942, he earned nearly $5,000 in book royalties that year) that Harper informed him that it was going to put together a second volume of his old essays for publication in 1943. Its title was to be *Benchley Beside Himself,* and that was a fair assessment of how its author felt when he found out that the book was going to include sixteen pages of photographs from his movie shorts. Looking at the photos of himself—curled up in his pajamas in *How to Sleep*, being stared at by an elevator full of people in *An Hour for Lunch*, sitting drenched in the bleachers in *How to Watch Football*—Benchley came to a painful realization. At age fifty-four, he no longer had the energy—or, more important, the will—to compete with his own past as a writer, a past that was now mocking him with irrefutable evidence. The plain truth was that he was now a motion picture funnyman who, once upon a time, had written humorous articles for magazines. And, for better or worse, he felt he had to face that reality, head on.

In December 1943, after signing a one-year contract with Paramount to work solely as a character actor in feature films, Benchley bluntly announced that he was officially ending his career as a writer. "I don't think I write funny anymore. I've run out of ideas," he said in a statement that was carried nationally by the Associated Press news service. "From now on I'm an actor. It's a lot easier and the pay is good." Benchley's decision prompted a flurry of reactions. Reviewing *Benchley Beside Himself* for the *New York Times*, S. J. Perelman wrote, "The Ice Age of American humor began the moment he stopped practicing letters. . . . The sad fact is that when Benchley went out of business, he forgot to appoint a successor. He just locked up the store and threw away the key. . . . God grant its author may be seized with sufficient remorse to desert the spurious trade he is plying on the Pacific Slope and return to the vineyard. Come back, Bob, all is forgiven." The *Herald Tribune* even ran an editorial about Benchley. "Many of our writers, once regarded as excellent humorists, live to a great age under the amiable but often pathetic delusion that their powers to create laughs are in no way diminished with the passing years," said the newspaper. "They are not critical enough to be bored with themselves. Mr. Benchley may be wrong, but his example is salutory."

For his part, Benchley didn't think he was wrong, and he didn't see himself as much of an example of anything except a man surrendering to his own self-made fate. "He had a theory that everyone tends to become the type of person they hate most," Nathaniel Benchley wrote—and that's what was now happening to him. In closing the book on his writing career, Benchley was surrendering to his worst fears about his own worth—and, in the process, beginning to close the book on his life as well.

18
Gute Reise

"I CAN HEAR HIM LAUGHING RIGHT NOW"

Gloria Sheekman, who lived at the Garden of Allah during the 1940s with her husband, writer and producer Arthur Sheekman, remembered the day in 1944 when Robert Benchley, returning from a torturous day's work at Paramount Pictures, stopped by her bungalow for a visit. "He seemed quite depressed," she recalled. "He was acting in a film called the *National Barn Dance,* and he was having a terrible time. He wasn't writing anymore, and he wasn't making his shorts anymore, either. 'Just look at me,' he said. 'What am I doing square dancing?' " Sheekman, who, as Gloria Stuart, had been a successful actress in the 1930s and had appeared in such films as *The Old Dark House* and *Frankenstein,* tried to cheer Benchley up. "I said, 'Bob, we all settle in many different areas—and what you're doing now makes people happy. You really ought to be more saturnine about it.' Well, as soon as I said that, a shadow went over his face. After a while, Bob left, and as soon as he was gone, I ran to the dictionary and looked up saturnine. I knew I'd used the wrong word, and I felt terrible about it, so I picked up the phone and dialed Bob's room. He answered, and before I could say anything, he said, 'I know, Gloria—you meant sanguine.' "

While it might well have been far healthier for Benchley to feel more sanguine about his fortunes, the sad truth was that "saturnine" was the proper adjective to describe his general state of mind in 1944. In April, Universal released *Her Primitive Man,* the last picture he'd acted in while under contract with MGM, and a film that he regarded as "the low point in my movie career." ("It is a hokum comedy in which I get chased around by a headhunter—very subtle stuff," he'd written Gertrude during the filming the previous November. "I hope no one goes to see it.") Between the numerous comedies in which he was acting—*Janie,* in which he plays John Van Brunt, president of the Chamber of Commerce, *Pan-Americana,* where he's a magazine editor, and the aforementioned *National Barn Dance,* in which he's a square-dancing ad executive—and his frequent guest appearances on radio variety shows, Benchley was one of the country's most recognizable comic personalities. Yet he found little pleasure in the work. "Look at me," he complained to a friend. "A clown, a comic, a cheap gagman. There's a career for you!"

Almost the only aspect of his professional life that seemed to matter at all to him was his work on behalf of the war effort. With Nathaniel in the Navy and Robert Jr., whose asthma had kept him out of the Army, working in a bomb plant near New York, and with numerous friends and colleagues putting their lives on the line (most prominently, Jock Whitney, who, while serving as a political affairs officer, was captured by the Germans in the south of France in August 1944; he escaped unharmed), Benchley was determined to help out in any way he could: bond drives, USO tours, radio broadcasts, armed services recordings sent overseas, anything at all. He was a fixture at both the Hollywood Canteen in California and the Stage Door Canteen in New York, where celebrities would come to give a boost in morale to the soldiers coming from and going to the front lines. During one of his weekly 1944 visits to the Hollywood Canteen, Benchley encountered a surprise admirer. "One of the boys came over to where I was sitting and signing autographs," he wrote to Gertrude, "and said that Shirley Temple, who was over in a corner working her fingers off, had asked to get my autograph for her, so I sent word back that I would give her mine if she would give me hers." (This meeting ultimately led to Benchley's being cast as Temple's uncle in the 1945 movie *Kiss and Tell.*) It was also at the Hollywood Canteen that Benchley received a memorably *unfriendly* greeting from an Air Force sergeant. "Last night a flyer came up and said he had a grudge against me. He said on one of his flights to Africa he kept cursing the uncomfortable bags of freight he had to sleep on and found out later that the bags were filled with copies of *Benchley Beside Himself.* He told me, 'That stuff isn't very funny when you have to sleep on it.' "

Inside Benchley and *Benchley Beside Himself* were so popular that the unexpected monetary windfall (his 1944 royalties totaled nearly $20,000) helped the ever economically baffled Benchley—with considerable aid from an accountant named Lewis who'd begun looking after his financial interests not long after MacGregor's death—to clear several major debts, among them a long-standing $10,000 loan he'd taken on his life insurance policy. With his Paramount contract paying him $1,750 a week and his radio appearances providing an additional $750 or $1,000, Benchley was, by the end of 1944, and for perhaps the first time he could recall in his entire adult life, almost "caught up—give or take a few stray bank loans and those friendly reminders about arrears payments from the Treasury Department that breeze through here every now and then."

The Christmas season in 1944, though, proved to be an especially depressing one for Benchley. Hired out by Paramount to MGM to play the role of a society columnist in the *Grand Hotel*–styled *Weekend at the Waldorf*, Benchley arrived on the set the first day of shooting and found himself on an exact replica of the Waldorf's entire lobby. ("Needless to say," he wrote Gertrude on December 7, "I expected to, and now am feeling, quite homesick.") It didn't help that his "costar" in many of his scenes was "a Scottie bitch, and I don't mean Ginger Rogers." (Someone probably thought it would be funny to see boulevardier Robert Benchley escorting a tiny dog down Park Avenue.) "In terms of humans, I really work with Constance Collier most of the time," he wrote. "I thought she was dead."

Even at the Garden of Allah, things were subdued. Because of limits on transportation and gas rationing, as well as a wartime curfew, most people were staying at home at nights and on the weekends. "The day before Christmas Eve, I walked past Bob's bungalow, and he had one little ornament hanging in the window," recalled Gloria Sheekman. "I went in to tell him how funny I thought it was, and in the course of the conversation, I asked him where he was going for Christmas dinner. 'No place,' he said. I said, 'Well, look, if you don't have any plans, why don't you come and have dinner with us?' " Sheekman, a gourmet cook who often prepared meals for members of the Garden citizenry ("I was kind of the den mother because I was the only one who could cook, so during the war everyone used to give me their food ration tickets and I'd take it from there"), didn't have to ask twice.

"I got back to my place, and about ten minutes later, Bob called. 'Is it okay if I bring Charlie?' he asked, and I said sure. Then he called again a few minutes after that and said, 'Listen, can I bring Dottie, too?' So there I was, two days later, cooking Christmas dinner for Robert Benchley, Charles Butterworth, and Dorothy Parker." Parker's husband, Alan, was with the Army Air Corps in England, and she had recently learned he was having an affair with an Englishwoman. Butterworth had just returned from a tour of military hospitals, where he'd had to try to entertain soldiers whose arms and legs had been shot off. And Benchley's son Nathaniel was soon to be shipped off to active duty in the Pacific. The three weren't exactly brimming with holiday cheer. "Dottie came in wearing tennis shoes, black stockings, a black skirt, and a black blouse. She just sat there and talked about her dachshunds all night."

Amid all this relative gloom, Benchley walked into the CBS studios on the evening of December 20 and turned in a stellar performance in the title role of a radio adaptation of James Thurber's short story "The Secret Life of Walter Mitty." No doubt one of the major reasons for Benchley's triumph in the production was that to a great degree, Thurber's Mitty, who compensates for the ongoing indignities of his mundane, browbeaten existence by imagining that he is daring and courageous, had been based on Benchley's bumbling Joe Doakes. Thurber openly acknowledged the influence. In a *New York Times* review of the posthumous 1949 collection *Chips off the Old Benchley*, he wrote, "Benchley beat me to a lot of things, including the Algonquin pigeons. . . . His day dreamer, cool and witty on the witness stand (1935) and in heroic peril (1932), antedated a little old day dreamer of mine named Mitty."

For his part, Benchley found Thurber's story a delight—so much so that back in 1940, when David Selznick was trying to get him to produce his own shorts, one of the projects discussed was the Mitty story. So when *This Is My Best*, a series which featured radio versions of writers' favorite works, asked Benchley if he wanted to play Mitty on the air, Benchley heartily accepted. Before the performance began, Benchley told the radio audience, "The story of the little man who, in his spare moments, dreams great dreams is the story of all of us. We're all heroes to ourselves, but we don't have Jim Thurber to tell our story." Benchley played Mitty not as the nervous, skittish type that Danny Kaye portrayed in the 1947 MGM musical comedy version, but as a meek, distant character much truer to Thurber's vision. (Thurber felt the same way; he praised Benchley's portrayal of Mitty, and vehemently protested the film version.)

On New Year's Eve 1944, Benchley made the rounds of Hollywood parties with Reginald Gardner, a British comedian best known for an act in which he successfully impersonated a piece of wallpaper. Eventually the two wound up at Gardner's house in Beverly Hills—"the Pub," as its owner called it—and continued reveling. Noticing that Gardner had a recording machine, Benchley put on a blank acetate and the two began to talk into the microphone, filling one side of the record with lewd, drunken conversation. "Benchley kept telling me we could drink ourselves sober," Gardner told Sheilah Graham, "And, eventually, we did—or at least we believed we did." It was now past nine in the morning, and Gardner asked Benchley if he would record "something he really loved" on the remaining side of the record. "He asked me for a Bible, and opened to Ecclesiastes, Chapter 13. I put a recording of a Debussy string quartet on another record player as background, and Bob began to read, from 'The Prophet sayeth' through 'Vanity of vanities, all is vanity.' It was amazing; he read it as though it had never been read before." Benchley finished the reading with a salutation for the new year. "This is going to be the greatest year for us all . . . so will you all please clap, or have clap, as we welcome 1945—if there is going to *be* a 1945. Only kidding, God, only kidding!"

The first few months of 1945 kept Benchley busy, if not particularly sanguine. Besides finishing *Weekend at the Waldorf* (he was the film's narrator as well as one of its featured players) and making a cameo appearance in the movie version of the hit radio series *Duffy's Tavern*, Benchley acted in both Paramount's *The Stork Club*, starring Barry Fitzgerald ("He is a sweet man and hates movies," Benchley wrote Gertrude) and Betty Hutton ("She joins us on the set this morning, if she feels in the mood. She is not a sweet girl"), and *Janie Gets Married*, the sequel to the hit film *Janie*. His radio and recording assignments—the latter done as "V-Disks," which were hurriedly pressed and shipped overseas for the entertainment of U.S. troops—were numerous as well. In February alone, his schedule ran like this: February 8, guest spot on *Dinah Shore*; February 9, guest spot on *Duffy's Tavern*; February 11, two recordings with Fannie Brice; February 12, one recording with Burns and Allen; February 14, one recording with Jack Carson and Arthur Treacher; February 16, one recording with Jimmy Durante; February 21, guest spot on *The Aldrich Family*; February 23, one recording with Danny Kaye; February 24, guest spot on *Suspense*.

At the Garden of Allah, Benchley and Butterworth were insepara-ble—and, most of the time, a bottle was in front of them. Albert Hack-ett recalled that on one trip to Hollywood for a writing assignment, he and his wife were staying in a bungalow next door to Benchley and Butterworth and could hear them drinking and talking when they went to bed around eleven. When the Hacketts got up the next morn-ing and left for the studio at eight-thirty, Benchley and Butterworth were still going strong. "All I know is, no matter what happened the night before, they never missed a day of work," said Natalie Schafer, who often furnished Benchley and Butterworth with Sunday "brunch"—an enormous pitcher of martinis at noon, followed, around four o'clock, by boiled or scrambled eggs. Still, not everyone found their endless drinking bouts amusing. One time, writer Elliott Nugent and his family were staying at the Garden, and he sent over a note. "When I hear laughter coming out of Bungalow 16," he wrote, "I know it's coming from comedian Charlie Butterworth and literary wit Bob Benchley, and I appreciate it very much. But my children, who have never heard of you, regard you as just a couple of noisy drunks."

In April, Nathaniel, en route to San Francisco, where he was due to ship out for active duty in the Philippines, came to Hollywood to visit Benchley. Marjorie made the trip with him (little Peter had been left back east with Gertrude), and all seemed well until, a few days after they arrived, Benchley got a severe nosebleed, which required a trip to the doctor. Benchley assured both of them that it was merely some recurring sinus trouble, but over the course of their weeklong visit Benchley was forced to have his sinuses "blown out," as he put it, several times. The night Nathaniel was due to leave, Benchley poured two small glasses of whiskey, looked at his son quite seriously, and said, *"Gute Reise"*–good trip. Given both world events and his father's own apparent health problems, Nathaniel sensed the gravity of the moment. When he got to San Francisco, he was told there was a week's delay in his orders, and that he should then report to San Diego. Nathaniel and Marjorie returned to Hollywood to spend more time with Benchley, and at that week's conclusion, Benchley took out the shot glasses again and they had the same *"Gute Reise"* drink. "This time it was obviously the last," wrote Nathaniel. "Or it would have been, if there hadn't been a further delay in my orders, which allowed me to get back to Hollywood for one more weekend. The third *'Gute Reise'* did it, and I was off. Under any other circumstances, it would by that time have been a joke."

What Benchley knew at the time, and was keeping not only from Nathaniel but from Gertrude and everyone else as well, was that he'd been diagnosed with cirrhosis of the liver. The cirrhosis was leading to some internal hemorrhaging, which was manifesting itself in the nosebleeds. And though he kept insisting to everyone that all he had was sinus trouble from all the bad air in California, his friends began to see changes not only in his physical condition but in his personality as well. Muriel King, a motion picture clothes designer and friend of Benchley's since the Algonquin days, told Sheilah Graham that she never saw him "cross or impolite" until 1945. While his doctors kept advising him to stop drinking, they also gave him prescriptions for Benzedrine as well as regular shots of vitamins B-1 and B-12. Propped up by the speed and the injections, he'd have enough artificial energy to make it through the day. Then, as he'd begin to tire in the evening, he'd start drinking, and, with increasing frequency, the evenings would become a complete blank. "He'd call the next day and sheepishly ask if he'd done anything nasty the night before," recalled Sheilah Graham. "One evening I was out with him and Butterworth, and I made what I thought was a harmless comment. Bob turned and, really viciously, said, 'If you don't like it here with us, why don't you just leave?' The first chance I could, I got up and did just that. The next day, I received a hardwritten note from Bob apologizing for his rudeness. But I'm not really sure he remembered what he'd said, or if someone else had told him what had happened."

Throughout the spring and summer, Benchley continued to pursue his now all too precarious lifestyle. About the only thing he cut down on was his radio work, partly because, with Germany's surrender to the Allies in May and Japan's surrender after the bombing of Nagasaki and Hiroshima in August, there was less call for recordings to be sent overseas. During this period Benchley finished work on what were to be his last two films: *The Bride Wore Boots*, starring Barbara Stanwyck, and *Snafu*, a comedy in which Benchley, receiving star billing for only the second time in his film career, played the father of a teenage soldier (Conrad Janis) returning from the war. The work did not go easily, mostly because of a variety of physical problems. During a heat spell in late July, Benchley required medical attention on the lot after he suffered several fainting spells; his blood pressure, which had already been too high in January, had jumped even higher. In August, he was treated for gout. The only positive aspect of his health was that, under strict supervision by his doctors, he cut down on his drinking, and for the time being at least the nosebleeds subsided.

By the fall, Benchley was sorely in need of rest. With a contracted unpaid "layoff" period from Paramount about to start, he decided to return to New York in October for, ostensibly, a vacation. Robert Jr.'s wife, Liz, had given birth to Benchley's first granddaughter, Elizabeth Darling Benchley, in July. They were living in New York, as were Marjorie and young Peter Benchley, who were anxiously awaiting Nathaniel's return from the Pacific in mid-November. Returning to his suite at the Royalton, Benchley went with Gertrude to visit the children, and he scheduled a few radio appearances to keep busy and bring in some income. He guested on the Philco show with Martha Tilton and Paul Whiteman, and appeared on Hildegarde Neff's *Hildegarde* program as well, and on October 27 he went before the microphones on CBS's *Report to the Nation* and performed "The Treasurer's Report"—the "routine" that had changed his career, and his life. It was the first time he'd done it since his radio show in 1940. It was to be the last time he ever performed it as well.

In early November, the nosebleeds began anew. One occurred while he was dining at Toots Shor's restaurant on November 7, and on November 8, after getting his nose cauterized by a doctor, he had another incident while seeing friends at the 21 Club. On November 9, he again went to see his doctor—and again, later that day, the bleeding started. There was a nosebleed on the morning of the 11th, but Benchley still managed to make his final theatrical performance— an appearance on *The Texaco Hour* in which, ironically, he read one of his oldest humor pieces, the "Opera Synopses" from his 1922 collection *Love Conquers All*. The next morning, he bled again, but it didn't stop him from trying to make his usual rounds. Actor John Carradine, a neighbor at the Garden of Allah, happened to be in New York at the time, and he ran into Benchley at the 21 Club. "He didn't look well at all," said Carradine, "and I asked him, not just as a point of conversation, but in earnest, how he was feeling. All he said was, 'I'm tired, John. I'm tired.' " When Benchley awoke on the 13th, he felt so bad that, without consulting his usual doctor, he went to another physician for a B-vitamin pickup shot. He didn't tell the vitamin doctor about his condition, and as soon as he received the shot, he started bleeding. Furious that Benchley had been deceitful with him, the physician made him lie down and telephoned Benchley's regular doctor, who told him to go back to the Royalton and not go outside for at least a few days.

Benchley stayed in his hotel room on the 14th and 15th, but, after telephoning Gertrude in Scarsdale and telling her that he felt "encouraged," he tried to go out on the evening of the 16th. He'd hardly been outside when the bleeding started again, and Benchley called Gertrude to tell her he thought he needed help. Frantic with worry, she telephoned Bobby, who raced over from his apartment to the Royalton. A doctor who happened to be in the lobby of the hotel went up to Benchley's room. The bleeding had stopped, but it was determined that Benchley couldn't be cared for properly at the hotel, and he was taken to the Regent Hospital on East 61st Street. There the doctor who examined him told Bobby that he feared life-threatening internal bleeding.

On Sunday night, after more severe bleeding, Benchley was given a transfusion, and around midnight he was moved from the Regency to the Harkness Pavilion at the Columbia-Presbyterian Medical Center in upper Manhattan. Gertrude drove down from Scarsdale and was told that Benchley was likely to need more transfusions. Bobby was tested, but his blood didn't match Benchley's type A, and the next day, the 19th, Benchley's two daughters-in-law started rounding up possible donors from among Benchley's friends. All in all, some forty volunteers, ranging from Roland Young to Gerald Murphy, showed up at the hospital offering to give blood.

Throughout that day, with Gertrude at his side, Benchley received transfusions and sedatives every few hours, but to little avail. "No dope could keep him quiet," Gertrude later recalled. "He just kept begging me to take him home." She left around eight in the evening, and when she arrived back at the hospital the next morning, she was told that Benchley had suffered a serious cerebral hemorrhage during the early morning and had lost consciousness. On the table by Benchley's bed was a book that the voracious reader had brought with him from the Royalton, a book entitled *The Practical Cogitator, or The Thinker's Anthology*. He apparently had read one essay called "Am I Thinking?" and in the margin by the title he'd scrawled, "NO. (And supposing you were?)"

Gertrude again spent the entire day in his room and drove home by herself the night of the 20th knowing the end was probably near. At 4:45 A.M., the night supervisor called her. "She said, 'Mr. Benchley is doing poorly,'" remembered Gertrude. "I said I'll be right there, and the nurse said, 'I'm afraid you won't be in time.' I went at about sixty down the parkway, and arrived at 5:20. He had died at 5:15, September 21; the only person with him at the end was an intern."

Nathaniel, who'd docked in California from the Pacific on November 15, had boarded a train going cross-country on the 17th, for a trip that was to take five days. He'd last talked to Marjorie during the day on the 16th, but, at that point, all she'd said was that Gramps had had some nosebleeds, as when they had seen him the previous spring. It wasn't until he arrived at New York's Pennsylvania Station at 2:00 A.M. on November 22 that he learned what had happened, and that his father was dead. The *"Gute Reise"* toast had, indeed, been their last. "Thursday was Thanksgiving," Gertrude later told a friend. "But not for us."

Given Benchley's enormous circle of friends and colleagues—and given Gertrude's distance from that circle—it was not surprising that the family chose a private funeral service. The service was held at the Ferncliff Crematorium in Hartsdale, and was attended only by the immediate family, and one very conspicuous guest from Benchley's past: Lillian Duryea. Wakes were held for Benchley on both coasts. In New York, Marc Connelly hosted a gathering at the 21 Club attended by Jock Whitney, James Thurber, Wolcott Gibbs, a slew of *New Yorker* people, and, as well, many of the old Algonquin Round Tablers, including Donald Stewart, who, as one of the few who'd actually lost a friendship with Benchley, felt especially grief-stricken. Benchley's death was the third, and most profound, passing of a Vicious Circle member. Heywood Broun had succumbed to pneumonia in 1939 at the age of fifty-one, and Alexander Woollcott had died of a heart attack during a radio broadcast in 1943; like Benchley, he'd been fifty-six. But neither of them had commanded the strong affection that Benchley had. "This time," noted author John O'Hara, "the party is really over."

"Not over," someone responded. "It's just that they're going to have to stay up late in heaven now."

"Yes," said Thurber. "They're staying up late, and what's more, they must be having the time of their infinities."

At Mike Romanoff's restaurant in Hollywood, Dorothy Parker, Charles Butterworth, Sheilah Graham, and the rest of Benchley's Garden of Allah friends, as well as assorted writers, directors, and actors, made their toasts of remembrance. Butterworth was practically inconsolable. Within a year, still depressed by the loss of his dearest friend, he was dead, the victim of a single vehicle car crash right along the dangerous crossing on Sunset Boulevard near the Garden. Both Sheilah Graham and Natalie Schafer believed the crash was deliberate.

Even in death, though, Benchley's humor persisted. Following the funeral service for him, Benchley's ashes remained at the Hartsdale crematorium while his family tried to decide on a burial place. "He had called me once from Hollywood one summer at Nantucket," recalled Gertrude, "and asked me to buy a lot, since I was there. He said he and both boys and Marge, all of whom were in California at the time, had the idea that Nantucket was the place they wanted to be buried. I asked if they were kidding, and thought no more of it. But, according to the boys, he'd meant it. There was a quote from Shelley, regarding the death of Keats, which went, 'It might make one in love with death to think that one should be buried in so sweet a place.' Apparently, he'd mentioned that quote several times to his friends in Hollywood regarding the island." (These words, from the preface to *Adonais*, refers to Keats's burial at what Shelley described as the "romantic and lonely" Protestant cemetery in Rome.)

In the spring of 1946, after Gertrude bought a plot for the family in the Prospect Hill Cemetery on Nantucket, she, Nathaniel, and Bobby, with the urn containing Benchley's ashes in tow, drove from

New York to New Bedford, then took the ferry to Nantucket Island. Before they went to the family's summer home in Siasconset, they stopped at the undertaker's office to deliver the urn and instructed the proprietor to bring it to the cemetery the following day for the ceremony. Several hours later, though, the undertaker called them. "I'm afraid there's been a mistake," he said. "The urn you gave me is empty."

Sure enough, the crematorium had given them the wrong urn—and there wasn't enough time to get the right urn before they had to return to New York a few days later. "You know," Gertrude told her sons with a smile, "I can hear him laughing right now."

It wasn't until July that Benchley's ashes were finally interred at the family plot in Nantucket. The headstone, inscribed by Nathaniel in remembrance of the one role his father cherished above all others in his remarkable, improbable life—that of a writer—reads simply:

—Robert Benchley

1889–1945

Appendix

BOOKS BY ROBERT BENCHLEY

Of All Things. Henry Holt, 1921.

Love Conquers All. Henry Holt, 1922.

Pluck and Luck. Henry Holt, 1925.

The Early Worm. Henry Holt, 1927.

20,000 Leagues Under the Sea or David Copperfield. Henry Holt, 1928.

The Treasurer's Report and Other Aspects of Community Singing. Harper and Brothers, 1930.

No Poems or Around the World Backwards and Sideways. Harper and Brothers, 1932.

From Bed to Worse or Comforting Thoughts About the Bison. Harper and Brothers, 1934.

My Ten Years in a Quandary and How They Grew. Harper and Brothers, 1936.

After 1903–What? Harper and Brothers, 1938.

Inside Benchley. Harper and Brothers, 1942.

Benchley Beside Himself. Harper and Brothers, 1943.

POSTHUMOUS COLLECTIONS

Benchley–Or Else! Harper and Brothers, 1947.

Chips off the Old Benchley. Harper and Brothers, 1949.

The "Reel" Benchley. A. A. Wyn, 1950.

The Benchley Roundup. Harper and Brothers, 1954.

Benchley Lost and Found. Dover, 1970.

Appendix

The Best of Robert Benchley. Avenel, 1983.

Benchley at the Theater. Ipswich Press, 1985.

SHORT SUBJECTS OF ROBERT BENCHLEY

1. *The Treasurer's Report.* March 1928.
2. *The Sex Life of the Polyp.* July 1928.
3. *The Spellbinder.* December 1928.
4. *Lesson Number One.* February 1929.
5. *Furnace Trouble.* February 1929.
6. *Stewed, Fried and Boiled.* March 1929.
7. *Your Technocracy and Mine.* April 1933.
8. *How to Break 90 at Croquet.* January 1935.
9. *How to Sleep.* September 1935.
10. *How to Behave.* April 1936.
11. *How to Train a Dog.* July 1936.
12. *How to Vote.* September 1936.
13. *How to Be a Detective.* October 1936.
14. *The Romance of Digestion.* March 1937.
15. *How to Start the Day.* September 1937.
16. *A Night at the Movies.* November 1937.
17. *How to Figure Income Tax.* March 1938.
18. *Music Made Simple.* April 1938.
19. *An Evening Alone.* May 1938.
20. *How to Raise a Baby.* July 1938.
21. *The Courtship of the Newt.* July 1938.
22. *How to Read.* August 1938.
23. *How to Watch Football.* October 1938.
24. *Opening Day.* November 1938.
25. *Mental Poise.* December 1938.
26. *How to Sub-let.* January 1939.
27. *An Hour for Lunch.* March 1939.
28. *Dark Magic.* May 1939.
29. *Home Early.* May 1939.
30. *How to Eat.* June 1939.
31. *The Day of Rest.* September 1939.

Appendix

32. *See Your Doctor.* December 1939.

33. *That Inferior Feeling.* January 1940.

34. *Home Movies.* February 1940.

35. *The Trouble with Husbands.* November 1940.

36. *Waiting for Baby.* January 1941.

37. *Crime Control.* April 1941.

38. *The Forgotten Man.* May 1941.

39. *How to Take a Vacation.* October 1941.

40. *Nothing but Nerves.* January 1942.

41. *The Witness.* March 1942.

42. *Keeping in Shape.* June 1942.

43. *The Man's Angle.* August 1942.

44. *My Tomato.* December 1943.

45. *No News Is Good News.* December 1943.

46. *Important Business.* April 1944.

47. *Why Daddy?* May 1944.

48. *I'm a Civilian Here Myself.* Fall 1945.

Shorts 1–6 made for Fox, 7 for Universal, 8 for RKO, 9–34 for MGM, 35–43 for Paramount, 44–47 for MGM, and 48 for the U.S. Navy.

Directors: 1–3, Thomas Chalmers; 4–6, James Parrott; 7, unknown; 8, Lee Marcus; 9, Nick Grinde; 10–11, Arthur Ripley; 12–14, Felix Feist; 15–30, Roy Rowland; 31–34, Basil Wrangell; 35–43, Leslie Roush; 44–47, Will Jason; 48, Harry Joe Brown.

All shorts were written by Robert Benchley except as follows:

How to Behave, Music Made Simple, How to Sub-let, and *An Hour for Lunch:* by Robert Benchley, Robert Lees, and Fred Rinaldo.

The Romance of Digestion: by Robert Benchley and Felix Feist.

See Your Doctor: story by Harry Einstein (Parkyakarkus), screenplay by Robert Benchley.

That Inferior Feeling: by Robert Benchley and Basil Wrangell.

Important Business and *Why Daddy?:* by Robert Benchley and Rosemary Foster.

How to Be a Detective, How to Start the Day, A Night at the Movies, and *An Evening Alone:* by Robert Lees and Fred Rinaldo.

How to Train a Dog: story by Mitzi Cummings, screenplay by Mitzi Cummings, Felix Feist, Alexander Van Doren, Walter Wise, Robert Lees, Fred Rinaldo, and Pete Smith.

My Tomato: by Paul Gerard Smith and Sam Baerwitz.

Appendix

Robert Benchley also appeared in *Boogie Woogie*, a June 1945 Paramount Technicolor short directed by Noel Madison.

FEATURE FILMS OF ROBERT BENCHLEY

The Sport Parade. RKO, November 1932. D: Dudley Murphy: with Joel McCrea, William Gargan, Marian Marsh, Walter Catlett.

Headline Shooter. RKO, October 1933. D: Otto Brower: with William Gargan, Frances Dee, Ralph Bellamy, Betty Furness.

Dancing Lady. MGM, December 1933. D: Robert Z. Leonard: with Clark Gable, Joan Crawford, Franchot Tone, Fred Astaire, Ted Healy and His Stooges.

Rafter Romance. RKO, January 1934. D: William Seiter: with Ginger Rogers, Norman Foster, George Sidney, Laura Hope Crews.

Social Register. Columbia, August 1934. D: Marshall Neilan: with Colleen Moore, Charles Winninger, Pauline Frederick, Alexander Kirkland.

China Seas. MGM, July 1935. D: Tay Garnett: with Clark Gable, Jean Harlow, Wallace Beery, Rosalind Russell, Lewis Stone.

Piccadilly Jim. MGM, August 1936. D: Robert Z. Leonard: with Robert Montgomery, Frank Morgan, Madge Evans, Billie Burke, Eric Blore.

Broadway Melody of 1938. MGM, August 1937. D: Roy Del Ruth: with Robert Taylor, Eleanor Powell, George Murphy, Judy Garland, Buddy Ebsen.

Live, Love and Learn. MGM, October 1937. D: George Fitzmaurice: with George Montgomery, Rosalind Russell, Mickey Rooney, Monty Woolley.

Foreign Correspondent. United Artists, August 1940. D: Alfred Hitchcock: with Joel McCrea, Laraine Day, Herbert Marshall, George Sanders, Eduardo Cinanelli.

Hired Wife. Universal, September 1940. D: William Seiter: with Rosalind Russell, Brian Aherne, Virginia Bruce, John Carroll.

Nice Girl? Universal, February 1941. D: William Seiter: with Deanna Durbin, Franchot Tone, Robert Stack, Walter Brennan, Helen Broderick.

The Reluctant Dragon. Disney-RKO, June 1941. D: Alfred Werker (live action), Hamilton Luske (animated sequences): with Frances Gifford, Barnett Parker, Clarence Nash, Alan Ladd.

You'll Never Get Rich. Columbia, September 1941. D: Sidney Lanfield: with Fred Astaire, Rita Hayworth, John Hubbard, Osa Massen.

Three Girls About Town. Columbia, October 1941. D: Leigh Jason: with Joan Blondell, Binnie Barnes, Janet Blair, Eric Blore.

Bedtime Story. Columbia, December 1941. D: Alexander Hall: with Frederic March, Loretta Young, Allyn Joslyn, Eve Arden.

Take a Letter, Darling. Paramount, May 1942. D: Mitchell Leisen: with Rosalind Russell, Fred MacMurray, MacDonald Carey, Constance Moore.

Appendix

The Major and the Minor. Paramount, August 1942. D: Billy Wilder: with Ginger Rogers, Ray Milland, Rita Johnson, Dianna Lynn.

I Married a Witch. United Artists, October 1942. D: René Clair: with Frederic March, Veronica Lake, Susan Hayward, Cecil Kellaway.

Young and Willing. United Artists, February 1943. D: Edward H. Griffith: with William Holden, Barbara Britton, Eddie Bracken, Susan Hayward, Martha O'Driscoll.

The Sky's the Limit. RKO, July 1943. D: Edward H. Griffith: with Fred Astaire, Joan Leslie, Robert Ryan, Elizabeth Patterson, Eric Blore.

Flesh and Fantasy. Universal, October 1943. D: Julien Duvivier: with Charles Boyer, Edward G. Robinson, Barbara Stanwyck, Robert Cummings, Betty Field.

Song of Russia. MGM, December 1943. D: Gregory Ratoff: with Robert Taylor, Susan Peters, John Hodiak, Felix Bressart.

See Here, Private Hargrove. MGM, March 1944. D: Wesley Ruggles: with Robert Walker, Donna Reed, Keenan Wynn, Ray Collins, Bob Crosby.

Her Primitive Man. Universal, April 1944. D: Charles Lamont: with Louise Allbritton, Robert Paige, Edward Everett Horton, Helen Broderick.

Janie. Warner Brothers, September 1944. D: Michael Curtiz: with Joyce Reynolds, Robert Hutton, Edward Arnold, Ann Harding, Alan Hale.

The National Barn Dance. Paramount, September 1944. D: Hugh Bennett: with Jean Heather, Charles Quigley, Mabel Paige, Pat Buttram.

Practically Yours. Paramount, December 1944. D: Mitchell Leisen: with Fred MacMurray, Claudette Colbert, Rosemary DeCamp, Cecil Kellaway.

Pan Americana. RKO, February 1945. D: John H. Auer: with Philip Terry, Audrey Long, Eve Arden, Jane Greer, Isabelita.

It's in the Bag. United Artists, April 1945. D: Richard Wallace: with Fred Allen, Binnie Barnes, Jack Benny, Sidney Toler, Grady Sutton.

Duffy's Tavern. Paramount, September 1945. D: Hal Walker: with Barry Sullivan, Marjorie Reynolds, Bing Crosby, Victor Moore, Paulette Goddard.

Kiss and Tell. Columbia, October 1945. D: Richard Wallace: with Shirley Temple, Jerome Courtland, Walter Abel, Porter Hall.

Weekend at the Waldorf. MGM, October 1945. D: Robert Z. Leonard: with Ginger Rogers, Walter Pidgeon, Lana Turner, Van Johnson.

Snafu. Columbia, November 1945. D: Jack Moss: with Conrad Janis, Vera Vague, Nanette Parks, Janis Wilson.

The Stork Club. Paramount, December 1945. D: Hal Walker: with Betty Hutton, Barry Fitzgerald, Don DeFore, Andy Russell.

The Road to Utopia. Paramount, December 1945. D: Hal Walker: with Bob Hope, Bing Crosby, Dorothy Lamour, Hillary Brooke, Douglass Dumbrille.

The Bride Wore Boots. Paramount, May 1946. D: Irving Pichel: with Barbara Stanwyck, Robert Cummings, Peggy Wood, Natalie Wood, Willie Best.

Appendix

Janie Gets Married. Warner Brothers, June 1946. D: Vincent Sherman: with Joan Leslie, Robert Hutton, Edward Arnold, Ann Harding, Dorothy Malone.

As detailed in this book, Benchley did a substantial amount of screenwriting, mostly on dialogue. His official on-screen credits, however, are limited to the following:

Sky Devils. United Artists, 1932. Coauthor, dialogue.

Murder on a Honeymoon. RKO, February 1935. Coauthor, screenplay.

Foreign Correspondent. United Artists, August 1940. Coauthor, dialogue.

The Reluctant Dragon. RKO, June 1941. Author, additional dialogue.

Selected Bibliography

Adams, Franklin P. *The Diary of Our Own Samuel Pepys*. Simon & Schuster, 1935.

Adler, Polly. *A House Is Not a Home*. Rinehart, 1953.

Ashley, Sally. *F.P.A.: The Life and Times of Franklin Pierce Adams*. Beaufort Books, 1986.

Astaire, Fred. *Steps in Time*. Harper & Brothers, 1959.

Bankhead, Tallulah. *Tallulah: My Autobiography*. Harper & Brothers, 1952.

Benchley, Nathaniel. *Robert Benchley*. McGraw-Hill, 1955.

———. *Speakeasy*. Doubleday, 1982.

Brown, John Mason. *The Worlds of Robert E. Sherwood: Mirror to His Times*. Harper & Row, 1965.

Case, Frank. *Tales of a Wayward Inn*. Frederick A. Stokes, 1938.

Connelly, Marc. *Voices Offstage*. Holt, Rinehart & Winston, 1968.

Cowley, Malcolm, ed. *Writers at Work: The "Paris Review" Interviews*. Viking, 1957.

Ford, Corey. *The Time of Laughter*. Little, Brown, 1967.

Gaines, James R. *Wit's End: Days and Nights of the Algonquin Round Table*. Harcourt, Brace, Jovanovich, 1977.

Gill, Brendan. *Here at the New Yorker*. Berkeley Medallion Books, 1975.

Graham, Sheilah, and Gerold Frank. *Beloved Infidel*. Henry Holt, 1959.

Graham, Sheilah. *The Garden of Allah*. Crown, 1970.

Grant, Jane. *Ross, the New Yorker and Me*. Reynal, 1968.

Guiles, Fred Lawrence. *Hanging On in Paradise*. McGraw-Hill, 1975.

Harriman, Margaret Case. *The Vicious Circle*. Rinehart, 1951.

Kahn, E. J., Jr. *The World of Swope*. Simon & Schuster, 1965.

———. *Jock: The Life and Times of John Hay Whitney*. Doubleday, 1981.

Keats, John. *You Might as Well Live: The Life and Times of Dorothy Parker.* Simon & Schuster, 1970.

Kramer, Dale. *Ross and the New Yorker.* Doubleday, 1952.

Maltin, Leonard. *Great Movie Shorts.* Bonanza, 1972.

Marx, Harpo, with Rowland Barber. *Harpo Speaks!* Bernard Geis, 1961.

Meade, Marion. *Dorothy Parker: What Fresh Hell Is This?* Villard, 1988.

O'Connor, Richard. *Heywood Broun: A Biography.* G. P. Putnam's, Sons, 1975.

Parker, Dorothy. *The Portable Dorothy Parker.* Viking, 1973.

Redding, Robert. *Starring Robert Benchley.* University of New Mexico Press, 1973.

Rosmond, Babette. *Robert Benchley: His Life and Good Times.* Doubleday, 1970.

Schwartz, Nancy Lynn. *The Hollywood Writers' Wars.* Alfred A. Knopf, 1982.

Stewart, Donald Ogden. *By a Stroke of Luck.* Paddington Press, 1975.

Sullivan, Frank. *Through the Looking Glass.* Doubleday, 1970.

Thurber, James. *The Years with Ross.* Little, Brown, 1959.

Wilson, Edmund. *The Twenties.* Farrar, Straus & Giroux, 1975.

Winterich, John T. *Squads Write!* Harper & Brothers, 1931.

Woollcott, Alexander. *Enchanted Aisles.* G. P. Putnam's Sons, 1924.

–––. *The Portable Woollcott.* Viking, 1946.

Yates, Norris W. *Robert Benchley.* Twayne, 1968.

Permissions

Permissions

Illustrations from *From Bed to Worse* by Robert C. Benchley, © 1934 by Robert C. Benchley, renewed 1961 by Gertrude Benchley. Reprinted by permission of HarperCollins Publishers, Inc.

Illustrations from *My Ten Years in a Quandary and How They Grew* by Robert C. Benchley and Illustrated by Gluyas Williams, © 1936 by Robert C. Benchley, renewed 1964 by Gertrude Benchley. Reprinted by permission of HarperCollins Publishers, Inc.

Illustrations from *After 1903—What?* by Robert Benchley and with Drawings by Gluyas Williams, © 1938 by Robert C. Benchley, renewed 1966 by Gertrude Benchley. Reprinted by permission of HarperCollins Publishers, Inc.

Illustration from *Benchley—Or Else!* by Robert Benchley and with Drawings by Gluyas Williams, © 1932, 1934, 1936, 1938 by Robert C. Benchley. © 1947 by Harper & Brothers. Reprinted by permission of HarperCollins Publishers, Inc.

Excerpts from "Up the Dark Stairs," "The Beginning of the Slump" (which ran under the heading "The Press in Review"), "Back to Journalism" (which ran under the heading "The Wayward Press"), and "One Thing and Another," by permission of *The New Yorker*, © 1925, 1927, 1928, 1940 Robert Benchley.

Excerpt from undated letter from Harold Ross to Robert Benchley, © 1996 *The New Yorker* Magazine, Inc. All rights reserved. Excerpt from two undated memos from Harold Ross to Robert Benchley, © 1996 *The New Yorker* Magazine, Inc. All rights reserved.

Permission was granted by the Estate of Robert Benchley to quote accurately from unpublished and published works under the Estate's domain. Other Robert Benchley material by permission of the Boston University Mugar Memorial Library Department of Special Collections.

Photo credits: Pictures 3, 10, 14, 15, 17, 25, 26, 27, 29, 31, courtesy of Culver Pictures. All other pictures courtesy Boston University Mugar Memorial Library, Department of Special Collections.

Index

Index

Index

Index

Index

Index

Index

Index

Index

Index